MW00438765

SOCIAL AND POLITICAL CHANGE
IN UTTAR PRADESH

EUROPEAN PERSPECTIVES

Social and Political Change in Uttar Pradesh

European Perspectives

Edited by

ROGER JEFFERY AND JENS LERCHE

MANOHAR

2003

First published 2003

© Roger Jeffery and Jens Lerche, 2003

ISBN 81-7304-500-3

Published by
Ajay Kumar Jain for
Manohar Publishers & Distributors
4753/23 Ansari Road, Daryaganj
New Delhi 110 002

Typeset by
Kohli Print
Delhi 110 051

Printed at
Print Perfect
Delhi 110 064

Contents

Tables

Maps and Figure

MAPS

Note: All the following maps are based on digitized data from a variety of sources. They have all been based on the 56 districts of UP as used in the 1981 Census. This allowed us to use the data collected by the University of Maryland project. Data from 1991 (based on the seven additional districts) have been allocated to the prior 56 districts. All maps, therefore, include data on what is now Uttaranchal. All the maps have been generated using ArcView. In the light of reasonable doubts about the quality of many of the sources, we decided not to suggest that relatively small variations are significant. Therefore districts are grouped into quintiles, according to the relevant variable, in order to show general tendencies.

Preface and Acknowledgements

This book has been longer in gestation than we would have liked. Its original title—UP: Towards the Twenty-first Century—reflected its origin in papers given at the fifteenth European Modern South Asian Studies Conference, in Prague, in September 1998. Not only has the Millennium overtaken us, but the unit we addressed then—Uttar Pradesh—has lost a portion of its land to the newly-created Uttaranchal. Some of our original analysis, based on the data available when these papers were written, has been up-dated, most obviously by the release of preliminary results from the 2001 Census. Wherever possible, in finally revising the chapters, we have taken note of more recent developments, political, administrative, academic and statistical. Fundamentally, however, we believe that these papers make a contribution unaffected by the fleeting nature of social and political changes over the past three or four years.

The editors wish to express their thanks to those who made the Prague conference possible, Professor Vaclav Jacek and Dr Jan Dvorak in particular. We also thank the contributors for their patience in coping with the delays in publication, which were not of their making. And we thank our families for their forbearance in allowing us to finish the editorial work, at the cost (as usual) of our obligations to them.

Contributors

JAYATI CHATURVEDI is Reader in the Department of Political Science, St John's College, Agra. She has been field-researching areas of 'identity-formation', 'construction of the Other' and iconization as means of identity-consolidation in a fragmented society. She is investigating how these concepts are determining the processes of political-mobilization and setting the political agenda in parts of contemporay Uttar Pradesh. She is also the co-producer of a documentary for Candian TV on the 'Vrindavan Widows' and provided inputs in the drafting of the Copenhagen Declaration.

CHRISTOPHE JAFFRELOT is a Director of Research at the University of Paris, France. His recent books include (edited, with Thomas Hansen) *The BJP and the Compulsions of Politics in India*, 1998, and *The Hindu Nationalist Movement and Indian Politics, 1925 to 1990s*, 1999.

PATRICIA JEFFERY is Professor of Sociology in the University of Edinburgh, UK, where she has taught and held research fellowships since 1973. She has carried out research on gender and social change in Bijnor District since 1982. Her recent books include (with Roger Jeffery) *Don't Marry Me to a Plowman: Women's Everyday Lives in Rural North India*, 1997; and (edited, with Amrita Basu), *Appropriating Gender: Women's Activism and Politicised Religion in South Asia*, 1998.

ROGER JEFFERY is Professor of Sociology of South Asia at the University of Edinburgh, UK, where he has taught since 1972. His research in UP since 1982 has focused on social demography and agrarian change, and is now concerned with education and social reproduction. His recent books include (with Patricia Jeffery) *Population, Gender and Politics: Demographic Change in Rural North India*, 1997; and (with Nandini Sundar and Neil Thin) *Branching Out: Joint Forest Management in Four Indian States*, 2001.

CRAIG JEFFREY has been Lecturer in Geography, University of Edinburgh, UK, since 1999. His research interests include the sociology of Indian development, education, corruption and agrarian change. His doctoral research focused on the social and political strategies of a rural elite in western Uttar Pradesh. He is currently (in collaboration with Roger Jeffery and Patricia Jeffery) involved in research in Bijnor and Meerut into the relationships among private schooling, household strategies and the local state.

JENS LERCHE is Senior Lecturer in Development Studies at the School of Oriental and African Studies, University of London, UK, where he has taught since 1994. Recent publications include (edited with Terence Byres and Karin Kapadia) *Rural Labour Relations in India*, 2000.

G.K. LIETEN is Profesor of Development Sociology and Child Labour at the Faculty of Social Sciences at the University of Amsterdam, Netherlands. He is also the chairperson of the Child Labour Research Foundation Irewoc (irewoc@pscw.uva.nl). He has published extensively on the effect of land reforms in Kerala and West Bengal, and on rural development in northern India and Pakistan. His recent books include *Development, Devolution and Democracy: Village Discourse in West Bengal*, 1996; and (with Ravi Srivastava) *Unequal Partners: Power Relations, Devolution and Development in Uttar Pradesh*, 1999.

STAFFAN LINDBERG is Professor of Sociology at Lund University, Sweden. He has done extensive research on agricultural change, health and development, and farmers' movements in India since 1969. He has previously published (with Göran Djurfeldt) *Behind Poverty*, 1976 and *Pills against Poverty*, 1980; (with Venkatesh B. Athreya and Göran Djurfeldt) *Barriers Broken*, 1990; and (edited with Árni Sverrisson) *Social Movements in Development*, 1997. He is currently director and co-ordinator of SASNET—Swedish South Asian Studies Network (http://www-sasnet.lu.se).

STIG TOFT MADSEN is Assistant Professor in International Development Studies, Roskilde University, Denmark. His recent books include *State, Society and Human Rights in South Asia*, 1996; and (edited) *State, Society and the Environment in South Asia*, 1999. His interest in UP dates back to 1974 when he became a student at Meerut University.

EMMA MAWDSLEY is a Lecturer in Geography at Durham University, UK. She has spent several years working on the issue of new states in India, especially Uttaranchal. More recently she has been involved in a major DFID-funded project looking at knowledge, power and development agendas within the global NGO community. She is a 2001–2 Fellow at the Carnegie Council for Ethics and Inter-national Affairs, and is currently researching middle class environmentalism in India.

JOANNE MOLLER has a Ph.D in anthropology from the London School of Economics, UK, based on 16 months' fieldwork (1989–91) in a village in Almora District, Kumaon, focusing on kinship and gender. She spent two years in Thailand conducting research into gender and rural industrialization. She has published work from both her Indian and Thai fieldwork, and has taught at Sussex, Manchester and Hull Universities, UK. She lives in Cambodia and works as a freelance consultant.

SIMON ROBERTS has a Ph.D in Social Anthropology from the University of Edinburgh, UK. He has established 'Ideas Bazaar', a small company that specialises in ethnography, and is currently undertaking research on mobile telephone users for The Work Foundation, the think tank previously known as The Industrial Society, which will be published in the Autumn.

PER STÅHLBERG is a doctoral candidate in social anthropology at Stockholm University, Sweden. He is working on a thesis on regional journalism in Uttar Pradesh, for which he has carried out fieldwork in editorial offices in Lucknow. The study is concerned with the occupational culture and everyday practice of journalism as a global profession in a particular cultural context.

JASMINE ZÉRININI-BROTEL was research scholar at the French Centre de Sciences Humaines in New Delhi in 1998–9. She is currently working with the CSH, the Paris Centre d'Études et de Recherches Internationales, the Delhi-based Centre for the Study of Developing Societies on a sociology of India's MLAs since Independence.

1

Uttar Pradesh: Into the Twenty-first Century

Jens Lerche and Roger Jeffery

With a population about one-sixth of the total Indian population, it is no wonder that UP has played a central role in Indian development.[1] Many national political tendencies—such as the constitution of modern farmers into a political force from the late 1960s onwards, the demise of the Congress in the late 1980s and the subsequent emergence of the Hindu nationalist BJP on the political firmament—were taken seriously at national level only as a result of having gained importance in UP.

Moreover, UP has been in a number of ways a microcosm of the Indian nation: marked regional differences within the state mean that most of the economic, social, cultural and political trends that characterize present-day India are played out within its boundaries. Economically, the booming regions of the west of UP contrast with the more backward parts of the east, which have only recently cast off semi-feudalism. Demographic transitions are much further advanced in the northern hill region (the core of the new state of Uttaranchal) than in the UP plains.[2] Politically, the farmers' movement developed in the west; environmental movements took root in the Garhwal Himalayas (now in Uttaranchal); and the infamous Ayodhya temple-mosque dispute was engineered in east UP.

In the twenty-first century, the political importance of UP is likely to be as great as ever, despite the loss of 18 per cent of its area and 5 per cent of its population to Uttaranchal. It is no coincidence that, during the 1999 national elections, both the prime minister of the outgoing BJP-led government, Atal Behari Vajpayee, and the leader of the opposition, the Congress party's Sonia Gandhi, sought election from erstwhile UP. Its political value is undiminished: it is still numerically important, and it still holds immense symbolic value as being at the core of the north Indian 'Hindi heartland'.

In economic and social policy, however, UP has long ceased to be an example for others to follow. Its social development record is dreadful, and in the 1990s it has become known as one of the main development failures in India. The states of Bihar, Madhya Pradesh, Rajasthan and UP have been described by the term 'BIMARU' (Bose 1988; see also Dubey 1992: 171) to designate the 'hungry belly' of 'sick India'. These states have very poor records of social development; high levels of illiteracy and infant and child mortality; poor health and education provisions; and markedly unequal gender relations. It has even been argued that, within the field of social development, BIMARU has now become BIU: Bihar and UP are being left behind while MP and Rajasthan have begun to show some signs of improvement (Ramesh 1999: 2127).

The rather abysmal record is all the more noteworthy as UP's economic growth ratio has not always been as bad as its social profile would suggest. True, compared to many other states in India, UP experienced low degrees of industrialization and urbanization in the fifty years after Independence. The state remains overwhelmingly agrarian: in 1991, 72 per cent of the economically active population was engaged in agriculture.[3] This core sector has done well, consistently registering growth rates in yields above all India rates between 1962–5 and 1992–5, at an apparently accelerating rate.[4] Yet estimates of Net State Domestic product per capita suggest that UP, at Rs 6,733 in 1996–7 (current prices) is much poorer than India as a whole (Rs 10,919), let alone Punjab and Haryana (Rs 18,213 and Rs 16,199 respectively) (Kurian 2000: 541). Compared with the rest of India, UP's economic performance in the 1970s was probably as good or better, but in the 1980s its per capita income grew more slowly than in India as a whole (Measham et al. 1999: 1366). Head-count estimates of poverty in UP are very close to all-India figures, better than those of Bihar and Orissa, but worse than those of AP, Karnataka, Gujarat or even Rajasthan (Drèze and Gazdar 1997: 48; Kurian 2000). Yet a wide range of indicators suggest that social development has been badly neglected throughout UP, even in the wealthier regions of the state.

The neglect of social development in UP is closely related to the entrenched class structure of the state, particularly the uncompromising character of its upper class and upper caste élite (Hasan 1998; see also Hasan 2001). This élite has proved resilient to social compromises. It has not shown the foresight to ease its dominant political position in order to accommodate the new social groups that emerged on the political scene from the 1960s onwards: first, the middle caste modern farmers and later, the politicized Scheduled Caste movements.

Outside north India, more often than not, various types of populist regimes have delivered benefits (land reforms, midday meals, improved health service, etc.) to poor low-caste groups in return for their political support. This type of development has gone furthest in states where the Left has been in power (Kerala, West Bengal) but has also had some impact in other states where low-caste support has been mobilized by a regional élite (e.g. in Andhra Pradesh, Tamil Nadu and Madhya Pradesh).[5]

In UP, the ruling classes have not gone down this route. During the 1970s and 1980s, the high-caste élite found it unnecessary to compromise as they were firmly in control. This was among other things due to the fact that the high castes constituted a much more significant proportion of the population than elsewhere in India. Brahmins, Rajputs of various kinds and Banias, Kayasthas and Khatris make up around 20 per cent of the UP population (Saxena 1985) compared to 3–5 per cent in states like Maharashtra (Ramesh 1999: 2127) (see also Table 1.5 later in this chapter). When their dominance over certain client social groups (Muslims, Scheduled Castes) finally collapsed in the late 1980s, it was too late for realignments. At this time, political alternatives had evolved both for the modern farmers and for the subaltern groups.

Today, the character of the social relations remains as uncompromising as ever. Violent defence of caste, class and gender privilege is commonplace in the state, as are the clear political fault lines along class and caste. The political competition between the old élites and the farming groups has not focused on winning over sections of the poor through populist measures. State spending on public health and education, which would benefit the population at large, is limited, and spending on the poorest social groups even more so. The UP government has been under pressure from the World Bank to restructure its finances and significantly has imposed user charges on health services, but not increased them on irrigation (*Hindustan Times* 25 December 2001). Nor has it been able to reform its power supply (*Hindustan Times* 27 December 2001).

Instead, rent seeking by people in power, their followers and the bureaucrats they promote has become the norm as conflicts between the various élites have spilled over into the bureaucracy. Promotions and sidelining of civil servants according to political loyalty is common-place, while the buying and selling of offices is reportedly intensifying. It is hardly surprising that, in the 1990s, even the line between the criminal and the political élite is reported to be breaking down (Anon. 1997a; Anon. 1997b; Anon. 1998).

The public sector problems are not limited to this. The UP state government is near-bankrupt, with debts well above the Indian aver-age. It relies on up-front reimbursement from the central government in order to solve its cash flow problems; it does not have funds to run development projects; and it cannot manage to spend the planned funds even if they are available (Kurian 1999: 19; Ramesh 1999). UP has historically failed to invest in developmental activities, spending less in 1980–1 than any other state except Bihar. Between 1980–1 and 1995–6, developmental expenditures in constant prices rose only by 35 per cent whereas non-developmental expenditure rose by 228 per cent, compared to all-India figures of 77 per cent and 177 per cent (Kurian 2000: 542). This growing failure to undertake developmental activities suggests that the problems associated with backwardness are more likely to grow than decline.

The result is an inefficient bureaucracy, where actual completion of stipulated tasks tends to count for less than individual enrichment. As shown by Drèze and Gazdar, this adds significantly to the low per-formance of the public sector within sectors such as health and educa-tion (Drèze and Gazdar 1997).

Consider also UP's sheer size and diversity. It is widely acknowledged that economic structure varies dramatically between its different re-gions. This means that class-based social mobilization at the level of UP as a whole is difficult. Likewise, social movements based on single issues find it hard to mobilize across regions, as do caste-based move-ments, since very few castes or minorities are represented all over the state. Maybe as importantly, no UP-specific identity appears to exist: people from UP rarely claim to be 'UP-ites' in the same way as people from Tamil Nadu are 'Tamil' and people from Orissa, 'Oriya'.

No UP-specific language exists to glue the population together and to give immediate political appeal to populist regional political parties. True, this is a slightly circular argument: after all, the constitution of a language as being different from others is also a political process. Oriya was, for example, only constituted as a language different from Bengali as part of the movement in Orissa for an independent state, separated from Bengal and Bihar. The point remains, however, that by comparison with other parts of India, there are few 'banal' signs of UP identity (Billig 1995). In the press (see Ståhlberg, this volume) UP is not a particularly marked category; despite the pre-eminence of articles with the by-line 'Lucknow', other UP news is not given much salience. Unlike in other states, the schools do not in general stress regional heroes such as Shivaji in Maharashtra (see Bénéï 2000).

The absence of a UP-specific language is better seen as a reflection of a more general attitude: just as for north Indians the Hindi spoken in UP is *the* Indian language, UP is *the* Indian state. People of the state tend to perceive themselves as the archetypal (north) Indian people; the state of UP as the geographical heartland of the Indian state throughout the ages. For UP Hindus, UP—with the temples at Varanasi and Mathura, and the pilgrimage centres in the UP Himalayas—was the heartland of Hinduism even before the current stress on Rama and his supposed birth-place in Ayodhya. For Muslims, UP is home to two of the most significant institutions, the seminary at Deoband and the Aligarh Muslim University.

In order to understand UP's current social, economic and political realities, however, a regionally disaggregated picture is essential.[6] As a big, unwieldy state, UP contains within it too many differences, and very few people from UP identify themselves with the state as a whole. Regional identities within UP have developed, fastest in the UP hills, where a separate Uttaranchal was established in 2000. In western UP, at least among the élite, there is a desire to capitalize on its more rapid agricultural and industrial development trajectory, and shake off what is perceived as the drag of the districts in the east and central regions. The Bharatiya Kissan Kamgar Party of Ajit Singh (the son and political heir of Charan Singh) thus has an independent 'Harit Pradesh' or Green State as part of its programme.[7] Bundelkhand has also seen the beginnings of regional mobilization. We will now consider in more detail the nature of regional variations in economic and social indicators, and thus the extent to which claims to regional separateness are valid.

TOWARDS A REGIONAL ANALYSIS OF UP

To what extent *is* UP an appropriate unit of analysis? UP is a colonial invention, but was incomplete when the British left. The geographical core is to be found mainly within the flood plains of the Ganga, Jamuna and tributaries to the east. These lands were subject to a series of invasions, particular since 1000 CE. After Muhammad Ghor defeated

Prithviraj near Delhi in 1193, Afghans, Rajputs, Jats and others moved across the region (Metcalf 1979). In trying to take advantage of the needs of imperial rulers for allies, supporters and revenue collectors, their fortunes fluctuated. As taluqdars and zamindars these groups eventually intermingled in complex ways (Metcalf 1979: 10). Although under imperial control for much of the Mughal period, UP was never a single unit of imperial administration.

As the British moved up the Ganga from Calcutta, territories around Varanasi were the first to fall under their sway, in 1775. In 1801 a swathe of districts surrounding Oudh (from Bijnor in the north-west to Gorakhpur, Azamgarh and Basti in the east) were 'ceded' by the Mughals to the British. Two years later a further band of districts to the west—the Doab, Jalaun, Hamirpur and Banda—were conquered, along with the southern part of Mirzapur. These 'Ceded and Conquered Provinces' were called the Upper Provinces from 1809. Hill districts were conquered during the Nepal War of 1816; Jhansi was then 'acquired', and the British organized these lands into the North-Western Provinces (NWP) in 1836. Oudh was finally taken in 1856 (Metcalf 1979: 48). After 1857 no further lands were taken into direct control, so the princely states of Benares, Chakbari, Rampur, and Tehri Garhwal remained under indirect rule until 1947. The rest of what is now Uttar Pradesh was administered as the North-Western Provinces and Oudh from 1877 to 1902, and then as the United Provinces of Agra and Oudh, known in brief as the United Provinces, from 1937. The state of Uttar Pradesh was formed in 1950, and it included the United Provinces and those princely states that were contiguous or within its borders. The external boundaries stayed the same (Reeves 1991: 29–30) until Uttaranchal was formed. No changes were proposed by the States Reorganization Commission in 1955 on the grounds that 'UP forms the citadel of Indian civilization, that UP is homogenous, and that large size will lead to economy in administration' (Ramesh 1999: 2128).

In sum, although a casual glance might suggest that some of UP's boundaries are 'natural', like the river Jamuna in the west, in fact they were socially created as political limits. Some boundaries—such as those that keep the peninsula of Jhansi in UP rather than in Madhya Pradesh—are more obviously invented. Linguistically, Hindustani (Hindi and Urdu) in its many forms is spoken inside and outside the state, with no clear breaks at the state boundaries. K.M. Pannikar's note of dissent to the States Reorganization Commission in 1955 attempted to combine sections of western UP with five districts from MP, precisely because the existing boundary had no clear rationale (Ramesh 1999: 2128). As with all borders and boundaries, then, administrative convenience and historical conjuncture have drawn lines on maps to define UP, lines with little relationship to breaks in social, economic or political realities, at least at the time they were first drawn.

How significant are the differences in historical experience after British conquest? Metcalf suggests that, under the British, the NWP experienced little substantive reform until the period from 1835–57, when there was considerable dispossession of the rural landed élite and some levelling down. By contrast, in Oudh the British were more careful and protective of the rights of the class that became their natural allies, the taluqdars and larger zamindars. Throughout the first half of the twentieth century far more land was under occupancy and other hereditary tenancy rights in the old NWP (around 50 per cent) than in Oudh (6–7 per cent) (Hasan 1989: 144).[8] Nonetheless, Metcalf suggests, in both parts of UP the social power of taluqdars and zamindars was largely undermined by indebtedness, the rise of under-tenants, and the new aggression unleashed by the National Movement of the 1920s and 1930s (Metcalf 1979). Obviously, other differences also contributed to economic and social change: two worth commenting on here are differences in agrarian structure and climatic and geographical differences—but it is worth stressing that neither of these show patterns that conform closely to the distinction between Oudh and NWP.

The west also experienced more concentrated investment in agricultural improvement in the colonial period, e.g. canals were built in the western Doab. These investments were partly dictated by geography; further east, the opportunities were less. But the British also believed that the sturdy farmer-yeomen of western UP would take advantage of the opportunities offered by canal irrigation in ways that would not be true further east. This was not entirely wrong, not because of any inherent racial advantage, but because less minuscule landholdings and a less harsh taxation of the actual tillers were the order of the day in the western region (Stokes 1978; Stone 1984).

Despite these other patterns of factors that affected social and economic change, the different treatment of the two regions undoubtedly also helps to explain the different patterns of land-holding that continued after 1947, with impacts on agrarian policy and patterns of social change (Whitcombe 1980).

ADMINISTRATIVE DIVISIONS AND REGIONS

Administratively, UP has been divided into changing numbers of districts, which have been combined in different ways into divisions and regions for specific purposes. A perennial complication of discussing and mapping regions within UP is that district boundaries have changed, slowly up to 1971 but increasingly rapidly since then. For the purposes of this book we will use data based on either the 56 districts of the 1981 Census or the 63 districts of the 1991 Census.[9]

A common shorthand for describing differences within UP (until 2000 and the secession of Uttaranchal) was to distinguish five regions: west, central and east UP, Hills and Bundelkhand. Table 1.1 allocates the 56 districts of 1981, the additional 1991 districts (given in bold), and the additional 2001 districts (given in italics) to these regions, but also divides west UP into two, north-west and south-west (see also Map 1.1).

Table 1.1: Regional Distribution of Districts in UP, 2001

Region	Districts
UP Hills	Almora, *Bageshwar,* Chamoli, *Champawat,* Garhwal, Dehra Dun, Naini Tal, Pithoragarh, *Ryudraprayag,* Tehri-Garhwal, *Udham Singh Nagar,* Uttarkashi
Western	*North-west:* Baghpat, Bijnor, Bulandshahr, Ghaziabad, Hardwar, Meerut, Moradabad, Muzaffarnagar, Rampur, Saharanpur
	South-west: Agra, Aligarh, *Auraiya,* Bareilly, Budaun, Etah, *Gautam Budh Nagar,* Etawah, Farrukhabad, Firozabad, *Hathras, Jiyotiba Phule Nagar,* Mainpuri, Mathura, Pilibhit, Shahjahanpur
Central	Akbarpur, Barabanki, Fatehpur, Hardoi, *Kannauj,* Kanpur Dehat, Kanpur Nagar, Kheri, Lucknow, Rae Bareli, Sitapur, Unnao
Eastern	Allahabad, *Ambedkar Nagar,* Azamgarh, Basti, Bahraich, Ballia, *Balrampur, Chandauli,* Deoria, Faizabad, Ghazipur, Gonda, Gorakhpur, Jaunpur, *Kaushambi, Kushinagar,* Maharajganj, Mau, Mirzapur, *Parrauna,* Pratapgarh, *Sant Kabir Nagar, Sant Ravidas Nagar, Shrawasti,* Siddharth Nagar, Sonbhadra, Sultanpur, Varanasi
Bundelkhand	Banda, *Chitrakot,* Hamirpur, Jalaun, Jhansi, Lalitpur, *Mahoba, Shahuji Maharaj Nagar*

Source: Census of India, 1971, 1981, 1991 and 2001.
Notes: The 56 districts of 1981 are listed in normal type, with the additional 1991 districts in bold and the additional 2001 districts in italics. The names of the additional 2001 districts are taken from Registrar General and Census Commissioner (2001). The districts comprising Oudh were the 1981 districts of Bahraich, Barabanki, Faizabad, Gonda, Hardoi, Kheri, Lucknow, Pratapgarh, Rae Bareli, Sitapur, Sultanpur, and Unnao.

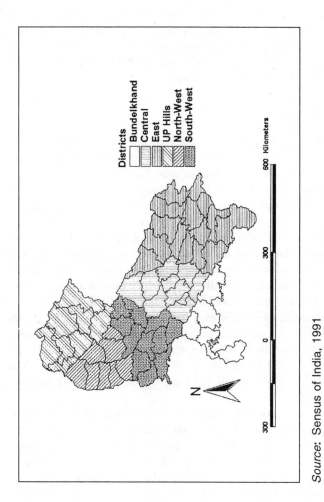

Districts

- Bundelkhand
- Central
- East
- UP Hills
- North-West
- South-West

N

300   0   300   600 Kilometers

Source: Sensus of India, 1991

Map 1.1: Regions of Uttar Pradesh, 1991

Together, the three first regions cover the UP Gangetic plains, while the hill region is UP's share of the Himalayan mountain region (also known as Uttarakhand, but granted statehood as Uttaranchal—with the addition of Hardwar district—by the BJP government). Bundelkhand is the UP section of the northernmost part of the central Indian plateau. In what follows we shall work with these simple groupings but also consider ways in which they need to be refined for different purposes. A key part of our argument is that the demographic, economic, political and social 'regions' that emerge from close attention to the empirical data only rarely overlap.

DEMOGRAPHIC PATTERNS

As Table 1.2 shows, the five basic regions are of very different population size, and the larger units mask some quite considerable variations. This is particularly the case in west UP where the north-west has developed differently from the south-west. The degree of variation in population growth rates is not large, but the benefits of a regional view are immediately obvious. Eastern UP has very low levels of urbanization, but is nonetheless as densely populated as north-west UP (which has almost three times the urban proportion as eastern UP). The UP hills (and to a lesser extent, Bundelkhand) are much less densely populated. Whereas UP's population as a whole grew as much in 1981–91 as in 1971–81, growth rates dropped in the UP hills, central UP and in Bundelkhand, while they rose in eastern and (marginally) in western UP. All the increase in the growth rate in western UP is accounted for by faster growth in the south-west; growth in the north-west (fuelled by migration to the Delhi hinterland of Ghaziabad and Moradabad) remained the highest overall, but growth there in 1981–91 was less than in 1971–81.

Population growth is a result of the net effects of fertility, mortality and migration, and these show very different patterns in the different UP regions. Fertility estimates for the UP districts are available for birth rates, completed family size, total fertility rates (TFR) and contraception prevalence rates (CPR). Table 1.3 is based on district-level fertility data, using data from the late 1970s as well as material for the 1990s that has recently become available (the 1991 Census data, and special surveys carried out on behalf of the USAID in 1995) (International Institute for Population Studies 1995; Tsui et al. 1997). It shows that the UP hills had much lower fertility than the rest of UP, and that

Table 1.2: Demographic Indicators for UP Regions

Region	Population (000s)		Inter-censal percentage population growth		Percentage urban		Population density (per square km)		Crude birth rate	
	1981	1991	1971–81	1981–91	1981	1991	1981	1991	1977	1987
UP hills	4,835	5,926	26.5	22.6	18.4	21.4	94	115	36	32
Western	39,350	49,548	25.7	25.9	23.8	26.3	479	603	42	39
North-west	*15,826*	*20,507*	*31.4*	*29.6*	*27.7*	*30.8*	*537*	*597*	*42*	*39*
South-west	*23,524*	*29,041*	*22.7*	*23.5*	*18.1*	*22.3*	*419*	*516*	*42*	*39*
Central	19,595	24,189	24.5	23.4	21.4	23.7	430	531	41	35
Eastern	41,652	52,721	25.6	26.6	10.7	11.6	484	569	43	39
Bundelkhand	5,429	6,730	26.5	24.0	19.9	21.3	185	229	42	38
Uttar Pradesh	110,863	139,112	25.5	25.5	18.0	19.8	377	471	42	38

Source: For population, population growth, per cent urban and population density, Census volumes, relevant years.
Note: Western UP includes south-west and north-west UP.

Table 1.3: Changes in Regional Fertility Differentials, UP, 1981–95

Region	Total fertility rate (TFR)			1995 Index of TFR	Contraceptive prevalance rate (CPR)		1995 Index of CPR
	1974–80	1984–90	1995	(1974–80=100)	1982	1995	(1982=100)
UP hills	5.1	4.1	3.1	61	18.1	48.2	266
Western	6.7	5.9	4.8	72	11.8	29.3	248
North-west	6.7	5.9	4.5	67	12.9	29.9	232
South-west	6.8	6.0	5.0	74	11.4	28.4	249
Central	6.3	4.9	4.6	73	12.9	22.9	178
Eastern	6.2	5.2	4.8	77	10.7	18.8	176
Bundelkhand	6.4	5.3	3.6	56	15.3	34.6	226
Uttar Pradesh	6.3	5.3	4.5	71	11.9	25.1	211

Sources: 1974–80 and 1984–90 total fertility rates from Mari Bhat (1996); 1995 total fertility rate and contraceptive prevalence data from Tsui et al. (1997); contraceptive prevalence rates for 1982 from Khare et al. (1982: 9–11).

Note: The 1995 estimate of TFR for Bundelkhand is implausibly low.

fertility had also declined very fast in central UP and in Bundelkhand. This latter finding is unexpected, given that (as will be seen later) economic and social changes in these regions have been slower than elsewhere in the state.

Table 1.4 shows estimates of mortality for children under 2 years by region, from the 1981 and 1991 censuses.[10] Child mortality on all measures is lowest in the hills. Beyond that, the anomalies are considerable. Census data for under-2 mortality suggest little regional variation among the remaining regions (they fall in a relatively narrow band, of 148–60 in 1981 and 106–12 in 1991). But overall, excluding the UP hills, Bundelkhand had the highest infant and child mortality rates, with especially high rates of male mortality, and north-west UP had the lowest rates. Given the very close relationship between falls in child mortality and later declining fertility, these figures are consistent with the conclusion that fertility may be declining quite fast in north-west UP, but they undermine even further the plausibility of the figures showing a rapid decline in fertility in Bundelkhand.

These different datasets together suggest that the UP hill districts are further through their demographic transition than the other regions of UP. In western UP, despite its reputation for a lack of social change commensurate with its economic changes (see further below)

Table 1.4: Changes in Regional Mortality Indicators, 1981–91

Region	q(2) 1981		q(2) 1991		1991 Index of q(2) (1981=100)	
	Female	*Male*	*Female*	*Male*	*Female*	*Male*
UP hills	105	109	82	82	78	75
Western	168	144	116	100	69	69
North-west	*151*	*132*	*101*	*90*	*67*	*68*
South-west	*180*	*152*	*127*	*107*	*71*	*70*
Central	165	155	114	107	69	69
Eastern	153	143	115	98	75	68
Bundelkhand	166	147	116	109	70	74
Uttar Pradesh	159	146	115	101	72	68

Source: q(2) for the 1981 Census: Registrar-General (1988); for the 1991 Census Rajan and Mohanachandran (1998).

Note: q(2) is the probability of a child dying before its second birthday (multiplied by 1000). Regional rates and ratios have been calculated from district estimates using weighted averages based on total district populations, though weighting should be by number of births, which are not available.

there are clear signs of demographic transition in the northern part, often masked by the lack of changes in south-west UP. The demographic evidence of differences between the rest of the regions is not consistent: demographic changes in the rest of UP seem to be slow and uncertain at best.

SOCIAL STRUCTURE

Evidence about how social structures vary across UP is limited. Here we shall consider only indicators of caste and community patterns, and gender relationships: we discuss agrarian classes in the section on economic development.

Membership of castes and religious groups is unevenly spread across UP (Tables 1.5 and 1.6). The most distinctive area is the UP hills. In a number of social and economic spheres, the hills display less inegalitarian social orders, while they are nevertheless rather backward economically. The UP hills are to an unusually large extent inhabited by high caste Hindus and members of the Scheduled Tribes.[11] Rajputs and Brahmans dominate the population to a greater extent in Almora, Garhwal and Tehri Garhwal (where they comprise 70–80 per cent of the population) but less so in Naini Tal and Dehra Dun, where immigration has had more impact.

Across the plains the most numerous single caste are the Chamars (also known as Jatavs). Extrapolating from the 1931 Census, we assume that they probably constitute at least 10 per cent of almost all districts; that in about 60 per cent of the districts they are the largest

Table 1.5: Basic Statistics on Social and Economic Variables by Region, 1991

(*in %*)

Region	Scheduled Caste	Muslim	Muslim and Scheduled Caste
UP hills	16.7	6.2	22.9
Western,	18.6	23.6	42.2
North-west	*17.5*	*34.8*	*52.3*
South-west	*19.4*	*15.7*	*35.1*
Central	26.4	15.1	41.9
Eastern	20.5	14.4	34.9
Bundelkhand	25.7	7.1	32.8
Uttar Pradesh	21.0	17.2	38.2
(Oudh	24.5	17.6	42.2)

Source: Census of India 1991.

Table 1.6: *Main Hindu Castes, with Approximate Percentage of the Hindu Population, 1931 Census, UP Regions*

(*in %*)

Region	Main Hindu Castes, in size order
UP hills	Rajput (48); Brahmin (21); Silpkar (17);
Western	Chamar (20); Brahmin (9); Rajput (8); Jat (6); Ahir/Yadav (5)
North-west	*Chamar (30); Brahmin (8),*
South-west	*Chamar (15); Brahmin (10),*
Central	Chamar (14); Pasi (12); Brahmin (10); Ahir/Yadav (10); Rajput (6)
Eastern	Chamar (15); Ahir/Yadav (14); Brahmin (12); Rajput (5)
Bundelkhand	Chamar (17); Brahmin (11); Rajput (4)
Uttar Pradesh	Chamar (15); Brahmin (11); Ahir/Yadav (9); Rajput (8); Pasi (3); Jat (2)

Source: Census of India, 1931, *United Provinces of the North-Western Provinces and Oudh.*

single caste; and that they form about 15 per cent of the population of UP as a whole. Some other agricultural castes (such as the Jats) are prominent in western UP but almost unknown east of Moradabad, and are more substantial in the states of Punjab and Haryana to the west. Others (such as the Pasi) are only found in the east. Brahmins are more prominent in the centre and east. The centre and east also have more members of the Scheduled Castes and fewer Muslims; in the west, the pattern is reversed. Bundelkhand, like the UP hills, has fewer Muslims and more Scheduled Castes. It has hardly any tribal population, relatively low levels of agricultural productivity, little industry, and displays deep social and economic divisions.

A commonly-used indicator of female disadvantage is the extent of excess female infant and child mortality. The incidence is greatest in the Gangetic plains; counter-intuitively, the UP hills also show relatively high levels of female disadvantage in child mortality (though not in infant mortality). Again, the figures for Bundelkhand are out of step, showing both higher mortality rates and lower levels of female disadvantage than the plains. But at high levels of child mortality, high male infant mortality rates mask discrimination against female children. As mortality rates decline, female disadvantage appears to worsen, but this does not necessarily reflect any change in behaviour towards young girls (Agnihotri 1997). This pattern certainly seems to make sense of these regional variations in child mortality differentials by sex, suggesting that discrimination against girls may be fairly similar across the state, masked by the higher mortality rates in Bundelkhand and the lower mortality rates in the UP hills. The data on degrees of son preference also show high levels across the UP regions, but the hills do show less son preference (fewer women reporting more boys than girls in their ideal family) than do the other regions, with Bundelkhand and the south-west showing the highest rates.

West-central UP has ten of the fourteen most masculine total sex ratios in the state. This pattern shows historical continuities with the districts declared 'blood-red' by the British administration in the 1870s during the campaign to eradicate female infanticide, and is also shown in statistics on juvenile sex ratios in all the British and post-Independence censuses (Jeffery et al. 1983; Miller 1981; Oldenburg 1992). There is little evidence of female infanticide since 1900, and the major contribution to the highly masculine juvenile sex ratios is that girls die from 'neglect' when they fall ill during the weaning period and up to the age of about 5. A further contribution to the overall sex ratios is the excess of female deaths in the age groups 15–35, attributable to maternity-related causes. Age-specific mortality for adult deaths is not available for the UP districts, so it is not possible to look at spatial variations in discrimination in health against adult women. Agnihotri suggests that female disadvantage is greatest in the central and east UP area, again an unexpected result, given that south-west UP has the most masculine total sex ratios in the state (see Table 1.7), and some of the worst in the country (Agnihotri 1997: 152, Annex. 5A).

Recently, data have become available on men's attitudes towards physical abuse of their wives. The data are drawn from only 5 districts, and we cannot draw firm conclusions about regional patterns of wife-abuse, but once again the differences between the plains and the hills are not as clear-cut as might have been expected. This may reflect the high rates of adult male out-migration from the hills, so that young women are more likely to be living in female-headed households (see Joanne Moller, this volume). On the other hand, Bundelkhand shows high rates of physical abuse of women, despite having almost as high rates of male out-migration as the UP hills. Nonetheless, as Agnihotri (1997: 315) points out, the significant links between 'women's seclusion and men's honour' are important in understanding the 'northern' demographic regime, within which all of UP (except the hills) falls (see Patricia Jeffery, this volume, on the customary legal position of women in north-western UP; also Mandelbaum 1988).

Table 1.7: Indicators of Female Disadvantage

	0–9 Sex ratio, 1971	Adult female literacy 1992–3	Index of son-preference	Married women working outside the home	Married women living in joint households	Percentage of husbands living away
N. hills	990	34.3	49.1	32.3	52.5	22.4
Western	867	26.6	58.1	9.0	58.6	3.7
North-west	872	33.0	51.9	6.8	55.1	2.6
South-west	866	23.2	61.4	10.2	60.4	4.4
Oudh plain	920	25.4	52.0	15.7	59.5	5.0
Bhojpur plain	932	19.9	58.1	12.3	74.7	20.9
S. uplands	890	19.8	64.0	19.1	71.3	9.5
Uttar Pradesh	903	24.3	56.6	13.4	63.8	9.8

Sources: Column 1: Census of India 1971; Columns 2–6 National Health and Fertility Survey (NHFS), reported in Mari Bhat and Zavier (1999).

Notes: The regions used in this table are those of the NHFS; the nearest equivalents are: UP hills = N. hills; West = NW plain + SW plain; Central = Oudh plain; East = Bhojpur plain; Bundelkhand = S. uplands.

ECONOMIC DEVELOPMENT

In the three plains regions, western UP (in particular, the north-westernmost part of this region around Meerut) is economically by far the most developed.[12] The ground for this was laid by canal irrigation during colonial times and the economic gulf was reinforced by post-Independence land reforms which, owing to the relative strength of the peasantry, succeeded in eliminating landlords more efficiently than elsewhere in the state. The major state-induced drive for increased agricultural production, the green revolution that started in the late 1960s, had a similar regional bias. As Hasan describes it, the western part of UP, together with neighbouring Punjab and Haryana, 'experienced the largest increase in rural capital investment, processing and small-scale industries in the green revolution era. By virtually all indices of growth and modernization, western UP achieved considerable progress, and by the early 1980s this region was substantially ahead of others in the state' (Hasan 1998: 88).

A class of surplus-producing middle and big peasants, tilling their land with family and paid labour, and investing in modern agricultural input and machinery developed in the west. Central and east UP, however, lagged behind. This division was reinforced by the related development of market towns and rural and semi-urban infrastructure in the west. Moreover, an industrial belt developed in and around Meerut division, neighbouring Delhi. Hence, in west UP today, urbanization as well as non-agricultural employment of the rural population is higher than elsewhere in UP. Agricultural productivity indicators are the highest in the state; so is agrarian investment, no doubt furthered by bigger landholdings, the links to the non-agricultural sector and the related, high non-agricultural rural income in the region. Poorer social groups of the region also appear to have access to less meagre incomes than their brethren elsewhere, as they have gained a foothold in the local urban economy and in nearby Delhi, as well as in brick kilns locally and in Punjab and Haryana.

Nevertheless, during the 1990s, several authors argued that the economic dichotomy between west UP and the rest of the plains has become somewhat less important and that such a dichotomy is a rather simplistic characterization of regional development in UP (Lerche 1998; Sharma and Poleman 1993; Srivastava 1994: 168, 170; Srivastava 1995: 230). We will show that the regional development trends are indeed more complex. Agrarian, industrial and urban developments combine in different ways to create a number of distinct regional patterns. Based on district-level statistical data covering the period 1961–91 regarding the economic, social and political developments in UP, it can be shown that in addition to east-west differences, a north-south divide exists.

This 'double divide' is not of recent origin. The districts running along the western and southern part of the Gangetic plain have long been considered distinct from the remainder of the state. Thorner and Han-Seng (1996) argued that, in the 1920s and 1930s, UP consisted of two agrarian regions. One, whose core was the Ganga-Jamuna Doab, stretched from the north-west of the state as far as Allahabad in the south-east. The other covered the old Oudh region and the districts east of it. For Thorner and Han-Seng, this characterizes the west and east UP regions, even if geographically the western region is a western-to-southern region and the eastern region is a northern-to-eastern region.

However, the meaning of Thorner's division line has changed during the last thirty years as a northern belt of districts has taken more of a lead agriculturally, while industrial development still is concentrated in the western and southern region. Moreover, the north-south divide has become stronger. Today, even in west UP, important north-south differences exist. While agriculture is well developed in west UP in general, agricultural *growth* is much more dynamic in the north than in the south. In fact, a belt of districts from the northern parts of west UP to the central parts of east UP is characterized by high growth rates in agriculture. Outside this northern belt, yield increases were lower during the green revolution. In the southern parts of west UP, agriculture continues to rely heavily on a drought-averse and less profitable crop mix. Since 1960, dryland crops such as millets have lost their significance in most parts of the state; rice has been superseded by wheat; and, in the most developed regions, sugar cane has gained ground.[13] Of these three most important crops, the north-south divide is particularly evident for the most profitable of the main crops, sugar cane.[14] Table 1.8 and Map 1.2 show graphically how the UP sugar cane belt stretches from a core area in the north-west to the northern part of central and eastern UP. There are both economic and political implications of this. The profitability of sugar cane growing is closely related to the government investments in sugar cane mills, and to the procurement prices for these mills, a price that is fixed each year by the government. The farmers of the north UP sugar cane belt are thus not only relatively prosperous, they also have significant political clout.

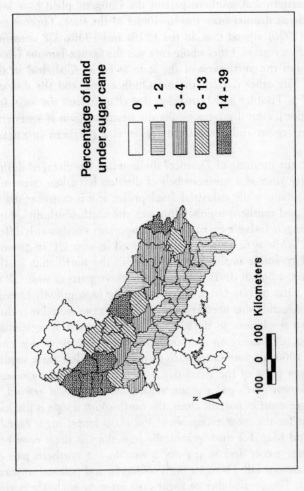

Percentage of land
under sugar cane

| 0 |
| 1 - 2 |
| 3 - 4 |
| 6 - 13 |
| 14 - 39 |

100   0   100   Kilometers

Source: Agricultural Situation in India 49, 2, May 1994.

Map 1.2: Percentage of Agricultural Land under Sugar Cane, 1991

Table 1.8: Indicators of Agricultural Development in UP

Region	Sugar area 91 as percentage of total cultivated	Wheat yields 1990–1 kg/ha	Wheat yields 1960–1 kg/ha	Wheat yields % growth rates 1961–91	Paddy yields % growth rates 1961–91
UP hills	5	1649	990	67	72
Western	13	2609	1099	137	149
North-west	*27*	*2635*	*1077*	*145*	*177*
South-west	*5*	*2597*	*1114*	*133*	*131*
Central	7	2128	973	119	152
Eastern	4	1917	794	141	155
Bundelkhand	0	1582	1133	40	4
Uttar Pradesh	7	2171	1001	117	143

Sources: 1961: Directorate of Economics and Statistics, Ministry of Food, Agriculture, Community Development and Co-operation. Government of India, 1970: *Estimates of Area and Production of Principal Crops in India, 1954–55 to 1964–65* (detailed tables) parts I and II.

1991: Rice and wheat: Economics & Statistics Division, State Planning Institute, Uttar Pradesh, Lucknow, 1997: *Statistical Abstract Uttar Pradesh 1992.*

1991: Sugar cane: *Agricultural Situation in India,* 49, 2, May 1994.

Note: 1991 Index of wheat yield, 1961=100

Table 1.8 and Map 1.3 also show wheat yields in 1991. The map reveals the west-east divide in UP agriculture, with districts in the western half of the state outperforming districts to the east. However, when we look at wheat yield *growth rates* 1961–91 (Table 1.8 and Map 1.4), a north-south line of division can also be gleaned. Seen together with the sugar cane data, the wheat yield growth rate pattern indicates that the agricultural heart of UP may be shifting. It used to be the districts running along the western and the southern part of the Ganga plan, but increasingly there is a new core covering both western and northern districts in west and central UP, and middle-to-northern districts in east UP. For rice, the highest yields back in 1961 followed a distribution pattern roughly similar to that of wheat. By 1991, a growth area covering northern districts of west and central UP had been established, even though this region had only partially overtaken the previous core in the southern west and central UP concerning yields (Map 1.5).

Industrial development in the state favours the same regions as agriculture used to, following a pattern close to Thorner's agrarian regionalization. Urbanization as well as the proportion of rural workers

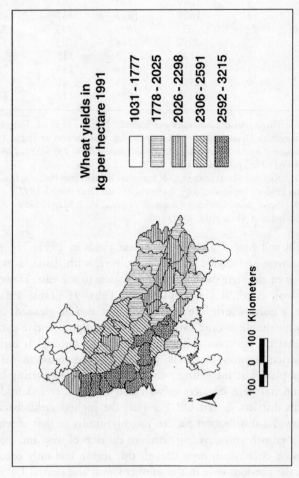

Wheat yields in kg per hectare 1991

- 1031 - 1777
- 1778 - 2025
- 2026 - 2298
- 2306 - 2591
- 2592 - 3215

100   0   100   Kilometers

Source: *Statistical Abstract Uttar Pradesh 1992,* Lucknow: Economics and Statistics Division, State Planning Institute, Uttar Pradesh, 1997.

Map 1.3: Wheat Yields in Kg per Hectare, 1991

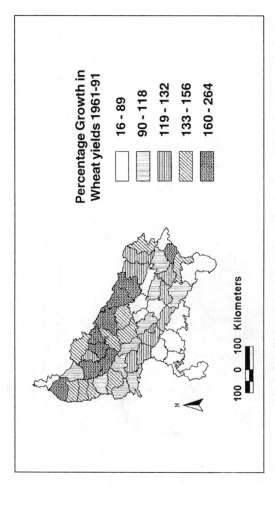

Percentage Growth in Wheat yields 1961-91

- 16 - 89
- 90 - 118
- 119 - 132
- 133 - 156
- 160 - 264

100   0   100   Kilometers

N

Source: 1961 figures: *Estimates of Area and Production of Principal Crops in India,*
1954–55 to 1964–65 (detailed tables) parts I and II, New Delhi: Directorate of
Economics and Statistics, Ministry of Food, Agriculture, Community Development and Cooperation, Government of India, 1967.

Note: No data are available for the districts in the UP hills for 1961 (except for
Dehra Dun and Naini Tal) so calculating growth rates for those districts for
1961–91 is impossible.

Map 1.4: Percentage Increase in Wheat Yields, 1961–91

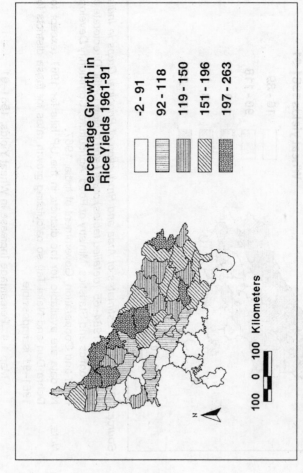

Percentage Growth in Rice Yields 1961-91

- -2 - 91
- 92 - 118
- 119 - 150
- 151 - 196
- 197 - 263

100   0   100   Kilometers

Source: As for Map 1.4.

Note: No data are available for the districts in the UP hills for 1961 (except for Dehra Dun and Naini Tal) so calculating growth rates for those districts for 1961–91 is impossible.

Map 1.5: Percentage Increase in Rice Yields, 1961–91

employed in manufacturing is highest in the north-west, and around the 'old' centres of western and southern UP.[16] The northern UP belt is overwhelmingly agricultural, even though agricultural development has created some ancillary industries. The exception is the north-west region, which combines agricultural growth with high industrial employment.

The social transformation of the countryside has taken place at considerable speed, particularly in the north-west. Traditional rural society included a number of marginal landowners and landless people who had their main income source from agricultural labour, traditional services and crafts. The old landlord-dominated areas of the east had a very high proportion of marginal landowners and agricultural labourers. Marginal landowners were preponderant mainly in the north-east and far east of the state, while agricultural labourers (with or without dwarf holdings) were more numerous in the south-east. In the west, on the other hand, with its somewhat less landlord-dominated landowning pattern, larger peasant holdings were more common, while a higher proportion of landless or near-landless labourers worked in non-agricultural traditional services and cottage industries, as opposed to agricultural labour (Registrar-General of India 1961; Thorner and Han-Seng 1996). Since 1961, however, the twin forces of industrial and agricultural development have led to the decline of the traditional service and cottage industry sector, and in the north-west it has practically collapsed. Simultaneously, according to a number of case studies, wage work in agriculture has also fallen steeply here, both as an effect of mechanization of agriculture and of the decreasing size of peasant holdings. Instead, a rapid increase in the proportion of rural non-agricultural wageworkers has occurred, particularly in the north-west where labourers have found employment as migrant workers in urban areas as well as in neighbouring states. Confusingly, retrenched rural cottage-industry workers are most often enumerated statistically as agricultural labourers, not 'rural workers' or 'manual workers'. In the north-west, the collapse of traditional non-agricultural rural occupations has been near total, and agricultural wage work has more than halved within the last forty years (according to local informants). This development is reflected in statistical accounts not only as a steep decrease in household industries employment (which was to be expected), but also as a steep increase in the proportion of agricultural labourers (see Table 1.9 and Map 1.6).

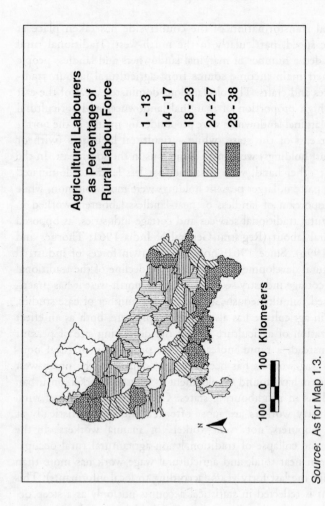

Agricultural Labourers
as Percentage of
Rural Labour Force

1 – 13
14 – 17
18 – 23
24 – 27
28 – 38

100   0   100 Kilometers

Source: As for Map 1.3.

Map 1.6: Rural Male Agricultural Labourers as Percentage of
Total Male Rural Labour Force, 1991

Table 1.9: Regional Patterns of Occupational Change in Rural UP

Region	Rural male cultivators plus agricultural labourers as percentage of rural male workers, 1991	Rural male cultivators as percentage of rural male workers, 1991	Rural male agricultural labourers as percentage of rural male workers, 1961	Rural male agricultural labourers as percentage of rural male workers, 1991	Landholdings less than 0.5 ha as percentage of total Landholdings, 1991
UP hills	77	70	3	7	47
Western	83	61	8	22	44
North-west	79	51	9	28	43
South-west	85	67	7	18	44
Central	88	71	9	17	50
Eastern	84	60	18	24	63
Bundelkhand	90	64	14	26	33
Uttar Pradesh	84	63	12	21	52

Sources: Columns 1, 2 and 4: Census of India 1991; Column 3: Census of India, 1961; Column 5: *Statistical Abstract Uttar Pradesh 1992*, Lucknow: Economics & Statistics Division, State Planning Institute.

The regional land-owning picture, on the other hand, has remained stable over the years. Agricultural growth between 1961 and 1991 has cut across regional differences in size of farm holdings without altering the regional balance (see Map 1.7): it is not only the somewhat richer peasants of the west who have developed economically. This said, it is clear that it is in the north-west that the highest growth rates have been achieved. Here, capitalist accumulation strategies go together with relatively big landholdings and easy access to non-agricultural incomes and markets, enabling proper investments to take place. Case studies from east UP, on the other hand, point out that the growth here is achieved by small landowners who have been enabled to pursue modern accumulation strategies as they have experienced a significant loosening of the economic and political dominance from their erstwhile landlords during the last decades. In addition, many relatively small ex-landlords have also embarked on capitalist agrarian strategies as opposed to relying on leasing out land.

The agricultural growth in parts of east and central UP has been achieved in spite of a number of constraints. The many very small peasants predominant towards the north and the east of these regions are constrained by their lack of capital. Moreover, rural economic infrastructure is less developed than in the west: for example, electricity supply to the important pumpsets is more erratic, and marketing structures are less beneficial to the peasants.[17]

The numerical and political strength of small and marginal peasants in the north-east probably provides the backbone for the recent agricultural growth in this region. In the south-east, the fact that this productive class is smaller, while there is a much higher proportion of rural labourers (see Map 1.6), gives a clue to the reason why growth has been less impressive here.

The two remaining administrative regions outside the main UP Gangetic plains are the hill region and Bundelkhand. In Thorner's scheme, the hill districts of Dehra Dun and Naini Tal were considered part of west UP, geographically as well as economically. Today, these districts form part of the north-west UP agricultural and industrial growth regime (see maps). The remaining hill districts belong to the lowest category of UP districts regarding both rice and wheat yields in 1991 (i.e. the lowest 20 per cent) and rank similarly low regarding degree of urbanization as well as non-agricultural occupations (except for household industries and religious trades).[18] In this mountainous

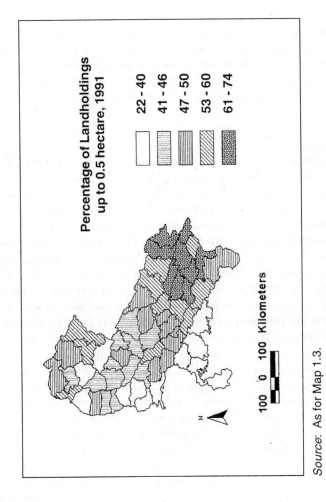

Percentage of Landholdings up to 0.5 hectare, 1991

	22 - 40
	41 - 46
	47 - 50
	53 - 60
	61 - 74

100 0 100 Kilometers

N

Source: As for Map 1.3.

Map 1.7: Landholdings of up to 0.5 Hectare as Percentage of Total Operational Landholdings, 1991

region with its concentration of high-caste Hindus, most households own some land, often tilled by female members of the household, while male migration is common.

Agriculturally, Bundelkhand can be seen as an extreme extension of the dry southern part of west UP. Thorner included Bundelkhand in west UP. Given the dry climate, agriculture in Bundelkhand is heavily dependent on investments that have not been forthcoming. Millets and other dryland crops are more common here than elsewhere in the state, and growth of wheat and rice yields were among the lowest of the UP districts between 1961 and 1991. Together with the low levels of mechanization in agriculture, and the strong bias towards agriculture in rural employment, this suggests that modern capitalist development has penetrated the countryside less than in the neighbouring districts of the Gangetic plains.

Bundelkhand and most of the hills districts are clearly outside the mainstream development patterns of UP. The UP plains cannot any longer—if it ever could—be summed up as 'the west versus the rest'. This is not least because parts of north UP that have commonly been considered economically backward have displayed impressive economic growth rates during the 1961–91 period. This represents an important correction of the traditional picture of UP's economic development.

Nevertheless, this correction should not be over-dramatized. In India, agriculture is often seen as a 'residual sector', providing a fallback position for those peasants who have not been successful in accessing more remunerative employment in other sectors (see, for example, Bhalla 1999: 46). This may also be true in UP. The virtually non-existent opportunities for non-agricultural employment in the northern parts of the state are likely to have provided a powerful impetus for small and marginal peasants to stick to their agricultural occupation. They try to develop it productively—even if the overwhelming rural character of the area (and particularly its poor economic infrastructure) also is a constraint to agricultural growth. In the south, where urban/migratory employment opportunities exist, labourers and marginal farmers tend to seek out more remunerative employment outside of agriculture, a move which may not further agricultural growth but which most probably alleviates poverty more effectively. It seems that only in the north-west region of the Gangetic plains have agricultural and urban/industrial growth developed a synergetic relationship.

POLITICAL REGIONS

The political map of UP displays a less regionally divided picture than the economy. Politics of the state has, in the 1990s, been dominated by the demise of the Congress party and the rise of three others. The BJP, the leading Hindu nationalist party, has at its core high-caste and business groups. Farming groups and the middle castes dominate the SP, and the BSP is a low-caste party led by an untouchable and projects itself as a party for untouchables, other low castes and Muslims. All three have been in power during the 1990s through a variety of coalitions. From 1996–2001 UP was governed by a coalition led by the BJP.

Many social and political movements champion regional causes or express the political interests of regional élites or subaltern social groups. The farmers union (BKU) is a major force in the Upper Doab region but not elsewhere, the (ultimately successful) movement for a separate state in the hills has likewise obvious regional limitations, and even the BSP with its national political agenda was initially limited to east UP.

However, the fact that important political decisions are taken by the state parliament in Lucknow creates a need for regional political interest groups to organize themselves at the state level, in spite of the existing regional differences. It is therefore not surprising that the double E–W and N–S divide that characterizes UP economically is not reflected in the party political structures of the state. Today, the three major parties, the BJP, SP and BSP, are 'all-UP' parties in the sense that they draw their support fairly evenly from all over the state. According to election data from the national elections of 1991, 1996 and 1999 (Election Commission of India 2001), this is particularly the case with the two biggest parties, the BJP and the SP. However, the BSP has also developed into an all-UP party. In 1991, its base was in the eastern and central regions of UP, most probably reflecting the breakdown of age-old social oppression in these regions as a result of the economic development, and related emancipatory processes among the oppressed. During the 1990s the BSP also gained more than a foothold in the western and northern districts, transforming itself, in the process, into an all-UP political party.

The need to mobilize different social groups across regional economic differences may even be part of the reason why political mobilization on lines of caste and ethnicity works well in the state. In UP there is a broad correlation between caste and class structures. The socio-economic position of small high-caste farmers of the hills and of high-caste landlords of the east may be quite different, but both these groups would tend to vote for the BJP. This party has tailor-made its political agenda to encompass high- and middle-caste groups all over UP by including in its policies support of a hill state as well as backing landlord supremacy in the east.[19] Another case in point is the BSP. Duncan has shown that BSP's support correlates strongly with the proportion of low-caste SCs and Muslims present in each constituency whereas the correlation with occupation is much less clear (Duncan 2000).[20]

This said, there are some regional political differences pointed out by Brass, among others (Brass 1997: 2406–7). He argues that this reflects the caste and ethnic composition of the regions—high-caste preponderance in the hills, high proportion of Muslims in Rohilkhand (the core of our north-west UP) and a high proportion of agrarian backward castes in the east—as well as political traditions and preferences. Modern farmers, for example, have since the days of Charan Singh flocked to the parties who could protect their interests, be it BKD, BJP or SP. The nature of Jat political mobilization in western UP (described by Staffan Lindberg and Stig Toft Madsen, and given a local context by Craig Jeffrey, in this volume) leads to very different political patterns from those led by Brahmins, Thakurs and Yadavs in central and eastern UP. Lindberg and Madsen, for example, show the tensions introduced into the operations of the Bharatiya Kisan Union led by Mahender Singh Tikait, by the inclusion of peasant farmers from eastern UP. Tikait was able neither to establish a formal bureaucratic party-like structure of command, nor maintain his dominance over the expanded movement through charisma and inherited office, which worked so well for him until the mid-1980s. Some of the reasons for this fracturing of the middle peasantry (at least for the Jats of north-west UP) are revealed in Craig Jeffrey's paper. He demonstrates the processes of differentiation that are emerging as the UP becomes an arena of conflict both between Jats and SCs but also among Jats. Jat farmers have clear interests in common (for example with respect to the maintenance of high procurement prices for sugar cane and wheat, or for reliable and virtually-free access to electricity). But they are also fractured by their informal political networks, their attempts to control the police, and their efforts to gain access to secure government employment.

In politics it is primarily at the level of social and political movements that regional differences express themselves. Several of the case

studies in this book bear witness to this social and political regionalization. The rise of the Bahujan Samaj Party (BSP) is one of the
most striking political phenomena of the 1980s and 1990s. As the
Congress party lost its previously dominant position, the BSP emerged
as the main political representative of Scheduled Castes (especially
Chamars/Jatavs). Over the same period the Bharatiya Janata Party
(BJP) managed to gain a leading position in representing the middle
and upper castes. The Janata Party and its inheritors (led in most years
by Mulayam Singh Yadav) has attempted to dominate the representation of Other Backward Castes (especially the Yadavs of eastern and
central UP) and attract the support of other marginalized groups
like the Muslims. These processes are explored in two papers, by Jens
Lerche, and by Christophe Jaffrelot, Jasmine Zernini-Brotel and Jayati
Chaturvedi.

Lerche discusses the ways in which caste and class are interlinked in
the politics of UP, developing his argument on the basis of case studies
of Muzaffarnagar and Jaunpur. A major conclusion of his paper is that
the possibilities for Scheduled Caste assertion, whether through the
activities of the BSP or in other ways, are heavily conditioned by specific local features. Crude contrasts between east and west UP are hard
to sustain in the face of detailed local enquiries. Jaffrelot and his colleagues focus on the problems posed to the BJP by challenges from
the SP (Samajwadi Party) led by Mulayam Singh Yadav, and the BSP.
Relative to other parts of India, the electoral potential in UP of a party
based around the high castes is relatively good. But as we have shown
in Table 1.5, if the Muslims and Scheduled Castes formed a coalition
they could make it virtually impossible for the BJP to come to power.
In practice, of course, for locally specific reasons, these groups are
divided, and (insofar as this is a meaningful concept) the 'anti-BJP'
vote was split in 1992, 1996 and again in 2002. With the loss of a
stronghold in the seats that have now gone to Uttaranchal, the BJP
needed to recreate a sense of Hindu unity, and to undermine SC and
Muslim unity, to return to power. Jaffrelot and his colleagues show the
party and its allies (notably the RSS and the VHP) worked at the state
level and in specific localities to achieve these ends. Only relatively
small groups within among the SCs (Balmikis in particular) seem to be
attracted by the BJP strategies of Sanskritization and co-option, and in
the 1999 Lok Sabha elections only around 5 per cent of SC voters
reported voting for the BJP (Verma 2001: 4454).

The other papers in this volume deal with different aspects of social, political and economic change, and together help to flesh out the general picture we have sketched in this introduction. Two chapters deal with aspects of gender relationships in different parts of UP. They provide depressing examples of the extent to which women are still excluded in various ways from full citizenship. Patricia Jeffery's paper discusses what might be one of the consequences of women's lack of functional literacy—their inability to access legal rights, in this case after divorce. Women in rural Bijnor knew little or nothing about the Shah Bano case, in which a divorced Muslim woman used the civil law to get financial support that she was not able to get under the Muslim Family Law, despite the considerable publicity surrounding the case. And far from there being major differences between Muslim and Hindu women (as the legal system proposes, and as the Hindu right-wing parties have been claiming was the case), in everyday terms their rights on abandonment, separation or divorce turn out to be very similar— and equally meagre.[21]

Joanne Moller's paper also provides a warning to those who would paint too rosy a picture of the relatively low extent of gender inequities in Kumaon (almost half of what is now Uttarakhand), compared to the rest of UP. Kumaonis consider they have social values and a way of life which is unique to themselves as hill people, and which distinguishes them from the dominant plains society. Nevertheless, as in the rest of the state, while girls form almost half the primary school population, in secondary schools they are one-third or less of the student body. Moller summarizes the local perceptions of the effects of schooling on young women. Schooling is supposed to make women 'difficult', immodest, lacking respect for their seniors, commanding their husbands and eager to set up a nuclear family, as well as lazy and unwilling to participate in the household work. Moller is sceptical about the ability of schooling to make major changes in women's life chances directly (as much of the development literature seems to suggest). Rather, women who have been to school benefit indirectly, as they form stronger bonds with their husbands and thus increase the strength of their new conjugal unit vis-à-vis their in-laws.[22]

The exceptionalism of Uttarakhand is only partly to be understood in terms of its physical environment. To be sure, the adverse agricultural conditions and extremes of weather probably engender differences in attitudes and behaviour amongst hill-dwellers, and the long tradition of male emigration to look for work in the plains has created a unique pattern of agricultural labour in the hills (with women playing major agricultural roles). Nonetheless, the major boost to Uttarakhand's political aspirations came as a result of the adoption of the Mandal Commission's recommendations in 1990. The caste structure of Uttarakhand—unlike the rest of UP at the time—had very few Other Backward Castes to benefit from the extension of reservations, and many Brahmins and Rajputs who would be adversely affected. Emma Mawdsley explores further the effects of this decision as well as the reactions to the police brutality against hill demonstrators when they reached Muzzafarnagar. Mawdsley also shows how relatively insignificant in hills politics the state political parties have been.

Three papers, in different ways, discuss the versions of modernity that can be discerned in UP. Kristoffel Lieten shows that in many respects, the desires and development perspectives of the poor are similar in parts of both west and east UP. He demonstrates the strong attachment by people from all castes and classes to that familiar 'modernity' characterized by a developmentalist state. As far as the poor are concerned, expansion in agricultural yields, egalitarian access to credit and other government programmes, and investment in infrastructure remain the highest priorities. As Lieten points out, it would be ironic indeed if the shift to 'post-modernism' in development planning (in particular, the rolling back of the functions performed by the state) were to overwhelm these demands for more government intervention.

The roles played by the mass media within social life generally help to maintain generalized orientations towards 'the modern'. Per Ståhlberg shows how the press in Lucknow is organized, and what kinds of news dominate the daily newspapers. He discusses the dualisms of modernity displayed by the conflicts and contrasts between the English- and Hindi-language newspapers. Though he does not extend his analysis to the kind of modernity that is emerging in UP, there are clear links between the ambivalences he discerns and the appeal of the Hindu right as a party that can transcend such dualisms. With a wealth of local detail, Simon Roberts ends the book by showing how cable television has become a dominant form of mass media in Varanasi. The availability of local news and political reporting has given new impetus to the traditionally male public political sphere in the city, but it has also enabled women to gain some access to a sphere that was previously closed to them. The burgeoning bourgeoisie is grasping the opportunities provided by these new means of communication, and in doing so, articulating new visions of the future. Roberts concludes by suggesting that this local study also supports what is a major theme of this book, the need to take seriously moves towards regionalization, not only between the Indian states but also within them.

In bringing together social, economic, political and cultural research, we believe we can make a useful contribution to debates on policy and progress in India's largest and most important state. But it is not our place to make specific proposals. As outsiders we have the advantage of distance in our perspectives on the state. Because we only come and go, we have no basis for political action. We can do little more than cheer from the touchline those who are attempting to overcome the inertia, increasingly combined with growing inequality and poverty, that has characterized the recent history of UP.

NOTES

1. In October 2000, the new state of Uttaranchal was formed from the districts of Hardwar, Almora, Bageshwar, Chamoli, Champawat, Garhwal, Dehra Dun, Naini Tal, Pithoragarh, Rudraprayag, Tehri-Garhwal, Udham Singh Nagar, and Uttarkashi. The 2001 Census reports population totals separately for the two units, provisional figures being 8.48 million in Uttaranchal and 166.05 million in UP. For our purposes in this book we shall deal with the old unit of Uttar Pradesh, except where we explicitly exclude the new state.

2. Whereas UP as a whole grew by about 25 per cent in the intercensal decades 1971–81, 1981–91 and 1991–2001, Uttaranchal's population also grew by 25 per cent in 1981–91 but by only 19.2 per cent in 1991–2001 (*Census of India 2001*: 42–3). Note, however, that within Uttaranchal, Dehra Dun and Naini Tal have experienced dramatic growth rates, largely through immigration, since the 1970s.

3. Measured as 'cultivators' and 'agricultural labourers' as percentage of 'main workers', according to the 1991 Census. The all India average was 64 per cent (*Census of India 1991*).

4. Measured, for example, as average value of yield (Rs /ha) (Bhalla and Singh 1997: A-3–A-4).

5. Unsurprisingly, in the latter case, land reforms have not been on the agenda.

6. Surprisingly, in an otherwise excellent survey article on mobilization patterns in UP, Hasan (2001) fails to provide a disaggregated picture.

7. West UP MLAs raised the demand for the separation of West UP in 1964. Brass notes, however, that at that time, the demand 'had no significant popular basis [and] was never taken seriously by the central government' (Brass 1994: 151).

8. For more details see Jafri (1985 [1931]) and Whitcombe (1972).

9. For a review of a number of case studies, see Lerche (1999).

10. The census authorities regard the q(2) estimates (the chances, out of 1,000, of a child not reaching its second birthday) as the most reliable of those they produce. Graduated figures have been used where these have been provided. The National Health and Fertility Survey uses different boundaries (so we are not using its data here). It shows

similar regional patterns of mortality but much higher levels of child mortality than does the 1991 Census.

11. In 1981, the UP hills held nearly 80 per cent of all UP's Scheduled Tribe population.

12. Meerut Division has changed its boundaries through time: in 1982, for example, it consisted of the Districts of Meerut (split by 2000 to create Baghpat), Ghaziabad (split by 2000 to create Gautam Budh Nagar), Bulandshahr, Muzaffarnagar, Bijnor and Saharanpur (split by 2000 to create Hardwar).

13. The reasons for this development may be summarized as follows. The crop-specific results of the green revolution as well as government policies made wheat growing in particular more profitable. The increase in irrigation enabled the replacement of 'dry' crops with more valuable 'wet' crops; and the high procurement prices for sugar cane set by the government led to a concentration on this crop in the few parts of the state where sufficient sugar cane factories existed.

14. Sugar cane is highly profitable provided it is grown within the catchment area of the large scale sugar cane factories paying the high cane rates fixed by the government as a result of political pressure from modern farmers.

15. Comparing the three decades between 1961 and 1991, the northern growth regime is particularly pronounced in 1971–81. During 1981–91, a more disparate growth pattern emerges (see Map 1.7). Upper Doab growth rates have flattened out while other northern districts are joined by south-eastern parts of east UP as well as eastern parts of west UP.

16. Agra in the west; several districts around the Kanpur–Lucknow area in central UP; and several districts around Varanasi in east UP.

17. Sharma and Poleman argue that a main factor in the increased productivity in the east is increased government investments in irrigation (Sharma and Poleman 1993). However, the main factor in irrigation today (providing the most feasible type of irrigation) is private tubewells powered by small electrical pumpsets, not large-scale government irrigation schemes.

18. Growth rates of these districts are not included due to date inconsistencies between the 1961–81 and the 1981–91 periods.

19. The decision by the BJP-led government to divide the SC and OBC reservations into sections, to limit the benefits accruing to the Chamars (in the SC category) and the Yadavs (in the OBC category) fit into this general strategy: see Verma (2001).

20. This also means that the BSP must straddle the very different political expectations of, for example, employees and small-scale businessmen of the west UP and the towns.

21. Some further idea of the public perception of women and their rights can be gained from Ståhlberg (2002a). He has shown how Mayavati, a prominent Scheduled Caste politician, was the target of sexual innuendoes. These were widely seen as undermining her claims to be able to remain as a responsible leader to her party (the Bahujan Samaj Party or BSP) and (for a while in the mid-1990s) as chief minister.

22. In rural Bijnor, by contrast, women who have experienced longer schooling are more likely to be living in joint households with their parents-in-law—in part because women who have been to school longer are more likely to marry into families with only one or two sons (Jeffery and Jeffery 1996).

2
Development Priorities: Views from Below in UP

G.K. Lieten

Peasant populations, Marx observed in the *Eighteenth Brumaire of Louis Napoleon*, are politically disunited. He compared them to a sack of potatoes, a collection of homologous magnitudes without a relationship. Their merely local interconnection pre-empts supra-local political organization: 'Each individual peasant family is almost self-sufficient; it itself directly produces the major part of its consumption and thus acquires its means of life more through exchange with nature than in intercourse with society' (Marx and Engels 1969, III: 478–9). Peasants, accordingly, were considered to be incapable of enforcing their class interests and they had to rely on outside leadership for their further liberation (or repression). Lloyd and Susanne Rudolph used this quotation to suggest that in the view of Marx, and of many contemporary social scientists, development involves a break with tradition. In their own view, development and modernization could be perfectly aligned with traditional views and structures. They rejected the notion that modernity and tradition are dichotomous and argued that

Indian peasants have found in traditional social arrangements some of the means to represent and rule themselves. . . . In any case, India has shown a strong propensity to transform rather than supersede traditional corporate structures, to move imperceptibly from traditional to corporatism without so marked an intervening individualist phase as the West is said to have experienced. (Rudolph and Rudolph 1967: 19, 23)

The construct of the traditional Indian village has been the dominant paradigm in the past. The 'village community' was perceived as the essence of rural South Asia. This view, expressed in major writings by, for example Baden Powell, Maine, John Stuart Mill and Metcalf, and to an extent also by Marx, was supplemented by numerous sociologists who have tended to see India, in an Orientalist way, as a conglomerate of villages in which reciprocity and aloofness from outside developments were the key elements. One of them wrote that village communities all over the Indian subcontinent have a number of common features.

The village settlement, as a unit of social organization, represents a solidarity different from that of the kin, the caste, and the class, and plays a vital role as an agency of socialization and social control. Each village is a distinct entity, has some individual mores and usages, and possesses a corporate unity. Different castes and communities inhabiting the village are integrated in its economic, social, and ritual pattern by ties of mutual and reciprocal obligations sanctioned and sustained by generally accepted conventions. Inside the village, community life is characterized by economic, social and ritual co-operation existing between different castes. (Dube 1955: 202)

These theories have been with us for a long period of time. Despite the obvious disappearance of the dormant village as described by Dube, there still is a considerable body of opinion in mainstream circles that the rural population, except for some of the more advanced areas, is embedded in traditional ways of thinking. There still is assumed to be a dichotomy between modernization and the cultural and cognitive make-up of villagers.

Recently, a related view has cropped up in post-modernist theorizing. In a number of respects, it has similarities with the neo-liberal approach, but its development vision is different.[1] It claims to speak on behalf of people who are being uprooted from their traditional culture and who only want to revert to those pre-modern traditions.[2] Although no trajectory towards the resurrection of the traditional village is spelt out, post-modernists have positioned themselves on the moral high ground as self-appointed defenders of the wishes of village folk.[3]

So far I have covered three assumptions about the development expectations of villagers in the process of transition from the traditional to the modern: the idea that modernization comes from outside; the idea that the alignment of tradition with the modern world is a congruous process; and the defence of the ancient. In this chapter I seek to cover that local field of development expectations.[4]

The intensifying processes of globalization have brought the impact of the capitalist development vision to practically every nook and corner of the world. UP is no exception. Despite its seemingly retarded state of development, the area has been the target of various development strategies. It was the cradle of the Community Development Projects in the 1950s, and, with Punjab, the focus of the green revolution in agriculture from the late 1960s onwards. Generally, the various government programmes (such as the Integrated Rural Development Programme, the National Rural Employment Programme, and the extension of infrastructure in the field of education, health, sanitation and transport) have brought the villages of UP ever closer to the world at large, and the world ever closer to the villages.

Not only in the more dynamic areas in the western region and the labour export zones in the east, but also in the more secluded areas in Oudh and the Lower Doab, villagers have come to experience changes that, in the western discourse, have been marked as 'development'.[5] In the local language, development has its equivalent. Depending on the connotation, it can be referred to as *pragati* and *unnati* (progress), *samriddhi* (growth), or just *vikas* (the generic term for development, evolution). The concept thus has a local meaning. It is, to use a postmodern phraseology in questioning post-modern assumptions, discursively embedded in local culture. The question, however, is to uncover what is meant by the development vision of the local people.

RESEARCH FORMAT

I was interested in the meaning of development for villagers as a sub-question of a more general study on local political dynamics in UP (see Lieten 1994, 1996a, 1996b; Lieten and Srivastava 1999). In order to uncover the social cognition and world views behind the public stance, I conducted three series of surveys in combination with in-depth interviews in different parts of UP. The purpose was to gauge the reaction of the people to the ambient ideological changes that have come with the process of social and economic modernization. Were there different world views and different perceptions of development? Was there an 'Indian' form of development expectations, and moreover, was this Indian form structured along communal, gender or class lines? Or on the other hand, were there, gendered and class divisions of universal visions?

The study was conducted in three different areas of UP between 1991 and 1996. The first area, in Muzaffarnagar District in the western zone, was chosen as an example of capitalist development. Dominated by sturdy Jat peasants, many of them big landowners, in the late 1960s this area availed of the new agricultural technology leading to the green revolution. The second area, Jaunpur district in the eastern region, had been under the dominance of Brahmin landlords, and was characterized by a reasonably tranquil small peasant agriculture. Its potentially fertile soil is increasingly put to productive use, but landlords are still wary of investment in agriculture and small peasants are still too poor to do so. The villages were at great distances from urban centres, both in space and in linkages. Work was also conducted in a third area, namely, in Rae Bareli, in the Oudh region of the state. Detailed findings on this third district are not included in this paper.[6]

In each of the three districts, one development block was selected, and within the block a study was made of the functioning of the panchayats of one sub-block (*nyaya* panchayat). Within the latter area, two panchayat villages were then selected for a detailed study of the various political, social, economic and ideational aspects of village life.

In 1993, I enquired the villages in about the perceptions of the functioning of the panchayats and of the socio-economic developments in general, interviewing a random sample of around 350 households.[7] These in-depth interviews were supplemented one year later by a random survey, checking the attitudes on important public issues among around 750 respondents. The latter will be referred to as the survey, the former as the sample. In addition, structured interviews with male and female respondents drawn from a random sample of 25 per cent households (397 in all, 202 males, 195 female) were conducted in the six gram panchayats to discuss how they viewed the existing and proposed changes in panchayat legislation.

The investigation, which might sometimes have seemed like an inquisition, involved a complex range of choices, and I took extra care to see that the answers noted were genuinely reflective of the stand of the respondent. Most of the respondents appeared to be able to engage in a discourse on general issues. This may lead us to the first important conclusion, namely the presence of a very high level of awareness and ideational commitment.[8] Rae Bareli, where the respondents were less candid in expressing their opinions, had for many years been the recipient of favours by the Gandhi family. The high level of response and the internal consistency in the other districts are probably also due to an underlying process of emancipation. As one of the respondents in Jaunpur said:

There is a hell of a difference from our fathers' time. We can now talk to you. Earlier, Brahmins told us not to talk to foreigners. Or they would have told you not to come here, or they would have come along. So there were a lot of fences built around us. Also, we had to feign beliefs that we did not have. We had to believe in *karma*, but our heart said no.

PERCEPTIONS OF THE PANCHAYATS

First I shall look at the way in which the people perceive the panchayat, its leaders and its works.[9] The panchayati system was erected in order to bring democracy closer to the people, i.e. to have a direct rapport between the elected members of the lowest development institution and their constituency. It has been operational since the mid-1950s, and one can therefore reasonably assume that it is an institution with which people are very familiar. It is the locus of local power politics and of the distribution of government largesse; increasingly, many government development and extension programmes are routed through the panchayats.[10]

After talking to all the panchayat members in around 35 villages in the three development blocks, I selected a sample of 350 households, and had wide-ranging discussions on various issues related to development, (national) politics, the functioning of panchayats, the gender question, etc. The opinions I heard were indicative of a more general world view that I assumed to exist. Since I have not quantified the answers—most items were discussed in an open-ended mode—I am not in a position to give an exact division of opinions, and shall only generalize where the spread of opinions warrants it.

Generally, it can be concluded that the poor are aware of the ascribed role of the panchayat for village development. Unfortunately, they say, the good intentions of the government break down at the local level where the corrupt local administration is hand in glove with the (high-caste) landowners. Panchayat meetings were hardly ever held, and if they were held, they were confined to a small band of supporters called by the *pradhan* (chairman), and the lower castes did not have the freedom to speak in these meetings.

References to the works executed by the panchayat were often accompanied by sneering remarks about the money that had gone down the drain. Numerous were the complaints that, although the expenses were duly entered into the books, most of the money in fact had lined the pockets of the *pradhan* and some of his friends, as well as those of the block officials, with a further cut for the bureaucracy at the higher echelons. It was often said that much of what comes from the government is snatched away by the powerful. The *bare log* (big people), at least in the opinion of the *chhote log* (small people), rule and act as they like. They do not believe in *nyaya* (justice) or in the difference between right and wrong. Dominant-caste politics are summarized as internecine factionalism and suppression of the lower castes. Brahmins in Jaunpur are said to have united and to be using their unity and their muscle power against the interests of the poor people. Similar stories abound in the taluqdari area (Rajput power) of Rae Bareli and in the Jat-dominated area of Muzaffarnagar.

It is remarkable, therefore, that four-fifths of the panchayat member respondents, whom I interviewed separately, believed in panchayats as the source of rural development. The reason, which needs to be explained at some length, is that they have accepted the intervening and enabling state and have more confidence in a (potentially) democratic institution than in the bureaucratic echelons of a state that is far from transparent. I therefore noticed a belief in the grand narratives of the *State* and of *Democracy*, unlike the assumptions made in postmodernist theory and in the NGO-world, that poor villagers do not trust either politics or the state.

There also seems to be a faith in the *Development Project*. I noticed a generalized expectation of beneficial development to come. Most respondents, despite all the complaints about deterioration in economic and social life, appeared to be confident that somewhere or somehow, circumstances could improve. They have witnessed dramatic changes over the last fifty years—official statistics as well as the narratives of the village elders attest to this—and generally have experienced improvements in indicators of economic, human and political development. They are generally hopeful of more development and progress coming their way. Poverty and inequality as the natural state of affairs, or as something that had been ordained by God, is overwhelmingly rejected. It was actually expressed by only a handful of elderly males and females. By and large, work is regarded as the fountainhead of social development, and labour and the fruits of labour are perceived as socially embedded.

Many of the poorer respondents are indeed quite convinced that the economic and political system prevents any further reduction in poverty: 'if poverty persists, it is because of the exploitation by capitalists [the rural rich], and their friends in the government', as some people suggested. It is difficult to judge how far ideas have spread, but references to big countries like the USA, the big business families, and all the traders and 'thieves' sitting in the government, were too frequent to be dismissed as merely minority opinions.

At the same time, most of the people—literates and illiterates, men and women, Brahmins, Thakurs, Muslims and Chamars—all believe in the capacity of the human race to eradicate poverty. Despite the antagonistic attitudes they expressed, and despite their added cynicism about political parties, in the assessment of most people positive expectations prevail. The government is still seen as the repository of development vision and development instruments.

Development through the institutions of the state, a position contrary to neo-liberal and post-modern thinking, has a wide acceptance in the villages of UP which I studied. It remains possible that this reliance on the state and its government has been imbued through decades of ideological guidance from above, and that the basic yearning of the people, pushed down behind the surface, is different. The argument has validity within a purely metaphysical sense. In the physical world, ideas and perceptions get shaped through the socio-economic environment. What people told us reflects the developmentalist Keynesian and Nehruvian agenda of the last half century.

DEVELOPMENT ALTERNATIVES: A PROBE

In the remainder of this article, I shall consider the development priorities that people have in mind when they visualize their future. Methodologically, research into this issue is faced with a vexed problem. The 'listening to' may all too often amount to 'suggesting to'. The problem exists even if the researcher painfully abstains from setting the agenda. The agenda all too often has been established by ongoing development initiatives, as I have suggested. To a simple question like 'what should the local government do?', one receives an answer that usually refers to ongoing development plans. The *tabula rasa* mind, speaking out on development from an indigenous and primordial state of mind, presupposes a virginity of experience that is never the case with living beings.

In their environment and in their life span, changes have taken place, programmes have been discussed, promises have been made, and innovative ideas have entered the village. And yet, a straightforward enquiry into the course of development often, at least initially, is answered by silence. When I asked the villagers about their priorities, it indeed turned out to be difficult to extract answers. For example, I asked all the respondents in the sample, and later also in the survey, to assign priorities to the work the panchayats should undertake. The answer was not infrequently that so many things had to be done, or that it was difficult to tell exactly what would be most beneficial. When pressed for an answer, the answers could be analysed to reflect a world view, but I was never sure whether the selected items were inclusive or exclusive of alternative items. For this reason, I later made a paired comparison (discussed later in this chapter).

The activity most frequently mentioned as necessary was a corrective one, deemed necessary in the distorted process of development and modernization: *nyaya*, the Hindi word for justice. The call was expressed across caste and gender, and often was accompanied by a defeatist reference to corruption (*ghooskhori*) and nepotism (*bhaibhatijavad*). Life experience has informed the villagers that the government has developed various modes of intervention, and that many of these modes should have come their way, but that the various instruments have been distorted by the village élite and the powerful people high up in the administration. This is probably the reason why direct financial support, which has moved to a high priority in (international) development programmes, particularly after the commitment to the micro-credit philosophy (see Hulme and Mosley 1997), was hardly ever mentioned during the course of the interviews.

The need for roads was also high on the priority list of the village population in all areas. Spatial mobility appears to allow better and cheaper access to the labour and commodity market and to the educational and health infrastructure. People seem to prefer more linkages with the outer-village life rather than fewer. Roads, which can be seen as metaphors of modernity, carry ideas as well as goods from urban to rural contexts, and suck the hinterland into the process of modernization. The other priority needs predominantly expressed by villagers were likewise needs of a public nature, and do not relate to productive investments. Water supply, electricity, health provision and education, in that order, were frequently expressed.

Two sets of priorities were class-specific. Among the richer households, including lower caste households that had experienced upward mobility and had some members with higher educational qualifications, the introduction of employment opportunities was rated highly; rural industrialization and irrigation facilities were also mentioned. Among landless labourers and small peasants, the call for land, or for the right to possess the land that had been allotted to them during Indira Gandhi's land distribution programme in the 1970s, almost equalled the call for *nyaya*. Inequality is contested. Unequal access to land finds its corollary in unequal access to the public space and in the caste system. Lower-caste and (near-) landless villagers generally find this state of affairs despicable. In the words of one of them:

The quality (*gun*) of all the people is similar, but in ancient times, something happened that divided society. Brahmins then captured more land, and imposed their rule on society. This can be reversed. Now, to end poverty again, everybody should be equal. If economic equality is there, caste equality will be possible. If land is given to the landless people, equality will be there.

Upon closer investigation, these priorities only partially reflect the official development priorities. Two items that my respondents frequently mentioned—justice and land reforms—have been excluded from the official development agenda. Villagers hardly ever mentioned some other items that are very high on the official development agenda, possibly constituting the core of the neo-liberal development paradigm. Among them were issues such as population control and micro-credit, and more general concerns such as eco-balance and gender-justice.

The findings from sample studies in the three areas were strengthened by a survey of around 750 respondents in which we set the terms of the discourse. The respondents were asked to prioritize their policy needs on the basis of five types of interventions extracted from the development debate. I presented five choices to the respondents: education and family planning,[11] more finances for local development works, redistribution of assets, a clean and just administration and, finally, employment generation. Each policy initiative had to be checked against the four other alternatives, and thus could get a score ranging from −4 to +4 depending on whether the alternatives were accepted or rejected.[12] The respondents were asked to compare each intervention with each other type separately, and to indicate their preference.

The juxtaposition of two development options informs us of their relative attraction. The aggregation of the respective scores tells us about their absolute attraction. Since I also had the socio-economic background of the respondents, the exercise allowed me to separate the preferences of the relevant groups. I have reported the results in terms of four socio-economic status groups: very poor, poor, middle, and rich and very rich families. The results have been aggregated in separate tables for the regions. I shall focus the discussion on the data of Jaunpur area in eastern UP, but occasionally shall also use some of the data relating to Muzaffarnagar, especially when the findings from that relatively developed area shed a different light on the discussion.

FOREMOST: A CLEAN ADMINISTRATION

In Table 2.1, I have illustrated the matrix of priorities in respect of fifty very poor households in Jaunpur. Take, for example, category IV (a clean administration). In all cases a clean administration is preferred to family planning and education; in almost all cases (46) it is preferred to more finances, and in 37 cases it even takes preference over employment generation. Yet in only 17 cases is it preferred over land reforms and other such structural interventions. Most poor household respondents thus preferred land reforms to other types of interventions. Only employment generation scored higher: 32 poor families opted for employment and 18 opted for land reforms.

We find in the rows that a mainstream government mechanism (more finances) received only 54 positive scores (out of a maximum of 50 x 4 = 200), most of them in comparison with population control and education. In the columns, we find that in 146 comparisons, more finance was rejected as the priority development strategy. The net score (positive minus negative) as recorded in the last column of Table 2.1 clearly reflects the poor opinion of development finances in comparison with, for example, land reforms and a clean and just administration. It appears that the priorities of poor people are radically different from the priorities of the government and of most development planners.

The most outspoken choice of the poorest people, in a negative sense, is against family planning (and education, but see note 11) as a direct instrument of welfare and development. Confronted with the numerous offspring of most parents, it is indeed not surprising that family planning is not a priority item. Although by and large it receives low priorities in all categories, the poorer the family, the lower the priority. This also applies to Muslims, who generally belong to the poorer sections and (unlike the myth constructed in the *Hindutva* discourse), generally have the same attitudes as Hindus.

One reason for adversity to family planning is religious. At least, so it seems, for the direct answer one always get is 'A small family is a good family, but *Bhagwan* gives more'. The argument that 'children are a gift from God' is very often heard. It is difficult to judge, but when such an explanation is given by people who are atheists (in the sense that they never pray and only have a vague sense of the Hindu pantheon), the explanation starts sounding more like an empty phrase.[13] For example, the mother of Jagdev initially told us that children are a gift from God, but in the end she gave a more mundane explanation of

Table 2.1: *Paired Comparisons of Development Priorities of Very Poor Households in Jaunpur (N = 50)*

	I Family planning and education	II More development finances	III Redistribution of wealth and assets	IV Just and clean administration	V Employment generation	Total	Net score	Relative score
I Family planning and education	—	16	2	0	0	18	-164	-3.28
II More development finances	34	—	10	4	6	54	-92	-1.84
III Redistribution of wealth and assets	48	40	—	33	18	139	78	+1.56
IV Just and clean administration	50	46	17	—	37	150	100	+2.00
V Employment generation	50	44	32	13	—	139	78	+1.56
Total	-182	-146	-61	-50	-61			

Note: The absolute score (positive minus negative preferences) divided by the number of respondents gives the relative score which can be any number between -4.00 (absolute rejection) and +4.00 (absolute preference).

why the 'production' has stopped. It could have stopped earlier if the family planning programme staff had helped her:

I understand what they say. If I have fewer children, they can be looked after in a better way, and if I have more children, they have to run around in old and torn clothes. But my father listened to them, and he died one year after he got sterilized. If they had given me one *bigha* of land for my children, I would have allowed them to operate on me. That would have been good, because I did not know how to stop it. In one year I even produced two children. Luckily now my sister-in-law is staying with us under the same roof, and so the production has come to a natural end.

The call for justice is closely related to the explicit expectations that poor people entertain. The correct implementation of different government plans would go a long way in helping them, but in practice the benefits are taken by the rich and powerful who have access to the government administration in headquarters towns, which are usually a tedious and long journey from the village. Government staff are widely seen as unresponsive and even callous in their dealings with villagers. They are said to have close links with the *goondas* and the *punjipati* (capitalists, rich people). The Village Level Worker does come to the villages, but mainly (if not exclusively) to the houses of the rich. To poor people he may offer the partial benefits of a scheme from which he will benefit more than the beneficiary in the end. Schemes that are decided at the village level, usually by the *pradhan*, are more likely to benefit the poor households whenever their representatives dominate the panchayat. In those cases, more hand pumps, subsidized houses, and investment loans have come to the neighbourhoods of the lower castes. The problem of corruption, remains, however, and constitutes the major reason for poor people not to set greater store by employment facilities: 'You can now talk to the officials, you can even talk to the police. Our sons have been educated, even more than the police, but the Brahmins and the Thakurs are sitting on their jobs. They had the money to pay the bribes. And if you can not pay the bribe, you have to continue doing the old jobs.'

Next to the cry for justice is the demand for land and land distribution from among the rich landowners. Access to land, and to employment that comes with it, are seen as a means to earn a living and to escape oppression. The rhetorical question is often posed by landless or near-landless villagers: how can there be *nyaya* (justice), and how can there be democracy and equality between the upper and lower castes so long as the access to land is polarized along caste lines? Even the homestead where poor families live is often without a *patta* (land ownership deed).

Among the landless, awareness of the necessity of land distribution is widespread. The ideological impulse given by the land reforms' movement of the CPI in the eastern districts in the 1950s and 1960s lingers on in the mind of many landless and near landless households. In Muzaffarnagar also, in the past the communists were a force to reckon with. But this influence does not explain the call for land reforms. Even in Rae Bareli, the complaint that land had not been distributed was often heard. There and elsewhere, the policies and messages of Indira Gandhi in the 1970s have struck deep roots. Ram Sarup, a backward-caste man without land, has become even more interested in land distribution since, in his view, landowners are nowadays reticent to give land on sharecropping (*batai*) basis. In a nutshell, he explains how development would potentially lead to empowerment from below, and why the requisite development plans without land reforms are coming to naught.

I have asked the *pradhan* to distribute the *gram sabha* land, but he does not listen to me. The land should be distributed. If we get land ownership, then we shall get freed from the clutches of the upper castes. The *pradhan* knows that also. The problem is that the people of the upper castes neither do work nor let the work be done, because if the work gets done then the backward castes will get equal status. Development cannot be allowed, that is what their interest tells them.

Land is still available. Some land is possibly on the grab from rich Brahmins, but most eyes fall on the commons. Most of this land that falls under the jurisdiction of the panchayat has been privatized in two ways. Some of it has been grabbed by the rich landowners. Some was officially allotted to landless families in the 1970s, but was usurped by the very same rich landowners. The cry for land therefore is more a cry for the possession of allotted land, and for the issue of deeds for *awadhi* (homestead) land.[14] Possession of allotments depends on luck, since powerful Brahmins, Thakurs and rich Muslims have often intervened to take possession of (part of) the land.

Land that has been allotted often remains in the hands of the *bare log*. The explanation follows simply from the existing balance of power. Although the land has been grabbed illegally, and although everybody knows who has done it, it is difficult to get the names. As one peasant said: 'They control so much of the village that they may do anything to us. That is why we keep mum. Yes, they have taken our land, but nobody is going to help us to take it back, and, moreover, we can survive as long as we work for them. It is either working for them on their conditions or to leave the village.'

The poor people in Jaunpur want justice and land. They obviously also want employment, but in comparison with the other groups they attach less importance to it. Employment opportunities are something that the rich people *apparently* are more interested in. As income rises, there is an increasing desire for employment. Of course, poor people would like to get employment, and many of them indeed would see it as their greatest achievement if a son could obtain a (secure) government job or even a job in the (less secure) private sector. From experience, however, they have learnt that except for the casual and lowly-paid menial jobs, the chances of getting a job are positively related with the income. The higher the income, the easier the access to the people who matter and the higher the bribe one can pay, if required. Employment, particularly in the better-paid and more secure market segments, is usually the preserve of the rich households. In fact, as Table 2.2 illustrates, the second highest positive score (+2.42) is in favour of employment generation among the 57 rich and very rich respondents.

The rich villagers are obviously dead set against land reforms. It is a little more puzzling to find that they do not necessarily want more finances either: prior to the devolution of finances for village development, they want a clean and less corrupt administration. This attitude

*Table 2.2: Paired Comparisons of Development Priorities
of Various Classes in Jaunpur*

Type of intervention	Type of Household			
	Very poor	Poor	Middle	Rich
Family planning and education	-3.28	-2.54	-1.14	-0.45
More development finances	-1.84	-1.64	-1.59	-1.44
Redistribution of wealth and assets	1.56	-0.37	-2.31	-3.36
Better and clean administration	2.00	2.72	2.83	2.84
Employment generation	1.56	1.82	2.22	2.42
Respondents (N)	*50*	*61*	*72*	*57*

Source: Village survey involving 240 respondents in 1994.

stretches across class, caste and gender. The preference for a clean and just administration in Jaunpur varied between +2.84 (rich peasants) and +2.00 (very poor families). Except for employment, where richer families can count on their reservoir of skills and educational achievements, in the matter of financial allocations, they are dependent on the arbitrary decisions of the bureaucrats. This may hurt, especially when the bureaucrats belong to, or are in patronage relations with, a different village faction. The priority of a just and clean administration is therefore absolutely foremost in the minds of those between the rich and the very poor. Often they do not stand to benefit from poverty alleviation programmes. On the other hand, since they have some income and property, they may become easy targets of greedy and vindictive bureaucrats. If they belong to patronage networks, protection may be had from a patron with direct links with the administration, but it remains a fragile position.

Economic Progress, Social Corrosion

Muzaffarnagar is one of the richest districts in the country. It has often been assumed that the spread of capitalism in agriculture, particularly in its green revolution form, will lead to polarization and pauperization. In comparison with the eastern district, material conditions of life are distinctly superior. The rich and middle peasants have profited from the sharp rise in agricultural prices and from the diversification in economic activities, for example sugar making and brick kilns. The poorer sections have not profited commensurately. The combined might of the dominant Jat peasants has kept them in a subordinate position. Fortunately for the underclass, they have been able to get work opportunities outside the villages, particularly in Delhi, and gradually they have come to take their share of the material progress. But on one issue, practically all the villagers are of one mind: despite economic progress (or because of it), the social quality of life has been deteriorating.

In view of the conflict between insecurity (*asuraksha*) and survival, most poor families are intensely aware of the potential role that the village administration could play in ensuring law and order and in providing justice and security. Muzaffarnagar happens to be the stronghold of the legendary peasant leader Tikait, who, in addition to having stood for just economic and political causes, has also been associated with the protection of Jat muscle power, intimidation and robbery (see Lindberg and Madsen, this volume). Understandably, the priority scores in Muzaffarnagar contain a clear message: the quest for a clean and just administration. Good governance is priority number one across class, caste and gender.

Depending on the socio-economic position, expectations like land reforms came up, but one type of intervention clearly dominated in the expectations of all sections: justice by a clean administration. The results on the Muzaffarnagar area (see Table 2.3) are indeed revealing. Even the rich peasants, who may be hand in glove with the state bureaucracy and the local power holders, had an absolute preference for the establishment of law and order before anything else: +3.40. The very poor people were unanimous in their priorities: the preference for a clean and just administration received a +3.37 score. The low-caste people, the landless Chamars, Pasis and Bhangis, often refer to *asuraksha*. They complain that the Jat *goondas* are moving around with pipe-guns, and that it is better to keep out of their way. The women complain that it is not safe to go to the fields to defecate, and that they may get accosted if they do not move in groups. People from all groups, male and female, complain that teasing, *dacoity* and kidnapping are so widespread that it is risky to have girls continue their studies in the nearby town after class V.

The discourse on insecurity and criminalization deals with virtual reality. The collective assessment of decreasing cordiality and increasing insecurity is likely to be based on real stories of the immediate neighbourhood, on twisted stories of adjoining villages, and invented stories of the wider area. In the case of the dominant castes, it is

Table 2.3: *Paired Comparisons of Development Priorities of Various Classes in Muzaffarnagar*

Type of intervention	Type of household			
	Very poor	Poor	Middle	Rich
Family planning and education	-3.16	-2.00	-0.06	-0.27
More development finances	-2.84	-2.78	-2.20	-1.60
Land reforms	+0.32	-0.50	-3.43	-3.73
Clean and just administration	+3.37	+2.76	+3.32	+3.40
Employment generation	+2.31	+2.52	+2.38	+2.20
Respondents (N)	44	94	68	30

Source: Village survey involving 240 respondents in 1994.

probably also induced by weakening caste dominance. Whereas hitherto there was compliance and order, nowadays there is some defiance and therefore disorder. The greater access that the lower-caste households now have to employment opportunities in the cities and to the lifestyles and world views that follow in their wake have upset Jat dominance. The city provides better educational facilities and employment at higher wages, and in addition, it is also freer of the injustice and the harassment that they have to undergo in the villages at the hands of the Jat, Rajput and Gujar landowners. In the words of one Chamar with a small morsel of land: 'Village life actually is only good for landed property holders. Here we are *ghulam* (slaves). In the city, there is no harassment on the basis of caste, which is good for us.'

The findings of Muzaffarnagar reflect distinctive class preferences as well. Very poor and poor villagers do not see much virtue in the effects of family planning and education. Especially the very poor families, but also to an extent the poor families, see more gain in redistribution of land. Middle peasants and rich peasants are vehemently opposed to this solution. Their clear-cut position against land reforms explains their moderately positive attitudes towards family planning and education. For many of them, the choice possibly amounted to a comparison between two evils: land power and muscle power through procreation have been traditionally associated in Jat culture.

The Government is generally not despised for what it does, but for what it does not do, namely its inactivity in eradicating corruption: 'When dishonesty will disappear, poverty will end.' Several statements, particularly those by poorer people, indicate that the government is doing its best, but that the middlemen have occupied the space at the delivery point, and that the all-pervasive corruption prevents the benefits from reaching the people.

Thus the government is assessed for what it claims to be doing, namely providing general facilities for rural development and target-oriented facilities for the poorer sections, and not for what the same government in practice allows to happen: the privatization of the common good. The priorities of the poor, it appears, are particular and personal, but also, unlike the assumption made by Chambers (1983: 148), general and abstract. They include higher agricultural production, equality, and infrastructure. They also include the eradication of corruption so that the benefits of the government schemes may reach the target group. This suggests that there is a need for more government intervention, not less.

CONCLUSION

The direction of development is the substance of political, ideological and scholarly debates. Theories of the past and the present have often assumed villagers to be longing for traditional values and institutions and to be wary of the modernizing state. Post-modernist writers have even started pleading for a fragmented and indigenous non-development. Others have argued that village India wants to enter modernity on the basis of its own age-old institutions and values, which includes caste and hierarchy. These theories amount to the acceptance of a non-universal development vision, which is the standard prescription of post-modernists for non-Western societies. Such acceptance has generally not been informed by field studies.

My field study suggests that a universal and traditional 'development' vision may exist in the rural areas of UP. The hundreds of villagers I met generally appear to have aspirations, hopes, wishes and visions very much akin to (and as variegated as) the views and aspirations in the more 'developed' parts of the world. The anti-modernist school of thought, which ascribes to non-European people an essential otherness, is strong on ethical assumptions and projections but poor on locally informed perspectives. By homogenizing and romanticizing the indigenous mentality it denies non-European people the variegated nature of development along a modernist path. Interventionist debates could therefore best be conducted along 'modernizing' lines.[15]

What people want is fairly obvious. Careful study of the world views of the people who inhabit the villages which are being sucked into the world of modernization reveals that they want to have more state intervention rather than less, and would prefer more development rather than less. By discussing four economic class categories separately, I have been able to illustrate the preferences that are dissimilar as well as the priorities that are similar for all groups. Most villagers, it turns out, attach the highest importance to a clean administration. Good governance is priority number one across class, caste and gender. As could be expected, the generation of employment scores reasonably high. At the other end of the spectrum, very poor and poor villagers do not see much virtue in the effects of family planning and education. Finances for rural development does not attract them either. The very poor families, but to an extent also the poor families, see more gain in redistribution of assets. Middle peasants and rich peasants are fundamentally antagonistic towards this solution.

The general conclusion is that rural UP looks for solace in more development rather than less, and in more government rather than less. But development programmes have also disappointed the villagers because those programmes by and large have fortified unjust and inegalitarian structures. Peoples' reactions are not to dismiss modernization, but to express their realism: many of the development efforts, including education and financial support, will continue to go awry unless the power structure is re-adjusted in the direction of more transparency, entitlement and democracy.

NOTES

1. The state is portrayed as a neo-colonizing institution that is bent on uprooting the people in rural India, the people of Bharat, from its community roots in self-centred villages. Foremost in the approach of the neo-liberal discourse and the post-modernist discourse is the attack on the state and its various institutions as the anchor in development strategies. The state has been downgraded as a bureaucratic, insensitive and self-centred institution. Privatization and freedom of action and activity have taken its place.

2. In the Indian context, Nandy (1987), Alvarez (1992), and Ananta Giri (1998) propagate this view. See also Escobar (1995).

3. In the wake of the ascent of post-modernism, it has become trendy to dichotomize the Western world view and the plethora of non-Western world views. Non-western mankind, per definition, has a different frame of mind, a different cultural ethos and a different perception of the way forward (or the way inward) of their society. These theories of a *fragmented essentialism* are usually argued in an opaque language, discursively overextended, but weak in empirical underpinning. These ideas have been further developed in Lieten (2001 and forthcoming).

4. The soliciting of the views from below often serves as a means to collect data to illustrate a development vision. A trail-blazing contribution was Salmen's *Listen to the People*, pleading for 'an effective way to bring people into the planning and implementation of programmes that affect their lives' (Salmen 1987: 125). His work, like Korten's and Cernea's, was indicative of the World Bank catching up with the participatory ideology which the NGOs, in the footsteps of Freire, Chambers and others, and they were proud to claim it as the new panacea (Korten 1990; Cernea 1991). Salmen has argued, on an underlying assumption of deficient knowledge among the managers of the official development organizations, that 'managers do not normally have an adequate understanding of the world they are trying to change. This understanding is primarily among the people who inhabit that world' (Salmen 1987: 126). The question which remains, and which is sought to be answered by 'listening to them' is how they could be made to become optimal players in the further extension of a capitalist development process.

5. For more on these changes, see 'Uttar Pradesh: Into the Twenty-first Century', this volume.

6. Rae Bareli is situated in between two other districts. Historically, the area has been associated with the taluqdars, mainly upper caste Rajputs and Muslims who, under the aegis of the British colonial administration, became despotic revenue collectors and landlords. The heirs of the taluqdars still hold sway over many villages in the area and have retained agriculture within semi-feudal bonds (see 'Uttar Pradesh: Into the Twenty-first Century', this volume for more on the historical roots of differences in social structures within UP). This area was selected for field work for another important reason. Its belongs to Amethi, which for many decades had been the electoral constituency of the Gandhi family, and which, especially during the regime of Indira Gandhi and Rajiv Gandhi, had been the target of government largesse. The findings on Amethi are generally in line with the picture prevailing in Jaunpur and Muzaffarnagar.

7. The sampling was done in such a way that in the end it included males and females, upper castes, lower castes and Muslims, and the various professions and constituted a fair reflection of the village population.

8. In Rae Bareli, the preliminary conclusion was that, in comparison with the other areas, the no-response frequency of around 10 per cent of the respondents was considerable. People who feigned ignorance or who were really not in a position to state their position on a number of normative statements almost exclusively belonged to the OBC and SC sections; one-third of them were males. I was given to understand that the issues were too difficult for them to grasp. The sub-text may very well have been that they did not consider it in their interest to oblige the interviewer.

9. For a more elaborate treatment, see Lieten (1996b) and Lieten and Srivastava (1999).

10. Panchayats, traditionally, were associated with a Gandhian perception of Indian villages. Since villages were conceived as having organizational coherence and harmony of interests, they were defended as a better and more indigenous alternative to the centrally-administered development structures. Time and again, however, official reports and scholarly research have illustrated how hierarchy, nepotism and inequality have incapacitated the village councils and have stifled their democratic functioning, sometimes even their functioning at all. A survey of the debates can be found in Lieten and Srivastava (1999: Chap. 1).

11. Combining education and family planning was based on their pairing as human development indicators, different from (for example) economic development projects. During the research, I soon realized that the combination was faulty. Both indicators should have been treated separately since they involve different decision making processes and different approaches. By the time I fully realized the flaw, the mistake could not be rectified. In the course of the interviews, I started paying more attention to family planning because I realized that education, although it was deemed necessary by many, was a dependable variable: as long as family sizes were large, education could hardly be afforded. I therefore opted to find out their stand *vis-à-vis* family planning.

12. The exercise required deft handling of the interview situation, but I am reasonably satisfied that the exercise was understood properly and that the respondents were genuine about their stated priorities.

13. The family planning teams make their rounds of the villages, looking for candidates for the operation. Their success remains limited, for a number of reasons. There are the bitter memories of the Emergency (1975–7) when coercive sterilization took place on a vast scale. There are health risks involved, and there are broken promises: people who were promised land, loans or gifts never received any.

14. Some of the members have received a *patta* during the regime of Indira Gandhi, but few of them have been able to take actual possession of the land. Illustrative of the type of land that has been distributed is the land which belongs to Bhulai Harijan, and which he is keen on showing: his supposed 1 *bigha* of land is located exactly in the middle of the Sai river. Some other *pattas* for which the ex-*pradhan* had taken a hefty amount of money, related to a non-existing cadastral number.

15. Lest I am accused of resurrecting the modernization theory, I have put modernization within quotes.

3

A Uniform Customary Code?
Marital Breakdown and Women's
Economic Entitlements in Rural Bijnor

Patricia Jeffery

Drawing on research in rural Bijnor District, this paper focuses on aspects of everyday gender politics in western UP. In particular, exploring marital breakdown enables me to raise questions about the relationship between formal law and theology on the one hand, and the lived realities of Muslim and Hindu women on the other; about the efficacy of the law in protecting women's rights; and about strategic priorities in the struggle for gender equity in India—all issues that were raised by the Shah Bano controversy.[1]

THE SHAH BANO CASE

Among the many activities initiated during the British colonial era were the classification of the Indian population on the basis of religious allegiance and the codification of indigenous legal systems and customary means of dispute settlement.[2] These included procedures for dealing with family life—such as marriage and marital breakdown, child custody, and property transfers within the family. Recent commentaries note that written texts were privileged over oral traditions and encoding the 'correct' legal framework entailed attempts to homogenize the diversity of 'customary practices'. Crucially, British civil servants consulting (male) religious experts assumed that family life was governed by religious texts. Thus, distinctive systems of 'personal law' were codified, despite considerable evidence of cultural parallels and religious syncretism. Further, official policy was that family life should normally be regulated by the authorities of the different religious communities.[3] After 1947, the Hindu Code was revised, despite opposition (Agnes 1995; Kapur and Cossman 1996; Kishwar 1994; Parashar 1992) but Indian Muslims are still (notionally) governed by the Shariat Law of 1937.[4] Thus the multiplicity of 'personal laws' remains—enshrining religious or communal divisions through the differing procedures, rights and obligations for Indian citizens of different religions.

The British rulers also developed systems of civil and criminal law applicable irrespective of religious allegiance, including the Criminal Procedure Code (CrPC). The Indian government's 1973 revisions of Section 125 of the CrPC enabled women who became homeless (for instance, after divorce or being ousted from a son's house) to press for maintenance from their ex-husband or their son. How, though, should Muslim personal law and the CrPC come into play in relation to the rights of divorced Muslim women?

After being divorced, Shah Bano, an elderly Muslim woman from Indore, appealed through the provisions of CrPC Section 125 for maintenance from her ex-husband.[5] He contested the case, claiming that it would be un-Islamic for a Muslim man to provide for his wife beyond the *iddat* period. After the case was adjudicated by the Supreme Court in Delhi in 1985, conservative Muslims argued that the Supreme Court judges had neither had the competence nor the jurisdiction to find in Shah Bano's favour or to make adverse comments about women's position in Islam. Indeed, during this outcry, Shah Bano felt compelled to dissociate herself from the judgement because she came to believe that it was contrary to Islamic law (Engineer 1987: 211–12). Rajiv Gandhi's Congress government permitted an independent Member of Parliament to introduce the somewhat curiously titled Muslim Women (Protection of Rights on Divorce) Bill, which became law in 1986. Under its provisions, it seems that Muslim *men* were protected from maintenance claims by ex-wives because Muslim *women* could no longer make claims under CrPC Section 125.[6]

Responses to the Bill became largely framed by Congress and conservative Muslim rhetoric emphasizing the constitutional protection of minority rights to govern their own domestic lives free from state interference and in accord with the (supposed) requirements of their religious beliefs. In opposing the Bill, the Hindu Right[7] also focused on minority rights, but to accuse Congress of cynically refusing to intervene in Muslim family law in order to retain the 'Muslim vote bank',[8] and of 'appeasing' Muslims by according them more rights than the majority Hindu population (for instance, by letting Muslim men evade the obligations entailed under CrPC 125). The conservative Muslim stance was viewed as confirmation that Muslim men victimize their womenfolk and that Islam is inherently oppressive to women (in contrast to Hindu men and the Hindu tradition). Soon, this was explicitly linked to the Hindu Right's increasingly assertive proclamations over the Babari Masjid in Ayodhya and to the wider communalization of politics, marked by Muslim vulnerability to physical and rhetorical attacks from the Hindu Right and by the electoral successes of the BJP in the 1990s. In terms of subsequent political developments, then, a minority rights and communal politics reading of the Shah Bano case clearly has considerable justification.[9]

Yet the Shah Bano case was certainly not just about minority rights and communal politics. At its core are crucial issues of women's economic entitlements. Liberal Muslims opposing the Muslim Women Bill asserted that generosity to ex-wives would not be contrary to the spirit of Islam or signify that Islam was endangered. Various feminist organizations not only opposed the Bill because it disadvantaged Muslim women *vis-à-vis* other Indian women, but attacked the negative comments about Islam in the Supreme Court judgement and highlighted the paltry sums normally awarded in maintenance: Shah Bano herself was granted just Rs 179.20 per month by the Supreme Court after a lower court had originally granted her Rs 25. Feminists also contested Hindu Right claims that Muslim women were especially disadvantaged and that the position of Hindu women was unproblematic, and they argued that the furore distracted attention from the inability of Indian women in general to ensure their financial security outside marriage. Such voices, however, became increasingly marginalized in the unfolding debate and by the Hindu Right's interventions.

Gender equity is enshrined in the Indian Constitution—but so too is freedom to practise religion. During the 1980s, the Indian government was swayed in turn by the contradictory demands of Muslim conservatives and the Hindu Right, for whom women were a crucial part of the terrain on which battles about minority rights and national identity were fought.[10] As the Shah Bano case demonstrated, religious freedom may be privileged over gender equity when the two conflict: 'community' self-regulation on matters covered by personal laws is a core element of religious freedom, yet the protection of religious freedom can have an extremely detrimental impact on women's rights (P. Jeffery 1999; Kapur and Cossman 1995).

Accounts of the Shah Bano case, however, are dominated by a focus on high-profile political, legal and constitutional issues. Little attention has been paid to the implications of the case or to the associated communalization of everyday and gender politics at the grass roots, my central concerns here. I want to make three main points in this chapter. First, the crucial parallels in the everyday domestic lives of Hindu and Muslim women in rural Bijnor, combined with case material on marital breakdown, challenge Hindu Right assertions that Muslim women are uniquely oppressed by their menfolk and victimized by Islam. Second, the Shah Bano case and the Babari Masjid campaign were highly significant in terms of local-level communal politics in Bijnor (Basu 1995b; R. Jeffery and P. Jeffery 1994b, 1997). Yet the Muslim Women Act appears to have had no impact on the economic situations of ordinary Muslim women. Third, and following from the first two, bringing local-level gender politics into the frame alongside the communalization of everyday politics poses dilemmas for feminist activism that attempts to mobilize rural women around issues of gender equity.

COMMUNITY AND GENDER IN RURAL BIJNOR

About a quarter of Indian Muslims live in UP, where they numbered over 24 million (or 17.33 per cent of the state's total population) in 1991 (Registrar General and Census Commissioner 1996: Table C-9). Almost two-thirds live in the rural areas, compared with the overall UP figure of just over 80 per cent. Muslims are under-represented in the most wealthy sectors: town-dwellers tend to inhabit particular residential areas and are especially associated with artisanal activities such as weaving and metal work; rural Muslims are generally middle or poor peasants, landless agricultural labourers or semi-skilled labourers (mechanics or weavers). When class is held constant, the similar domestic arrangements, property rights, linguistic patterns and diet of north Indian Muslims and Hindus, and the distinctive flavour of South Asian Islam are striking, despite the divisions connected with the aftermath of Partition and the recent communalization of politics (Ahmad 1973, 1976, 1981; M. Hasan 1991, 1997; Mann 1992).

Bijnor District in western UP seems less affluent than districts to the west which have had canal irrigation since about 1900; but on most criteria of social and economic development it is rather more 'developed' than eastern UP. At about 32 per cent of the rural population, the rural Muslim population in Bijnor District is proportionately one of the highest in UP.[11] Broadly speaking, kinship and marriage, residence and property ownership, gender politics and demography among rural Muslims and Hindus alike reflect what Dyson and Moore have called the 'northern demographic regime' (Dyson and Moore 1983). The following sketches the position of young married women, for whom marital breakdown by separation or divorce is most salient.

Productive resources, especially land, are owned (albeit inequitably) and managed by men. Women—whether as daughters or as wives—scarcely ever own land, irrespective of community or class (Agarwal 1994). A girl normally depends on her father and brothers to meet the costs of raising her and arranging her marriage. At all levels of the class hierarchy, the most honourable form of marriage requires the bride's parents and their wider kin network to provide a dowry. This can entail major outlays for clothing and jewellery for the bride and members of her husband's family, household goods—bed, bedding, cooking utensils, etc.—and, among Hindus, cash.[12] On marriage, the bride normally migrates to her husband's village. If the mother-in-law is alive, the new bride can expect to spend some years sharing a cooking hearth, subject not only to her husband's controls but also to those of his mother.

It is crucial that a woman bears children, yet the physiological processes associated with fertility and childbearing (sexual intercourse, menstruation, pregnancy, childbirth and post-partum bleeding) are matters of shame (*sharm ki bat*) and/or of pollution (locally termed *gandagi*). Moreover, Muslims and Hindus alike express a preference for sons over daughters, largely grounding their views on parental anxieties about providing dowries for daughters and on the importance of having sons to ensure support in old age. This part of UP—and northern South Asia in general—is notable for very masculine sex ratios, attributable to differential care of young boys and girls and to high rates of maternal mortality.

Whilst a young married woman's work may be trivialized by her in-laws (and even by herself), she plays an important economic role in the well-being of her husband's household, cooking, child-rearing, caring for livestock or working in the family fields. Variations in women's work relate to the class position of the household, whether Hindu or Muslim, as well as to life cycle changes. In the wealthiest households, controls over women's mobility beyond domestic space are evidenced in seclusion practices known locally as purdah; women will work almost wholly in and around the home. Somewhat poorer households may endeavour to keep their womenfolk engaged in activities based around the home, generally unpaid work for the household, although some women earn small sums of money by spinning cotton thread or stitching clothes for neighbours. Women in the poorest households may be compelled to seek employment as domestic servants or field labourers for the richer households. Poor, and usually elderly, widows (or women with husbands who earn insufficient incomes) may practise as *dais* (traditional birth attendants), a low-status occupation associated with pollution (R. Jeffery and P. Jeffery 1993a). Most rural women are not well-placed to support themselves: very few have the schooling or training that could enable them to earn enough to become economically independent.[13]

Post-marital residence norms have important social consequences for married women. Unlike her husband, a young married woman is separated from the networks of kin and friends she established during childhood. Nevertheless, her parents and brothers continue to be concerned for her. Partly, this is reflected in the things they continue to present to her. Indeed, Hindu and Muslim women describe their 'income' (*amdani*) as the foodstuffs (grain, sugar products), jewellery, clothing and cash (and very occasionally livestock) sent by their natal kin after the rice and wheat harvests, at festivals, when they give birth, when their children are married, and when there are marriages and births in their natal household. Usually, however, such gifts are neither regular nor sufficient to furnish all their requirements and provide them with a route to economic independence. Indeed, women whose parents and brothers are financially straitened may receive little or no such 'income'.

Some features of domestic life suggest that many Muslim women may be somewhat better placed than the typical Hindu woman in rural Bijnor. While son preferences are expressed irrespective of religious community, maternity history and census data from the study villages indicate that sex ratios are markedly less masculine among Muslims than among Hindus (R. Jeffery and P. Jeffery 1997: 68, 230–5).[14] Among Muslims, dowry demands and dowry harassment of young married women, the fear of which plagues Hindus, are very rare and Muslim dowries do not include cash, unlike those among Hindus. Hindus arrange their children's marriages beyond the village and usually at some distance (25–30 km was common); women are usually married into households where they know no one and only rarely are two closely related women married into the same village. Muslims generally arrange their children's marriages within a smaller geographical radius (about 3 km or less, and even within the village) and/or with people who are already closely related. This does not guarantee a woman's well-being after marriage—but Muslim women are normally less cut off from their natal kin than Hindu women. Married Hindu women normally receive visits from their brothers; many are never visited by parents (particularly the mother); and they rely on their husband or brothers to accompany them to their natal village for visits. Many married Muslim women can walk to their natal village—maybe with their children or another married woman—and it is not uncommon for even their mothers to make the reverse trip. Dense marriage networks enable a Muslim woman's parents to have considerable information about a potential groom and his close relatives before agreeing to a marriage—and to exert pressure if their married daughter is mistreated, although many Muslim women see this as a rather ambiguous benefit because parents cannot easily be spared knowledge of their marital troubles.[15]

Basically, though, a married woman—whether Muslim or Hindu—is the responsibility of her husband and his kin, who should continue to provide for her throughout her life, meeting her daily living expenses for food, clothing, medical care and so forth. Young married women are very unlikely to own productive resources or have incomes that permit independence. They continue to obtain some social and economic support from their natal kin, but are basically dependent on their husband and his kin. Young married women's room for self-determination in their affinal village is severely circumscribed by their lack of economic and social power in their own right (P. Jeffery and R. Jeffery 1996a: 1–37). Close marriage and lower dowry do not add up to greater autonomy for Muslim women, but they probably do make the negotiation of dependence somewhat easier for them. Few Hindu or Muslim women in rural Bijnor, however, regard their dependence as problematic and many fear the 'responsibility' (*zimmedari*) that independence (*azadi*) would entail (P. Jeffery and R. Jeffery 1994a, 1996b; R. Jeffery and P. Jeffery 1993b). The limitations of women's dependence, however, are starkly exposed by marital breakdown.

Marital Breakdown

Conversations with women in rural Bijnor suggest that marital bliss is somewhat elusive. Women often resent how they are treated by their husbands, their mothers-in-law and other in-laws. Many women complain that they cannot visit their parents as often as they wish, that they are required to work extremely hard and yet their efforts are inadequately appreciated, and that marital violence is commonplace. Nevertheless, few marriages end in separation.[16] Most separations occur in the first few years of a marriage, when there are few, if any, children. Beyond that, though, it is impossible even to hazard rates of marital breakdown. It is a 'shameful matter' (*sharm ki bat*) and we often learnt of separations or marital difficulties by chance, when querying gaps in women's maternity histories, when old marital conflicts became part of people's weaponry in contemporary disputes, or when young women returned to their natal village and became the focus of gossip. Our most detailed data relate to the 88 key informant couples.[17] Among them, about 6 per cent of the key informant women had experienced separation: one Muslim woman and three Hindu women were in second (or later) marriages and another Muslim woman had been 'divorced' by her husband but had returned to live with him (see P. Jeffery and R. Jeffery 1996a: 142–54 for more details). This figure cannot be extended to the populations as a whole, of course; nor can these cases give a reliable indication of which spouse is more likely to initiate the separation or of differential rates of marital breakdown, say by economic position or community.

While these cases and the others we learnt about vary in their specifics, there are some common features, whether they occurred before or after the Shah Bano case. Formal divorce procedures are hardly ever deployed: few people take marital disputes to secular law courts and Muslim couples are unlikely to take their case to a *qazi*. Rather, informal kin- and village-based mechanisms are central, both in trying to prevent marital breakdown and in dealing with it once it happens. These 'customary' and taken-for-granted procedures may not relate closely to stipulations laid out in theological treatises or in the statute books of the Indian state—and focusing on how people customarily respond to marital problems and marriage breakdown demonstrates further important parallels between Muslims and Hindus in rural Bijnor.

AVOIDING MARITAL BREAKDOWN

Marital breakdown is far more than a 'shameful matter' and the economic as well as social prospects facing separated women help explain why women often devote considerable energy to avoiding it. Recent discussions emphasizing the importance of disaggregating the household and of focusing on intra-household negotiation give some leverage here (Agarwal 1997; Kandiyoti 1988, 1998; Sen 1990). Sen views households as characterized by 'cooperative conflicts', because members have some interests in common and others that differ. Negotiations over conflicts reflect the parties' perceptions of their interests, contributions to the household and entitlements: the outcomes normally benefit those parties with least to lose in the 'breakdown position' (when the household itself dissolves) because they have the greatest bargaining power. Similarly, Agarwal outlines the differential bargaining power and different 'exit options' of household members. Against Sen, though, she argues that women's failures to strike bargains seemingly in their interests should not be interpreted as acceptance of their situations, for there is evidence aplenty that South Asian women critique their situations. An 'overt appearance of compliance' is a 'survival strategy' (Agarwal 1997: 24) for women who lack economic power (productive and other resources, independent income) and social capital (social support networks after marriage migration, socially sanctioned and gendered styles of bargaining that put men at an advantage) within the household and beyond. This is similar to Kandiyoti's view of the 'patriarchal bargains' struck when women weigh up the short- and long-term costs and benefits of complying with or resisting their situations. Gender inequalities change through an individual's lifetime and the relatively powerless young married woman can anticipate a more powerful position as mother-in-law in later years—provided she toes the line meanwhile (Kandiyoti 1988).[18]

Men do not lightly or frequently oust their wives from the marital home. The labour intensity of work plus the gender division of labour mean that households need able-bodied adult women just as they need men. Men also need wives to bear sons to support them in old age. That said, a separated man does not lose his home or his land (if any) and he is not usually socially shunned in his natal village, unless he has a reputation for extreme violence or heavy drinking. A separated man can generally find a second spouse more readily than a separated woman—although parents may be reluctant to marry their daughter to a man with a record of marital breakdown and such men's second wives are generally widowed or separated women.[19]

These considerations apply to Muslim and Hindu men alike, yet a central element of Hindu Right anti-Muslim rhetoric is the 'triple *talaq*', which they allege means that Muslim wives are routinely being repudiated on a whim (by implication, in contrast to Hindu women).[20] Crucially for my argument, such communal contrasts are not supported by the Bijnor data. Few men of either community initiate a separation; when they do so, it is generally through informal means such as despatching their wife to her natal village or failing to collect her after a visit there. The triple *talaq* is simply not part of Muslim men's everyday repertoire—any more than secular law courts are of Hindu men's.

In rural Bijnor, however, women's exit options make marital separation even less attractive for them. Remaining in an uncongenial marriage often seems the least worst option when set beside the fate of a separated woman. Several key informants and others—Hindu and Muslim alike—presented their marital problems as seemingly offering no realistic option but to endure the difficulties. Take Anisa, for example.[21] After she was widowed, her parents wanted to safeguard her future, so they arranged her marriage to Ahmed. About four years later (in 1991), her situation was miserable, because her in-laws taunted her about her second marriage, beat her, refused to let her visit her parents, and insulted her relatives when they visited. How could she escape this situation? She had virtually no contact with her parents and little prospect of rescue from that quarter:

If I didn't think of the children, I'd just die. But then I realize there's no one who would care for my children. They'd end up running from one place to the next being beaten. . . . My first husband never even slapped me with his four fingers, but this one beats me daily. . . . On occasion, I've considered taking poison. But then I think about the children. Anyway, the villagers would say it was an unlawful death. (P. Jeffery and R. Jeffery 1996a: 255)

Generally, it is considered inappropriate for parents to become involved in their daughter's marital problems. Indeed, unhappily married women often say nothing to their parents, because they are ashamed or wish to protect their parents from knowing about troubles from which they should remain aloof, as Kavita's account illustrates. Since before her marriage in the late 1980s, Kavita's husband had been having an affair with his older brother's wife. In order to avoid trouble from the couple, Kavita had adopted a policy of silence—both in her in-laws' home and to her parents:

The last time I visited my parents, my husband complained to them that I fight with him a lot. So my mother asked me why I fight with him. She told me to remain silent and not interfere with him whatever he might do. But how could I tell my parents about my husband's affair and the beatings? I've never said a thing about it to my father when he visits me here. How could I tell him about such a wicked matter? I couldn't tell my mother either. Even if I got the courage to do so, my mother wouldn't be able to say anything to my father. So what would be the point? (P. Jeffery and R. Jeffery 1996a: 230)

Parental interventions considered unwarranted or excessively frequent are roundly criticized and create annoyance among their daughter's in-laws. A married daughter is in 'her own' house and is expected to deal with her own difficulties. Nevertheless, parents often do become involved if they consider their daughter cannot resolve or escape her marital problems without their support—a clear recognition of the young married woman's lack of social and economic power. For instance, when news came one evening in 1990 that Brijpal's daughter had taken rat poison after a dispute with her husband, Brijpal took a party of his young male relatives to threaten his son-in-law (P. Jeffery and R. Jeffery 1996a: 192–6).

Sometimes a woman's parents make considerable efforts to achieve a reconciliation or make it possible for their daughter to tolerate her lot. Shankar's sister, for instance, was married to a man who spent all his earnings on drink. Shankar and his two brothers provided her with money, grain after each harvest, and clothing, so that she could remain in her in-laws' village with her children (P. Jeffery and R. Jeffery 1996a: 190). Often interventions were occasioned when a daughter visited her parents and refused to return to her husband's home until her in-laws had been confronted. A violent husband would be admonished and told that his wife would not return to his house until he mended his ways. A man whose father made unseemly advances or whose mother stirred up trouble—criticizing his wife's work, demanding that she bring more goods from her parents, taunting her because she has failed to bear any sons—might be told that his wife would not return until he guaranteed good treatment in future.

It is not unusual for a young woman to live in her parents' home for several months while these negotiations and threats take their course: Afsana spent nine months in her parents' home in 1982, Zebunissa was in her parents' home for over a year throughout our fieldwork in 1990–1; Promilla reported staying in her parents' home for about a year in the mid-1970s, while Jayavati was back in her widowed mother's house for much of our 1990–1 fieldwork (P. Jeffery and R. Jeffery 1996a: 159–60, 178–9, 197–9, 219–23). The husband and members of his close family may make several visits before the young woman is returned to her marital home.[22] Occasionally, a prominent person from the woman's natal village may mediate: Kunwar Satya Vira in Dharmnagri has enabled several young women to stand firm in refusing to rejoin their husband, as in the case of Sudesh's daughter (P. Jeffery and R. Jeffery 1996a: 132–3). The pressure on a woman's in-laws may include threats of legal action, but they are rarely implemented: local people fear involvement in the legal process, even when their case is strong, because they believe the police and the judiciary to be corrupt.

MARITAL BREAKDOWN AND WOMEN'S ECONOMIC VULNERABILITY

When marriages break down, they generally do so before the wife has sons of an age to support her. Irrespective of who initiated the separation, the woman must leave the home she has shared with her husband: it is his home, not hers. She cannot even remain in her husband's village. Separated women do not obtain ownership or usufruct rights in their ex-husband's land (or other property), any more than they have rights in the marital home; nor do they receive maintenance payments from their ex-husbands or in-laws. Few women have the education to enable them to enter the labour force on favourable terms.

Formally, Muslim women seem better placed than comparable Hindu women because of the *mehr* (the cash settlement by a Muslim man on his wife, specified in the marriage contract). Sometimes, the husband should give some or all of the *mehr* immediately. More commonly, the *mehr* is deferred and the husband is expected to give it only if he initiates divorce; the woman who initiates separation forfeits the *mehr*. In the event of divorce, the *mehr* notionally provides the separated woman with economic security. There is no parallel among Hindus, which is perhaps why *mehr* does not figure in the Hindu Right's anti-Muslim discourse.

Muslim women in rural Bijnor were, however, sceptical about the *mehr*.[23] Many saw little sense in claiming it while living with their husband, since it would be spent on the food and clothing they were already receiving. Even if the *mehr* were given, it could not provide long-term economic independence. A quarter of the key informants did not know what their *mehr* was. Of those who did, just one mentioned a *mehr* of Rs 15,000, another ten mentioned sums between Rs 1,000 and 8,000, and five said their *mehr* was the '*mehr Fatimi*'[24] comprising 125 silver rupees. For the remaining third, the *mehr* was less then Rs 500 (for more than half of them it was under Rs 100 and

several were just Rs 25). Several women said they had already consumed far more than their *mehr* was worth in their husband's home.
Others said that their *mehr* was the focus of banter: Hashmi (whose
mehr is Rs 125) said 'My husband laughs and says "How much is the
mehr anyway? I can give it whenever I wish!" ', while Khurshida told us,
'My father-in-law teases my husband, saying, "Give Khurshida her
Rs 25—it's a very heavy *mehr!*" '

In any case, one-third of the key informants (disproportionately those
with the highest *mehr*) had 'forgiven' or 'renounced' (*mo'af karna*) the
mehr, mostly under pressure from their husbands. For instance, when
Zubeida was being married to her deceased older sister's husband, the
proceedings were delayed for four days because of her step-father's
insistence that the *mehr* be Rs 5,000. Yet, Zubeida was forced to renounce the *mehr* later (P. Jeffery and R. Jeffery 1996a: 111–12). Two
women had forgiven the *mehr* voluntarily in order not to place their
husband in debt, while nearly a quarter could not recall if they had
forgiven it or not. The general view was 'But the *mehr* is only forgiven—who is giving it?' and 'The *mehr*? Who gives it? They all make
you forgive it.' Not one woman had received her *mehr*, either when her
marriage was consummated or later: as one women put it, 'No one at
all gives it. Enough! [*bas!*] There must be one or two men somewhere
in the world who give it!'

Even after divorce, women claimed, the *mehr* is not given. Several
said that people are now 'tying' their sons-in-law with a 'price tag'
(*raqam*, meaning a large *mehr*) to prevent them from initiating divorce, particularly if the marriage is between non-kin—but they saw
little point if wives are compelled to renounce the *mehr*. Others said
divorced and separated women are unlikely to receive the *mehr*, even
when they have not forgiven it: 'But what is the benefit of *mehr*? If a
man is going to leave his wife, he'll do so, no matter how much *mehr*
has been set.' The *mehr* was sometimes shrouded in uncertainty as well
as cynicism: 'I forgave it on the first night. But I've heard that *mehr*
forgiven on the first night is not understood to have been forgiven in
law. If it is forgiven a few days after the wedding, then it is considered
forgiven. I do not really know. But here in the village, who gives the
mehr? They don't give the *mehr* even if they do give *talaq*!'[25]

In rural Bijnor, then, Muslim women are not protected from marital
breakdown or from financial insecurity after it by the *mehr*. A separated woman could not live an independent life on the basis of the
mehr—but none of the separated Muslim women we knew had

received their *mehr* in any case. In practice, no woman—whether Muslim or Hindu—is likely to receive financial support from her ex-husband.[26]

In other parts of the world, where women's property rights, agricultural work or educational levels permit economic independence, women may establish female-headed households after separation (or widowhood) (Chant 1997). South Asia as a whole, however, seems to be characterized by an aversion to such households. The northern areas, in particular, are marked by low levels of female-headed households.[27] For women in rural Bijnor, separation usually entails returning to their natal kin, at least in the first instance.

DEPENDING ON THE NATAL KIN

A woman's natal kin will probably have been contributing to her material well-being already, but her dowry and the other items presented to her may no longer be accessible. Foodstuffs will have been eaten, cooking utensils may have been requisitioned by her mother-in-law. Clothing may have been worn out or presented to an affinal relative and jewellery sold to pay off a debt or buy medicines, or presented to her husband's sister. Cash may have gone on daily expenses or on large-scale expenditures, such as installing a tubewell or refurbishing her house. Sometimes, a woman's parents threaten reprisals, but there is generally little hope of retrieving even a small portion of the items they presented to her, even if they have not been consumed.

Further, the woman who visits her parents and tells them of her marital problems could not have carried enough with her—apart from her jewellery perhaps—to support her for more than a few days. Those, such as Dilruba, who feared that their marriage might collapse, might have persuaded their parents to store the foodstuffs and cash they presented rather than send it to them in their husband's home:

For the past two years, I've been leaving the things at my mother's house so that I could buy my own necessities there. . . . Last Eid, for instance, I received 2 kg of sugar, 10 kg of unrefined sugar, 5 kg of rice, and 2 kg of flour. I just brought the sugar and left everything else at my mother's house. When he [Dilshad] divorced me and put me out of the house, I went to my mother's home. I sold some unrefined sugar and rice so that I could buy what I needed. Now I'm returning after six days, and my mother and my brother each gave me 10 kg of wheat. I've left it all in my mother's house. What could I do with it if I brought it here? (P. Jeffery and R. Jeffery 1996a: 151)

A few women had stored jewellery in their parents' home, because they suspected their parents-in-law or husband had designs on it—but the woman whose husband fails to collect her from her parents' house is more likely to have nothing salted away. In any case, even Dilruba's forward-planning would not provide long-term economic independence. Basically, a separated woman, whether Muslim or Hindu, faces almost certain penury unless she can persuade her natal kin to support her. Certainly, they are generally the separated woman's best source of support—though not necessarily a very good one. Women whose marriages break down are often blamed for failing to adjust to their in-laws' requirements, for bringing shame on their natal family and for damaging the marriage prospects of their unmarried siblings—unless they can plausibly argue that the whole sorry affair resulted from their in-laws' evilness. Moreover, once a daughter has been provided with a dowry, she should not make further substantial claims on her parents' property, and certainly not on her father's land (if any). Periodic out-lays for gifts to her as a married woman are of a very different order— in quantity and in how they are perceived—from meeting the expenses of a separated woman living permanently in her natal village again. Food, clothing, medical expenses on a daily basis for her and any chil-dren who accompanied her, and possibly educating her children and arranging their marriages, would exceed her parents' and brothers' expectations of their financial obligations. She would be not just a financial burden, but one wrongfully consuming the entitlements of her brothers, their wives and their children. Her natal kin, then, may provide shelter and support only grudgingly and temporarily.

DEPENDENCY IN ANOTHER MARRIAGE

Even women acting decisively to end an unhappy marriage cannot ensure that they retain control over their destiny thereafter, for their natal kin generally make haste to place them in new 'marriages'. Among Hindus, these new unions do not involve full marriage rituals; among Muslims they may. Locally, though, the pair are usually regarded as married and their children are considered legitimate.[28] This outcome, however, does not necessarily offer attractive prospects for either party.

The preferred marriage for men is with a previously unmarried woman whose natal kin provide her with a dowry. The separated woman can-not meet the former criterion—and her natal kin may not meet the latter one at all or to the extent that makes her an attractive match. Sometimes, natal kin put together a modest second dowry, but they are unlikely to have retrieved any items from the first one and they may be unable or unwilling to foot another substantial bill. Chet Ram was widowed in the mid-1980s; his second wife had been married to an impotent alcoholic and had spent three years in her natal village after refusing to return to him. A few months after she married Chet Ram, her parents presented him with Rs 200, a watch and some cloth (Chet Ram had presented her with no clothes or jewellery at the time of their marriage). Of the separated key informants, however, she is the only one remarried like this: the separated woman (and sometimes also the widow) is more likely to become a 'bought bride', when her new husband 'takes a bride for a price' (*bahu mol-lena*), particularly if her brothers or another male go-between organize a second match for her. In the late 1970s, Taslim bought Tahira from his sister's husband who lived in Tahira's natal village. Rohtash paid Rajballa's brothers Rs 800 in the late 1970s, while Lalit had obtained seven wives in this fashion, including Lakshmi for whom he paid his cousin (MBS) Rs 2,000 in about 1980 (P. Jeffery et al. 1989: 39–41; P. Jeffery and R. Jeffery 1996a: 231–44). In 1981, Muni left her violent husband and sheltered in the home of a cousin, whose husband sold her for Rs 2,000 to her current husband.

This is certainly not an approved method of marrying. Usually the man has been unable to arrange a conventional marriage, because he was widowed and already has children or was considered too old by parents with young marriageable daughters, or because he was deserted by a first wife who accused him of mistreatment, or had some social or physical disability, or was extremely poor. The woman herself can expect little or no economic and social support from her natal kin. Bought brides come empty handed (*khali hath*), without a dowry or the other gifts associated with the typical bride. They rarely visit their natal kin or receive visits from them and are very poorly placed to protect themselves, whether from taunting neighbours or marital violence. Yet remarriage is the most likely outcome for the separated woman: in the four study villages, just three women had been separated for several years without being remarried.

It is thus hardly surprising that women and their natal kin strive so hard to prevent marital breakdowns. The social and economic prospects for separated women pale in comparison with an approved dowry marriage—perhaps even in the face of considerable discord. The similarity in Muslim and Hindu women's experiences of economic dependency in marriage and economic vulnerability after marital breakdown is a key point here. Contrary to stereotypes, Hindu women in rural Bijnor are not less vulnerable to being left in penury by their husbands than Muslim women are. The types of problems women report, the efforts they put into achieving reconciliation, their reliance on natal kin and the centrality of kin-based mechanisms for dispute resolution, are common across the board. So, too, are the outcomes when the marriage breaks down: women's lack of entitlements in the ex-husband's household, their temporary reliance on their natal kin, and their probable remarriage in circumstances that may prove no better (and may even be worse) than the first marriage.

LEGAL REFORM AND GENDER POLITICS AT THE LOCAL LEVEL

Adherents of organizations such as Tablighi Jama'at work to expunge 'cultural' and 'religious' syncretism from Muslim practice in South Asia (Gardner 1999; Metcalf 1999). On the other hand, the loyalty of Indian Muslims to the Indian nation has often been questioned by the Hindu Right, whose rhetoric is replete with contrasting stereotypes of Hindu and Muslim (Bacchetta 1993, 1994; Basu 1995a; M. Hasan 1988). In rural Bijnor, ethnic differences are indeed signalled in dress styles, aspects of religious belief and practice, and stereotyping (Jeffery 2000b). Yet, if we focus on micro-level everyday life, the proposition that Muslims and Hindus are inherently different flies in the face of social complexity. Identifications cross-cut one another in confusing and conflicting ways. People's behaviour—for instance, in the sphere of gender politics—cannot be neatly glossed as 'Muslim' or 'Hindu'. In other words, there are 'multiple patriarchies' cutting across the boundaries of reified religious communities (Sangari 1995).

Nevertheless, much of the discourse surrounding the Shah Bano affair—whether emanating from the Hindu Right, conservative Muslims or the state—played on assumptions that Muslims and Hindus are (or ought to be) essentially different. Moreover, the communalization of contemporary Indian politics has had severe consequences for the attainment of gender justice. I shall touch on just two of the issues that arise here: the role of legal reform and how feminists can engage with the state; and the grassroots mobilization of women around issues of gender equity.

In the early years after 1947, there was widespread optimism that the state would act to protect its citizens, and that legislative reforms and government planning could achieve social justice. The disillusionment already in evidence by the late 1960s was exacerbated by the damning evidence of the gulf between women's constitutional rights and their daily lives, presented in the report of the National Committee on the Status of Women in India in 1974. Other events in the 1970s and 1980s—for instance, the notorious Mathura rape case—left many feminists in deep doubt about the state's capacity to be an effective and reliable ally for women, not least because agents of the state—whether local policemen, national and state legislators or senior judges—have so often been implicated in actions inimical to women's interests. The stock-taking surrounding the fiftieth anniversary of Independence sparked further analysis among feminists about achievements and failures and about strategic priorities in the light not just of communalized politics but also the economic developments of the 1990s, such as structural adjustment, economic liberalization and consumerism (Agnes 1995; Agnihotri and Mazumdar 1995; Butalia 1997–8; Kapur and Cossman 1995, 1996: 232–83; Sangari 1995).

Throughout these debates, the Uniform Civil Code (UCC) has been a recurrent and contentious theme. The report on the Status of Women in India had addressed the matter in the mid-1970s (National Committee on the Status of Women 1975: 57) and, until the Shah Bano case, the replacement of the separate systems of personal law by a single gender-equitable UCC was a central demand of feminists in India. The Hindu Right, however, appropriated the idea of the UCC during the Shah Bano controversy, a move that seriously compromised feminist positions on legal reform. If feminists supported the UCC and opposed the Muslim Women Bill, they would risk being co-opted to the agendas of the Hindu Right and antagonizing many Muslims by intervening in community affairs. Not to press for gender-equitable legislation pertaining to family matters, however, could leave unchallenged personal laws that are all premised on gender inequity.

Not surprisingly, feminist activists in India remain divided over how to define the key issues and how to campaign for gender equity. Can they tackle gender issues without marginalizing other dimensions of inequality (caste, class, community)? Can they rely on reforms coming from within 'communities'? Should they concentrate on legal reforms? If so, what form should these take (Anveshi Law Committee 1997; Gangoli and Solanki 1997; Working Group on Women's Rights 1996)? Should feminists focus on legal provisions within the framework of women's dependency in marriage, maybe pressing for larger maintenance payments (which are notoriously difficult to enforce) or for once-off rights in matrimonial property (which might be easier to enforce, but would not be relevant for women married to poor men) (Agnes 1992; Parashar 1997)?

Or does a focus on women's rights to maintenance perpetuate the presumption that women are (or should be) dependent on their husbands? Perhaps, indeed, the focus on the UCC falls into the trap of framing issues of gender equity solely in terms of women's position in the 'private' sphere of the family. Perhaps the emphasis should be on enabling women to attain the economic viability outside marriage that would be a better long-term remedy for their disempowerment within marriage. The recent unearthing of the National Planning Committee's 1938 Report of the Sub-committee on Woman's Role in Planned Economy has highlighted how this (albeit contradictory) document contained not just recommendations for a UCC but also emphasized women's role as productive citizens, whose work would both give them economic rights and benefit the nation (Banerjee 1998; Chaudhuri 1996; Kasturi 1996). Yet government policy since 1947 has largely approached women as members of families, as mothers and as family planning and welfare targets, but not individual citizens and workers. So, should feminist activism target state policies on employment and training?

Then again, beyond questions of which emphases are most appropriate in relation to government policy and legislation, are feminist activities best focused on the state, given its history of failures? Lest I be misunderstood, I am not advocating disengagement from the state. That would give *carte blanche* to pressure groups unlikely to have women's interests at heart. Further, at the very least, the law plays important symbolic and normative roles in stipulating what is permissible or intolerable, and so it is vital that the many gender (and other) inequities in the legal system be removed. Yet it is also crucial to ask how much priority and energy should be focused on legislative reforms and on the state at the centre. Even when the framing of legislation apparently points towards the eradication of gender inequities, implementation that is itself gender-biased may undermine the purpose.

Marital breakdown in rural Bijnor is just one case in point. Prior to the Muslim Women (Protection of Rights on Divorce) Act, Hindu and Muslim women alike had no customary right to maintenance after marital breakdown and they relied on support from their natal kin or from a new husband. None of the separated Muslim women we knew had received the *mehr* or received support from a *qazi* to enforce their claims. Few women, Hindu or Muslim, could have afforded to employ lawyers and make maintenance claims under CrPC Section 125; after all, Shah Bano herself could pursue her claims in the courts only because of financial support from her adult sons. The CrPC Section 125 played a very limited role in preventing women from becoming destitute after marital breakdown. In practice, then, the Muslim Women Act's removal of Muslim women's rights to appeal through CrPC Section 125 had little direct negative impact on the *economic* situation of Muslim women in rural Bijnor. Nor did the Act differentiate the economic positions of Hindu and Muslim women in practice. (Formally, though, it clearly did, and the wider impact of the affair on local communal politics should not be under-estimated.) Briefly, Muslim and Hindu women's economic insecurity in the event of marital breakdown has remained comparable.

In other words, what practical effects would a gender-equitable UCC—or indeed other legislation focusing on gender issues—have on most ordinary rural Indian women's experiences of family life? Even in a situation of *formal* legal equality, there is no guarantee that *substantive* equality would result, without interventions in local-level social, economic and political processes beyond the legal domain, such as inequalities in access to property, income and entitlements in everyday practice. In rural Bijnor, there already is a (fairly) 'uniform customary code' with respect to gender politics at the domestic level, one that stacks the cards against women, especially young women. Many feminists would argue that empowering and mobilizing women is the most effective remedy for this sort of issue (see, for instance, Molyneux 1998; Moser 1989).

Yet this will be difficult in rural Bijnor. For one thing, essentialized gender differences and the naturalization of many aspects of everyday family life limit the critical reach of women's complaints. Women do not question the propriety of marriage migration, for instance, yet it seriously disempowers them in their husband's household. The efforts people put into preventing marital breakdown reflect most women's lack of realistic options beyond dependency within the household. Few women are likely to mount far-reaching challenges to their best source of support and well-being—albeit not always a very good source, and one that is often a source of misery too. Further, within the household, women's interests do not coincide, and individual women's perspectives shift in the course of the life cycle. Moreover, women's lack of social capital in their affinal villages puts them into weak positions in the wider community, making it difficult for them either to mobilize or to withstand backlash (P. Jeffery 1999, 2000b; P. Jeffery and R. Jeffery 1996a: 1–37, 1999: 136–8). Women's resistance, then, is largely individualistic and sporadic 'everyday resistance' rather than organized activism (Scott 1985).

Crucially here, the communalization of Indian politics and people's heightened awareness of communal identities mean that mobilizing women across the communal boundary would be no simple matter. The impact of the Shah Bano case and the Babri Masjid campaign was felt locally, through communal violence, Muslim fears and Hindu assertiveness. During our research in 1990–1, many Hindu men cited the Shah Bano case as evidence of Hindu victimization, of Muslim appeasement, and the justice of the Babri Masjid campaign. Indeed, Muslim women and men in Bijnor discussed the Shah Bano case in relation to communal politics, not the rights of Muslim women. In Bijnor town, women of the Durga Vahini (the women's organization affiliated to the Vishwa Hindu Parishad) were crucial in the events that led up to the communal disturbances and curfew in October 1990 (Basu 1995b; R. Jeffery and P. Jeffery 1994b, 1997). At the village level, Muslim and Hindu women and men engage in communal stereo-typing and distancing (P. Jeffery 2000b) and gender and communal differences are marked in access to facilities provided by the local state, such as health care and schooling (P. Jeffery and R. Jeffery 1999). Women's allegiances around communal identities hamper the transla-tion of their complaints about their everyday situations as women into activism across communal boundaries. In western UP there are few NGOs and even fewer women's groups that might facilitate women's mobilization and empowerment (unlike in some other parts of South Asia, perhaps most notably Bangladesh). Currently, too, the workings of local political parties, whether communal or not, provide little scope for optimism either (Omvedt 1993). Of course, this is not to fore-close the possibility that NGO activism, political parties, or indeed government-sponsored changes, might widen the opportunities for significant changes at some stage.

The Shah Bano case certainly had a momentous impact on India's recent political history: the constitutional dilemmas it raised are un-resolved and the scars of communal disturbances remain. Yet the case has tended to divert attention from the need to tackle gender politics at the grass roots, not just within the formal legal realm and by focusing on the state at the centre. Rights and obligations during marriage and after marital breakdown are not narrowly legal matters amenable to simple legal resolution. They are intensely political issues, and customary procedures for dispute resolution reflect power imbalances at the micro-level. Crucially, most rural women in north India lack entitlements to economic resources and they are relatively powerless in the domestic arena and beyond. Without far-reaching changes at that level, women's formal legal rights are likely to remain a dead-letter.

NOTES

1. An earlier version of this chapter appeared as Jeffery (2001). The research on which this chapter is based has been done with Roger Jeffery and I am grateful to him for comments on this paper. Our thanks go to all the people in Bijnor who were so generous with their time; to our research assistants (Swaleha Begum, Radha Rani Sharma, Savita Pandey, Chhaya Pandey, Zarin Ahmed and Swatantra Tyagi); and colleagues in Edinburgh, Kuala Lumpur, Amsterdam, Oxford and Prague, and to Jens Lerche for comments on earlier versions of this paper. We are grateful to the Economic and Social Research Council (UK), the Moray Fund of the University of Edinburgh and the Overseas Development Administration (UK) who funded our research; none of these organizations is responsible for the opinions expressed here.

2. The British also codified vocabularies and grammars of local languages, systematized place names and engaged in extensive geographical and geological surveys. For more on this see, for example, Appadurai (1993), Cohn (1987), Ludden (1993), and Pandey (1990).

3. The state's non-involvement in the 'private sphere' was (and still is) notional, of course. Prior to 1947, several instances of state involvement generated widespread debate and opposition: on sati (widow immolation) and the age of consent see Parashar (1992: 17–76); Sangari (1995); Sarkar (1993).

4. In Pakistan, by contrast, revised legislation passed in 1961 as the Muslim Family Laws Ordinance attempted to enhance the legal rights of Muslim women by reducing some of the most overtly discriminatory provisions of the 1937 Shariat legislation. Implementation and enforcement have, however, remained partial at best: see, for instance, Chipp-Kraushaar (1981) and Mumtaz and Shaheed (1987: 57–9). Periodically since 1961, and again in 1999, the Ordinance was the subject of conservative legal challenges, which were counter-challenged by feminist organizations (Women's Feature Service 1999).

5. The following provide useful accounts of the case: Chhachhi (1991); Engineer (1987); Z. Hasan (1989, 1993, 1994, 1999); Kishwar (1986); Kumar (1993: 160–71); Mody (1987); Palriwala and Agnihotri (1996: 511–19); Pathak and Rajan (1989).

6. Certainly, the most widespread interpretation was that Muslim women's rights were being undermined. There is some ambiguity, however, because the Act requires that a Muslim man provide his ex-wife with fair and reasonable provision and gives space for some legal decisions in which Muslim women obtained sizeable lump sum payments. In West Bengal, for instance, Mukhopadhyay (1994) reports that

some women obtained legal aid and some had successfully claimed maintenance through the Criminal Procedure Code. After the Muslim Women Bill was enacted, Muslim men facing claims from their ex-wives made counter-claims that they were under no obligation to pay maintenance. Engineer (1999) reports a case in Mumbai in which the judges used the Muslim Women Act to argue for long-term maintenance for a divorced Muslim woman. In response to such outcomes, Syed Shahabuddin introduced a private member's bill in the Lok Sabha to prevent this (Agnes 1996).

7. The 'Hindu Right' comprises several organizations also known as the 'Sangh Parivar': the Rashtra Swayamsevak Sangh (RSS or National Volunteer Corps), the Bharatiya Janata Party (BJP) and the Vishwa Hindu Parishad (VHP).

8. The notion of a somewhat mythical 'vote bank' revolves around the assumption that groups of people, such as Muslims, vote en bloc in local and national elections because their leaders can deliver their followers' votes. Indian Muslims tended to vote for Congress until the late 1980s, but sizeable numbers also voted for parties championing the interests of the urban working classes and the rural dispossessed, especially in recent years.

9. For discussions of the Ayodhya affair and the communalization of politics, see Basu and Kohli (1998); Basu et al. (1993); Chakravarti et al. (1992); Engineer (1991); Gopal (1991); M. Hasan (1997); Jaffrelot (1996); Ludden (1996); van der Veer (1994); Vanaik (1997).

10. For discussions of how women are iconized in relation to the nation or community, the role of women activists in the Hindu Right, and how organizations of politicized religion advocate conventional family roles for women, argue for the importance of personal law in 'defining' community, and use gendered stereotypes in communal politics, see Bacchetta (1993, 1994, 1996); Basu (1993, 1995a, 1999); Z. Hasan (1989, 1993, 1994, 1999); Jeffery and Basu (1999); Kandiyoti (1991); Sarkar (1991); Sarkar and Butalia (1995). The complex interplay between gender and national or ethnic identities is an issue not only in India but also more generally. See, for instance, Anthias and Yuval-Davis (1992); Moghadam (1994a, 1994b); Yuval-Davis (1997).

11. Since 1982, Roger Jeffery and I have been working in rural Bijnor, in two Hindu-dominated villages, Dharmnagri and Nangal (populations then about 750 and 4,000) and two Muslim dominated villages, Jhakri and Qaziwala (populations then about 350 and 3,000). For more details on economy, demography and social organization see P. Jeffery et al. (1989); P. Jeffery and R. Jeffery (1996a); R. Jeffery and P. Jeffery (1997). For other accounts of villages of the western UP plains, see Raheja (1988, 1995); Raheja and Gold (1994); Wadley (1994). For northern India more generally, see also Chowdhry (1994); Mandelbaum (1986), (1988); Sharma (1980).

12. Parents cannot always achieve this ideal, and those who fail to save for their daughters' marriages are subject to widespread censure or pity. I am leaving dowry escalation and dowry harassment to one side here.

13. According to the 2001 Census, the rural literacy rate in Bijnor for females aged seven and above was 22.5 per cent (the urban rate was 38 per cent).

14. We should also note, however, that Muslim women generally experience somewhat higher levels of fertility and child deaths (though not necessarily higher than low-caste and poor Hindu women), largely due to their concentration in the lower levels

of the economic hierarchy and their position as an ethnic minority (P. Jeffery and R. Jeffery 1999; R. Jeffery and P. Jeffery 1997).

15. I discuss *mehr* below, in the context of marital breakdown.

16. The term 'separation' covers cases of marital breakdown, including the minority of formal divorces. I leave widowhood on one side here as the antecedents and consequences are normally somewhat different from separation/divorce. Widowhood does not necessarily reflect acrimony between husband and wife (and possibly wider kin); a young widow may remain in her husband's village (and possibly be married leviratically to her husband's brother) or return to her natal kin and remarry, or be permitted to remain with them as a widow. Widowhood, though, is more commonly experienced by older women, who will probably remain in their husband's village and expect to be supported by their adult sons. For more on widowhood, see Chen (1998); Chen and Drèze (1992, 1995a, 1995b); Chowdhry (1994: 74–120, 356–77); P. Jeffery and R. Jeffery (1996b: 231–73); Kolenda (1987a, 1987b: 288–354); Vatuk (1990, 1995); Wadley (1994: 25–9, 154–62, 1995a, 1995b).

17. In 1982–3 (with follow-ups in 1985 and 1990) we concentrated on Dharmnagri and Jhakri and selected key informant couples from a range of class and caste positions, in which the wife had recently given birth or was pregnant; in 1990 we added Nangal and Qaziwala and selected additional key informant couples with the wife aged between 25 and 35 and who covered a range of educational experiences and marriage distances. There are almost equal numbers of Muslim and Hindu key informant couples. Among the key informants, four women and eight men had experienced widowhood by 1991. For more details see P. Jeffery et al. (1989: 233–7); R. Jeffery and P. Jeffery (1997: 32–4).

18. Agarwal (1997) and Kandiyoti (1998) both address 'rationality' and the extent to which women understand the bases of their subordination or are submerged in false consciousness, but I do not have the space to discuss this further here.

19. To use the term 'marriage' for such second unions is somewhat problematic as they would rarely meet formal legal definitions of marriage, even though local people generally regard them as 'marriages'. Later I discuss second marriage from the woman's viewpoint.

20. Hindu Right discourse suggests that Muslim men are sexually rapacious and liable to replace their wives frequently and/or to indulge in polygamous unions. Polygamy is very uncommon in Bijnor, but is slightly more frequent among Hindus (for whom it is not legal) than among Muslims (for whom it is permitted). Polygamy is usually connected with the infertility of the first wife. The 'victimized Muslim woman' discourse also includes claims about seclusion and lack of education, as well as the specific issues central to the Shah Bano case. See, for example, Bacchetta (1994).

21. The pseudonyms here are the same as in P. Jeffery et al. (1989), P. Jeffery and R. Jeffery (1996b) and R. Jeffery and P. Jeffery (1997).

22. If the problem is disputes with the husband's parents or brothers and their wives, both the daughter and her husband may live in the woman's natal village to preserve their relationship, e.g. Mamta and her daughter Rani (P. Jeffery and R. Jeffery 1996b: 224–6).

23. This is based on discussions with our Muslim key informants as well as many other Muslim men and women in rural Bijnor.

24. This is the *mehr* specified when Fatima, the daughter of the Prophet Muhammed,

was married; it is sometimes called *sharia mehr*. Silver rupees are more valuable than contemporary coins of the same face value.

25. It seems to be common for Muslim women not to receive their due according to Islamic law. Other accounts of contemporary practices with respect to *mehr* in India include Agarwal (1994: 227–8, 260); Agnes (1996); Ahmed-Ghosh (1994: 178–80); Engineer (1992: 111–13); Husain (1976: 119–37, 193–4); Jacobson (1976: 185, 207, 1995: 187); Jeffery (2000: 57–9); Mann (1994: 154–6, 1992: 69); Papanek (1982: 24–5); Singh (1992: 81). For historical sources see Ali (1832: Vol. 1, 345); Blunt (1969: 198); Crooke (1921: 75); Kozlowski (1989); Metcalf (1992: 139–42).

26. We can note the irony of conservative Muslim claims to orthodoxy over the issue of maintenance of ex-wives during the Shah Bano controversy, since Muslim women commonly do not receive financial entitlements over which there does not seem to be doctrinal dispute.

27. For instance, older widows hope for support from their adult sons, while young widows will probably either be remarried (either leviratically in their deceased husband's village or from their natal village). Widows occasionally inherit land, but most do not. In relatively wealthy families with daughters but no sons, a female-headed household is averted by the 'in-living son-in-law' (*ghar jamai*) who moves to his father-in-law's home and runs the farm. Typically, women who inherit land, either as widows or as daughters, cannot manage or cultivate their farm effectively: women cannot plough (although they do many other agricultural tasks) and their mobility beyond the home is limited. Thus, they normally rely on male kin.

28. By contrast, some widows remained with their natal kin for many years without being pressured into remarriage.

4

Responses to Modernity
Female Education, Gender Relations and Regional Identity in the Hills of Uttar Pradesh

Joanne Moller

INTRODUCTION

In the development world and literature the education of females is considered to feed directly into national development, and to produce far-reaching benefits for the families and communities in which they live. Some go so far as to say that 'the education of girls may well be the highest-return investment available in the developing world' (King and Hill 1993: v). Female education is seen by international development experts to benefit women personally by playing a crucial role in improving women's quality of life and raising their status. On the individual level, education and literacy are said, among other things: to give women a voice and the language with which to express their needs, interests and concerns; to make women self-reliant and increase their self-confidence and self-esteem; to enable women to take better care of themselves and their families, and to be able to make decisions concerning their own lives. It is assumed that greater literacy can provide women with greater autonomy in their daily lives and increase their status and standing in their local communities.

In India, equal access to education for females is not a new idea. Since the nineteenth century social reformers have advocated educating girls, appealing to progressive regions and upper-caste groups, and thereby generating an atmosphere favouring girl's education (Desai 1995: 23–4). Although initially the spread of women's education was restricted to a small élite, with Independence came new provisions that aimed to give women equal rights of access and opportunity in education, and thus equal participation in the development process. According to the Constitution's directives, within 20 years there should be free and compulsory education for all children to the age of 14. Due to many cultural and economic obstacles, and to failures to reach girls, Scheduled Castes and tribal peoples, this goal was not realized. Over the past four to five decades there have been several shifts in policy on women's education and development (Desai 1995; Elliott 1984). Unfortunately, most of these efforts have not significantly expanded educational opportunities for girls and women: three-quarters of Indian women do not know how to read or write (Bennett 1991: 109).

Progress in female education, as well as economic and social development, has been especially slow in north Indian states. Uttar Pradesh lags behind the rest of India in a number of important aspects of well-being and social progress. The region has especially high levels of mortality, fertility, under-nutrition, illiteracy and social inequality, and a slow pace of poverty decline (Drèze and Gazdar 1997: 33–40). With regard to female literacy, the state has a particularly poor record. In Uttar Pradesh only 25 per cent of females aged seven years or older was able to read and write in 1991. This number falls to 19 per cent for rural girls of the same age group, and goes as low as 8 per cent for Scheduled Caste girls in rural areas (ibid.: 43). Moreover, significant variations exist between regions. Within the old UP, one of India's most backward states, lay the Himalayan region, which is comparatively progressive in key areas of social development and well-being. Despite economic underdevelopment and higher than state average poverty rates, the eight hill districts of Garhwal and Kumaon, referred to jointly as Uttarakhand (and the core of the new state of Uttaranchal), have lower rates of mortality, fertility and illiteracy. Furthermore, when it comes to gender-related social development indicators the Himalayan region stands out as relatively favourable to women. Uttarakhand is the only region of erstwhile UP where the female-male ratio is above unity, where female children have a survival advantage over male children, and where female labour-force participation is high (24.2 per cent compared to the state rate of 5.3 per cent in 1981). Regarding female literacy and schooling, Himalayan girls fare better than their plains sisters, with a crude female literacy rate of 24.1 per cent and 40.7 per cent of girls between 5 and 14 years of age attending school. These figures are in contrast to the all-UP rates of 14 per cent and 21.1 per cent respectively (Drèze and Gazdar 1997: 58–9). It has been suggested that the relatively rapid expansion of female literacy in the Himalayan region and the lamentably low levels of progress in other regions of Uttar Pradesh can be understood in terms of degrees of gender inequality. Uttarakhand displays less patriarchal gender relations than is characteristic of other parts of erstwhile UP (Drèze and Gazdar 1997; Drèze and Sen 1998). But what of the expected effects of this spread of female education? Involving women in the development process through education has not been an easy task, especially in India. Recent studies have highlighted the inequities in women's educational access and achievement and the multiple factors affecting girls' education such as gendered socialization, gender ideologies and patrifocal kinship structures and ideologies (see Bennett 1991; Chanana 1990b; Mukhopadhyay and Seymour 1994). Furthermore, the benefits assumed by the development world to result from female education have been seriously questioned. Drèze and Sen claim that education and health can be valuable to a person's freedom in several ways, one of which is through its 'empowerment and distributive roles' (Drèze and Sen 1998: 15). Greater literacy and educational achievement of disadvantaged groups, including females, can increase their ability to resist oppression, organize politically, and get fairer treatment all round. Moreover, it can have positive effects on relations within the family, as there is evidence that better education, and in particular female education, contributes to the reduction of gender-based inequalities and can give women more voice and agency within the family (Drèze and Sen 1998: 15, 160). However, recent studies raise doubts about whether education really is a route to the realization of female autonomy and a catalyst for social change. Indeed in some areas, far from altering people's ideas of women's role in society, female education is in fact regarded as a means to enable women to fulfil their domestic roles better. Though schooling does seem to effect a woman's ability to influence other's decisions covertly, and may make kin aware of an educated women's increased bargaining power, these studies conclude that schooling does not inevitably result in increased female autonomy (Basu 1996; Jeffery and Jeffery 1996; Jeffery and Basu 1996). Moreover, the issue of female autonomy is itself problematic: not only are definitions of female autonomy culturally specific, but rural Indian women may not regard autonomy as desirable. Given this situation, can we expect education to contribute to the uplift of women's social status and their empowerment (Chanana 1990a; Jeffery and Jeffery 1994; Karlekar 1994)?

This chapter examines attitudes towards post-primary education for females in a rural community in the Himalayan foothills of Kumaon.

It looks at perceived effects of secondary and higher education on domestic authority and gender relations and on regional identity. Focusing on the societal perceptions of the aims and consequences of female education, the paper gives particular attention to how notions of different kinds of women—especially daughters and daughters-in-law—shape people's opinions about the education of girls. By way of conclusion the paper considers whether women are experiencing more 'autonomy' and whether or not gender inequalities within the Himalayan region are being gradually eroded.

The views presented in this paper belong primarily to high-caste residents of Silora village (a pseudonym), Almora district. Silora is situated on the crest of a 2,000-metre high ridge at approximately 16 km distance from Ranikhet town. Silora's population is made up of 73 per cent ploughing Brahmins, 22 per cent Thakurs, and 5 per cent Harijans. In the early 1990s, nuclear households, which comprised 44 per cent of an 87-household sample, represented the dominant type in Silora (see Moller 1993: 53–5 for more details).[1] The average land holding was 24 *nalis* (about one acre or half a hectare). Apart from agriculture, horticulture and animal husbandry, migrant employment is a significant income source with 50 per cent of income-earning men living away for employment purposes, and more than half of all village households with at least one male member engaged in migratory employment.[2] In all respects Silora is representative of villages in Uttarakhand (see Nanda 1991).

EDUCATION IN KUMAON

Modern education in Kumaon began in the nineteenth century when the British encouraged the establishment of schools, especially in Almora district (Swarup 1991: 15). Since that time Kumaonis have regarded education to be the primary means to a brighter future and as a means of mobility into a higher social class. In 1981, Almora district had a comparatively high literacy rate, standing at 38 per cent compared to the state figure of 27 per cent. At this time the male literacy rate was approximately 56 per cent and the female literacy rate 20 per cent (Swarup 1991: 53). By 1991, literacy rates had risen to 63 per cent and 33 per cent respectively (Samal 1993: 89). This compares very favourably with the UP figures of 47 per cent and 17 per cent in 1981, and 55 per cent and 26 per cent in 1991 for male and female literacy respectively (Nanda 1991).[3]

As in other parts of India, the considerations involved in educational decisions are very different for males and females. The economic incentives for male education are strong. The value placed on education for males is largely due to the population pressure on relatively unproductive land. Agriculture alone cannot support hill families, and so hill men invest a lot of effort in securing public service and army jobs, for which education is a prerequisite. Improved education enhances a boy's employment prospects, and parents have a high stake in the economic advancement of their sons. To this end, every household will try to see at least one son through to high school graduation. Thus, for males a good education level is seen as a prerequisite for highly coveted public sector government jobs. Those with salaried, usually white-collar, jobs are known as *serviswalas*. Salaried work can be in the private or public sector, but becoming a government employee is valued most highly. To become a public servant means success, as a government job provides a regular and assured income for life, job security and a pension in old age. In contrast, private sector jobs do not carry so much status, and are regarded as insecure and temporary.

Not only is a well educated, comfortably employed son expected to provide well for his parents but he is also highly sought after on the marriage market and can attract offers of marriage from families who are willing to offer high dowries for a match with their daughters. The desirability and celebration of the *serviswala* is given ultimate expression and unequivocal confirmation in the form of the present day groom's wedding attire. Whereas in the past the groom wore a yellow *dhoti* and a long white or yellow *kurta*, the contemporary groom wears a three-piece suit and a tie.[4] The white-collar *serviswala*, the epitome of the successful modern man, is the groom *par excellence*, the husband and son-in-law that every girl and parent dreams of.

Education for females, however, is considered less important and Kumaoni girls face the same barriers to secondary and tertiary education as in other parts of South Asia (Khan 1993). In Silora, primary education and basic literacy for girls is generally valued and considered necessary. This seems to be confirmed by the trend for the proportion of females educated up to primary level to equal if not exceed the proportion of males (Swarup 1991: 52–3). However, many people consider primary education to be sufficient, and during secondary schooling the girls' drop out rate is quite high (see Table 4.1).

Although people are aware of the benefits of education, and even

Table 4.1: Enrolment by Age Groups in Kumaon Division, 31 March 1988

(*in %*)

District/Division	6–11 Primary level		11–14 Junior high school level		14–18 Higher secondary level	
	Boy	Girls	Boys	Girls	Boy	Girls
Almora District	55	45	69	31	79	21
Pithoragarh District	57	43	65	35	66	34
Naini Tal District	60	40	57	43	66	34
Kumaon Division	57	43	65	35	70	30

Source: Adapted from Joshi (1988: 345).

though poorly educated mothers stress the need of educating their daughters better, the common view is that females belong in the home and fields. In a society where, irrespective of social status and class, females constitute the agricultural workforce and are the backbone of the local subsistence economy, the exigencies of agricultural work often dictate whether or how much education a girl receives. Daughters are frequently pulled out of school in order to perform household duties, collect fuel and fodder and help with crop production either during agriculturally busy seasons or permanently. And, aside from economic considerations, parents are also concerned for the moral well-being of their daughters. The purdah system is not as strong in rural Kumaon as other parts of north India, and the secondary school that serves Silora village is only 1.5 km away Nevertheless, some parents will not allow their daughters to continue secondary education because of the 'social dangers' (Bennett 1991: 115) associated with male school teachers and students, and most rule out the possibility of tertiary education because colleges are far away from the village.[5]

Beyond these economic and socio-cultural factors and considerations, attitudes towards secondary and higher education for females are in fact relatively ambivalent. In the subsistence farming communities of the Kumaon hills, where women perform most of the agricultural, animal husbandry and domestic work, and men out-migrate in search of employment, conflicting attitudes are held regarding the desirability of secondary and higher education for out-marrying and in-marrying women. There is a tension between the desire to educate daughters and the desire that daughters-in-law are not so well educated. But one person's daughter is another's daughter-in-law and *vice versa*.

DAUGHTERS, DAUGHTERS-IN-LAW, *HEEROINS* AND *PADHI-LIKHIS*

The perceived benefits of giving a girl secondary and higher education differ depending on whether one is considering the issue as a parent or parent-in-law. Whereas post-primary education for one's daughters is desirable, finances permitting, extended education for a daughter-in-law is viewed with scepticism. Kumaoni villagers seem to be responding to this form of modernity in a culturally familiar and telling manner. Villagers interpret secondary and further education for females in terms of prevalent assumptions about different kinds of women. The desirable aspects of education are personified in the cherished out-marrying daughter while the educated in-marrying daughter-in-law represents the less desirable and more threatening influences associated with this form of modernity.

It is true that to many families a daughter constitutes a burden, as a dowry must be supplied at the time of her wedding. Moreover, as it is very rare for rural women to take salaried employment for which educational qualifications are necessary, and since she will move away at marriage anyway, her natal family may be reluctant to invest in her education. At the same time, some parents do recognize the contribution that education can make to the quality of a daughter's life, and are motivated to support her schooling by a basic concern for the well-being of a daughter in her own right (Drèze and Sen 1998: 136).

Daughters and sisters are highly and positively thought of, and despite the marked preference for sons in India, daughters do enjoy affectionate and intimate relations with their parents and siblings, and are bestowed with love and attention by their mothers (Dhruvarajan 1989: 105–6; Madan 1989 [1965]: 87; Egnor 1986). In Kumaon, the out-married village daughter, known as *celibeti*, is accorded high status, conceived of as a bestower of well-being and embodiment of auspiciousness and prosperity, and is the most welcome of guests (see Moller 1993: 178–85). This positive model of the out-marrying woman informs attitudes as to the beneficial influences of continued post-elementary education for females.

According to some people a woman is 'educated' if she has completed five to eight years of schooling. However, more commonly it means someone who has obtained at least a high-school pass, if not a Bachelors degree or higher. Such a female is referred to as *padhi-likhi* (educated female). In Silora nowadays most girls are educated until eighth grade and a growing number are actually completing secondary education. Extended schooling is, however, considered to have a detrimental impact on a female's disposition and conduct. Educated women are said to be obstinate, strong headed and outspoken (*tej*), and education is thought to develop a female's self-confidence and independence of spirit (see Vatuk 1972: 78). This is a slight concern for a girl's parents, but only insofar as it effects her future behaviour as a daughter-in-law, and educated daughters do not seem to be viewed as a threat or a challenge to the authority structures within their natal homes (cf. Ullrich 1994). In preparation for her status and position as a daughter-in-law in her marital home, the adolescent daughter is 'trained' to be a hard and efficient worker and to go about her tasks capably and obediently. Though the disposition of a girl is a cause for concern for parents-in-law, ultimately it is not a main worry for parents. Parents want their daughters to live comfortably and happily in their husband's house, and being a good daughter-in-law may make relations with her senior in-laws less difficult. However, parents also want their daughter's needs and wishes to be attended to, and the qualities which education is believed to engender in a female may be advantageous in ensuring that they are. Indeed, the common explanations offered for why a woman or her natal kin (especially her mother) should want to cast spells onto her husband—to ensure she is favoured by her husband or that he remains under his wife's authority—is to achieve these very same objectives! To some degree, therefore, the characteristics that education is assumed to encourage in a female are seen to increase a daughter's potential for authority within her conjugal home, as well as equipping her better to manage incidents which may arise there.

The main benefits of giving a girl secondary education are linked to her marriage prospects, and, to some extent, female schooling has become a prerequisite for marriage and a matter of prestige (Vlassoff 1996: 232). Since education is linked to social standing and prestige, to have an educated daughter is also a matter of pride and reflects well on the household's standing. If one's daughter has attained a high level of education, one can aspire to marry her well into a wealthy and high status house. Parents hope to educate their daughter well in the hope that she will secure a groom from a 'good house' (*thik ghar*), and it is assumed that the more highly educated a girl, the better her chances of marrying into such a family.

Customarily, the groom should be more educated than the bride. If she has a high-school pass, her husband should at least have a Bachelor's degree or some other diploma. If the groom has a Bachelor's or Master's degree it is assumed that he will have a good job (or good job prospects) and that his family is wealthy enough to have enabled their son to study so far. Furthermore, a daughter with a good level of education is a better match for a white-collar husband who may also be in a better position to help his wife's family were adversity to strike (Moller 1993: 170). A woman's educational achievements are so important an ingredient for securing a good marriage partner that families frequently lie about their daughter's qualifications (see also Jeffery and Jeffery 1994: 153–4). The parents of one woman in Silora lied to the prospective groom's family by stating that their daughter had a high-school pass, where in fact she had only a fifth-grade pass. The groom's family would not necessarily have found this suspicious, as the girl's father was a senior teacher of Sanskrit. The groom had a Master's degree. Recently, ten years after her wedding, this woman has expressed anger at her parents for not having allowed her to study more. Now that her husband's business has collapsed, she would like to get a respectable job to ease their difficult financial situation. Her parents, who are upset and confused by her resentful letters, can only respond 'but we married you well'.

Daughters also want to marry well into a *thik ghar*. Many educated daughters express dislike for the prospect of a life of sweat and toil after marriage, and dream of the perfect husband, the *serviswala*, who will take them away to live a life of ease (Jeffery and Jeffery 1994; Jeffery and Jeffery 1996). As one 19-year old Brahmin girl said: 'The work here is *ganda* (dirty) especially for those who have studied; we do not want to do this work, and what is the use of studying if all you are going to do is carry this stuff [manure] around on your head. If one has a good husband then he will take you away with him on service. If not then you have to do what the *sasu* (mother-in-law) says.'

However, most girls do indeed experience a life in which they rarely see their husbands, who, as migrant workers, spend most of their time in one of the towns or cities of the plains. They live with their parents-in-law and their offspring in a mountain village, and they work and work.

When they can afford it, parents encourage daughters to pursue their studies because this shows that the family is 'modern' and improves a woman's chances of marrying into a 'good house'. However, these very same people, as prospective and actual parents-in-law, have more ambivalent feelings about receiving an educated woman into their house as a daughter-in-law. It is a well-known fact that in north India the in-marrying daughter-in-law is seen as a threat to the solidarity of the joint family and as a messenger of inauspiciousness and misfortune. This same model of the in-marrying woman underlies Kumaoni villagers' ambivalence towards educated daughters-in-law. An educated bride usually brings an ample dowry and increases the groom's family's status within the local community. Her higher educational status, however, is seen as a challenge to existing gender and power relations within the household as well as a threat to the Pahari ethos, regional identity, and way of life. The educated bride is identified as the harbinger of the menacing changes that are thought to accompany higher female education.

Whereas the daughter-sister is constructed as benevolent and auspicious, the in-marrying woman is potentially disruptive and a carrier of inauspiciousness. This is not to say that the in-marrying woman is not seen to have any redeeming features. Indeed, the *bwari* also represents positive potential as a conduit for wealth in the form of the dowry and affinal gifts thereafter, and as the provider of progeny and labour. The *bwari* is the prime worker in the household and her labour ensures the fertility and productivity of the household estate. Nevertheless, the negative construction of the daughter-in-law is predominant and frequently overrides any positive potential the new bride may represent. The woman enters her husband's house and village as an outsider, despite being classified thereafter as an insider. She brings with her the dangers associated with outsiders.[6]

As in other parts of South Asia, in Kumaon the daughter-in-law, the stranger who joins the household, is associated with many negative qualities: she is seen as a risk to the house's reputation if her sexuality and procreative capacities are not contained, and as a threat to the unity and stability of the joint patrilineal household unit (see Madan 1989 [1965]: 219; Das 1976; Vatuk 1972; Bennett 1983). Men and senior women always blame in-marrying women for household conflicts and the break up of the joint family. And, should a son behave disrespectfully towards his parents, or act against their wishes, that is often blamed directly on the spiteful machinations of a manipulative daughter-in-law. A main concern is that the new bride will win her husband's affection and convince him to set up an autonomous household unit, or, that after the birth of children, the tension and antagonism between sisters-in-law will intensify, resulting in premature and undignified partition. The in-marrying woman is also thought of as a conveyor of inauspiciousness and misfortune, and an agent of supernatural danger (Bennett 1983; Das 1979: 99; Parry 1989). In Kumaon, during the first year of marriage the new bride is not supposed to stay in her conjugal place during the two 'black months' of the year (mid-August–September and mid-March–April). During these months her husband's senior agnates must not see her face since this may bring them misfortune. And, if there is an illness, or if livestock should die or some other misfortune should befall the house after the daughter-in-law's arrival, she is often held responsible. It is also the in-married village woman who is suspected of casting spells (*jadu*) onto her husband, or of transporting them from her natal kin with her dowry; it is she who is accused of sorcery and considered to be a potential witch.

In addition to deeply distrusting the daughter-in-law, senior kin, and the mother-in-law in particular, complain, as they have done for generations, about how far short their *bwaris* fall of the ideal. The mother-in-law wants a modest, obedient and malleable *bwari*, a diligent and efficient worker who will work the land, feed the cattle and keep the kitchen hearth burning. She wants her *bwari* to be *kirshan* (skilful, efficient, hardworking). However, mothers-in-law universally complain that *bwaris* are lazy and parents-in-law moan that *bwaris* show no respect to their elders. A *bwari* is supposed to be modest, deferential and respectful before her senior conjugal kin, thereby reinforcing and maintaining the gender and power relations within the household and larger kin group. As one woman explained, '*bwaris* should fear their *sasu* and *sasur* (parents-in-law), because only then will any work get done'. In-marrying women have always been seen as threatening, senior conjugal kin have always complained about their *bwaris*, and conflicts have always existed within extended joint households. However, educated daughters-in-law (*padhi-likhi bwaris*) are considered to be even more dangerous than less educated sisters-in-law. Although an educated daughter-in-law can enhance the family's status, she is seen as a threat to existing power and gender relations within the family.

Increasingly, young men prefer educated women for wives. Silora men explained that being educated and literate are desirable qualities for a wife and mother as she can help her children in their education and so make for a brighter future. Educated women (*padhi-likhis*) are said to have good manners, to speak and dress well, and to be more sophisticated than their less educated rustic sisters (see Vatuk 1972: 80). There is also an element of personal pride involved as one's own status is confirmed and increased by having secured an educated woman in marriage. Parents are also keen to acquire an educated *bwari*. Such a match confers prestige and status within the locality, signals the formation of affinal ties with high status people, and anticipates the prospect of a suitably copious dowry. However, a conflict of interests exists between wanting to marry your son to an educated girl because of the wealth and status such a match brings, and the realities of village and family life in which in-married women are expected to perform physically demanding agricultural work and to conform to the model of a 'good' *kirshan* daughter-in-law. As one 56-year old woman told me, 'earlier, most women were illiterate but now educated girls are wanted, but not too educated!'

Daughters-in-law who are 'too' educated are not desired because, as mentioned above, secondary and higher education are assumed to effect detrimentally a female's character and behaviour. Irrespective of whether an educated woman actually feels or behaves differently from less educated woman, it is widely held that she is different, and that education has developed inappropriate qualities that are regarded as undesirable in a daughter-in-law. Consequently, the educated daughter-in-law is considered to pose an even stronger threat to existing gender relations and power structures within the household than is a less educated daughter-in-law. Secondary and tertiary female education is given as the explanation of changes in domestic relations. Education is explicitly identified as the cause of perceived conflicts and changes in relationships between a husband and wife, between junior and senior kinswomen, and between a woman and her senior conjugal kin.

Argumentative and confrontational, educated daughters-in-law are said to demand attention, to answer their seniors back, and to be disrespectful and immodest. The following quotes illustrate these points. One woman explained:

Nowadays everyone has to give daughters-in-law *khushamad* (flattery, attention) otherwise there will be arguments. Her mother- and father-in-law and husband must keep her content.

And an elderly man moaned:

A *bwari* should, however, cover her head in front of her father-in-law, but now she even combs her hair in front of us!

And another explained that:

Whereas, in the past, quarrels between husbands and wives frequently occurred, resulting in divorce, nowadays with educated daughters-in-law, the conflict is between the son and his wife versus the parents/parents-in-law.

Furthermore, an educated daughter-in-law is deemed more likely to forge a strong alliance with her husband and to persuade him to break off from his parents and set up a nuclear family of their own. Perhaps this is because an educated woman is assumed to have better powers of persuasion than a less educated woman. Or, perhaps a son's preference for an educated wife, and therefore a companion in marriage (see Vatuk 1972: 80), is seen to make him more compliant to his wife's wishes. Whatever the reason, it would seem that educated daughters and their husbands are thought to be capable of fearlessly flouting the authority of seniors. One elderly man told me that juniors, especially daughters-in-law, are supposed to fear their elders, but that now 'a mother-in-law fears her *bwari*, and a father fears his son'.

In-laws have always complained about their son's wives and blamed them for trying to divide the joint family. Not only are these reproaches part of the Indian mother-in-law's almost institutionalized right to complain about her daughter-in-law. They are also part of older people's more general tendency to compare their view of the present as a time in which the world is upside down, with their (somewhat spurious) image of the past as a time when things were as they should be. What is interesting, however, is that it is higher levels of female education that is identified as the cause for changing fault lines of inter-generational tension and conflict within the home.

Educated women are also said to be arrogant and proud, and unwilling to put their hands to physically demanding, manual agricultural or domestic work. These qualities curtail a mother-in-law's control and authority over daughters-in-law. They also exacerbate conflicts between sisters-in-law. *Padhi-likhis* are said to use their educated status to set themselves apart from other women, and are criticized for not co-operating in agricultural work. In extended households in which there is no mother-in-law and property has not yet been divided, senior sisters-in-law (*jethani*) resent their educated junior sisters-in-law's (*deorani*) reluctance or refusal to do agricultural work. Not only is the junior denying the elder sister-in-law her rightful authority as a senior, but the latter resents such inequalities and feels that it is due to her hard work alone that the undivided ancestral land is maintained in cultivable condition. Furthermore, as was repeatedly pointed out to me, it is not that educated women do not know how to do field work, but that they use their superior education as an excuse not to do it. As soon as the ancestral land is partitioned, many, though not all, educated daughters-in-law take up agricultural work on their own plots with uncharacteristic zeal, when previously they had done none.

Significantly, in all of the above cases it is a woman's higher level of education, and the alleged increased confidence and obstinacy it engenders, that is identified as the cause for these changes. A woman's 'difficult' behaviour, her expressions of immodesty, her lack of respect for her seniors, the presumed command she wields over her husband coupled with her eagerness to set up a nuclear family, as well as her laziness and unwillingness to participate in the household work, are explained by and blamed on her level of education.

The characteristics attributed to *padhi-likhi bwaris* are exemplified in the construction of the woman as *heeroin*, and educated daughters-in-law are frequently referred to as *heeroins*. *Heeroin* (heroine in English) is the term for the Indian actress/film-star. *Heeroin* has negative and positive connotations. In some contexts to be called a *heeroin* is to be identified with the superior beauty and perfection associated with legendary movie stars and is therefore a compliment. When the new bride (*dulhin*) appears dressed up in her wedding finery people may comment 'doesn't she look like a *heeroin* in her new sari' or 'look at the *heeroin!*' The new bride is allowed, and indeed expected, to wear make-up, special saris and her gold jewellery in her conjugal home (*sauras*) for the first few weeks after the wedding. One old woman said 'a new daughter-in-law's work (*kam*) is to show off her *phaishan* (fashion), what else!' When travelling between her conjugal and natal homes soon after the wedding, the new bride will travel dressed up in her wedding finery. A *dulhaini* is considered to be auspicious and women always stop to watch one pass by. In this context the *heeroin* is positive, and propitious. However, the new bride is permitted to enjoy this role for a limited period only. When it is time, the *bwari* will slip into her *dhoti*. Soon this becomes tatty and worn and she is just another village wife, another pair of working hands in the fields.

Though to be like a *heeroin* is desirable in the context of the wedding, *heeroin* can also be a derogatory term and this is mainly how it is used regarding educated daughters-in-law. In this use of the word, a *heeroin* is a woman who wears nice saris, nail-varnish and make-up, sits around looking pretty, and enjoys strolling around (*ghumna*) with her husband. On the face of it, these may seem to be desirable and enviable qualities, the stuff that dreams (and movies) are made of, and women may actually dream of living such a life. However, in Silora the *heeroin* is the polar opposite of the much praised and valued *kirshan*. *Heeroin* refers to an in-married woman who does not work but spends all of her time tending to her appearance. *Heeroins* are ladies of leisure and luxury, and, according to Silora women, lazy, conceited and arrogant. In Silora it is not socially acceptable for village wives not to work; only visiting *celibetis* are entitled not to work. Ultimately, *heeroin* is a comment on what is not valued in a woman in Silora: in daily life the term is used as a device by which to denigrate in-married village women and as a sanction on diversions from what is considered to be normal and acceptable behaviour. The following is an example of such disparagement concerning a new *bwari* and her inability (or unwillingness) to do any agricultural fieldwork. A Silora Brahmin had recently married a Kumaoni woman from Lucknow. He too was living in Lucknow, where they had their wedding. They returned to the village in the autumn, at harvest time. The new wife was obviously a university educated and city woman: she was always well dressed and wore make-up. One day, during their visit, the husband took his new wife out to the fields to do some work, which involved the harvesting and transporting of *marua* (*Eleusine coracana*). Whilst in the field she said she could not do the work, and that she did not know how to hold or use a sickle (*datuli*). Some older women who were watching and listening from a courtyard just above the field ridiculed her: 'You don't know how to use a sickle? Haven't you ever cut vegetables before? You use it like a knife!', they jeered. Others exclaimed, 'don't they [*padhi-likhis*] have any shame not to do any work?', and one woman said, 'I don't know what it is about these *padhi-likhis*; they do not want to do this work, as if they are somehow above it.' The young daughter-in-law was never to be seen again in public. For the rest of her stay the husband harvested alongside his mother. Other women criticized the young wife's behaviour and labelled her a *heeroin*.

As Seymour (1995) says, then, with education for women (especially higher education) has come, on the one hand, an increased desire for such education, and on the other, concern over the perceived challenges to the patrifocal system that accompany it. A tension both for and against female education exists because of the different consequences the education of daughters and of daughters-in-law is believed to bring. This tension is linked to gender constructs of out- and in-marrying women and to the differing wishes and expectations parents and parents-in-law have of different female family members.[7] Hence, although the education of daughters and daughters-in-law has the potential of enhancing the status of both their families, and is therefore considered desirable for those who can afford it, educated daughters are not perceived to challenge domestic authority structures, whereas

educated daughters-in-law are. This association of the negative consequences of secondary and higher female education with the daughter-
in-law, and not with the revered daughter, is consistent with the prevailing model of the in-marrying woman as potentially disruptive.

However, not only does the educated in-marrying woman represent
an especially potent challenge to existing domestic gender and power
structures, she also represents a threat to the Pahari ethos and way of
life. The effects of education on the female character in the form of
in-marrying women are thought to be contrary to and incompatible
with the social values and way of life which Kumaonis consider to be
unique to themselves as hill people, and which they identify as distin-
guishing them from the dominant plains society. Just as the in-marrying daughter-in-law is conceived of as an agent of disruption and
messenger of misfortune, so the educated daughter-in-law represents
the vehicle through which the contaminating immoral influences of
plains society enter and undermine the essence of Pahari village culture
and identity.

FEMALE EDUCATION AND REGIONAL IDENTITY

Kumaonis are suspicious of people of the plains (*deshis*) and are dis-
approving of many of the customs of plains society. They identify
implicity the plains (*desh*) with the city or town (*shahar*), and the hills
(*pahar*) with the village (*gaon*). Consequently, the eating habits, moral
behaviour, styles and fashions observed in the urban centres of the
Ganga plains are defined as plains customs. Regarding themselves to
be not only morally distinct, but also morally superior, Kumaonis believe they have preserved moral and social values long since corrupted
in the plains by modernity. Amongst other things, plains people are
thought not to respect and care for their kinsfolk and to live anony-
mously in nuclear families. Any new 'bad' habit or trend is usually
attributed to having come from the plains. Furthermore, plains people
are said to be rich (*mota*) people who value social difference and inequality. And, whereas wealth does not entitle a person to superiority
or authority over others in Kumaoni village society, plains people are
perceived to be engaged in a continual contest of one-upmanship.
Consequently, plains people are perceived as arrogant and pre-
occupied with showing off their wealth and standing.

As hill people, Kumaoni villagers consider themselves to have distinct social values and mores that they share among themselves and

which mark them off from the dominant plains society. These distinctive markers, as well as their self-proclaimed moral superiority over plains people, are fundamental to the negotiation and formation of a Kumaoni identity and sense of self (Moller forthcoming). Among the features considered distinctive to hill people, and directly opposed to plains society, is the value given to the notion of equality.

Silora villagers give ideological stress to the notion of equality, and this value informs inter-household relations within the village community (Moller 1993: 108–34). Villagers from 'Twice-born' castes emphasize that all high-caste co-villagers should be, or at least should appear to be, *barabar* or on the same level, equal. On the surface, and going by appearances, it is very difficult to tell who is wealthy. Women wear the same shabby *dhotis* day in and day out until they are almost in shreds.[8] Womenfolk from the more wealthy households work in the fields and collect fuel and fodder from the forest just like other women. The furnishings and decorations of the houses are relatively uniform. Berreman says of Sirkanda villagers that 'some are honestly poor, some learned to make a show of poverty' (Berreman 1963: 219), and this applies to Silora too. This kind of equality can be defined in terms of sameness and non-difference with regard to economic standing, political authority, lifestyle and social conduct (see Foster 1965: 303). Such egalitarianism can be called a 'pragmatic egalitarianism' which 'leads people to mute expressions of difference to which they are nevertheless sensitive' (Cohen 1985: 33).[9]

For example, Silora villagers express approval of the fact that the social relations of production are more fair and egalitarian than in the plains. 'Here people do their own work (*apna kam*) and there is no shame (*sharm*) in this.' And, despite the problems involved in ploughing and cultivating their terraced fields and the low yields, villagers speak almost boastfully about the Pahari people's way of farming. As one man explained: 'In the plains if people are rich they will not do the fieldwork but will hire *naukars* (servants). Here in the hills, be they rich or poor, they do their own work; they are *barabar* (equal).'[10]

This putative egalitarianism is presented by Paharis as a means of expressing their difference from plains society. Although this is a simplified image, it is one which can become a rhetorical expression of Pahari virtue, and which can feed back into their own sense of self.

This ideological stress on equality (*barabar*) underlies the condemnation of displays and expressions of wealth and economic, as well as social, difference. Social pressures exist to ensure that people conform to recognized norms of behaviour, and those who go beyond the norm are criticized and mocked for trying to be bigger and better than anyone else. People who visibly differentiate themselves in terms of material wealth, lifestyle or social conduct are considered arrogant and scorned for putting on airs of superiority. Such attitudes, behaviour and social pressures, which stem from the notion of keeping everyone even, *barabar*, are most clearly demonstrated when we examine consumption patterns, partially expressed through attitudes about *phaishan* (fashion, style, or trend), and ideas about women and work.

One of the easiest and most obvious ways of expressing economic standing is through one's appearance. It is assumed that a person must be relatively wealthy to be able to afford such luxuries over and above basic daily necessities. Clothing tailored in up-to-date styles and materials, as well as hairstyles and beauty accessories, is *phaishan*. The trend and style-setters for young people in particular are the Hindi film stars, locally referred to as *heeros* (film actors) and, as described above, *heeroins*. *Phaishan*, I was told, is based on imitating television and film stars. Young men copy those *heeros* who are, or who represent, *seths* (wealthy men), thereby proclaiming to others that they come from a good, wealthy house (*thik ghar*). By extension, these styles are inextricably associated with the 'service class', urban lifestyle and in particular with plains society. Accompanying the styles and fashions come sets of attitudes and behaviour that are considered by most village adults to be alien and inappropriate to village life and hill society in general.

Dressing up, or showing off one's *phaishan*, is permitted on occasions like weddings, but is not appropriate for daily living. 'Dressing up' is considered pretentious and concomitant with putting on airs of superiority and difference. One young woman told me that if she were to put on a nice sari, other women would comment sarcastically: 'become big have you? Showing (off) your *phaishan* are you?' (*twil bari hai gai chai? Apan phaishan dikha ha chai?*).

Similar issues come to the fore in relation to women and work. A specific type of lifestyle and modes of behaviour are expected by all women within the village. Strong social pressures exist to ensure that individuals do not steer off course into behaviour considered unacceptable and unbecoming of wives of the village. In Kumaon women are the main agricultural workers. Their load is very heavy and they always look busy. Indeed, it is not good for a woman to wander around aimlessly: she must have a purpose in her movements. For an in-married woman life in the village means work. Work is central to a woman's life and self-worth. Other women judge a woman by how well she works, how efficient and skilful she is, and how strong she is. Someone who is a good and efficient worker is referred to as *kirshan*. A woman who is considered by others to be *kirshan* is respected and admired, but perhaps also envied.

Kumaoni women are aware that they are crucial to the local agricultural economy. As one woman said, 'Here woman is everything. Without women there is nothing here' (*'Ya shaini sab ch'*). They are also aware that they contribute much more to the local agricultural economy than plains women commonly do. One woman said: 'Hill women do everything: they look after children, do the cooking and work in the fields. In the plains, women do house work and men work on the land.' Despite what any one woman may feel, and in other contexts many complained about the pain and suffering (*kasht* and *dukh*) of a woman's life in the hills (see Moller 1993: 42–6), when contrasting their lives to that of plains women, they represent their situation as the better of the two. Village women take pride in their physical strength and consider their mobility a kind of freedom not enjoyed by their sisters in the plains. Going out to the fields or forest, for young daughters-in-law in particular, is a relief and release. On one trip to the forest a young woman said: 'Our way of life is better than that of the plains women. We go out; they just sit around in the house and they are not very strong in the body.' Though women generally consider themselves to be suppressed (*daba*), they value the fact that they are not confined to the house all day. One woman explained, 'we women here are not restricted: we go to the forest, the house, here and there. We are not confined, we are free (*azad*)', and as another woman proudly declared: 'Here women work, not as they do in the *desh* where they just sit around.'

Women work out of necessity. They are responsible for ensuring good harvests with which to nourish household members. However, women are in another way 'forced' to work. Where in plains society the seclusion of women is seen as a mark of prestige and economic security, in rural Kumaon for a woman not to work in the fields and forest is taken as an attempt to try to set oneself apart as socially superior, and as such is condemned. There is an enormous amount of social pressure placed on women by other women, to work, or to look as if they are working. A woman who does not work, or who does not work well, or who does not work as much as others think she should, is teased and ridiculed. And indeed, even if a woman wanted to ease her workload by purchasing wood, for example, other women would mock her. A 50-year-old Brahmin woman said to me: 'I get tired and worn out from carrying wood from the forests, but if I were to buy wood for my stock, people would say "can't you even manage to carry a bundle on your head?" People would tease me and call me names.'

As a wife of the village a woman is expected to work. I recall one Brahmin woman's discomfort when she visited the village. Her husband is employed with a private bus service in the nearby town of Ranikhet, where she and her family live. They visit Silora very rarely. On this occasion she and her husband had returned to the village for several weeks to observe mourning for her father-in-law's death. This woman has never worked in the fields and forests, having lived in the bazaar ever since marriage. When she returns to Silora she says she feels embarrassed and spends as much time as possible indoors, out of sight of her '*jethani* and *deorani* people' (her sisters-in-law). She said to me 'it doesn't look good if, while they are working, they see me sitting around'. Other women tease her when they walk by saying '*baithi chai?*' (sitting are you? i.e. No work to do?). For a village wife not to work is somehow not acceptable; it gives cause for comment. The only married woman seen sitting around without any work, and who is not teased for it, is the *celibeti*, the out-married village woman.

The educated in-marrying woman, through her association with the negative qualities of the *padhi-likhi* and *heeroin*, is seen to exemplify traits, conduct and values that are strongly equated with the urban way of life, and, by extension, are considered typical of plains society and therefore alien to hill society. Just like *heeroins*, urban women and plains women, educated daughters-in-law are considered obstinate and confrontational; they are thought to disregard existing gender and power relations in the household, to forge strong 'companion-like' relationships with their husbands, and to favour the establishment of nuclear families. Furthermore, educated daughters-in-law are assumed to take pleasure in showing off their social superiority through their *phaishan*. They are seen to have a predilection for a life of leisure and to refuse arrogantly to perform agricultural work, behaviour which directly mirrors that of plains people, is repugnant to hill people, and defies their egalitarian ethos. Moreover, the model of the typically vain and lazy *heeroin/padhi-likhi* fundamentally contravenes the image of the ideal village hill woman, the *kirshan*. Therefore, the *padhi-likhi bwari*, like the *heeroin*, represents the antithesis of the social values, morality and way of life of hill people and hence the Pahari identity and sense of self.

CONCLUSION

This paper has presented data that link aspects of Kumaoni socio-cultural traditions to attitudes regarding post-primary female schooling. We have seen that those qualities which development specialists hope, and villagers assume, women gain from education are considered by a woman's parents to be potentially beneficial for their daughters in their conjugal home. To some extent this affords opportunities to women to undertake post-primary education. However, these same qualities are viewed by parents-in-law as extremely undesirable in a daughter-in-law. The extension and promotion of post-primary education among Kumaoni women raises a number of questions.

The main question is whether or not women fare better in their conjugal homes because of their education. Though it is difficult to identify objective and standard indicators for female autonomy (Jeffery and Basu 1996) the following points touch upon some pertinent issues. There were no cases in Silora of a couple separating from the joint family as long as both of the husband's parents were alive. Nevertheless, educated daughters-in-law, and especially university educated women, are expected to receive better treatment from their husband's mother than less educated women (see Krengel 1997: 185), though this is more likely if her husband lives locally too. This situation of a highly educated daughter-in-law living with her in-laws is not very common, however, as very few university educated women actually live regularly in the village. Most of them accompany their husband to his place of work. In recent research Krengel suggests that this is becoming a more common phenomenon in rural Kumaon, and that it is perhaps also applicable to a man and his high-school pass wife. She reports that, compared to a decade ago, despite or in response to a threefold increase in dowry expenses, there has been a weakening of internal household authority structures, resulting in the exposure of new conflicts. Young men who are migrant workers are apparently refusing parental marriage arrangements, and more couples are insisting that the wife follow her husband to the city where he works. Though this is still the exception, it represents a significant shift. Krengel suggests these changes have come about as a result of male migration to the plains. However, it might be, as Basu (1996: 69) suggests in relation to intentional fertility decline, that the increasing educational levels of both man and wife as a united team, and the new shared aspirations that such education nurtures, are important contributory factors. Krengel (1997: 185) also reports that whereas in the past it was rare to find women disposing of money, today most women dispose of at least small amounts of money. Whether this is as a result of increased female educational levels, I cannot say.

A rather ironic result of increased education is that it eventually promises to undermine the economic basis of Kumaoni society. If more girls are educated to higher levels, and if they do not want to perform fieldwork or if they insist on accompanying their migrant husbands, local agriculture will lose its primary labour input. In a region where women are the agricultural workforce, this is an important consideration. This will evolve especially if parents-in-law's ability to mobilize the labour, and control the living place, of educated daughters-in-law progressively diminishes. Given that access to post-primary education for women is only a relatively recent phenomenon, it is difficult to anticipate how, as better educated daughters-in-law make the transition to mothers-in-law, agricultural work and the performance of other domestic tasks will be affected.

It is also important to ask to what extent educated women themselves consider they obtain a passport to a 'better life' as a result of their education. Girls generally enjoy attending secondary school, but are also aware that after marriage they will probably be expected to behave like women who have not received such an education. The freedom and contact with a world beyond the house and village, which secondary education affords, is denied to them in their conjugal home. Indeed, it could be said that life in the conjugal home could potentially be made more difficult because of a girl's educational qualifications, as parents-in-law perceive an increased need to preserve the family's existing authority structures and ideas. During my fieldwork, young women expressed frustration at the prospect of such constraints and thus did not perceive that higher education necessarily yields concrete improvements in their future life. Nevertheless, girls value highly the fleeting taste of liberation that post-primary education can give them and, if Krengel's intimations are correct, in some way the seeds of change have been sown.

It is important to remember, however, that female education is not the only source, and educated women are not the only agents, of social change in Kumaoni villages. Contact with the urban centres of the plains and the migrants who work and live there are other significant sources and agents (Krengel 1997). Just as in-marrying educated women are considered to be harbingers of negative change and a threat to the reproduction of an homogenous regional identity, male migrants and the migration process itself are thought to pose similar threats. However, just as female education is a double-edged sword, so too is migration. Both processes certainly are seen as a means of strengthening one's standing locally and towards the outside and of doing away with the stigma of being unsophisticated peasants (Krengel 1997: 183). But male migrants and in-marrying *padhi-likhis* are also seen as conveyors of new attitudes, values and practices which are considered to have the potential to undermine Kumaoni villagers' cultural distinctiveness and regional identity.

Female education in Kumaon is leading to autonomy, but not in the way anticipated by policy makers and development specialists. It is not developing women's autonomy as individuals, but it does seem to enable them to form stronger bonds with their husbands and thus to increase the strength of a conjugal unit *vis-à-vis* the in-laws. While the Western model of individual strength is false, there is nevertheless increasing autonomy of a unit. This new conjugal autonomy is, however, only true to the extent that males and females actually forge allegiances when previously they had not. Though difficult to prove, this at least is Kumaoni villagers' perception and, as others have noted, an emerging tendency.

NOTES

1. These figures are similar to those recorded for other villages in Kumaon in the 1960s (Fanger 1980: 300) and 1980s (Krengel 1989: 103).
2. The data in this paper were gathered during 15 months of doctoral field work in Almora District between 1989 and 1991 and a field visit between December 1993 and January 1994. Doctoral studies at the London School of Economics, including field research in Kumaon, were generously funded by an Economic and Social Research Council Competition Award (1988–92). An earlier version of this paper was presented to the 'Gender Issues and Social Change' panel at the 15th European Conference on Modern South Asian Studies, Prague, 8–12 September 1998. The Department of Social Anthropology, University of Manchester and a British Academy Overseas Conference Grant funded attendance to the conference.

3. These figures can not be treated as definitive, however, as different sources give different rates. Samal, for example, quotes another source which say that the state female literacy rate in 1991 was 20.92 per cent (Samal 1993: 90).

4. In some parts of Uttarakhand grooms still wear the *dhoti-kurta* outfit. However, during my fieldwork I saw only one groom so dressed as compared to about six '*serviswala*' grooms.

5. Although daughters living with relatives in urban centres may attend universities more easily, for village girls this is not possible, as it would involve regular travel. The only resident village daughter to continue tertiary education between 1989 and 1991 did so by taking a correspondence course.

6. For more details on high-caste ideas about the dangers associated with affines and 'outsiders' in Kumaon see Moller (1993); Moller (forthcoming); and Moller (in press).

7. This double standard in ideas regarding the desirability of education for daughters and daughters-in-law is akin to those held about by working women by middle and upper class Punjabi Delhi residents (Chanana 1990a). According to the latter, working women are no longer stigmatized, a view shared by men and women alike. Nevertheless, Chanana notes that when daughters-in-law go out to work the aged have to shoulder the responsibility of looking after the household and grandchildren. Therefore, in some cases people feel that their daughters-in-law escape the drudgery of housework by taking a job. However, these very people seem to take a different stance regarding a woman's education and career when their own daughters are involved. Though they feel that their daughters should be able to earn and become economically independent to face any contingency, they do not actually expect them to work (Chanana 1990a: 87).

8. Traill, over 150 years ago, remarked that hill people in general are 'extremely indifferent in regard to the state of their everyday apparel, and continue to wear their clothes till reduced to mere shreds and tatters' save on festive occasions (Traill 1980 [1828]: 212).

9. Several factors account for this ideological emphasis on 'being the same'. The *pattidari* land tenure system and the notion of brotherhood (*biradar*) both express and are based upon a principle of equality (see Parry 1974). More importantly, however, is the fact that Kumaoni villages are not sharply stratified as villages are in the plains: there are no large landlords as exist in the plains of Uttar Pradesh. In the early 1980s holdings below one hectare constituted approximately two-thirds of the total holdings in the hill region of Uttar Pradesh, and approximately 80 per cent of the total land holdings in Almora District (Butola 1992: 124). The phenomena of large individualized landholdings, and of landlords and the accompanying inequalities so characteristic of the plains system, do not exist in Silora or Kumaon in general. A relatively even pattern of land distribution among village Brahmins and Thakurs has remained, and high caste Silora villagers have, in recent history, been small owner-cultivators and have not been in a position to offer allegiance to a landlord or master. Moreover, no landowner is free from working the land: every household still cultivates its fields with family labour. Consequently, these owner-cultivators have enjoyed a degree of economic autonomy, control and security which has contributed to an independence of spirit and fierce self-reliance (see Berreman 1963: 353; Randhawa 1970: 30–1), which in turn translates into a general dislike of any local, or external, form of leadership. Village-wide acceptance of formal leadership and authority is

absent in Silora and people resent others trying to tell them what to do. As one man said to me, 'as many hearths there are, that is how many leaders there are'.

10. While the division of agricultural labour may, in men's opinion, contrast favourably (as more egalitarian and fair) with that in the plains, men do relatively little farm work and the main inequalities lie not among men or between the castes, but between men and women.

5

Divided We Stand: Identity and Protest in the Demand for a Separate Hill State in the UP Hills

Emma Mawdsley

INTRODUCTION

In August 2000, Uttar Pradesh experienced a momentous change. Its northern Himalayan region was formally separated and recognized as the new federal state of Uttaranchal. In one day, UP lost around 20 per cent of its geographical extent (but only some 4–5 per cent of its population, given the lower population density of the mountains). The creation of a separate hill state had been on the political agenda ever since 1991, when a Bharatiya Janata Party (BJP) government of Uttar Pradesh had passed a resolution in its favour. But the origins of the demand can be traced back to the 1940s and the transition to Independence. The issue became more pressing after mid-1994, when an explosive mass mobilization brought the subject to national attention. In 2000, after a significant struggle, the Bill creating the state of Uttaranchal was passed in the Lok Sabha. As well as having obvious substantial consequences for both the hill region and UP itself, the achievement of separation has important implications for the whole country. It has encouraged and revitalized old and new regional movements elsewhere in India, and helped set in motion a renewed debate on federalism and political devolution.

Successive central governments of India have tended to be hostile to the break-up of existing states and the formation of new ones. The reasons for this include the deep traumas and tragedy that accompanied Partition, and persistent anxieties about the fundamental unity of this most heterogeneous of nation states (Corbridge 1995; Harrison 1960; King 1997). Nehru and other senior nationalists wanted to prevent the states succumbing to traditional affiliations of religion, ethnicity or regional culture, and to represent 'rational(-izing)' and 'modern(-izing)' constituents of the body politic instead. Although various changes were made to state boundaries between 1950 and 2000, and several new states were created, such alterations were conceded very reluctantly (Brass 1994). Over this period, different regional movements have deployed a number of tactics in order to achieve territorial autonomy. These include various degrees of armed insurrection, nonviolent protests, appeals to the political, economic and/or strategic logic of separation and so on. Like other social movements, the *range* of such tactics open to each regional protest (or elements within it) may change over time, but are linked to the specific cultural, political and material resources available to it. The *choice* of tactics, on the other hand, will be influenced by the 'field of opportunities' within which particular demands are being articulated—in other words the political environment in the region, state and/or Centre, and the shifting openings and closures that this may present (Escobar 1992; McAdam et al. 1996).

This paper explores some of the physical, symbolic and rhetorical devices that were deployed to support and 'legitimate' the demand for a separate Uttaranchal state, and the political environments within which these demands were made.[1] Many 'objective' differences exist between the hills and the plains regions of UP, including language and regional culture,[2] but during the early struggle these differences tended to be downplayed while other identities and images were emphasized or exaggerated. This paper does not seek to offer a straight-forward history of the regional movement; nor does it analyse the degree to which these images and identities correspond to 'real life' in the hills (which would in any case be a rather dubious enterprise). Rather, it is an examination of some of the principal claims made during the regional mobilization about hill, state and Indian identity, and how these related to the mobilization. Particular attention will be paid to the way in which the Uttaranchal region was argued to be *united* on the basis of geography (rather than caste, language or religion); *different* from the rest of the state of Uttar Pradesh; but nevertheless *integral* to the nation state of India. The analysis also takes up some of the contradictions inherent within these identity constructions, and how they were dealt with. More serious ruptures in the idea of a united hill population are examined briefly at the end, in relation to caste, community and subregion. The paper focuses on the first two years that followed the explosion of mass protest in the hills, roughly from 1994 to 1996.[3] Since then, of course, many changes have taken place within the movement and in the wider political context—including the creation of the state. This particular study is, therefore, very time- and place-specific, but the theoretical approach (which draws on a range of social movement theories) is widely applicable to analyses of contemporary regional movements. Moreover, although this paper was originally conceived before Uttaranchal was created (and there was no guarantee that such an event would happen), it provides an important history to some of the tensions and difficulties that have since been apparent within and between UP and Uttaranchal. These include the tensions between the hills and the *terai* areas; the battles over the location of the capital; and the issues around the substantial Punjabi Sikh community (Mishra 2000; Ramakrishnan 1998).

THE REGIONAL MOVEMENT: A BRIEF BACKGROUND

Uttaranchal is made up of Garhwal in the west and Kumaon in the east. In the late eighteenth and early nineteenth centuries, Gurkhas invaded from the east and conquered the hill region, but in 1815 they were defeated by the British, who wanted to halt their incursions into the *terai* region. The Treaty of Sigauli established a border with the Gurkhas, and returned to the son of the previous ruler most of the western half of the region, which then became the princely state of Tehri Garhwal (Rawat 1989). At Independence, a combination of nationalist pressure and the *Praja Mandal* (a popular movement) ensured that Tehri Garhwal, like the other princely states, was absorbed into the newly formed India (Bhatkoti 1987; Guha 1989), and the region became a part of Uttar Pradesh.

Kumaon has a longer relationship with the plains, having been annexed by the British in 1815 with a view to trade with Tibet. A strategic part of the eastern half of Garhwal was added to this, and was renamed British Garhwal (Rawat 1989). Initially these two areas were ruled together as a Non-Regulation Province because of their mountain geography and unusual social and cultural systems. However, in 1891, the colonial government decided to merge Kumaon and British Garhwal with the North-Western Provinces and Qudh, despite petitions from the Kumaoni élite. In 1947 Kumaon achieved Independence as part of the United Provinces (as it then was), thus remaining administratively and politically connected to the plains.

The possibility of separation was debated throughout the first four decades of Independence (Rau 1981; Sah 1993). The case was unsuccessfully raised before the States Reorganization Commission in the early 1950s (Government of India 1955), but continued to be brought up periodically by different political leaders, intellectuals and academics during the 1960s and 1970s. A number of rallies and meetings took place over this period, but it was not until the 1980s that there were signs of more significant popular support for the idea. In 1979 the Uttaranchal Kranti Dal (UKD) was formed, a single-agenda political party for the creation of a hill state, and in 1986 it won its first seat in the Legislative Assembly of Uttar Pradesh.[4] Several regional and state units of different political parties also started to express their support for separation between the hills and the plains. These included the Bharatiya Janata Party (BJP), the Janata Party (JP) and the Communist Party of India (CPI). In 1991, the BJP Government of UP passed a resolution in the Legislative Assembly in favour of a separate 'Uttaranchal'.[5] Although this undoubtedly gave the movement impetus, it was a rather empty parliamentary gesture. Constitutionally, the central government alone can permit the creation of new federal territories, but when the motion came to the Lok Sabha in Delhi, only 1 of the 119 BJP MPs supported it.

The real turning point in the history of the demand came in 1994, with the development of a new phase of mass support. In 1993 the Samajwadi Party-Bahujan Samaj Party (SP-BSP) coalition had been elected to power in UP, representing an uneasy combination of lower caste and OBC interests.[6] The SP-BSP initially supported separation for Uttaranchal (and, indeed, passed a Resolution in the Assembly in favour of the plan in early 1994). But they quickly ran into massive opposition in the hill region over different legislation, proposing 27 per cent reservation in education and government posts for Other Backward Castes in the state. The problem lay in the fact that a uniquely high proportion of the hill population are upper castes (around 74 per cent), compared to the rest of the state, in which the upper castes constitute a more usual 17 per cent of the population. Only 2–3 per cent of the hill population are Other Backward Caste, compared to around 37 per cent in the plains (Hasan 1998).[7] The legislation, if applied blanket-fashion to the state, would mean that the majority of the population in this already-poor region would be denied a huge proportion of the government jobs and educational opportunities previously available to them. Growing discontent over this OBC legislation turned into a massive and explosive demand for a separate state after the SP-BSP government first turned a deaf ear to the hill people's grievances, and then responded with considerable violence to their mostly peaceful protests. The reason for the SP-BSP's antagonistic stance was almost certainly based on a narrow political calculation of the electoral benefits this would bring. By depicting the issue as a chauvinistic high-caste struggle over reservation, rather than one over development and regional issues, the state government could enhance its reputation as a champion of the backward castes (Mawdsley 1996). The result was several years of avoidable turmoil, disruption, injuries and deaths.

Although the OBC reservation issue was critical in triggering protest in the hills, the transition to a mass regional movement cannot be explained solely in terms of this piece of legislation, nor in terms of the political circumstances in the state at the time. Rather, after decades of neglect and/or exploitation by successive state governments, the insensitive reservation legislation was felt by many to be the final straw. It was widely argued that the unequal relationship between the hills and the plains was responsible for the backwardness and poverty of the Uttaranchal region. Local people felt that they had borne the costs of inefficient and/or environmentally-damaging development projects without reaping the benefits. With their own state, they argued, planners and bureaucrats would be drawn from the hill population, or at least resident in it. They would be more aware of the needs and conditions in the hills, and would also be more accessible to ordinary people. Furthermore, politicians would remain within the hills rather than move down to Lucknow, making it easier to contact them and monitor their (in)actions. The result would (theoretically) be a more accountable, transparent and efficient government, in which local people would have greater voice, and development projects would be more suitable to their needs.[8]

Although inevitably the frequency and degree of protest declined over time, the first year was remarkable for the depth and spread of action. The vast majority of the hill population was involved in the demand, totally disrupting and overwhelming almost every aspect of life in Uttaranchal.[9]

IDENTITY AND PROTEST IN THE
HILL REGION OF UTTAR PRADESH

A significant feature of the movement over 1994–6 was its decentred and genuinely grassroots nature—initially at least, it was in many ways a truly *jan andolan*, or people's movement. Given the poor communications in the hills and the lack of a single undisputed leader, the degree of consensus on many issues was quite remarkable. Many aspects of hill identity were open to multiple (and sometimes contradictory) interpretations and the dominant themes did not go uncontested. Nevertheless, it was still possible to identify certain 'mainstream' discourses around identity and protest: *unity* (within/of the hills); *difference* (from the UP plains); and *loyalty* (to India).

Through these three interconnected arguments, protesters aimed at building a case for the legitimate separation of Uttaranchal from UP, while seeking to reassure the Centre and the rest of India of the region's commitment to the federal Union. These themes were constantly played upon and emphasized in interviews with various leaders; through letters, articles and petitions written by people within the region; through the graffiti, placards, banners and slogans that accompanied the protests; through the poems, songs and street plays that were composed and performed; and in the specific forms of protest that were deployed during the agitation. At the same time, other images and identities were downplayed or disowned by the 'mainstream' of the regional movement.

HILL IDENTITY

A vital claim made during the struggle was that the regional demand was based on the geographical differences between the hills and the plains of UP. What is interesting here is the omission (or playing down) of the hill region's social, cultural and/or linguistic differences with the plains. These include its unusual class and caste structures (Berreman 1963; Joshi 1990); various cultural and religious practices (Nand and Kumar 1989); and the Garhwali and Kumaoni languages (Joshi and Negi 1994). These 'traditional' affiliations were recognized to be important, but denied to be the primary motivating factors for the agitation. Instead, the vast majority of protesters argued that their demand was based on the need for a more geographically homogenous state, which would in theory prompt greater administrative viability and political accountability. This can be seen as an appeal to the rationalizing and modernizing discourse of the Indian state, and specifically its role as planner and developer of its territory and people (Chatterjee 1986). It took into account, and perhaps encouraged, a growing recognition in the Centre that administrative efficiency and political viability might also be legitimate reasons to divide up some of India's 'mega-states' (see also Khan 1992). At the same time, it was an explicit repudiation of the idea of separation based on parochial regional identities—a signal designed to reassure those who continued to bear Nehruvian-nationalist fears about the fragmentation of India. Some protesters suggested forging links with other non-secessionist regional groups such as those in the north-east, Jharkhand and Chhattisgarh. But most leaders within the movement sought to distance themselves from these groups on the grounds that, unlike the Uttaranchal movement, they were ethnic or religious in origin. Kashi Singh Airi, the leader of the UKD, claimed:

Our demand for statehood is based on geography. Our situation is completely different to the plains. Our movement is not based on caste or religion. We are not ethnically-motivated like Khalistan or Gorkhaland. Everyone from all eight districts, whatever caste, community or religion, is an Uttaranchali. (*Nainital Samachar*, September 1994: 'Interview with Kashi Singh Airi')

These assertions were embodied in certain forms of protest, notably marches and demonstrations in towns around the region. Various groups who did not belonging to the high-caste majority of the region (including Sikhs, Muslims, Van Gujars, Bhotiyas, Scheduled Castes and OBCs) were encouraged to join the marches under banners proclaiming their minority, but nevertheless *hill*, identity. For example, in 1994 the President of the Sikh Forum of Dehra Dun told reporters that they were in total support of the movement:

Gyani Sujan Singh said that the Garhwal and Kumaon Divisions have traditionally remained peaceful. The virtues of communal harmony and secularism had its birth in this region. He said that the people living in the hills are unitedly demanding Uttaranchal State irrespective of religion, caste and creed. He said that the Garhwalis and Punjabis (allegedly 40,000) residing in Dehra Doon live in perfect harmony with one another. (*Himachal Times* 2 September 1994: 'Doon Sikhs support Uttaranchal demand')

In September 1994 members of the Gorkha community also took out a large procession in Dehra Dun. Their leaders stated that, 'The Gorkhas have been living in the Uttaranchal for years. It is their land and since they are part of the society of Uttaranchal, the Gorkhas cannot remain insensitive to this unprecedented mass agitation' (*Himachal Times* 25 September 1994: 'Massive procession by Gorkha community').

A second set of arguments concerned the 'moral' justification of the demand for a separate state and the essentially 'virtuous' nature of the hill people who were involved in the movement. These ideas found expression through idealized representations of hill individuals and society in comparison with the rest of UP. The situation of women in the hills received particular attention—although interestingly, most of these comments came from men.[10] Again, the reality was and is far more complex than this. Nevertheless, the following villagers' comments are indicative of arguments that could be heard and read all over the hills during this period: 'Women are safe in the hills—our mothers, daughters and wives can go safely to the market and the jungle'; 'I and my brother are in the military. If we leave, whether that be for five or ten years, then our women will be safe. In the plains a man would have to stay with them'; and 'We are safe here. Our women wear lots of gold, but in the plains it would be snatched away by *dacoits.*'

Caste unity was also frequently stressed, but although it is true that there is far less caste-motivated violence than in the plains, as we shall see below, these assertions are still open to dispute. Again, though, the following statement, made by an elderly village Brahmin woman, was representative of arguments made by high castes all over the region: 'We have Harijan brothers here. I have given land for sharecropping to them, but I never demand the produce. This makes me happy. We live in brotherhood here. In the plains it is very different.'

When a local UKD leader in Mussoorie was asked about the relationship between Dalits and the upper-caste Hindus in the hills and how that might change with the creation of a separate hill state, he was at pains to argue that the region was one of caste harmony (although his patriarchal schema was rather revealing): 'No, there will be no problems, not even between high and low castes. We have good relations with the Harijans. We call [the older ones] "Uncle" and "Aunt". We respect each other. Even when Untouchability was at its height in India we still had good caste relations in Garhwal. We always give them respect, protection and help, and they work for us' (Interview 23 September 1994).

Related to this image of a virtuous society was the emphasis on the (supposedly) non-violent nature of the struggle. The forms of protest that were widely used were readings of the *Ramayana*, relay hunger strikes, processions, *dharnas*, *rasta* and *rail rokos*, *bandhs*, *jail bharo andolans* (mass courting of arrest), effigy burning, and so on. *Nukkad nataks* (street plays) and *jan jagrans* (awareness raising programmes) also helped promote the movement and certain themes within it. These methods are instantly associated with Gandhi and the Independence struggle. When deployed in contemporary social mobilizations they can be read to allude to a unity of virtuous purpose by a politically disempowered mass against a physically powerful but morally empty foe. The emphasis on non-violence highlighted a popular consensus that, by doing so, the Uttaranchal movement was maintaining the moral high ground with both the Centre and the state. But despite the claims to non-violence, and the best efforts of many people, the movement did have its violent moments.[11] Several organizations divided on the issue, including the UKD. Although the majority of people in the hills were not in favour of aggressive protest or armed struggle, there was a widespread feeling that in the past the government had only responded to a regional movement when it turned violent. However, whatever the facts, the movement's leaders and spokespersons maintained consistently that it was peaceful. Vinod Chamoli of the (local) BJP argued that: 'One bullet would undo the *tapasya* the people of the Uttaranchal have done, and it would damage our image as great patriots, non-violent and loyal citizens' (*Himachal Times* 1 November 1994: 'BJP leader, 16 women released').

The unity between Garhwal and Kumaon was also stressed and their political, historical and cultural rivalry downplayed. For example, every year in Kumaon the Khaturwa festival is celebrated, marking the historic victory of a medieval ruler of Kumaon over his Garhwali counterpart. In 1994, an effigy of Mulayam Singh Yadav (then the Chief Minister and leader of the Samajwadi Party) was burnt instead of the traditional figure of the vanquished Garhwali opponent, underlining the coming together of the two sides of the hills in the face of a common enemy. As the agitation developed, efforts were made to try and emphasize the common situation and experiences of the two sub-regions, including their shared mountain geography and their economic and political marginalization by the rest of the state.

Notions of landscape and identity were also prominent in these debates. The plains, most said, were hot, dirty and dusty, where 'even a glass of water can make you sick'. In contrast, peace, silence, fresh air and fresh water marked the hills. One village man summed up a widely expressed sentiment: 'We people who live here are one hundred times better off than in the people in the plains. We have rights that they don't—fresh water and air, and natural resources. There is peace here.' This physical description of the hill region took on more significance when it was allied to a cosmological reading of the hill landscape. The Uttaranchal region is known as *Dev Bhoomi*, the Land of the Gods, and is considered one of the holiest parts of India, attracting tens of thousands of pilgrims a year. The landscape is heavily sacralized through its association with great historical and mythological events described in various religious texts and poems (see Haberman 1994; Nelson 1998). A 'naturalized' link was constructed between these readings of the landscape with the supposedly high moral character of hill people and society. Because the hills were so pure, it was argued, so too were its sons and daughters. Uttaranchalis, it was repeatedly claimed (in conversations, letters, articles, speeches and so on) were of 'good' character—honest, straightforward, peaceful, patriotic and loyal. This is why, many people said, Garhwali and Kumaoni servants are so popular in the plains: everyone knows they can be trusted.

But there is something of a paradox in both of these physical/environmental and cosmological interpretations of landscape and society. In the first place, hill society is strongly influenced by the so-called 'Little Tradition', especially in rural areas (Nand and Kumar 1989). Some beliefs and practices edge towards those more commonly defined as tribal, and hill people are widely perceived as being culturally 'backward' rather than 'high' Hindus. Similarly, although the mountain air, water and forests were celebrated in one context (their purity compared to those of the plains), on the subject of development it was the ecological degradation of the hills that was stressed. However, these alternative interpretations were played down as protestors sought to harness Brahminical or 'mainstream' Hindu notions of the 'Holy Himalaya' to the cause of a separate hill state, as well as (depending on the circumstances) allied discourses of environmental purity.[12]

DIFFERENCE FROM THE PLAINS OF UTTAR PRADESH

Acting as a foil to these constructions of hill identity were the representations of plains people and society. The plains were generally seen as an area of disorientation and danger. Some people said that it was dangerous even to walk in the plains because of the volume of traffic there. The following sorts of comments were common: 'People don't know about Lucknow. Whenever they go there they are cheated'; 'In newspapers we read so many times what is happening in the plains, but we are in peace here. We don't know about plains people, how they work, their customs and ways of living'; and 'In the plains there are different kinds of people who deceive each other, and life is greatly disturbed.'

The relationship between the hills and the plains of UP was often represented through colonial metaphors of exploitation and brutality. Many hill people claimed that the UP government had forfeited its moral right to govern the region because of its economic exploitation of, and colonial attitudes towards, the hills. Particular events were also set within the colonial discourse, notably the Muzaffarnagar affair. In this, at least 10 people were killed and 17 women were raped and molested by the security forces when their convoy of buses was stopped on its way to a rally in Delhi. This was widely likened to the infamous Jallianwala Bagh massacre in 1919, with Mulayam Singh Yadav being called another General Dyer. Attention was drawn to the fact that the policemen found no weapons on the buses they stopped, and accusations were made that Mulayam Singh ruled only by force of arms. Some Garhwalis likened the SP-BSP regime to *their* pre-Independence experience, which, if not as bad as British imperialism, was by 1948 a much disliked autocratic princely regime.

In November 1994, a mass demonstration was taken out in Dehra Dun 'to protect women's honour and to protest *against the state government's failure to do so*'. The implication was that the 'political settlement' between a state and its citizens was not being honoured—what right did the SP-BSP have to rule when it could not protect its own people, or even initiated unsanctioned violence against them? Such arguments about the unfitness of the SP-BSP to rule helped justify many of the unilateral actions that were taken in 1994–5, such as the (failed) attempts to set up parallel governments in the hills, the economic blockade in the region, and the sending back of college and job candidates to the plains (*Himachal Times* 27 August 1994: 'Anti-reservationists send interviewees from plains back').

In an ironic continuity of imperial discourses on degeneracy in the tropics, from which the cool hills were a refuge (Kenny 1995), a number of hill people suggested that rising crime and alcoholism amongst them was the result of the growing influence of dissolute plains culture and people. 'Luxury' tourism, for example, was condemned in a number of articles, pamphlets and speeches for its association with wasteful luxury, unregulated hotel building and black money (amongst other things). One long-time opponent of 'five star tourism' in the hills is Sunderlal Bahuguna, and others who were keen to talk about the need to preserve the 'cultural heritage' of the hills now joined him. Nevertheless, despite the rhetoric, it would seem likely that envy (of outsiders' control of profitable tourist industries) was also a factor in generating the discontent (Rangan 1996).

Another cultural image that the mainstream sought to harness to the movement was the condescending stereotype of hill people as gullible and stupid, and the anger and humiliation that this provoked. The derogatory term 'Pahadi' (a mispronunciation of 'Pahari') has similar connotations to the more familiar insult, '*jungli*', often used for tribal peoples. The following comments, made by two village women in Tehri Garhwal, echo many similar ones that were heard at this time: 'Hill people are very simple in their living and their clothes. They like to live in peace. That is why outsiders say we are nothing and have contempt for us'; and 'Uttaranchalis are being called backward people. It is being said that we are traitorous. That's why plains people are being narrow-minded about us. We are being called "Pahadis" and "backward" and this upsets us.'

Leaders tried to turn this around by instilling pride in the Pahari identity with slogans like, 'We are Uttaranchali; we are Pahari'.[13] These strategies helped mobilize, channel and maintain anger and discontent, stimulating many into support and/or action. However, a number of people were concerned by the antipathy growing, and being encouraged to grow, between Uttaranchal and the rest of the state. On occasions, leaders such as Kashi Singh Airi tried to argue that their quarrel was with the UP government and not its people.

UNITY WITH INDIA

The third 'theme' was the attempt to win sympathy and support from the central government and the rest of the population of India. A vital part of this was the portrayal of the movement as 'non-threatening', as the following slogan highlights: '*Bharat desh rahe akhand, lekin rahenge Uttaranchal*' (India should not disintegrate, but we want Uttaranchal). On every banner the '*Jai Uttaranchal*' written in one corner was matched by '*Jai Bharat*' in another. This reflected the anxieties as much as the ambitions of the hill people that the movement should be recognized as constructive and not subversive. Various arguments were used to demonstrate that the creation of Uttaranchal would benefit the region *and* the nation. For example, in one interview Kashi Singh Airi stated:

The borders of Uttaranchal are international with Nepal and Tibet. We have the responsibility of safe-guarding the environment for the people of Uttar Pradesh and whole sub-continent of India. . . . If the forests and environment of the Himalaya are damaged, it will result in disaster for the whole of India. . . . If the people of the Uttaranchal are rich they will be strong and they will be able to face the Chinese or other enemies. (*Amar Ujala* 18 September 1994: 'Interview with Kashi Singh Airi')

The spirituality of the hills was also used to emphasize the historical and mythological unity of Uttaranchal with the rest of India. As noted above, the hill region is one of the holiest places in the geo-cosmography of Hinduism, and forms one of the cardinal points of the body of *Bharat Mata*. This unity with Hindu India was repeatedly stressed. To take just one example, Chandi Prasad Bhatt, of Chipko fame, argued that: 'The Uttaranchal region of the Central Himalaya which is the source of the Ganga and Yamuna along with dozens of other perennial North Indian rivers, is also the fountainhead of Indian culture and spirituality in which crores of Indian citizens have reposed their faith' (*Himachal Times* 8 December 1994: 'Appeal for support to Uttaranchal issue').

One image and argument that was constantly raised and promoted was that of the hill people's loyalty to the Indian nation state, especially in terms of their military record. Uttaranchali soldiers, it was widely claimed, were the first into Kashmir during the upheavals of Partition and Independence. Were it not for them, it was said, India would have lost this state to Pakistan—a nice play on their commitment to India's unity as loyal citizens given their regional demands. Others pointed out that two hill regiments were the first to fight the Chinese in 1962, and that the then Chief of Staff was an Uttaranchali. Although it is unlikely that the Uttaranchal would have ever witnessed serious armed insurrection (as in north-east India, for example), it is significant that this was very rarely even held out as a threat. One intellectual and author associated with the movement explained that: 'Once people talked about us in a different way—comparing us to the terrorists of Punjab. But we have been successful in peacefully conveying our message to the people and to the Government of India. We have never given any cause for the accusation to arise that we were treasonable.' (Interview 23 September 1994). This claim became more significant after rumours circulated that the movement has been infiltrated by various national and international terrorist organizations, including Naxalites and the Pakistan secret service (*Indian Express* 18 October 1994: 'Uttaranchalis' no to armed struggle').

One symbolic strategy was the use of particular places and dates that were imbued with regional, and sometimes national, meanings. For example, in November 1994 a number of intellectuals, NGO and *sarvodaya* workers, and other leaders of the movement came together in the Anashakti Ashram in Kausani, Kumaon, to discuss the progress of the agitation and to some extent to try and redirect/coalesce the movement. They suggested a list of dates on which the Uttaranchal movement ought to organize particular demonstrations. The specifically regional and national resonances of these events and figures could be clearly read to refer to aspects of the contemporary struggle. Amongst these were:

- 24 December: The birthday of Chandra Singh Garhwali, a great hero of the region. He was an NCO in a colonial hill regiment who, in 1930, refused to fire on a group of unarmed Pathans taking part in a freedom protest in Peshawar.
- 11 January: The date[14] in 1948 on which two activists were killed in Kirtinagar in the course of the popular *Praja Mandal* struggle in Tehri Garhwal.
- 13 January: Marking the success of coolie-begar movement in 1921.
- 2 February: The inception of the 1984 anti-liquor campaign.
- 24 April: The date of a famous Chipko incident at Mandal, Chamoli in 1973.
- 2nd of each month: The killings of protestors at Mussoorie and Muzaffarnagar occurred on 2 September 1994 and 2 October 1994 respectively.

The 'utilization' of these dates and their associated events and characters emphasized the continuity of the regional struggle with past social movements that were 'virtuous' and/or sanctioned by the state or the pre-Independence nationalist movement. The celebration of the actions of Chandra Singh Garhwali, for example, acted as a reminder that the hill people were committed to Indian freedom and unity.

However, by late 1994 or early 1995, anger with the Centre was starting to mount as it continued to take no action on the Uttaranchal issue. The dualistic imagery of 'difference from the plains/unity with India' was not dropped, but other more oppositional discourses concerning the central government also started to make their way into the movement. The procession of effigies being burnt gave a clue to the growing disenchantment with the Centre—at first they were usually of Mulayam Singh Yadav and Mayawati (the leaders of the SP and BSP respectively),[15] but by December 1994 they included the Prime Minister, P.V. Narasimha Rao. After the immense disappointment and anger that followed the BJP's decision not to support Backward Area status for the hills in 1996, effigies of Kalyan Singh, the former BJP Chief Minister, were also burnt all over the hills. When the BJP's then national President, Atal Behari Vajpayee, came to Dehra Dun he was bombarded with fruit—apparently the first time this had happened to him in a political career of over forty years. It was also demonstrated in the changing slogans being shouted: *'Asli hatyara kaun hai jo Dilli me maun hai. Kendra prant hatyara hai—ye Uttaranchal ka nara hai'* (The real killers are the ones who are silent in Delhi. The central government is the murderer—this is the slogan of Uttaranchal).

At the most extreme were the occasional allusions to secession, which could provide a 'lever' in the struggle, if a controversial and potentially dangerous one. Indramani Badoni, a major figure in the UKD, was quoted as saying that unless the Centre took a decision soon, India would end up disintegrating like the Soviet Union (*Himachal Times* 7 August 1994: 'UKD agitation till demands not [*sic*] met'). The growing tensions between the region and the Centre were also demonstrated in the run-up to the 1996 general elections. Some agitators felt that no one in the region should vote, and politicians should not be allowed to file nominations. One slogan ran, 'No separate state—no elections'. But many more felt that this was sending out the wrong message as their quarrel was with the state government and not the Centre, and they should not be trying to antagonize or divorce themselves from politics at the Centre.

DIFFERENCES AND DIVISIONS

Many of these images and identities could have been 'played out' in a number of other ways—there was nothing inevitable about the ways in which they were constructed and presented. But although they were clearly flexible and contingent, there was a strong sense of internal coherence. As noted before, given the lack of central direction in the movement and the obstacles to transport and communication in the mountains, the convergence on many issues was quite remarkable. The degree to which disparate groups and areas came together on particular subjects indicated not just a commonality of experience, but also a shared appraisal of the political opportunity structure within which their demands were being articulated. But although there was much genuine unity in the hills, these arguments did underplay important differences and divisions, as recent events have shown in the quarrels, tensions and political negotiations that have accompanied the delimitation and establishment of the new state. There is not the space to analyse this in any detail, and the following section touches very briefly on three examples: caste, community and sub-region in the period 1994–6.

CASTE

Some Dalits, especially younger urban-based men and women, supported the regional movement. They argued that the whole region would develop faster and better under a separate state, and that all sections of society would benefit from this, albeit probably unevenly. This was very much the argument from intellectuals and many ordinary people in the movement. But despite claims to the contrary, caste violence is not unknown in the hills, and casteism was not absent from the regional movement. Bharat Dogra, for example, chronicled the following events:

In Narendranagar, an official of the home guards named Harilal was insulted after being dubbed 'reservation-wala'. His face was blackened and he was taken around the town in this condition. In Vikas Nagar a settlement of Harijans was attacked. Shops of cobblers were burnt down in Uttarkashi and in Pauri. In Dehra Dun the office of the Bahujan Samaj Party was burnt. The Harijans of Simkhet village, near Pauri, were threatened and asked to leave their village. In Uttarkashi District a Harijan named Gabru was forced to have his hair cut and worse after the insult, he was forced to join the protest in which he had no interest. Later several Harijans protested against this to the DM [District Magistrate] but no effective action has been taken to the time of writing. (Dogra 1994: 3130)

An opinion column written by a retired Army Colonel in Dehra Dun included this extraordinary statement:

Since intelligence is a basic human attribute, is partly heritable and also varies with ethnic groups, a couple of generations down the road the Indian nation shall thus become intellectually bankrupt, all the more so since the least intelligent and economically backwards have a habit of attaining high reproductive capability. . . . Do we want our coming generations to inherit 'Genetic Bad Luck' through rule of reservations and minority status? (*Himachal Times* 20 November 1994: 'Politics of reservations')

Perhaps not surprisingly, many Dalits interviewed expressed indifference or opposition to the regional movement, with the following comments being typical of many responses to our questions:

We don't have anything to do with it. It doesn't matter to us who is ruling or not . . . it makes no difference to us. People are becoming crazy demanding a hill state. What will they do with Uttaranchal? There is nothing here, everything is imported from outside. Only the water is running here, but we are getting everything else from the plains. We hear all this noise—everyone is shouting 'Give this, give that, come here, go there', but I don't know anything about all of this. . . . We just buy grains to eat. I only hear '*Zindabad, Zindabad*'. We watch them raising slogans and dancing on the buses—that's all I know. (Interview 18 November 1994)

Some of this opposition was due to the fact that the Dalits were generally amongst the worst hit by the agitation as their income sources gradually dried up. There was less private labouring work available, government employment schemes and construction activities were severely curtailed, and the poorer members of the community suffered especially from the rising prices that accompanied the agitation.

The issue of caste antagonism in the hills was not confined to that between upper and lower castes. Historic and more recent rivalries and alliances within and between Brahmin and Rajput caste groups also affected the configuration of the movement, especially in Kumaon.[16] Here Brahmins are divided into 'higher' and 'lower' Brahmins, humorously known as *bari dhotis* and *chhoti dhotis*. Traditionally the *chhoti dhotis* have formed a strong and exclusive caste group, antagonistic to the Thakurs (Rajputs) and the *bari dhotis*, while the Thakurs and *bari dhotis* have tended to be allies. *Chhoti dhotis* are widely stereotyped as narrow, casteist and parochial in their outlook, and it is popularly held that for this community, caste overrides all other political affiliations. One academic commentator suggested that the agitation in Kumaon was strongly influenced by these affiliations and antagonisms in terms of the patterns of protest and support for different leaders and factions. Thus for example, N.D. Tiwari, the former Congress Chief Minister of UP and a *chhoti dhoti*, received strong support from others within his group and from his area, but much less from elsewhere in Kumaon or Garhwal or from amongst other traditional group rivals (N.D. Dhoundiyal 1994, pers. comm.).

COMMUNITY

As we have seen, many in the movement were especially concerned to argue that all communities were equal and that the movement was in no way inimical to minorities in the hills. But the few 'militants' were vociferous in their protests. First and second generation immigrants from the plains (principally Punjabis) now dominate business in many towns, leading some to talk about 'banning usurpers', or stopping the sale of land in the hills to those who do not belong there. As the lines of the agitation deepened and the issues became more intractable, these aggressive assertions seemed to be on the increase. Of the Muslims I was able to speak to, a number felt that they already suffered discrimination in the Uttaranchal, and that this would worsen if a separate state was created with its massive upper-caste Hindu, and largely BJP-sympathetic, majority. A Muslim woman told me, 'This is just like the Freedom Struggle. When India was under the British, all Indians came together to fight for a free India, but afterwards everything was different' (Interview 18 December 1994).

Adopting a different strategy to many Muslims, who mostly kept a low profile, a number of Sikh communities organized visible and vocal support for the movement (mentioned earlier). However, the ambiguity of their position was demonstrated in the following statement made by a traders' organization (many of whose members would be Sikhs and Backward Castes) which suggests that all was not as harmonious as the leadership and others sought to portray:[17]

The Doon Udyog Vyapar Mandal has cautioned the citizens of Uttaranchal against the conspiracy of some elements who want to divide people on the basis of their origins. They said that all people in the Uttaranchal were Uttaranchalis. The trading communities of Dehra Doon fully supported the demand for a separate hill state, and would take out a rally to prove it, but said that some vested interests were indulging in mischief to try and weaken the movement. (*Himachal Times* 13 November 1994: 'Traders caution people against mischievous elements')

More recently, the place of Sikhs within the hill state has become a major issue through the question of land ceilings, and the inclusion of the *terai* district of Udham Singh Nagar, which has a high proportion of Sikhs, and whether it should have been included within the new state.

SUB-REGION

Another challenge to the homogeneity of the movement at this time was the matter of regional difference within the Uttaranchal itself, notably in terms of the traditional divide between Kumaon and Garhwal. The transport links between Kumaon and Garhwal are limited, and it is generally harder to travel east-west in the hills than it is to travel north-south. Administrative arrangements reflect this, and the two areas have separate Commissionaries. Historically, the two regions were often at loggerheads, and even today marriages between Kumaonis and Garhwalis are rare (A.J. Rawat 1993, pers. comm.). The effects of their separate medieval and pre-Independent histories continue to be felt in the rivalry between the two areas. Particularly important are the differences arising from Kumaon's longer relationship with the administrative and professional élite in the plains because of its colonial history, and the impact this has had on patterns of caste consolidation and affiliations in the area.

The stereotypes each hold about the other were indicative of tension. A typical Kumaoni description of a Garhwali is of a quarrelsome and less civilized hot-head. Garhwalis on the other hand frequently describe Kumaonis as smooth and untrustworthy. These differences were evident in the regional movement in a number of ways and at a variety of levels, including the length and type of agitation, the primary focus of the demands, and the competition over where the capital of the new state should be.

There was also considerable tension between the richer *terai* area and the mountains proper. In a meeting organized by the UP Government Kaushik Committee in Kashipur in early 1994, for instance, some participants asserted that if the capital was to be Kashipur or Ramnagar (also in the *terai*), then *and only then* should the *terai* area be included within the Uttaranchal state. If it was to be Garsain, or any other hill location, then Kashipur should remain with the rest of the Uttar Pradesh (Government of Uttar Pradesh 1994). Without the advantage of the capital, in other words, many inhabitants of the *terai* were unhappy at the prospect of becoming a part of a potentially poor and/or 'hill-focused' state. More recently (after the period with which this paper is concerned), the debate over the inclusion of the new *terai* district of Udham Singh Nagar, with its substantial Sikh population, became headline news. It threatened to halt all proceedings on the separate state (*Frontline* 18 July 1998: 'A confrontation in the Terai'; *Frontline* 1 August 1998: 'A climbdown'; *Deccan Herald* 20 September 1998: 'Hardwar remains in UP, Udham Singh Nagar goes to Uttaranchal').[18]

Although the Garhwal/Kumaon and the *terai*/hills distinctions form the main regional splits in the Uttaranchal, these are by no means the only geographical divides. Old rivalries and distinctions continue at a variety of scales, between 'British Garhwal' and Tehri Garhwal, between the different districts, and even beyond that. Thus, a name that people from Tehri have for those from the 'interior' (Chamoli, Uttarkashi and high Tehri) is *budera*, meaning uneducated and uncivilized. Songs I heard in the high valley above Chamiyala denigrated the Jaunsar region, and it seemed that every place I visited had its own demonology of places.[19]

CONCLUSION

Social movement theorists have long recognized the flexibility and 'situatedness' of identity construction in relation to physical, rhetorical and symbolic forms of protest. In the case of the Uttaranchal regional movement, we have seen how certain readings of the cultural, geographical and historical 'resources' upon which the hill people could draw, were emphasized, while other possible readings were downplayed. Thus the long martial tradition in the hills was rarely invoked as a threat (through the possibility of the Uttaranchalis taking to armed insurgency), but the history of service within the Indian Army was repeatedly stressed. The environmental and development benefits that might accrue to the region and the nation were played up, while the cultural and even linguistic differences tended not to be highlighted. While the Pahari/non-Pahari split between the hills and the plains of UP was raised in many contexts, religious, ethnic and citizenship ties with the rest of India were emphasized. Thus, very few in the region argued for an approach to the Centre based on their right to a cultural-linguistic state, but drew instead upon ideas of an improved democratic structure and faster and more appropriate development. This would, they claimed, strengthen both the region *and* the nation environmentally, financially and strategically (Mawdsley 1999). This talk of 'construction' is not to imply that these arguments are artificial in any way, but to recognize that they are the outcome of both deliberate and tacit decision-making and must be situated in specific contexts. As contexts change, so to do the grammars and strategies of resistance. Thus, since the creation of Uttaranchal, and the growing tensions that have emerged between the hills and the *terai* areas, there is an indication that more is being made of social, cultural and linguistic differences between the mountains and the lowlands.[20]

In terms of the political environment, it is clear that the success of the Uttaranchal movement was not the result only of the persuasiveness of the arguments, images and discourses deployed. The major political parties are now willing to consider such territorial changes as a possible option—even when they are in government. The reasons for this apparent responsiveness to territorial change, which marks quite a shift from the attitude taken over much of the last fifty years of Independence, include the vast growth in population (the larger states are now more populous than many countries), and the concomitantly increasing difficulties of administering such unwieldy territories. While this may be seen as a constructive context in which to discuss state formation (see Khan 1992), another reason for the shift in attitudes is less positive. This is the recent growth of coalition politics, and the encouragement this has given to the short-term political expediency that appears to be driving the position of many parties on this and other issues (Mawdsley 2002). But whatever the case, regional movements like that which divided UP in August 2000, are obviously reflexively engaged with a changing political opportunity structure in India, in which the formation of new states has entered the arena of *realpolitik* as never before, reflecting significant changes in political attitudes to territory, autonomy, development and democracy in India today.

NOTES

1. I would like to thank Staffan Lindberg for his comments on the paper originally presented at the 15th European Modern South Asian Studies Conference in 1998, and Roger Jeffery for his help in formulating this paper. The research was funded by the Economic and Social Research Council and Cambridge University, for which I am very grateful. The British Academy kindly contributed to my travel costs to the conference.
2. See Lerche and Jeffery (this volume) on other aspects of hill exceptionalism.
3. The paper is based primarily on fifteen months' field work in the UP hills between 1994 and 1996. I lived in one village for about five months, carrying out detailed questionnaires, rapid rural appraisal and participant observation. Much of the rest of the time was spent travelling around Kumaon and Garhwal, interviewing and talking to a wide range and number of people, as well as observing and participating in events in different parts of the then UP hills. My sincere thanks to the many people who talked to me, helped me and allowed me to stay with them. I met with enormous hospitality and generosity throughout my stay in India, as I have on all subsequent visits.
4. Since then it has never won more than two seats in the hill region (out of 19 during the 1990s, although the number of MLA seats is now 70 for the new state Assembly).

5. 'Uttaranchal' is the name that the BJP gave to the region, although many activists wanted the name 'Uttarakhand'. There are semantic differences between the two, but the re-naming is more of a political exercise through which the BJP has sought to assert a special relationship with the regional demand.

5. See Lerche (this volume) for more on the Bahujan Samaj Party.

7. See Table 1.6 in the first chapter of this volume for more details.

8. These ideas are examined in more detail in Mawdsley (1999: 197).

9. Any search of the newspaper archives over this period will reveal this, especially the *Amar Ujala* and *Dainik Jagran*, as well as all the major English-language newspapers. See also *Economic and Political Weekly*, *Frontline*, *India Today* and *Sunday*. An Uttaranchal web site (run from Canada) has extensive archives and information, including on events since the creation of the new state of Uttaranchal: http://www.geocities.com/RainForest/Vines/7039/index.html.

10. See Moller (this volume) for further discussion of how hill people distinguish hill women from plains women.

11. Compare Amin (1995) on the events in Chauri Chaura in 1922, and the discourse and historicizing of violence and non-violence during the freedom struggle.

12. The links (or lack of them) between conceptions of ritual and 'actual' purity and pollution are extremely complex. For an excellent discussion, see Nelson (1998).

13. There is, in fact, some ambiguity in the term 'Pahari' as it can denote quality, such as Pahari ghee and Pahari wool.

14. There is some disagreement over the exact date. Guha (1989) puts it at 9 January 1948.

15. See Ståhlberg (2002a) for more on Mayawati.

16. In Garhwal too, there is a hierarchy of Brahmin castes, dependent upon names, myths of origin, claims to previous status under the Rajas, who was explaining the system and so on. However, these distinctions had not taken on as much political importance that they had in Kumaon, probably because of the influence of the British in the latter area.

17. The statement also clearly shows up the symbolic and performative dimensions of the protest marches.

18. In fact, both districts are currently part of Uttaranchal, despite opposition from political groups in Haridwar.

19. See Moller (this volume) for more on insiders/outsiders.

20. As yet, there has been little academic analysis of these issues. The most accessible English-language material (descriptions and commentaries) can be found in the archives of magazines like *Frontline*, *Sunday* and *India Today*.

6

The BJP and the Rise of Dalits in Uttar Pradesh

*Christophe Jaffrelot, Jasmine Zerinini-Brotel
and Jayati Chaturvedi*

Given the number of seats it had won in UP during three of the four
Lok Sabha elections in the 1990s—51 in 1991, 53 in 1996 and 56 in
1998, though only 29 in 1999, Uttar Pradesh remains at the core of
the BJP's strategy. The BJP came to power in the state for the first time
in 1991, riding the Rama wave. Only two years later, it proved unable
to recapture power and was swept aside by a coalition of the Samajwadi
Party and the Bahujan Samaj Party, two parties rooted respectively
in what came to be known as the OBC and 'Dalit' vote banks. This
setback and then the incapacity of the BJP to win a majority in the
1996 assembly elections have pushed it to reconsider its position to-
wards·these sections of society. Its direct bids at building an alliance
with the BSP in 1997 were part of this attempt to project a new face,
like its efforts to give a greater representation to Dalits, whether in the
party's organization or through the allotment of tickets at the time of
elections.

However, such changes—still discrete—have been at the root of
tensions in the BJP's state unit. Prior to the emergence of the Scheduled Castes, the OBCs had been striving to strengthen their position
inside the upper-caste-dominated BJP in UP. Under the banner of Kalyan
Singh, the party's first Chief Minister in 1991–3, and again 1997–
2000, a strong OBC lobby had indeed started to emerge since the
1980s. Kalyan Singh took over from a Brahmin as president of the
UP unit of the BJP in 1984, and other OBCs contested positions of
power traditionally ascribed to the upper castes. The path trodden by
the party's upper echelons was somewhat reminiscent of the strategy
of support pieced together by the Congress party in the 1970s and

1980s. It consisted in forging an alliance of upper-castes and Scheduled Castes—an 'alliance of extremes' as Paul Brass calls it[1]—to keep the OBCs at bay. This strategy was strongly resented by Kalyan Singh who accepted the agreement with the BSP only reluctantly.

For other reasons, the RSS also disapproved of this tactic. It has always been adverse to any 'casteist' politics, and it remains imbued with an organicist, Brahminical world view in which Sanskritization is seen as the main avenue for social mobility.[2] In UP, this line of reasoning is well illustrated by the activities of one of the most recent RSS creations, Sewa Bharti. Essentially paternalist and negative of the Dalits' new-found ways of expressing their difference, Sewa Bharti is certainly more acceptable to many in the BJP than the alternative strategy that relies on making alliances with the BSP.

THE BJP IN UTTAR PRADESH: AN UPPER-CASTE AND OBC LEADERSHIP?

Bruce Graham has underlined the support drawn by the predecessor of the BJP, the Jana Sangh, from the urban upper-caste middle-class electorate (Graham 1990). In its first years, the BJP quite thoroughly relied on this combine of Brahmins and Banias (Zérinini-Brotel 1998: 72–100). The need to expand the support base was recognized by the Hindu nationalists as early as in the 1960s but was then unsuccessful because of the creation by Charan Singh of his own party, which attracted Jats and many OBC castes. In 1967, the Jana Sangh won 99 seats. Then its MLAs included 19 OBCs, 23 Scheduled Castes, 19 Brahmins, 21 Rajputs and 9 Banias. In 1962, by contrast, out of its 49 MLAs, 28 belonged to the upper-castes and only 7 came from the OBCs and 7 from the Scheduled Castes (Tripathi 1997: 141). But in 1969, the Jana Sangh won only 49 seats, compared to the 98 won by Charan Singh's Bharatiya Kranti Dal, which captured most of the votes of members of the low castes.

The BJP did not try again to attract the latter until after 1990. Even then, it came as a reaction to an external factor: the Janata Dal's policy of reservation for the OBCs. The choice by the V.P. Singh government to dig out and implement the Mandal Commission Report became the main line of political polarization in UP in the early 1990s. The staunch opposition met from the upper-castes can be explained by their sense of vulnerability, driving them to discern in it a direct threat to their economic survival. Intermediate castes that had been excluded by

Mandal, such as the Jats from western UP and the Tyagis from eastern UP,[3] were also agitating strongly against the Janata Dal. For the BJP, the danger was double. On the one hand, it could lose its upper caste support, should it choose to stay aloof from the controversy. On the other, it was also running the risk of alienating the OBCs, accounting for more than 40 per cent of the population and among whom a small fraction had started supporting it, in Oudh in particular. Because of the implementation of the Mandal Report, the BJP came up with a policy of re-unifying the Hindu vote beyond caste barriers by using the Ayodhya issue. The Ramjanmabhoomi movement had been launched by the Vishwa Hindu Parishad in the mid-1980s and had received, at that time, only tepid enthusiasm. It now provided a useful plank for the BJP, which seized it as a convenient political expedient for reunifying the differentiated parts of Hindu society through a common goal and against a common Other, the Muslim. OBCs and Dalits were invited to forget about their sub-identities and to merge themselves in the Hindu *samaj* or nation.

This move followed the ideological tenets of the *Sangh Parivar*. Its conception of society as an organic whole has been put under considerable stress by the assertion of individual identities by the OBCs and the Scheduled Castes. The rejection by these groups of Sanskritization as a valid avenue of social promotion and their proposal of alternative means (reservations and Ambedkarization) was not acceptable to the *Sangh Parivar*, to which this emancipatory attitude was a dangerous fracture in what would otherwise according to the Sangh, be a harmonious whole.

In the general context of OBC assertion in northern India, upper-castes who had been in charge of building the BJP in the state were not ready to give up their dominant position precisely at a time when the party had started gaining ground. Relying on the Ayodhya movement and its religious mobilization, the party did not open up to low-caste people. The profile of MLAs elected on the BJP ticket from 1985 onwards shows that the BJP's social composition did not undergo a real change. In 1989 the number of seats won by the BJP in the Assembly elections went up by four times—though it was still below 60—and the party's representatives still chiefly had an élite background.

In 1985, an overwhelming thirteen of the BJP's 16 MLAs were either landowners or self-employed lawyers or businessmen, who often owned land (see Table 6.1).[4] By 1989, the economic background of the BJP MLAs showed a sharper differentiation. Landowners still accounted

Table 6.1: *Economic Background of BJP MLAs in 1985, 1989 and 1991 Vidhan Sabhas*

Occupation	1985	1989	1991
Agriculture	37.50	26.86	26.78
Lawyer	12.50	20.69	14.73
Doctor	0	3.45	1.34
Business	31.25	26.86	22.32
Teacher	12.50	8.62	12.50
Social worker	0	3.45	0.89
Other	0	0	0.89
Unknown	6.25	12.06	20.53
Total	100	100	100
N	(16)	(58)	(224)

Source: *Uttar Pradesh Vidhan Sabha, sâdasiyon ke jivan-parichay*, 1985, 1989 and 1991.

for the major part (27 per cent) in equal numbers with businessmen (27 per cent), but the proportion of lawyers had increased from 12.5 to nearly 21 per cent. These figures tend to show that the BJP could claim the true inheritance to the Jana Sangh's 'middle world' electorate:[5] when the BJP started gaining ground in UP, it still appeared as representing the landowners, professionals, traders and small industrialists who had supported the Jana Sangh. By 1991, at the core of the Ramjanmabhoomi movement which was supposed to expand the party's base beyond the twice-born, more than half of the party's MLAs were either business-men (22.3 per cent), lawyers (15 per cent), teachers (12.5 per cent) or doctors (1.3 per cent). The share of agriculturists had dropped below 25 per cent. However, nearly all of the BJP's white-collar representa-tives still had a foothold in the countryside. In 1989, 60 per cent of the businessmen of the BJP claimed to own some land, though they rarely tilled it themselves.

The rise in MLAs coming from the 'business' community is a major characteristic of the BJP in UP—and in northern India in general.[6] One can point to the lack of precision of the category subsumed in the word 'businessmen', ranging from *dukandar* (shopkeepers) to in-dustrialists. Admittedly, whether they come from its lower or upper economic ranks will certainly imply different concerns. Yet some iden-tical social values will also be found among them, pointing to a similar culture shaped by the fact of belonging to a business community, struct-ured around 'the principles of corporatism and of family solidarity' (Graham 1990: 159).

Another significant aspect of evolution is the rise in the proportion of MLAs identifiable as educationists. Whereas 2 of them could be found in 1985 and 5 in 1989, by 1991 as many as 28 MLAs from the BJP, nearly 14 per cent, claimed to be teachers or educationists. Obviously the BJP's commitment to evolving a new curriculum reflecting the values of *Hindutva* is exerting some attraction over people involved in teaching. This is in tune with the fact that the *Sangh Parivar* at large is interested in reshaping the mind of India and has taken advantage of the Vajpayee government to penetrate institutions dealing with education and research. Murli Manohar Joshi, the Minister for Human Resource Development, who happens to be from Allahabad—his constituency in UP—has managed to reorganize the Indian Council of Social Science Research and the Indian Council for Historical Research and place men of his choice in control.

TOWARD A DILUTION OF UPPER-CASTE DOMINANCE?

While the BJP managed to win an ever-larger number of rural seats, one must be careful in concluding on the BJP's ties with the *mofussil*. A confrontation of the economic and the caste background of BJP MLAs suggests that its rural appeal is limited to the upper and middle castes.

As Table 6.2 shows, it was not until 1993 that the percentage of BJP MLAs coming from the upper-castes went down below the 50 per cent mark, but this change was not accompanied by a significant rise in the share of the OBCs: they remained below 20 per cent, ten points less than the percentage of OBCs in the Vidhan Sabha (Table 6.3).

Interestingly enough, though the percentage of Scheduled Castes elected on a BJP ticket dwindled in 1993, the party actually managed to increase slightly its relative share of OBC representatives. The good performances shown by its OBC candidates indicates that a large section of the OBC population was not aligning with the SP-BSP alliance. Kurmis and Lodhis, who accounted for the earliest OBC core support of the BJP in UP, were re-elected in 1993 in numbers very similar to 1991. Most of the Gujjars, Kewats, Sainis and Sainthwars achieved the same, showing a tendency in the party to select those candidates who were on the fringe of the Yadav-dominated OBC movement led by the Samajwadi Party. Though some Yadavs were elected on BJP tickets from 1985 onwards, their number was never very significant compared to their relative strength in society. Projections of the 1931 Census, the last one to incorporate caste, show the proportion of

Table 6.2: Caste Break-up of BJP MLAs in 1985, 1989, 1991, 1993 and 1996 Vidhan Sabhas

	1985	1989	1991	1993	1996
Upper castes	56.25 (9)	56.9 (33)	51.12 (113)	46.6 (83)	50.54 (88)
Brahmin	6.25	20.69	19.91	14.04	16.66
Rajput	18.75	15.52	19.00	19.10	22.41
Bania	12.50	12.07	7.24	8.98	6.89
Kayasth	12.50	5.17	2.26	1.68	1.72
Khattri	—	3.45	1.81	2.24	1.72
Bhumihar	6.25	—	0.45	—	0.57
Tyagi	—	—	0.45	0.56	0.57
Intermediary castes	—	—	3.16 (7)	3.93 (7)	4.59 (8)
Jats			3.16	3.93	4.59
Other Backward Classes	31.25 (5)	18.96 (11)	18.1 (40)	19.06 (34)	21.66 (36)
Yadav	12.50	1.72	2.26	1.12	2.87
Kurmi	—	5.17	5.43	5.61	5.17
Lodhi	12.50	5.17	4.97	5.05	4.59
Gujjar	—	—	0.90	1.68	1.15
Kewat	—	1.72	0.90	0.56	1.15
Mallah	—	—	—	—	—
Kacchi	—	—	—	—	2.29
Saini	—	—	2.26	2.24	—
Sainthwar	—	—	0.90	0.56	0.57
Gadariya	—	—	—	—	0.57
Jaiswala	—	—	—	0.56	—
Rajbhar	—	—	0.45	—	1.15
Other	6.25	5.17	—	1.68	1.15
Scheduled Castes	12.50 (2)	22.41 (13)	25.80 (57)	19.07 (34)	21.82 (38)
Chamar	6.25	5.17	4.52	5.05	4.02
Valmiki	6.25	—	0.45	0.56	—
Dhobi	—	3.45	4.07	0.56	2.87
Kori/Koli	—	6.89	3.16	3.37	3.45
Pasi	—	—	2.71	1.68	1.15
Khatik	—	—	1.35	1.12	1.72
Baiswar	—	1.72	0.45	0.56	—
Bahelia	—	—	0.45	0.56	—
Dharkar	—	—	0.45	—	—
Shilpkar	—	—	1.35	—	1.72
Gond	—	—	0.90	1.12	1.15
Dohare	—	—	0.45	0.56	0.57
Kureel	—	—	0.45	0.56	—
Other	—	5.17	4.97	3.37	5.17
Sikh	—	1.72	0.45	0.56	1.15
Unknown	—	—	1.35	10.67	1.15
Total	100 (16)	100 (58)	100 (221)	100 (178)	100 (174)

Source: J. Zerinini-Brotel's fieldwork. Numbers figure within brackets.

Table 6.3: *Percentage of OBC MLAs in the UP Vidhan Sabha, All Parties*

Castes and communities	1985	1989	1991	1993	1996
OBC	19.20	22.80	25.20	29.90	24.00
All others	80.80	77.20	74.80	70.10	76.00

Source: As for Table 6.2.

Yadavs in the state's Hindu society at over 10 per cent, while Kurmis stood at 4 per cent and Lodhis at about 2.5 per cent. Therefore Lodhis and Kurmis are benefiting from an actual over-representation in the BJP's ranks while Yadavs are under-represented. Smaller Backward Castes are also over-represented with relation to their proportion in UP society.[7]

The modus operandi of the BJP is more or less the same in the case of the OBCs and the Scheduled Castes. The party tends to select candidates from the lower OBCs and the non-Chamar Scheduled Castes, small castes, not so politically aware or economically affluent. Since the 1960s castes such as Yadavs, Kurmis and Lodhis in the OBC category have benefited from economic development and increasing political representation and power. Among the Scheduled Castes, Chamars and their western UP counterparts, Jatavs, have benefited the most from policies of reservation in the administration. The economic status of Chamars has risen steadily over the last 30 years. With development has come political awareness and these castes have played a strong part in political movements and parties. The support of the three main OBC castes used to go to the peasant parties, whether Bharatiya Kranti Dal, Lok Dal or Janata Dal, while Chamars used to stand with the Congress.[8] The split in the Janata Dal in the late 1980s and the emergence of the Yadav-dominated branch as the major player, gave the BJP a chance to corner Lodhi and Kurmi votes. Its projection of Kalyan Singh, a Lodhi, as the party's main figure in the state con-siderably helped it win their acceptance. In fact, until Kalyan Singh's ascent, only three 'Backwards' had been chief ministers in UP, all for only a short span of time.[9] As far as the Scheduled Castes are concerned, the Chamars (and especially the Jatavs) are quite firmly with the BSP (Mayawati herself is one of them). The *Sangh Parivar* therefore has evolved a strategy of focusing on the small castes of Untouchables such as the Bhangis (sweepers) and the Mangs (basket weavers). These groups are more responsive to BJP overtures as they resent the Jatavs cornering the major benefits flowing out of the policy of reservations.

For the BJP, the constitution of a solid base of support around Kurmis and Lodhis was nevertheless not sufficient and the same dilemma applies with regard to the Scheduled Castes. With the bulk of the Chamar vote going to the BSP, the BJP could only hope to win over the less influential castes among the Scheduled Castes. The social work undertaken among the Most Backward Classes such as the Mallahs, Gadariyas, Gosains, which the BSP had left on the edge of the movement, and the BJP's targeting of those Scheduled Castes which used to oppose the Congress in the 1980s—such as the Khatiks, the Bhangis and the Pasis—have borne some fruit (see, for instance, Brass 1997; Pai and Singh 1997). But surveys made during the 1996 elections tended to show that the proportion of Scheduled Castes supporting the BJP was very marginal—below 9 per cent, with the core support for the party still coming from the upper castes and, significantly, from non-Yadav OBCs.[10] These figures discredit the BJP's proclaimed success at 'social engineering', all the more so when compared to the Congress party's 21 per cent of SC vote or the United Front's 12 per cent. By contrast, 67 per cent of the upper castes of UP voted for the BJP in the 1996 Lok Sabha elections (CSDS opinion poll, as reported in *India Today* 31 May 1996).

While the OBCs have not made significant inroads among the BJP MLAs and in the party apparatus, Kalyan Singh has been able to promote them within his government. There is a striking difference in the composition of the first two BJP cabinets he headed in 1991 and the one formed in October 1997, again headed by him. As Table 6.4 shows,

Table 6.4: Representation of Castes and Communities in BJP Governments in UP

(*in %*)

Castes and communities	June 1991	July 1991	October 1997	February 1999
Forward castes	49.90	57.45	48.40	49.21
Intermediary castes	5.55	4.25	3.22	4.76
Other Backward Classes	22.22	21.28	29.05	31.76
Scheduled Castes	16.67	8.51	16.12	7.94
Muslims	5.55	2.13	—	3.17
Sikhs	—	2.13	—	—
Unknown	—	4.25	3.22	3.17
Total	100	100	100	100
	N = 18	N = 47	N = 31*	N = 63

Source : As for Tables 6.2 and 6.3.

Note: *The allies induced in the government in October 1997 have been excluded from this list, counting only BJP ministers.

the number of OBCs had risen in the 1990s and they had then cornered some real influence in UP, whereas their allotment of power in 1991 was token.

In terms of the portfolios secured in Kalyan Singh's first government, while 89 per cent of upper-castes were awarded cabinet or ministerial postings with independent charge, half of the OBCs had positions of the same rank. In his second government, expanded only a month later, 67 per cent of the members from the OBC were at least of ministerial rank without independent charge, against 41 per cent of upper-caste ministers. The less prestigious positions were granted to two Scheduled Castes and one Kurmi. Contrasting with this, in the 1997 BJP government 55.5 per cent of the OBCs were of state cabinet rank. The figures seem to show that Kalyan Singh had promoted the formation of a lobby centred on his own power. This lobby tried to prevent the upper caste command from taking positions detrimental to them, a situation that created a rift on many crucial issues.

While the upper-caste leadership of the BJP was favourably inclined towards the institution of quotas for women in elective bodies, the OBCs of the party implicitly joined hands with those of other parties, who feared that such a move would reduce the share of the Backward Castes. They asked for a quota for OBC women. The tensions raised by the tentative implementation of 33 per cent reservations for women in the central and legislative assemblies are reflections of the rise of OBCs inside the BJP in UP and to their conflict with the upper-caste leadership. To show his refusal of the Bill in its current form and seek the introduction of a separate quota for OBC women, Kalyan Singh is said to have strongly backed the attempts of a BJP MLA to organize members of the backward classes across party lines (*The Pioneer* 21 November 1996).

The tension had already become obvious during the campaign for the Assembly elections of September 1996, when Kalyan Singh wanted to give tickets to many more OBCs. The upper-caste lobby and the RSS, however, resisted his move. When the results of the elections fell well below the BJP's expectations, he blamed the RSS, and argued that the four organizing secretaries of the party—key figures with an RSS background who were all Brahmins, coincidentally—had paid more attention to upper-caste candidates during the election campaign. Soon after, Govindacharya, one of the party general secretaries, was appointed convenor of a committee which was in charge of examining the reasons for the party's setback. He concluded that 'BJP's penetration in the society is still incomplete' and argued for a strategy of 'social engineering', that is, the promotion of non-élite groups within the party apparatus and the nomination of more OBC candidates at the time of election.[11] This suggestion was immediately criticized by Bhanu Pratap Shukla, the editor of *Panchajanya*—the Hindi mouthpiece of the RSS based in UP—who advocated the relevance of D. Upadhyay's old theory of 'society as an organic entity' (cited in Tripathi 1997). Murli Manohar Joshi also reacted strongly on behalf of the Brahmin lobby of the UP BJP. This lobby, comprising Brahma Dutt Dwivedi and Kalraj Mishra, was favourably inclined towards making a deal with the BSP. Starting in late 1996, all-India leaders—including Suraj Bhan, the Deputy Speaker of the Lok Sabha who headed the Scheduled Caste front of the BJP for a long time—conducted negotiations in Delhi (Tripathi 1997). Mishra was kept informed, but not Kalyan Singh. Instead, the latter's supporters campaigned against such an alliance. Ganga Charan Rajput, a Lodhi like Kalyan Singh and close to him, was especially vocal.

The rift between Kalyan Singh and the upper-caste lobby led by Kalraj Mishra and Lalji Tandon was further accentuated by the former's 'coup' against the Mayawati government in October 1997, which resulted in breaking an alliance carefully woven by the upper-caste lobby.[12] As Chief Minister, Kalyan Singh further alienated his upper-caste colleagues by promoting the Lodhis in the state apparatus and projecting himself as a backward class leader. On 25 April 1999, he addressed a 'backward rally' where 'he urged the OBCs to ensure the election of backwards, no matter which party ticket they stood on' (Gupta 1999). A few days later, 33 dissident MLAs sent their resignation to the BJP President, Kushabhau Thakre, to protest against the continuance of Kalyan Singh as Chief Minister. Interestingly, they were all from the upper castes, except one Yadav and one Scheduled Castes member.

Kalyan Singh may try to project himself as an OBC leader merely for electoral reasons, without adhering to any ideology of empowerment and social transformation. A teacher by training, he followed the path of Sanskritization by learning Sanskrit and graduating in literature. His biographer emphasizes the fact that 'he uses so many literary words that it seems that he is delivering a speech even in informal talks' (Tripathi 1997). Beyond this Sanskritized ethos, so different from the behaviour of other OBC leaders such as Mulayam Singh Yadav or Laloo Prasad Yadav, he subscribes to the RSS social views. With great perception his biographer writes:

Kalyan Singh is preaching the pro caste system ideas of Deen Dayal Upadhyaya [the RSS-trained ideologue of the Jana Sangh] at a period which has become a strong harbinger of Ram Manohar Lohia's anti-caste system ideas. . . . The problem of Kalyan Singh is that in spite of being well aware of these ideas of Lohia and agreeing with them from inside, he is unable to express them. Instead he has to adhere to Deen Dayal Upadhyaya's ideas like: 'People make divisions from castes. But caste is a part of our body and the body cannot be divided'. . . . But Kalyan Singh is in favour of enhancing backwards' share in power. He is also a symbol of elevation of castes and Sanskritization by emulation and adoption of high caste attributes. But alongside, his politics also involves keeping close contact with lower castes. (Tripathi 1997)

Kalyan Singh stands mid-way between Sanskritization and social revolt: he aspires to be accepted by the upper castes he is emulating, and at the same time he wants to dislodge them. This ambivalence is a result of the contradictory influences he has undergone since his youth: on the one hand he has been brought up in an Arya Samaji milieu and took part in RSS *shakhas* since childhood. On the other hand, he is a Lodhi and proud of his caste. He took part in the activities of the Lucknow-based Lodhi-Nishad-Bind Unity Front, whose convenor is none one other than Ganga Charan Rajput. He also contributed Rs 10,00,000 in 1992 to the Awanti Bai Trust, which was formed to exalt the memory of Awanti Bai, the Lodhi queen of Ramgarh principality (Mandla District in Madhya Pradesh). In 1857 she had fought the British and died a 'martyr' on Dussehra day. The effort to Sanskritize oneself and, at the same time, promote pride in one's own caste is not contradictory. Kalyan Singh's father, Chaudhury Tej Pal Singh had adopted the Kshatriya surname, Singh, for which the Lodhis had carried out a long struggle, but they were not only imitating the Rajputs, they were proud of being as strong and prestigious as them, as testified by Ganga Charan Rajput: 'This tribe [the Lodhi] may be culturally and socially backward but it is fearless and irrepressible. Especially those who belong to the Mahalodhi sub-tribe are comparable to the Kshatriyas. These people are in general very generous but intolerant towards injustice' (cited in Tripathi 1997).

While the BJP upper-caste leaders tend to favour alliances with Dalits, Kalyan Singh looks at the promotion of the latter as a potential threat. It would be overly simplistic to say that he has not made any attempts at winning over Scheduled-Castes voters, but the fact remains that he has strongly mouthed a rejection of Dalit emblems and tried to counter every Dalit breakthrough. Certainly, it recognized a page of

Dalit history through the funding of beautification work at the Jaunpur fort built by Raja Bijli Pasi. But this cannot balance the BJP's protests against the strict implementation of the Dalit Atrocities Act, where it came together with Mulayam Singh Yadav to denounce the 'victimization' of OBCs at the hands of the BSP. The figures in Table 6.4 show that Scheduled Castes have been the first casualty of the rise of OBCs in the BJP organization. Their numbers in the government have actually diminished in proportion to both 1991 governments, a confirmation that the fracture line in the BJP's unit in the state is centred around which strategy to adopt towards Scheduled Castes.

To sum up, two trends are visible in the BJP's strategy towards the lower castes. For one, there is a strong tendency to maintain the upper-caste domination, marginally mitigated by an attempt, pushed by the party's high-command in Delhi, to select some more candidates from the lower castes at the time of the elections. It also implied projecting some Dalits to high positions in the state and making new alliances with the BSP, which recalls the 'coalition of extremes'. For another, there is a tendency for OBCs inside the BJP to consolidate their own positions of power against the upper-castes as well as the Dalits, according to what one could term the 'Kalyan Singh model'. These two opposing trends have been generating great tension in the party and bringing to the fore divisions along castes lines between the upper-caste leaders of the party, in favour of the first type of strategy, and the backward castes, led by Kalyan Singh.

The opposition between the OBC group (supporting Kalyan Singh) and the upper-caste lobby crystallized in relation to the attitude that had to be adopted towards the Dalits. Intimately linked to this issue is the question of what kind of identity the *Sangh Parivar* is adopting towards Dalits, namely how it is responding to the BSP's theme of Ambedkarization.

THE BJP'S ANSWER TO AMBEDKARIZATION

Most of the BJP mainstream leaders are belated and unconvincing converts to 'social engineering', but the actions of the BSP, aimed at having Dalits take stock of their differentiated constituency, have made them uneasy. Their organicist conception of Hindu society has certainly been touched by the assertiveness of Dalits, rendering complex the formulation of a policy towards them. The Chamars seem to be especially problematic from the BJP's point of view, in the sense that they do not respond eagerly to attempts to co-opt them in the Brahminic fold. As one Dalit activist put it, 'the BJP is trying hard to attract Scheduled Castes by giving them positions in the party, by giving them ministerial postings, but it is not really successful because Brahminism is based on a hierarchy which exploits Scheduled Castes'.[13] For most Scheduled Castes, the BJP still remains an upper-caste party wanting to subdue their endeavours at breaking free from oppression. They point out their distinct social and religious traditions to explain that they cannot vote for the BJP. Studies of political mobilization during the Ramjanmabhoomi movement have shown that Scheduled Castes did not participate as much as other Hindu castes, and certainly much less than upper-castes. Either they did not feel so much empathy towards Ram, or theirs were desires 'more fundamental than the defence of a religious community' (see Lieten 1996).

As a result, the BJP's efforts at projecting a few select Dalit faces in UP and on the national scene do not seem to be taken for granted by Dalits.[14] A major move was nevertheless made in April 1998 with the nomination of a Dalit Governor of UP, Suraj Bhan. The induction of an active BJP politician and an outsider to UP was sought by the RSS to make up for the lack of Chamar figures in the party state unit and government.[15] This decision contradicted the constitutional tradition that has been not to appoint as Governor someone with an active political background. But obviously Suraj Bhan was expected to work as an ally of Kalyan Singh, not as a watchdog of the Centre. Suraj Bhan has shown great dynamism in assessing the performance of schemes concerning Scheduled Castes, such as reservations, or the virtually unused SC/ST MLA's Forum in the state assembly (*Hindustan Times* 10 August 1998). As a result the BSP perceived him as a direct threat to their stronghold.

In spite of this, and of the party's efforts, it seems very unlikely that more Dalits should turn towards the BJP. If they leave the BSP or stay aloof from it, the Congress party seems to be a much more likely choice to them because it does not bear the weight of Sanskritization and Brahminism. Actually, the BJP's attempts to enrol Dalits and con-solidate a vote-bank among them have been successful with those groups that have not followed the path of Ambedkar's reformist ideology. To a large extent, communities that have adopted it have progressed both economically and socially and reassessed their relation to Hinduism. On the contrary, Valmikis, Pasis, Koris and Khatiks, who constitute the BJP's main Scheduled-Caste supports and are easy to mobilize, are still widely under the influence of Hindu religion and social practices.[16]

The *Sangh Parivar* meets especially great difficulties in communicating with the Chamars. As one respondent put it, 'the politicians from the BJP [who come from] the Scheduled Castes are different from those who are elected on a BSP ticket . . . the language they speak is different, their clothes are different, they wear *dhotis* like others [BJP politicians], in their speeches they always say "Sri Ram" '.[17] If one wouldn't go so far as invoking dress as a criterion of distinctiveness of BJP Scheduled-Caste MLAs, there is certainly a case for the different language and religious practices of many of them. An interesting case in point is that of a Balraj Pasi from Naini Tal, who drew a lot of attention during the Ramjanmabhoomi movement. Coming from a family with a safe business background, he cannot be said to truly represent his community in the hills, whether Pasi or Shilpkars, who usually work as agricultural labourers in very harsh conditions. His fierce defence of the Ram Mandir movement as leader of the Bajrang Dal from the district was also quite in contrast to the apathy of the Scheduled Castes in general on that matter.

Interestingly enough, this discrepancy between how Dalits see BJP Scheduled-Caste politicians and how these wish to be seen is also present in the minds of the politicians. The reference to Dr Ambedkar has now become a universal necessity even for BJP leaders.[18] Suraj Bhan has made it a point to ensure his respect of Ambedkar is acknowledged. 'Let me tell you that while I was Deputy Speaker of the Lok Sabha, I demanded the house in which Ambedkar lived in Delhi be converted into a national museum.' Even more interestingly, he went as far as saying 'I am a *bhakt* of Ambedkar myself and would ensure there is no discrimination against that great architect of the Constitution' (*Rediff News* 2 June 1998). Since Ambedkar has become the main symbol of Dalit assertion, it is not surprising that the new Dalit figure of the state should have had to clarify his position with regard to him. But in *bhakti*, a devotee is supposed to 'avoid all thoughts not associated with god and do all things in his name alone'.[19] This was obviously not the case with Suraj Bhan who, in his extensive tours of UP, had chosen to give Ambedkar a low profile. Suraj Bhan was not projected then by the BJP's top brass in the state as a Dalit but as a 'measured and competent leader of BJP'.[20] They sought to play down his positions in favour of the Scheduled Castes as mere humanism and devotion to society.[21]

There is obvious discomfort among the BJP regarding the heritage of Dalit mobilization. Work on the Ambedkar villages—one of the schemes started by Mayawati for modernizing villages with a high proportion of Dalits—slowed down during Kalyan Singh's second term, because in the minds of many BJP leaders more than just crucial development work, it was biased. As one BJP MLA put it, 'after Mayawati left the government, the work got slowed down, not stopped. I was in favour of this scheme and of its being carried on because if a good road is being made up to an Ambedkar village, it also benefits the other villages along the road. But people in the party are not in favour of that for some reason.'[22] The UP government also announced its decision to cancel the creation of new districts sanctioned by Mayawati which had been given names of characters related to the Buddha or to Dalit history. Programmes that have become attached to the Dalit movement have to be dealt with by other parties too. But to the BJP they come as a hurdle in its smoothing of all forms of landscape in the Hindu community. It is still unwilling to acknowledge the distinction of many Dalit practices and tries to drown them. Examples of this are recurrent. The complete ban on cow-slaughter it propounded in its manifesto for the general elections of 1996 can also be analysed as a further example of its lack of understanding of the social practices of Dalits. As has been pointed out, Scheduled Castes and Scheduled Tribes would suffer the most from it as they are the greatest consumers of beef, ahead of Muslims (Ilaiah 1996).

The *Sangh Parivar* pays only lip service to Ambedkar: it is not willing to fight the BSP by using the same means. Its natural strategy for circumventing Dalit assertiveness remains rooted in the Hindu nationalist ideology, that is Sanskritization with an organicist overtone. This approach is the RSS' favourite, and the OBC lobby finds it preferable to that of accommodating Dalit leaders since it may be more effective at defusing Scheduled Caste mobilization. The activities of Sewa Bharti are a case in point. To understand them better, we chose to study the organization at the grass roots level, in a place where caste conflicts are especially acute and where Ambedkar's ideas have found a breeding ground: Agra city.

THE WELFARIST STRATEGY OF SEWA BHARTI IN AGRA

The Chamars represent the largest caste of Uttar Pradesh, with 12.7 per cent of the population (as against 9.2 per cent for the Brahmins) according to the 1931 Census. But they are an even larger proportion in Agra because the shoe-making industry—for which the city is well

known—attracts caste-fellows from the neighbouring villages. According to the 1991 Census, the Scheduled Castes were 2,40,726 out of
9,48,063—that is, about one-fourth of the population. Probably, two-
thirds of the Scheduled Castes of Agra are Chamars (according to
Owen Lynch the Jatavs represented one-sixth of Agra in the 1960s)
(Lynch 1969: 214).[23] If we go by the figures Rosenthal gives, the Scheduled Castes, with 18 per cent of the population of Agra city, were
second only to the Banias (22 per cent) and ahead of the other twice-
born castes (Brahmins and Rajputs, on 12 per cent) (Rosenthal 1970).

Gradually, shoe making brought Chamars some prosperity, while
the other Scheduled Caste groups, the Bhangis (sweepers, also called
Valmikis) and the Khatiks (meat-cutters) remained much poorer. This
economic development has generated a kind of Chamar middle-class
coming from the small layer of entrepreneurs within the caste as well as
from reservations.[24] But caste stigmas have remained. This contrast
between some socio-economic mobility and a very low status, besides
a steady increase in education, has fostered feelings of frustration and
political consciousness. The Chamars first claimed that they were
Kshatriyas descending from the royal lineage of the Yadavs or Jatavs,
the name they started to adopt in the first years of the century (Lynch
1969). This claim reflected the pervasive dimension of the ethos of
Sanskritization. However, the Jatavs quickly moved away from it. Their
emancipation from the value system of the upper-castes was largely
due to the influence of Ambedkar, who came twice to Agra—the last
time in 1956, the year of his death, to inaugurate a Buddha temple,
still in use. The inroads his political parties, the Scheduled Castes
Federation and the Republican Party of India, made in Agra in the
1946, 1952, 1957 and 1962 elections were largely due to the Jatav
voters.

This political tradition declined after the 1960s because of the Congress' capacity to co-opt Jatav leaders such as B.P. Maurya.[25] But the
Bahujan Samaj Party has substantially reactivated this tradition since
the 1980s, so much so that the party won 32 seats to the municipal
corporation out of 80 in the 1995 elections, as against 35 to the BJP.
The Congress has been relegated to fourth position with only 2 seats
(the Samajwadi Party got 4). These figures suggest that there is no
room left in Agra for a catch-all party: caste conflict is the order of the
day and the Dalits and the upper-castes are engaged in a proxy war
through the BSP and the BJP.

In the 1990s, two episodes have been especially illustrative of these caste tensions with strong political connotations. First, in June 1990, in Panwari, a peri-urban village (close to Fatehpur Sikri), a Chamar wedding procession was attacked by Jats who objected that Untouchables had no right to pass their neighbourhood that way. This reaction triggered off a riot that required the intervention of one of V.P. Singh's ministers, Ajay Singh, the Janata Dal and Jat MP of Agra. Since he did not side with his caste fellows, his action further alienated the Jats from the Janata Dal.[26] A few weeks later, the 'Mandal affair' led them to identify themselves with the upper-castes, since they very much resented not having been classified as Other Backward Classes by Mandal. The Jats of Agra—as elsewhere—therefore started to vote for the BJP.

The second episode that was responsible for further crystallizing the upper-caste versus Dalit conflict happened in 1997, when Mayawati was in office. As chief minister she launched a large-scale scheme of Ambedkarization. It consisted, among other things, of raising statues of Ambedkar in the Dalit *mohallas* of Uttar Pradesh (for more details, see Jaffrelot 1998a). In the periphery of Agra, again, Jat leaders resented this move, which was intended to refashion the public space along ideological lines. Some of them started destroying the statues. Soon afterwards, Mayawati's government was dismissed because of the withdrawal of BJP support. The BSP cadres reacted by desecrating temples and breaking idols in villages surrounding Agra (mainly in the Khandauli and Sadabad areas). Interestingly, one of the Jat leaders who had already played a major role in the 1990 incident, Chaudhury Babu Lal, had just launched a movement called Savarn Svabhiman Manch (the High Castes' Self-Respect Movement), reflecting the growing identification of the Jats with the upper-castes, the *savarn*. In November 1997, he reacted strongly to attacks on temples and declared that 'the loot following the breaking of idols [was] part of a well thought out BSP conspiracy. . . . Our decency should not be considered a weakness. If people who attack temples and break idols [do not] control themselves, then we [will] have the courage to have a physical fight with them' (*Amar Ujala*, Agra edition, 6 November 1997).

These developments made the *Sangh Parivar* even more fearful of the impact of the BSP, which posed a threat to its very project of creating a Hindu *rashtra* transcending caste divisions in an organicist perspective. But it was not likely to cope with this threat, since its Agra branch is probably even more dominated by upper-castes than its branches in any other city of UP because of the locally large proportion of Banias and Brahmins, two groups which are traditional supporters of Hindu nationalism. Among the Banias, the diamond merchants contribute significantly to the funding of the *Sangh Parivar*. Ramesh Kanta Lavaniya, a Brahmin who is one of the founders of the Jana Sangh in Agra, explains that the party relied primarily on a team of five, of whom two were Banias and two Brahmins.[27] Even today, the caste composition of the BJP corporators reflects the upper-caste profile of the party. Of the 35 BJP members of the municipal corporation, 22 are from the upper-castes (including 10 Banias and 7 Brahmins), 10 from the OBCs and 3 from the Scheduled Castes (including only 1 Jatav).[28] Therefore, the *Sangh Parivar* has resorted to two different strategies. The first consists in fostering solidarity between upper-castes and Dalits, as Hindus, against so-called threatening Others, the Muslims. This approach has been used repeatedly by the *Sangh Parivar* since the 1980s. In 1982 Meerut riots, Muslims were attacked by Bhangis, who, allegedly, had been paid by upper-caste Hindus for taking part in the attacks (according to some testimonies, Rs 200 were paid for each crime committed) (Engineer 1982). A similar scenario unfolded in the 1987 Meerut riots when 'Chamars and Bhangis joined upper-caste Hindus to loot and burn down' Muslim shops and houses in return for money and alcohol (Engineer 1988: 29). Even if the Scheduled Castes fight Muslims for what they get from the upper-caste Hindus, this violence is bound to crystallize their hatred for the Other and to routinize this antagonism. Apparently, Untouchables have attacked Muslims in a more spontaneous manner in recent years. For instance, Paul Brass shows that in Kanpur, the Khatiks and the Pasis played a part in the riots that followed the destruction of the Babri Masjid (Brass 1997: 204–59).

In Agra, the *Sangh Parivar* resorted to this technique during the Ramjanmabhoomi movement, after the first assault against the Babri Masjid in 1990. The ashes of those who had died in the events were transported in procession all over India, and in Agra this *Asthi Kalash Yatra* was taken through neighbourhoods which were inhabited by Scheduled Castes and Muslims. Hindu nationalist cadres succeeded in triggering off a riot in which the former attacked the latter (Gyaneshwar and Jayati Chaturvedi 1996). This strategy of the worse kind, however, could not be resorted to so easily after the BJP lost in UP, Madhya Pradesh and Delhi during the 1993 state elections. Then the voters seemed eager to punish the party for unleashing communal violence, especially after the demolition of the Babri Masjid in December 1992.

The *Sangh Parivar* therefore concentrated on another strategy based on social work among the Dalits. Social welfare has always been one of the main activities of the RSS. Its first public action in 1926, which was carefully selected by its founder, K.B. Hedgewar, consisted of providing essential supplies (especially drinking water) to the devout in the Nagpur region—the birthplace of the RSS—who were taking part in the festival of Dussehra. The RSS also protected them from those priests known for cheating the worshippers (Andersen and Damle 1987: 34). Its network of disciplined activists lent itself well to this kind of activity. Later it often intervened in the same way when natural or political disasters occurred. For instance, it set up a Hindu Sahayata Samiti (a Hindu mutual aid society) in 1947 to clothe and house in camps the refugees fleeing West Pakistan. Similar efforts were deployed in the 1990s on behalf of the Pandits of Kashmir who were accommodated in camps at Jammu and Delhi. Similarly, RSS volunteers have made a name for themselves by aiding the victims of floods, earthquakes, plane crashes or train accidents.

This propensity to help co-religionists in order to foster Hindu solidarity acquired a new dimension when it became a technique for integrating and maintaining poor Hindus in the community. This technique was made more systematic and institutionalized with the creation of Sewa Bharti in 1979. Sewa Bharti is not even an offshoot of the RSS: it is one of its departments, like the one in charge of coordinating the movement's publicity. Its motto is 'social welfare is my duty' and its main official objectives are

(1) to eradicate untouchability, (2) to imbue people with the spirit of service and unity, (3) to promote and perform literary, cultural, social and charitable activities among the poor and our underprivileged brothers who live in run-down districts and, (4) to serve the economically needy and socially backward sectors by contributing to their physical, educational, social, moral and economic development without distinction of caste, language or region, so that they gain self-confidence and are integrated into society. (Anon. n.d.-a)

Beyond these laudable claims, Sewa Bharti's ideological purpose is to divert the Dalits, who are naturally appreciative of charitable work, from egalitarian ideologies and to assimilate them into a 'Hindu nation'. This scheme has proved particularly worthwhile for Hindu nationalists since the Dalits were aspiring to emancipate themselves rapidly and neither the RSS nor its affiliates had ever succeeded in putting down roots among the Dalits. It was difficult for a movement dominated by high castes to reach this population set apart by many socio-cultural features (such as caste awareness and social habitus).

Sewa Bharti opened dispensaries, started ambulance services providing virtually free medical assistance, and put a strong emphasis on education. Vans with video equipment visit needy neighbourhoods and slums to promote 'moral and cultural education'. Among the films shown we find the *Ramayana* and *Mahabharata*, which had tremendous success when broadcast on nation-wide television. More importantly, Sewa Bharti offers children free education (much appreciated by their parents) longing through Sanskrit Kendras and Bal and Balika Samskar Kendras.

Samskar designates a rite of passage but also, more generally, everything that shapes the personality of the individual from childhood onwards (Kapani 1992: 43). In Hindu tradition, 'to have good *samskar*' usually means having no vices (not smoking or drinking alcohol, for example), having very polished manners, even following a vegetarian diet, in short, imitating the Brahmins. This is a Sanskritization process. The RSS's uses of the term '*samskar*' reflects its aspiration to reform mentalities in line with the high Hindu tradition and, more specifically, to infuse Hindu awareness and national discipline. It reinterprets the concept of *samskar*, which it adapts to its own needs, presenting it as a vector of Sanskritization for the low castes. Many Untouchables enter *shakhas* to learn how to live a disciplined life, in which they recognize good *samskars*.

The ability of Sewa Bharti to propagate a conflict-free conception of society and its attempts at maintaining the Dalit in the logic of Sanskritization are clearly reflected in its activities in Agra. The city has been a priority area for Sewa Bharti because of the strength of the Dalit movement. While the organization is active in 292 of the 780 towns and cities, and in about 500 of the 3,900 officially registered slums of Uttar Pradesh (Das n.d.: 18), it covers 70 out of the 200 slums of Agra (Anon. n.d.-b : 10). In 46 of these 70 slums, Bal and Balika Samskar Kendras are active.[29] As in any of these schools, before teaching begins the children recite the *Gayatri Mantra*, which Brahmins recite at sunrise and sunset. That Sewa Bharti teaches such an upper-caste ritual to Untouchables is revealing of its obsession with Sanskritization. Many other of its activities reflect the same objectives. For instance, Sewa Bharti associates Scheduled Caste members in Hindu festivals from which they used to be excluded, or did not celebrate publicly, like Raksha Bandhan. Makar Sankranti, a festival marking the day when the sun begins its northward ascent from the tropic of

Capricorn—Makar Rekha—is also celebrated the same way by Sewa Bharti. This festival is traditionally celebrated with alms-giving, not necessarily to beggars but to anyone less privileged than the alms-giver. In Agra as elsewhere, Sewa Bharti has started mass feeding of Dalits from *Sewa Bastis* (the slums where the organization is active) on Makar Sankranti day. They are usually given *khichdi* because it symbolizes the ultimate synthesis of rice and various kinds of *dals*, a model of social synthesis put forth before the Dalits to show them that they must aim to assimilate in Hindu society to form a *khichdi* incapable of separation in all times to come.[30] Similarly, Sewa Bharti organizes *Kanya Puja*, the worship of girls, in Dalit *bastis*, whereas this ritual used to be strictly reserved for Brahmins. Its activists pay due respect to Dalit girls whose feet they wash. The *havan* is one of the rituals that Sewa Bharti performs even more systematically in the Dalit *bastis*. Dalits are always associated with this Vedic ceremony for which the organization usually builds a *pith*, a good means for counteracting the construction of Ambedkar statues in the competition of the symbolic monopolization of social space.

These activities are all part of the same attempt to contain the growing influence of the BSP by maintaining the Dalits within the logic of Sanskritization. One of its local cadres considers that 'the BSP is so strong because of caste feelings. This is not good for the country. . . . The BSP is separating the Jatavs from the mainstream [of society].'[31] In other words, for this Sewa Bharti activist, the BSP is destroying a social system that is supposed to be harmonious and which prepares the ground for national unity, the Hindu *rashtra*. Such a discourse is revealing of the pervasive influence of the *Sangh Parivar's* organicist view of the nation.

In Agra, the cadres of Sewa Bharti are probably the staunchest advocates of this organicist brand of nationalism among the *Sangh Parivar* activists. The chief of the Braj branch of Sewa Bharti,[32] Krishna Das, repeatedly uses organicist metaphors to justify the need to help the downtrodden: 'we don't call them either Dalit or Harijan; we believe that they were part of the Hindu society who have remained ignored for some reasons, like some part of the body is ignored or ailing. To serve it is natural *dharma*. If the big toe is hurt the hand rushes to it. No need to mistrust it. With this objective we have started our service work [*sewa karya*].'[33] The metaphors of the body are never intention-free, as Schlanger has shown so well (Schlanger 1971). Here, they echo the Vedic view of society and the *Rig Veda* origin myth that describes how society is born from the sacrifice of the primeval man, when the Brahmin proceeded from his mouth, the Kshatriya from his arms, the Vaishya from his thighs and the Shudra from his feet (Renou 1956: 99).

This strophe lends itself to an organicist view of society and can therefore be used by upper-caste nationalists eager to promote a united Hindu *rashtra*. It obviously relies on the logic of social hierarchy: the feet cannot compete with the head in terms of status. And this is precisely the image of the relief given to the feet that comes to the mind of Krishna Das. Similarly, the man in charge of the Agra unit of Sewa Bharti explains that in a family of four brothers 'if one of the brothers is weak, then the three others get together and help him'.[34] It is not just by chance that these men use such images: they are conditioned by the schema of the four *varna* as an ideal arrangement. Correlatively they do not acknowledge the existence of Untouchables. They never use words such as Harijans or Scheduled Castes. They prefer to say *abhavgrast*, the deprived, or downtrodden. Thus, Sewa Bharti is less interested in emancipating the Dalits than in converting them to an active Sanskritization by displaying compassion (*daya*), one of the key words of the organization.

In Agra, this approach has been rather successful with the Bhangis. This caste—probably the lowest among the Scheduled Castes—has shown a propensity for Sanskritization for a long time. It was incited to do so by the Arya Samaj as early as the late nineteenth century, and this is how its members started to adopt a new name, that of Valmiki, the *rishi* who authored the *Ramayana*. The Valmikis have not benefited from the same socio-economic mobility as the Jatavs, whose commanding attitude they resent very much, especially because they have cornered most of the valuable reserved posts in the administration. The Valmikis might have been more favourably inclined towards Sanskritization because they were still very much dependent upon the upper-castes. They obviously appreciate the work of Sewa Bharti because they value its paternalist attitude. For instance, they lend themselves to surprising exercises such as the yearly visits to their houses by cadres of Sewa Bharti who inspect them and then classify the families according to the cleanliness of their homes and their compliance with religious orthodoxy (the *om* symbol in display is a plus point in this competition). Those who occupy the first five ranks are publicly rewarded.[35] Of course, the Valmikis primarily support Sewa Bharti because it provides them free schools and free medicine.

The way Sewa Bharti finances these institutions is interesting because it shows that upper-caste people do mobilize for helping Sewa Bharti to defuse the Dalit mobilization. This organization needs money to pay for its expenditures: in Agra, its activities represented Rs 4,66,400 a year. Half of this amount was spent in the schools, whose cost cannot be covered by the fees: the pupils pay Rs 2 to 5 a month whereas the teachers—when they are not housewives or retired people—earn Rs 250 a month. The money comes from donations. During the first trimester of 1998, Sewa Bharti received Rs 1,38,868 in that way. Its monthly mouthpiece gives the list of the donors with the amount of their contribution (*Sewa Sankalp* April 1998: 15–16). This list enables us to identify the social profile of the patrons. Banias are overwhelmingly overrepresented among them: 66 out of 101 donors, a figure to which one must add 8 private companies probably owned by Banias.[36] This social profile can be explained from two points of view. First, the Banias have always patronized charitable institutions because they were richer than the others, but also because they had to do so for status. In his study of another Uttar Pradesh city, Allahabad, C.A. Bayly points out that they used to finance religious festivals, the building of temples, bathing *ghats* and *dharamsalas* (Bayly 1973: 83). During the colonial period, however, the British incited the Indian notables to allocate their funds to philanthropy-oriented institutions (Haynes 1987). Sewa Bharti combined both dimensions, the religious and the social, and it may be one of the reasons why Banias make donations. In Agra, Sewa Bharti has been given a large house by a Bania couple for establishing an orphanage. The wife said that she had been inspired by god (indeed her guru had told her to do so), an argument upon which the local chief of Sewa Bharti, himself a Bania, commented by emphasizing that 'donating is in the blood of the merchants. It is a part of their nature. Because we will get *Moksha* [Salvation]. That is the motivation.'[37] The husband justified this donation by stressing the fact that his forefathers had done the same, generation after generation—his grandfather had patronized the foundation of a college in the same spirit of dedication to the public.

Besides this interpretation in terms of social duties and religious motivations, one can see the gifts of the Banias to Sewa Bharti as a contribution to the preservation of the social status quo. Patronizing public institutions by rich notables has always been conceptualized not only in terms of duty and status but also as a means for defusing the potential revolt of the plebeian elements (Brown 1998: 118). In India, the charitable activities of institutions such as the Lion's Club or the Rotary Club—not to mention those with a Christian orientation— have perpetuated this tradition. In India these clubs attract mostly upper-caste, conservative people from the middle class and the business world. They explicitly define their mission as oriented towards 'preventing the disintegration of society' and the promotion of 'a feeling of brotherhood and commitment towards the service of society'.[38] Interestingly, these clubs operate more or less the same way as Sewa Bharti: they also celebrate Raksha Bandhan with poor people, establish schools for them and so on. And like Sewa Bharti, they attract the urban middle class, mainly with a business class background.

Thus, the Banias patronize Sewa Bharti probably for two reasons, socio-religious duties and motivations on the one hand, and a desire to maintain the social status quo on the other. They undoubtedly share the concern of the Hindu nationalist movement regarding the mobilization of the low castes and perfectly understand the utility of an institution like Sewa Bharti. But can it be efficient? Its Sanskritization agenda seems to be workable with some castes such as the Valmikis in Agra, but in contrast to this special relationship, the Jatavs are allergic to Sewa Bharti, whose attitude they regard as condescending. While the Valmikis tend to vote massively for the BJP, the Jatavs remain en bloc on the BSP's side. The paternalist strategy of Sewa Bharti and the RSS at large may hinder the mobilization of some of the Scheduled Castes, but their claim for more equality is bound to intensify.

THE BJP DALIT LEADERS IN AGRA

Many BJP leaders consider that the welfarist strategy of Sewa Bharti and the *Sangh Parivar* at large may not appeal to the low castes and help the party to broaden its base as much as 'social engineering'. In Agra, this line of thought has been mainly directed towards the Dalits, since they were in larger numbers. The party has no hesitation in co-opting dissidents from other parties, including the BSP, even though this move is always highly resented by the grass roots workers who view these dissidents as unscrupulous time-servers and feel that away from seats of power they themselves worked for the organization but that, now closer to power, they are being pushed aside by people with no RSS background.

The case of the BJP MLA who has been elected in the only reserved

seat of Agra (Agra West) is very revealing in that respect. Ram Babu
Harit had been elected a corporator on a BSP ticket in 1989 but he
shifted to the BJP in 1990 and became MLA in 1991, before being
re-elected in 1993 and 1996. A Jatav, son of a shoemaker, born in a
RPI-oriented family, he passed his MBBS and became a medical pract-
itioner. He read Ambedkar during his youth but joined the RSS as
well as the BJP in 1990 for ideological reasons: 'The BSP is fanning the
flames of anger but the BJP and the RSS act as bridges' he argues, and
according to him they show the right direction because 'only when the
Scheduled Castes and the Savarns join hands and eradicate whatever
defect they may have, this problem [casteism] can be solved.'[39] Ram
Babu Harit's discourse is full of Gandhian overtones. He suggests that
what the BSP proclaims 'can be said with love' and that the only true
revolution 'takes place in man's heart':

Maharishi Valmiki, who was a criminal, meditated and became a Maharishi.
Angulimal was a *dacoit* and a *thug*. A *sadhu* who was not afraid of him asked him
to say Ram. He did so and was transformed.[40] Ashok did war and then *sewa* for
others. His transformation was so great that even those whose relations had been
killed by him before accepted him as king. This revolution is required on the
part of the privileged, the *savarns*. The weaker sections should also feel that
something is being done for us, by the Sangh. The Dalit community also has the
duty of keeping its programme constructive. . . . So revolution really is what is
there in the mind. What kind of change is there in the conscience: to fight evil,
not to drink or to gamble.

This Gandhian kind of discourse naturally reflects the strong sense
of Sanskritization that inheres in RSS training: Ram Babu Harit is full
of praise for the *samskars* that are taught in the *shakhas*. At the same
time, he is a strong supporter of the caste-based reservation policy and
opposed to quotas on an economic basis as advocated by the *Sangh
Parivar*:

When the Mandal riots took place, caste Hindus [sic] said that casteism should
end. When there'll be no caste, there'll be no dispute. This is the responsibility
of the *savarn* to finish the caste system. On the economic basis, things will not
work out because the District Magistrate or the Tehsildars have to certify that
this fellow is economically backward. They would give the certificates to people
who do not need them. They would be *savarn* and give them to other *savarn*.

In addition, Ram Babu Harit differs from the official line of the RSS
when he considers that the quotas had to be extended to the OBCs, at
least to the Most Backward Classes. Not only that, but he is also a

member of the Advisory Committee of the Jatav Maha Panchayat of
Agra District, a caste association, and he is an admirer of Ambedkar.
In his office, the portrait of Ambedkar is displayed next to that of
Hedgewar, Golwalkar and Upadhyaya.

The same kind of contradiction is evident in the discourse of Baby
Rani Maurya, the Jatav woman who was elected mayor of Agra on a
BJP ticket in 1995. In addition to Golwalkar, her office has a portrait
of Gandhi and her father-in-law, who initiated her into politics, and is
a strong proponent of Ambedkar's views—a legacy she tries to articulate herself.

Obviously, the BJP has been obliged to co-opt Dalit leaders with a
new kind of background. So far, its candidates for the reserved seats
had been trained on the RSS *shakhas*, or had no real political ideology.
Under pressures from the BSP, the party has been obliged to induct
new kinds of leaders with more militant views, people who do not
believe in the organicist definition of the nation: they have read
Ambedkar and belong to caste associations. Inevitably, this new blood
will dilute the BJP's doctrine, and one may wonder what the Hindu
rashtra will then look like.

Low-caste politics obviously poses a major threat to the *Sangh Parivar*
in Uttar Pradesh today. As Zoya Hasan has shown, this state was the
one in which the Ramjanmabhoomi movement was the most intense
and contributed most to the electoral rise of the BJP (Hasan 1998). Yet
the *Hindutva* identity did not crystallize in such a way that it could
transcend the divisions of caste. The project of forging a Hindu *rashtra*
has become a remote perspective for that reason and the BJP had to
evolve a new strategy in reaction to the rise of the Samajwadi Party and
the BSP as early as 1993.

The upper-caste leaders of the UP unit first restored the old Congress-
like 'coalition of extremes' by making an alliance with the BSP, but they
had to face the opposition of Kalyan Singh. He feared that it was a
means of sidelining the OBCs and eventually he broke this 'marriage of
convenience'. This OBC lobby which gradually gained some influence
within the state BJP, has now been reduced to ashes with the eviction
of Kalyan Singh from the BJP. The change of Governor has also put a
stop to pro-Dalit schemes other than those led by upper caste leaders.
In March 2002 the BJP reverted to the previous strategy of allying with
the BSP.

By and large, the *Sangh Parivar's* policy towards Dalits can be summarized by two key words, Sanskritization and co-option. The first is
well illustrated by the work of Sewa Bharti in the Dalit *bastis* of Agra.

The second, which has been epitomized by the 'coalition of extreme' pattern, finds its crudest expression in the recruitment of former BSP leaders who can be fielded by the BJP at the time of elections because of their local popularity. In both cases, the Hindu nationalist movement tries to defuse the growing assertiveness of the Scheduled Castes or, at least, to preserve the interests of the *savarn*. Whether these tactics will be sufficient remains to be seen. Sewa Bharti has not been able to take root among the Jatavs—and more generally among the Chamars who still vote for the BSP—and the Sanskritization process may also prepare the ground for egalitarian claims: after all, when Dalits imitate the Brahmins, it is also to become 'like them'. So far as co-option is concerned, they are also bound to dilute the *Hindutva* ideology (and probably more quickly) since the new-comers bring with them Ambedkarites or socialist ideas which do not fit into the RSS brand of nationalism. At the most, the *Sangh Parivar* may slow down the emergence of egalitarian claims in the political arena of Uttar Pradesh, but these claims may well soon become the dominant creed. Even in this state the long term effects of the 'Mandal affair' are more dramatic than are those of the 'Mandir affair'.

NOTES

1. Paul Brass suggests that the Congress 'coalition of extremes' might have been a well-thought-out attempt at short-circuiting the OBCs, who are the real threat to the upper castes. See Brass 1980.

2. This view reflects the RSS's deeper commitment to a society in which no group should be allowed to come out as a separate unit. For more details, see Jaffrelot 1999, Chap. 1.

3. Neither Jats nor Tyagis were OBCs but they expected to benefit from the reservation policy on social grounds, considering their position not to be much different from that of Yadavs or Kurmis in terms of education. Jats were later included in the OBC category.

4. One of the two lawyers and three of the five businessmen declared agriculture as an alternative to their main occupation.

5. See Graham's definition of the Jana Sangh's electorate as a 'middle world' of petty traders and businessmen (Graham 1990: 159).

6. For an analysis of the BJP's ambiguous stand on business, industrialization and capitalism, see Hansen 1998: 291–314.

7. Parallel to the over representation of the upper castes among the BJP MLAs, over 64 per cent of the members of the state executive committee, as of February 1999, come from the upper-castes, essentially Brahmins (nearly 40 per cent). Scheduled Castes account for about 4 per cent, while OBCs are slightly more numerous with about 18 per cent of the committee's members.

8. Yet in the case of Chamars in particular, such a following could vary—their rejection of the Congress in the elections following the Emergency is an example. Nevertheless, one can assume that until the 1990s, Chamars were *in general* behind the Congress, as Yadavs, Kurmis and Lodhis were *in general* behind the peasant parties.

9. Though the first of the three, Charan Singh was a Jat, he nevertheless symbolizes the first foray of Backward Classes into UP politics, at the height of the first anti-Congress wave in 1967. The second incursion was made in 1977 at the height of the Janata Party wave, and the third, more pervasive, in 1989.

10. Such are the results of a survey carried out by the Centre for the Study of Developing Societies, presented in Chandra and Parmar 1997.

11. Cited in Tripathi 1997. For more details, see Jaffrelot 1998b.

12. Kalyan Singh succeeded in engineering enough defections in the Congress, the BSP and the Janata Dal to form a government of his own without needing BSP support.

13. Interview with Jag Mohan Singh Verma, Lucknow, 26 December 1998.

14. See for instance its support to the Telugu Desam Party Lok Sabha speaker, K.C. Balayogi.

15. Suraj Bhan has been elected several times on a BJP ticket from Ambala (Haryana). There were only 8 Scheduled Castes in the BJP government in UP in March 1997.

16. Interview with a founding member of the Ambedkar Mahasabha, Lucknow, 9 April 1999.

17. Interview, Lucknow, 25 October 1998.

18. For the importance given to Dr Ambedkar in Dalit mobilization, see Singh 1998.

19. For Benjamin Walker, '*bhakti* is unremitting' (Walker 1983: 139).

20. Interview with Lalji Tandon, Lucknow, 20 October 1998.

21. Ibid.

22. Interview, Jai Pratap Singh, MLA from Bansi, Lucknow, 26 October 1998.

23. According to the 1931 Census, the Chamars represented one-fifth of the Hindu population and 28 per cent of the Scheduled-Caste population.

24. Nandu Ram points out that 'the economy of the shoe-manufacturing which once linked them with the international market has borne two classes, of *bare admi* (big men—factory owners, politicians and bureaucrats) and *karigars* (craftsmen and poor workers) among the Jatavs' (Ram 1995: 247).

25. Interview with B.P. Maurya in Delhi, 7 November 1997.

26. Interview with Ajay Singh, Delhi, 10 November 1998.

27. Interview with R.K. Lavaniya, Agra, 8 November 1997. Lavaniya became mayor of Agra in 1989.

28. These figures come from interviews in the Municipal Corporation.

29. Seva Bharti has also set up tutorial centres for students from needy families and electricity and electronics apprenticeship courses for adolescents who have dropped out of the school system. Girls are invited to attend dressmaking centres with the goal of making their families 'economically self-sufficient'.

30. Interview with Ashok Aggarwal, the RSS man in charge of the local branch of Sewa Bharti in Agra.

31. Interview with Inderjit Chauhan, Agra, 30 October 1998.

32. The RSS has divided UP into four regions, one of them being Braj, with its headquarters in Agra.

33. Interview with Krishna Das, Agra, 29 October 1998. Krishna Das also says: 'See,

for example, the part of a body. That is my foot. If there is something wrong with it, I'll look after it.'

34. Interview with Ashok Aggarwal, Agra, 28 October 1998.

35. Christophe Jaffrelot attended one of these competitions in a Valmiki *basti* in November 1998 during the 'Sewa Bharti Week' in Agra.

36. The same over-representation is in evidence in Aligarh (where half of the 20 donors are Banias) and in Bareilly (where 40 of the 63 donors are Banias) (*Sewa Sankalp* July 1998: 15).

37. Interviews in Agra, October 1998.

38. These quotes come from speeches made on the occasion of the foundation of a new branch of the Rotary Club in Bhopal (*Madhya Pradesh Chronicle* 1 August 1998).

39. Interview with Ram Babu Harit, Agra, 3 November 1998.

40. The Angulimal story is very famous and common, repeated in many school textbooks: one day Angulimal waylaid a lone travelling *sadhu*. Angulimal looked horrendous with a garland of human fingers of his hitherto victims round his neck. Yet he noticed that the *sadhu* was not scared of him. Thus began a conversation between the two, and Angulimal's heart was changed.

7

Hamlet, Village and Region: Caste and Class Differences between Low-Caste Mobilization in East and West UP

Jens Lerche

One of the most important political developments for poor people in UP in the 1990s has been the emergence of the Bahujan Samaj Party (BSP). The BSP is a party headed, run and voted in by the lowest castes. Its central thrust is to fight against the hegemony of the high caste minority and for the emancipation and rule of the Dalits (Scheduled Castes, 'Untouchables'[1]), backward castes and other minorities. It runs a fierce and, from the point of view of the high castes, extremely provocative anti-high caste propaganda machine. The party's core constituency is made up of Scheduled Castes (SCs), and the BSP is generally seen as the SC's party and inheritor of the Ambedkar movement's mantle.[2] Nevertheless, its attempt to mobilize the majority of society (*bahujan samaj*: 85 per cent of the population) against high-caste rule (*manuvadi*: 15 per cent) is continuously stressed.

The BSP gained prominence when it formed part of a winning coalition with the Samajwadi Party (SP), based on low- and middle-caste support in 1993. This had a direct impact on social processes in UP. From 1993 to 1997 some of the dominant features of rural UP were social protests and high profile clashes between SCs and dominant land-owning caste groups. The assertiveness of SCs increased dramatically as processes of emancipation unfolded among them.[3]

Since 1993, the BSP has been able to see its own charismatic leader, Mayawati, a woman from the 'Untouchable' Chamar caste, occupying the position of Chief Minister three times. In 1995, it formed a minority government, supported by Congress and the BJP, which lasted four and a half months. In 1997, it entered a formal power sharing arrangement with the BJP. This meant it held the chief minister's post for six months.

Thereafter the arrangement broke down and the BJP took over the government. The 1997 Mayawati government, in particular, challenged the existing high-caste bias within the state apparatus by interfering politically with the civil service, extensively sidelining upper-caste officials and placing SC employees in as many powerful positions as possible. Simultaneously, it embarked on a programme of 'Ambedkarization' of public life by naming parks, libraries and new districts after SC heroes, and supporting the installation of Ambedkar statues all over villages and towns in UP. It also dramatically sped up the channelling of funds to 'Untouchable' communities via government programmes. Together with the BSP government's extreme outspokenness against caste oppression and high-caste dominance, this had a strong politicizing effect.

After the downfall of the 1997 Mayawati government, issues concerning the SCs have stayed in the mainstream political agenda and Mayawati became Chief Minister again in 2002. Even parties like the BJP, who have their core constituency among the oppressors of SCs (a number of landholding communities, among other groups), are now making some concessions towards the low castes, albeit in a watered-down form.

The BSP was not the first party to support SCs. Most importantly, the Congress party has historically traded votes against some concessions to the SCs. Its maintenance of a special quota of government jobs for SCs[4] has meant that, today, SC hamlets commonly boast of one or more of their sons (rarely daughters) having become civil servants—no mean achievement for a social group at the bottom of society. In UP, the SP similarly attempted to achieve a pro-SC image during the early 1990s as it implemented certain pro-poor and pro-SC policies like special development programmes for selected hamlets, the so-called Ambedkar village scheme, and the reservation of a proportion of posts of *pradhan* (village head) for SCs.[5]

The emergence of the BSP is best understood as part of wider emancipatory processes that SCs in UP have gone through during the last few decades. Since the 1970s, there has been a rise in the political profile of low-caste rural labourers and, in reaction to this, increasing atrocities against them. During the 1980s, the patronage structures of the UP Congress party, which encompassed upper-class high-caste, as well as low-class SC and religious minorities, crumbled, as more clear-cut caste and class based politics developed. This formed part of the background to the unique emergence of a low-caste party as a major political player in the state.

It can be argued that this politicization process relates to certain economic developments. Since the 1960s, the green revolution and an increased availability of non-agricultural occupations for labourers have, in many parts of UP, led to a partial breakdown of patron-client based labour relations and social relations in the countryside. A certain degree of economic and social delinking at village level between the dominant land-owning groups and their erstwhile workers took place, loosening the labourers' extreme economic dependence on their employers and hence transforming the social and economic basis for the patron-client ideology among SCs (Lerche 1999).[6]

The economic changes initially only affected western UP, but from the mid-1970s onwards, east UP has experienced similar developments, albeit from a lower level. This may be an important reason why low-caste politicization originally (in the 1960s) was limited to west UP but in the late 1990s the electoral support of the BSP was roughly equal in east and west (Brass 1997).

The specific shape and timing of the SC movement owes a lot to the general move in UP towards more forthright caste, and class, based politics in the late 1980s.[7] In this context, the BSP was the only party that engaged with the immediate problem of caste-based social oppression.[8] The existing overlap between caste and class hierarchies added strength to this approach. Struggles against social oppression and economic exploitation tended to go hand in hand, even though the overlap was by no means total: not all SCs are assetless labourers.

The low-caste and low-class nature of the support base for the BSP is borne out by post poll surveys collected by the Centre for the Study of Developing Societies (CSDS, Delhi) Data Unit. Assuming that the data are reasonably reliable,[9] the following picture emerges. In the UP parliamentary election in 1996, 59 per cent of all SCs and 10 per cent of all other low castes (in the government classification used, Other Backward Classes [OBCs]) voted BSP, as opposed to less than 2 per cent of the upper-castes. Looking at income indicators, the BSP was the largest party among the very poor (36 per cent) and the poor (24 per cent), and the smallest party among the wealthiest (1 per cent) (Kumar 1999: 824–5).[10]

The present study looks in more detail at the emancipatory processes among SCs, and explains differences in levels of politicization and political activities amongst them. Until now, all studies of low-caste mobilization and low-caste politics have focused on west UP (e.g. Brass 1985; Lynch 1969; Pai and Singh 1997). This is a serious bias consid-

ering the economic and social differences between west UP and the
rest of the state.[11] The present study takes a first step towards correct-
ing this, by comparing existing west UP studies with developments in
a village in eastern UP.

The focus of the village study is on how economic and political
developments have led to different types of action and reaction among
the local groups of SCs and other low-caste people. Through this, a
more solid but also more diverse picture of emancipatory processes
and their background emerges. Hence, the focus is both on regional
differences and on social differences within a specific locality, which
enables us to specify as well as question some of the earlier assessments
of the BSP phenomenon and low-caste emancipation in UP.

Meerut District, West UP

Jagpal Singh and Sudha Pai conducted the only published rural field
research on low-caste politics in UP in the 1990s (apart from my own).
They studied four villages in Meerut District (Pai and Singh 1997,
Singh 1998; see also Pai 2000) where (unusually) the numerically and
politically most important caste group was Jatav or Chamar. Jatavs
were, to a large extent, already mobilized and emancipated when the
BSP emerged in 1993. They formed the core of the west UP SC
mobilization around the Republican Party of India (RPI) in the 1960s,
and in what Singh terms the 'second phase' from the late 1970s to the
1990s (Singh 1998). Singh and Pai stress the role of Jatav intellectuals
from the 1970s onwards. A product of reserved quotas for SCs in
education and government employment, they became the leaders of
the broad-based Ambedkarite movements that developed in Meerut
from the 1970s onwards (Pai and Singh 1997; Singh 1998). The second
phase movements appear to be mainly concerned with socio-cultural
issues, instilling self-respect among Dalits (Singh 1998), and in mainstream electoral politics (Pai and Singh 1997).

A second conclusion of Pai and Singh relates to the dominance of
the BSP by Jatavs. The BSP is seen as primarily a Jatav party. Some of
the other sixty-five SC castes do not support it at all; and only some of
the Most Backward Castes (MBCs), the most backward of the OBCs,
do. In fact, most MBCs appear to be supporting the BJP, a party normally associated with traders, upper-castes and dominant landowners.
In UP, the BJP attempts to broaden its base away from these groups by
successfully fielding MBC candidates for political offices (Pai and Singh

1997; Singh 1998). These findings are consistent with the CSDS UP sample which suggests that 74 per cent of Chamars (including the Jatavs) support the BSP, while only 15 to 21 per cent of the MBCs do so (Kumar 1999).

DEOGAON, JAUNPUR DISTRICT, EAST UP

My case study is of Deogaon, a village in Jaunpur District of east UP, north of Varanasi.[12] As in much of east UP, the two main land-owning groups of the district are high caste ex-landlords and their middle-caste former tenants. Service castes and agricultural labourers of the district have, since the 1920s, been influenced by caste movements propagating the cutting back of those services to their high-caste masters that emphasize their oppression. The main SC caste, the Chamars, have, at least from then onwards, been involved in socio-religious self-esteem movements like the worship of the Chamar saint Raidas; limiting certain services to the Thakurs; and in a few more overt political movements (Cohn 1954). During the last thirty years, both the Ambedkar movement and the communist agricultural unions have had activists based in the district. Nevertheless, the level of low-caste and low-class political activity is fairly low compared to some other eastern districts where various communist outfits have been much more active. In Jaunpur, until recently, social relations have been couched in patron-client terms, and they still are in some parts of the district.

Deogaon village is 5 km south of Jaunpur, the old town that gave the district its name, and borders on a smaller market town to the east and the river Sai to the north and west. It covers 35 sq km, including wasteland along the river bank. There are 740 households in the village. A 'village' is a revenue unit, not necessarily a functional unit; and Deogaon consists of thirty-two hamlets and a number of isolated mini-settlements (one to four houses) each surrounded by fields or in other ways spatially separated. Most caste groups live in separate hamlets, with limited social interaction: twenty-two of the hamlets are single-caste hamlets.

Deogaon village is dominated by upper-caste Thakurs. The overall caste distribution is presented in Table 7.1. Of the altogether twenty castes, Thakurs, Yadavs and Chamars are the most important, both numerically and as social actors.

At Independence, the Thakurs were at the apex of extremely strong dominance relations based, originally, on their conquest of the area

Table 7.1: Population Distribution of Deogaon by Caste

Caste grouping	Population (households)	Dominant caste within the caste grouping	Population (households)
Upper castes	170	Thakur	115
Other Backward Classes	175	Yadav	153
Most Backward Castes	157	Lohar	28
Scheduled Castes	223	Chamar	205
Muslims	15	Pathan	15
Total	740		516

Source: Fieldwork data.

and on their colonial land rights. They saw themselves as *rajas* and all the groups who worked for them, their *praja*. Since then, their undisputed rule has eroded. Following land reforms, their former Yadav tenants have acquired around half their land, and the introduction of universal franchise gave this group access to local political power as well, through control of the position of *pradhan*. Meanwhile, the Thakurs have made inroads in the wider non-agricultural job market, particularly in the government sector.

Village labour relations have changed dramatically since the 1960s. About 240 of the Deogaon households (32 per cent) work as agricultural labourers. They belong primarily to the Chamar caste (SC) (68 per cent), but also to other SCs and MBCs such as Rajbhar and Pal. Village crafts and services are still performed by designated service caste households.

In the late 1990s, the people of Deogaon voted along caste lines. All SC castes of the village supported the BSP together with all but one of the MBCs. The MBC Pals supported the SP, a party that got its main support from the OBC Yadavs. The upper-castes were staunchly BJP, with a handful of Thakur households still following a voting pattern that used to be common and are voting Congress.

For the lower castes, their political support of the BSP (and, in case of the Pals, for the SP), reflects a varying degree of empowerment. Some of them are effectively barred from casting their vote and some groups care more than others about this. Similarly, some are in a good position to make use of the new political support they enjoy, some are not; and some appear to have found ways of enhancing their position without such outside support. These differences reflect divisions between hamlets as much as between castes, and relate also to intra-hamlet solidarity and differentiation. This will be highlighted in the following through the cases of a number of Chamar hamlets, and through the cases of selected MBC hamlets.

CHAMARS FROM STATION PAR HAMLET

All villagers consider the core of the revenue village to be its main Thakur and Brahmin hamlet, Madhya Deogaon, where the first Thakurs settled 400 years ago. Today, in Madhya Deogaon, the land belonging to the fifty-eight Thakurs and Brahmins is nearly fully irrigated by tube wells, and all upper-caste farmers make at least partial use of tractors. While most of them are only small and medium landholders, practically all of them are also employed in government service or business.[13]

According to both labourers and landowners, each of the Madhya Deogaon landowners originally brought his own Chamar labour households to the area and settled them on his land; the worker was *niji*: he 'belonged' to his landowner and worked for him on a permanent basis. At Independence, the Chamars moved to a strip of land at the nearby railway where they established what is now the main Chamar hamlet of the revenue village, the Station Par hamlet with eighty-six households. With a few exceptions, the Madhya Deogaon landowners still only employ Chamars from here.

However, labour relations have changed dramatically during the last forty years. In 1993, the Madhya Deogaon landowners estimate that, compared to the 1950s, their use of agricultural labourers had fallen by around a half. This was due to technological development in agriculture,[14] smaller landholdings, increased participation of landowners in production, and increased availability of non-agricultural employment for the labourers. The Chamars state that during the 1970s and 1980s, non-agricultural work has become the main source of income for most labourers.[15]

The labourers' ties to particular masters and to specific working conditions have also become looser. Today, most labourers still work for certain landowners on a priority basis, but this involves only negligible obligations for most of them.[16] The traditional content of the *niji* term thus disappeared decades ago, but the term itself only lost its currency between 1993 and 1998. Today, it is no longer used nor acknowledged among Madhya Deogaon Thakurs and Chamars.

The partial occupational de-linking since the 1960s has transformed social relations between the two groups. In the 1970s, this was further enabled by ideological if not practical support from the Congress party to fight against poverty and social oppression. The Chamars no longer accepted the harsh 'master and patron' rule by the Thakurs. Instead, they began to develop an interest group approach, and since 1972 have gone on strike regularly (approximately every third year) for higher wages in agriculture. Moreover, they have stopped participating in Thakur ceremonies that served to emphasize their inferiority. Since the emergence of the BSP on the political scene, they have also managed to use their increased political clout to call a halt to most routine beatings, rape and the occasional murder of Chamars by Thakurs. Also, since the advent of the BSP, younger Chamars have started reacting against daily abuse and routines that emphasize their inferiority (seating, drinking and eating arrangements, greetings, and ways of talking). Finally, whilst as recently as in 1993 there was palpable appreciation of the patronal role of the Thakurs and an admiration of those Thakurs who fulfilled their patronal obligations, this had disappeared by 1998.

The Chamar hamlet today is firmly behind the BSP. This political–ideological unity is of recent origin. During the 1970s and 1980s, some of them had supported the radical Ambedkar movement, while others were more in line with the Congress (I). For example, a little under half of the hamlet converted to Buddhism after a visit by Ambedkar activists in 1976.[17] Opposed to such radical statements, support for Congress (I) was the political expression of the patron-client ideology: the party represented both the Thakur employers and the Chamars.

The present unity of the hamlet has strengthened the Chamar agricultural labourers in their struggles with their employers. In 1994, their longest strike to date led to a 33 per cent wage hike; and abuse, violence and rape appear to belong to the past.

These changes have also had organizational implications. The Chamar hamlet has its own caste organization. Their hereditary caste headman (chaudhury) led the strike action in 1972 and was killed by the Thakurs in the process. This led to the institutionalization of a collective bargaining process, with the caste leaders negotiating the demands of the Chamars with the Thakurs. If no compromise is reached, the Chamars might stop working until the Thakurs give in or until they decide to call a halt to the strike. The Deogaon Chamar caste panchayat thus works, in this respect, as an informal local labour union.

Parallel to the change in its tasks, the Chamar caste panchayat has also undergone some organizational changes. Basically, the organization is rather loose. It operates without by-laws or a written agenda. Caste meetings for the full hamlet are held whenever deemed necessary, usually less than once a year. Between these meetings, the institution is centred on a chaudhury and 'six respected men', while broader hamlet communication takes place though informal neighbourly or card-playing groups, etc. The 'six respected men' are chosen for an unspecified period of time. They represent different parts of the Chamar hamlet. The chaudhury position is, in principle, inherited, but when the grandson of the headman killed in 1972 was caught taking bribes regarding a dispute he was to settle, he was sacked and a new one was selected. Moreover, in the early 1990s, the Chamars decided to have two chaudhurys, from two different parts of the hamlet, in order to keep the hamlet united.

However, the emergence of a local BSP leader in 1994 made the old caste organization redundant. The leader, a widow in her thirties, single-handedly negotiated with Thakurs and secured decisive support from the police during a major strike in 1994. Since then, relations with the Thakurs—as well as government institutions—have been negotiated through her and the BSP. The chaudhurys still exist but are not consulted on political matters. In fact, they are also rarely consulted on issues hitherto within their realm, such as dispute mediation within the community. The BSP leader has taken over these functions too: she has in effect taken over a chaudhury position adjusted to the society of the 1990s.

There are also limits, however, to the unity of the Chamar hamlet, not surprisingly, because it is differentiated economically and socially. Chamar government servants from the hamlet are in a different position than the rest, both economically and socially. Migrant workers in reasonably safe jobs are also considered to belong to an upper stratum of the hamlet. Those who work locally and in nearby towns as casual labourers and, during the peak season, as agricultural labourers, form the bulk of the lower section. Households which are in debt relations to their employer are seen as being in the worst position, and within this group the handful of persons who have accepted seasonal agricultural contract work for the Thakurs represent the rock bottom.

Different degrees of dependence on the Thakurs have often led to splits within the community. The poorest households may break ranks during strike actions. Thakurs have also successfully put pressure on the poorest and most dependent Chamars in order to make them give false witness statements accusing other Chamars of crimes committed by Thakurs. This happened after the murder of the Chamar leader in 1972. The few Chamars in long-term work relationships with the Thakurs also attend their employers' *pujas* as required, and we even encountered a case where one of them followed the patron-client pattern by asking 'his' Thakur to mediate in a conflict within the Chamar hamlet. This all goes against the present spirit of the hamlet but is accepted as being a consequence of the poverty-related dependence on the Thakurs of the concerned households.

The well-to-do Chamar government servants, on the other hand, want to have as little to do with the Thakurs as possible, and close ranks with their community in conflict situations. One reason for this is that caste oppression by Thakurs is aimed at all Chamars, and thus also threatens the position that the upwardly mobile civil servants attempt to build.

The BSP has helped the vast majority of the already quite politicized Station Par Chamars to achieve a position where they see themselves as liberated from social oppression: they have become emancipated citizens or, as they express it themselves, they can now hold their head high.

CHAMARS FROM LAUKRI HAMLET

The interaction between the six Chamar hamlets of Deogaon is limited. No meetings, social functions or caste-based organizations unite them. The Chamars of the other hamlets are generally in a weaker position than are their Station Par brethren. One extreme case is that of the Chamars from the Laukri hamlet. This relatively small hamlet of 24 households is fully surrounded by Thakur fields, leaving the inhabitants open to physical intimidation, and they live in a state of constant interference and control. In the early 1990s, the Yadav pradhan of Deogaon attempted to undermine the Thakurs' threat of a physical boycott of the hamlet by building a public road to the hamlet, but the Thakurs can still close down access at will.

The Laukri Chamars support the BSP and vote for it when not intimidated about voting. The electoral success of the BSP has meant the end of actual violence against them, but they do not expect their situation to improve significantly as long as they are surrounded by Thakurs.

CHAMARS FROM BARA KURWAN HAMLET

Bara Kurwan hamlet comprises sixty-five Chamar households. They used to work both for their 'own' Thakurs from the nearby Kurwan hamlet and for Thakurs from other villages. In 1982, a work gang from here dug a canal for a group of Thakurs from the nearby village of Godhana who were not 'their own', and got cheated out of their pay. As a consequence, the labourers boycotted the 1982 wheat harvest for the Godhana Thakurs. This brought the Thakurs on the offensive. They started visiting the hamlet at night, threatening to abduct people. In 1983, the Thakurs arrived in three or four jeeps, picked up four men and beat them up, accusing them of stealing a tractor battery from their nearby brick kiln. They returned once more and attacked a boy and his mother, but were forced back. The Thakurs mobilized among themselves by spreading the rumour that the Chamars had attacked them in the brick kiln, returned in large numbers and set fire to the hamlet, killing one person and injuring several, and stealing chickens and goats.

Two or three days after the incident some Chamars from a neighbouring hamlet who had supported the Kurwan Chamars were poisoned while working for the Thakurs, but survived. The law machinery took up the atrocity, not least because the local Superintendent of the Police was from a Scheduled Caste. The Chamars received some compensation on the spot (Rs 100 to 6,000), but the sympathetic SP was soon transferred. The Godhana Thakurs lodged a counter-claim accusing eighteen Chamars of burning a shed in the brick kiln. Both court cases have been dragging on ever since. In 1993, a military recruitment officer promised to arrange jobs for a number of youth from the hamlet if they dropped their case, but they refused. During the Mayawati regime in 1997, the case was speeded up again, only to return to semi-hibernation when the government fell.

Following the atrocity, the Kurwan Thakurs came at night and expressed their sympathy for their 'own' Chamars. They were even helpful in rebuilding their houses but did not go so far as to support them publicly. The Chamars reacted by stopping any work for outside Thakurs, and scaling down work for the Kurwan Thakurs as much as possible. Instead, they now work on their very own small plots of land, in the local market, or as migrant workers. As they put it: in order to avoid Thakur harassment one has to avoid the Thakurs.

In 1993, the Kurwan Chamars did not dare to speak out against the

Thakurs except in the depths of their own hamlet. They had not developed a discourse of open resistance comparable to the Station Par Chamars'. They had never gone against their 'own' Thakurs; in fact, they had reinforced the patron-client relationship by accepting their support against outside Thakurs. After the 1997 Mayawati regime, people of this hamlet did become more outspoken, but in a much less articulate way than the people of Station Par.

This difference can also be seen in how these hamlets coped with upper-caste attempts to stop them from taking over small plots of land allotted to them as part of the implementation of land ceiling legislation. In the 1980s, the Chamars from the Station Par hamlet complained in writing to the District Magistrate about Thakurs not vacating their plots. Their complaint was ignored, but at least they reacted against the illegal behaviour of the Thakurs. The Chamars of the other hamlets did nothing. During the Mayawati regime in 1997, the Station Par hamlet and the Kurwan hamlet finally received their plots, but the Laukri hamlet did not. After the fall of the BSP government, the ownership of the Kurwan plots is once again being disputed.

The general election of 1998 served to demonstrate the different degrees of freedom obtained by the different Chamar hamlets. The election took place while the BJP was in power in UP and, according to the local Chamars, little was done to ensure their free access to the polling booths. All Station Par Chamars voted anyway, under the leadership of their local BSP activist. Most men from Kurwan also voted but the women did not find it safe to go to the polling booth. So, while no-one was directly hindered from voting, the threat of harassment was sufficient to ensure a low Chamar turnout.[18]

MUSAHAR, KAHAR, RAJBHAR, LOHAR AND PAL

Many of the other low-caste groups working for the Thakurs are still tied very closely to their 'rajas'. Compared to the Chamars, they do not have the strength of numbers; they may live in isolated clusters within the Thakur hamlets, making them vulnerable to the physical might of the Thakurs; and they do not have the same outside political support as the Chamars.

The group that is most closely tied to the Thakurs is the Musahars (SC). In Deogaon, Musahars are perceived to be among the lowest ranking SC castes and are, among other things, said to be mice eaters. All eight Musahar households of Deogaon are employed as agricultural labourers by a Thakur from Laukri who is the biggest landowner of Deogaon (he owns 80 acres of land), and who maintains feudal relations with his employees. In the early 1950s, the Thakur settled the Musahar families on his estate, establishing *niji* relations with them. These relations are still functioning in the old ways today.[19] According to the Thakur, he engaged the Musahars as it had become a matter of prestige to show that 'uncivilized' Musahars would respond well to kind treatment. The 'kindness' consists of an unmitigated master-servant or patron-client relationship. While the Thakur makes no bones about how a firm hand is needed in order to keep Musahars at their work (abuse, slapping), he is proud of having treated them as his 'own people'. For example, he gave them the land they were originally settled on, and when they were later given government homestead land, he added one *bigha* (0.66 acre) as the government allotment was not sufficient.

We were unable to solicit any opinions on the BSP from the Musahars, who were the only group in Deogaon not prepared to relate to us except through their patron. No BSP-inspired emancipation appeared to have taken place here.

Another of the most oppressed and poorest groups is the Kahars (MBCs). The women of the Kahar households perform tasks within the Thakur houses, including water-carrying, while most men work as agricultural labourers or coolies in towns. There are nineteen Kahar households in Deogaon, ten of which are from two segments of the Thakur hamlet of Madhya Deogaon. All of the Madhya Deogaon Kahars serve Thakur households in their traditional capacity in a beck-and-call relationship with no firm occupational boundaries. They are asked to do all kinds of tasks at all times. The Thakurs perceive them as their closest clients nowadays, and the Kahars are suitably deferential and obedient in public and perform their specific water-carrying duties at Thakur ceremonies. On their own, however, they confide that they support the Mayawati regime and see the Station Par Chamars as their political leaders—even though at the last election, they were forced to vote for the local Thakur candidate.

The Kahars are only one of many Most Backward Castes supporting the BSP. The very poor twenty-five Rajbhar households (Laukri and Kurwan), living off agricultural labour and migrant work do too, even though they are critical of the special treatment the SCs have got from previous government throughout the years. The not so poor (but by no means well off) Lohar '*prajas*', repairing agricultural tools and implements for the Thakurs, do likewise. Of the twenty-eight Lohar households, fifteen live in a segment of the Madhya Deogaon Thakur hamlet and the rest in Thakur hamlets in and around Kurwan. While most have stopped working for the Thakurs, their history as the *praja* of the Thakurs and the fact that they live inside Thakur hamlets are sufficient for them to maintain animosity towards their former masters—but also to keep this as low-key as possible.

The Pals are in a different position. There are thirty-five Pal households in Deogaon, in three hamlets independent of the other main settlements. Pals are said to be shepherds, but goat keeping plays no major role for them in Deogaon. The conditions of the Pals vary considerable. In the ten-household hamlet outside Madhya Deogaon, most households are very poor, surviving mainly through agricultural labour and the cultivation of small plots of land (of less than one acre). The biggest Pal hamlet near the river Sai benefited from the land reforms as its members were allotted land that Thakurs had previously registered falsely in their names in order to avoid paying land tax. Of the twenty households, ten own between 1.5 and 3 acres of land, and more than a third of the households have been able to invest in electrical pumpsets and threshers. The remaining households work as daily labourers in Jaunpur and elsewhere. The five Pals from the last hamlet near Laukri are also doing relatively well: one is a government servant, and four are migrant factory workers.

In spite of economic differences, all Pals vote for the same party, namely the Samajwadi Party. They see themselves as being close to the Yadavs, who are the SP's core supporters, and they bear no particular grudge against the Thakurs. Most of them do not depend on the Thakurs economically, and none of them live in Thakur-dominated hamlets. Moreover, the BSP is not seen as helping the upwardly mobile within this caste, and the poor members of the caste see the pro-OBC policies of the SP as more relevant to them than the anti-Thakur policies of the BSP.

CONCLUSION

The success of the BSP can be seen as a result of the development of class relations in the countryside. The break-up of patronal labour and social relations which has followed on from the economic developments of the last thirty to forty years has been accompanied by a break with patronal ideologies. Low-caste labourers are now in the process of reshaping their social and political identity. It is somewhat paradoxical that while structural developments operating along class lines laid the groundwork for the present emancipatory processes, their new political identity is being expressed in caste terms. This development is facilitated by the role of caste in politics in India in general, by the fact that the sole party focusing on their struggle against social oppression, the BSP, took a caste-based point of departure, and, not least, by the general overlap between caste and class.

Our detailed study from east UP indicates that both the petty bourgeoisie of government employees and rural manual workers within the Dalit castes support the BSP, so that class-based solidarity is overruled by caste solidarity. This unity appears to be based on a common struggle against caste oppression, an oppression that hits all low-caste people, independent of class.

Class shows in a different way, though. The BSP may be a radical party, but if so it is a radical petty bourgeois party, founded by government servants, and its official policy is to transform all SCs into self-employed persons and civil servants, not to develop a radical policy for workers' rights. It is therefore only natural that it does not concentrate on issues of class-based exploitation by local dominant-caste landowners. Such issues may be of major importance for a high proportion of the SCs, but not for the SC élite. However, whereas it appears that in Meerut District the movement is heavily dominated by the Dalit intelligentsia and does not involve itself in Dalit workers' struggle, the east UP case points towards some involvement in strikes and land struggles. The class character of its policy is thus more ambivalent in the east, as class conflicts are dealt with as part of caste conflict.

This broader, less sectarian approach to politics held by the BSP in the east also expresses itself in other ways. Judging from the Jaunpur case, the MBCs are closer to the BSP in the east. I would argue that this is due to wider differences in the social fabric of society between east and west. Social relations based on landlordism have historically been more widespread in the east, with a wide proliferation of *praja* or servicing castes as well as agricultural labourers. These relations also survived for longer than in the west, where full-fledged landlordism has been a rare phenomenon since Independence. Finall economic development in the east did not gain pace till the late 1970s and the 1980s, followed only then by a breakdown of patronal ideologies. It is not surprising that this led to somewhat different political trajectories in the east and the west.

Not only did the political emancipation of the lower castes begin later in the east; it also took a more unified shape than in the west. I argue that the basic conditions for Dalit or Chamar grass roots movements to establish themselves as strongly and exclusively as in the west were lacking. No sizeable independent Chamar petty bourgeoisie, similar to that already existing in west UP in the 1960s, has developed in east UP. The emancipation of rural SC labourers—the basis of any Dalit rural grass roots movement—is a recent phenomenon following the partial delinking of labourers and landowners during the 1970s and 1980s. Instead of an exclusive Dalit discourse, the anti-high-caste landlord ideology of pre-Independence land struggles (then led by OBC tenants) gained strength among SCs and MBCs as patron-client based relations broke down, not least due to the continued attempt by the Thakurs to maintain a strategy of oppression.

As the Deogaon example shows, the emancipatory gap between various Chamar hamlets is not much smaller than that between some of the MBCs and the Chamars. High-caste oppression ensures that the most important issue for the low-caste groups in Deogaon is this common enemy, not the differences between Chamars and MBCs. The MBCs as well as the Chamars see the BSP as their best bet for emancipation. Supporting the BJP, as the majority of MBCs do in west UP, is ruled out, as it would turn the wheel back to old patron-client politics: the BJP is the party of the very Thakur landholders whose dominance the MBCs are against.

Caution should, however, be taken in generalizing findings from villages in two districts. Variations exist, obviously, within these wide regions. In west UP, conflicts between low castes and high-caste landowners appear to be most pronounced in the westernmost districts of the Upper Doab, which also happen to be the most economically developed (Lerche 1999; Singh 1992; Srivastava 1999). There are also similarities regarding SC activities in some of these districts (Aligarh [Brass 1985], Agra [Lynch 1969], and Meerut). On the other hand, SCs are less organized in the likewise economically developed district of Muzaffarnagar, just north of Meerut. Within west UP, the main differences are, however, between the extreme west and the rest: in Bijnor District, class relations are less polarized (Jeffery and Jeffery 1997), and in Bulandshahar, patronal ideology apparently is still dominant (Gupta 1998).[20]

In east UP, fewer recent studies of rural social relations exist. But they all point to increased political activity among the low castes, and do not describe a split between Dalit and other low castes in local level politics during the 1980s and early 1990s (Pathak 1987; Sharkar 1993; Srivastava 1989; 1999). The east UP material does not allow us to draw any inter-regional conclusions. There is little doubt, however, that the dominant low-caste political development trajectory of this region differs from that of the extreme west.

The BSP must have reached the same conclusion in the late 1980s and early 1990s, when it started to concentrate its activities in the east. There, its *bahujan* alternative appears to have been readily accepted by both SCs and MBCs seeking political support for their emancipatory processes. Accordingly, it achieved its 1993 election victory through support from the east and the south of UP; only afterwards did the Dalits of west UP join in.

The UP low-caste movements are best understood as different, regionally specific, low-caste movements that came together in the 1990s. The main difference between the BSP's success and previous low-caste mobilizations in UP is that for the first time, the low-castes of the eastern regions have taken part in this development. This is a major break with earlier mobilizations, and has transformed the low-castes into a statewide political force. Whether the alliances behind the success of the BSP last or not, the recent emancipation of rural low castes in the east has left its mark.

NOTES

1. Opposed to the terms 'untouchable', 'ex-untouchable', 'Harijan' or 'Scheduled Caste' (SC), 'Dalit' is an explicitly political term. It refers to the untouchable group but 'implies demands for social justice and empowerment' (Sharma 1994: 14). The term 'Dalit' is, however, not in common use in UP; Harijan and SC are more commonly used by the people themselves. The present paper will use the terms interchangeably.
2. Dr Ambedkar is commonly seen as the founder of the modern untouchable movement, from the 1920s onwards.
3. News magazines as well as more scholarly journals followed this development in great detail, see for example *Frontline* and *Economic and Political Weekly* during these years.
4. A quota system for SCs was first introduced in 1934. The Congress party became its main guarantor after Independence (Mendelsohn and Vizciany 1998: 131).
5. For an outline of pro-SC policies, see Mendelsohn and Vizciany (1998).
6. See Mendelsohn (1993) for an extreme version of the delinking argument, and Lerche (1998) for a critique.
7. See Hasan (1998) for a discussion of UP politics in the 1980s and 1990s.
8. The communist parties, for example, did not give much priority to struggles against caste-based social oppression, as their main interest was to build an alliance between rural workers and small, medium and sometimes even big peasants against feudal landlords and the state. In the light of the success of the BSP, the CPI(M) and its agricultural labour organization have admitted that the low priority given to struggles against social oppression was an error (Lerche 1999).

9. Neither the methodology used in the survey nor its coverage are reported (Kumar 1999).

10. The 1998 UP Lok Sabha election figures are somewhat less polarized, see Kumar (1999: 824–5).

11. UP is conventionally divided into five main regions: east, west, central, Bundelkhand (south) and hills (north), though in some respects it makes sense to divide the West into north-west and south-west (see Introduction). Here, we are only interested in the plains of UP (east-west-central). The central region is omitted as our data are from the eastern and western regions.

12. During a 12 months stay in India in 1992–3, two assistants and I conducted six months' fieldwork in Deogaon and a village in Muzaffarnagar District of west UP, backed up by extensive touring of the districts where the villages were located. The research assistants were two sociologists: Mr Prakash Deo Singh, and Ms Rajashree Ghosh. Mr Indu Shekhar (also a sociologist) joined the research team during the last two months. The follow-up visits in 1995/6 and in 1998 were both of a month's duration. During these visits, Prakash Deo Singh again acted as research fellow.

13. All Thakurs own some land, and none of them work as agricultural labourers. Their landholdings average around 2 ha (5 acres), and no very big landowners stand out. 90 per cent of the households have one or more household member employed within the government sector.

14. Specifically, the introduction of motor driven tube wells (from the mid-1960s), tractors (from 1970) and motor driven threshers (from the mid-1970s).

15. Apart from coolie work in nearby markets and cities, around 40 per cent of their households are engaged in government service, business, or factory work. In 1998, male agricultural labourers were employed primarily during the peak seasons of paddy transplantation and wheat harvesting. In between, casual agricultural labour was carried out by women and old men. Migrant workers only return to work in agriculture during the peak seasons.

16. For most households priority relations nowadays function as an employment insurance in return for which they have to perform certain tasks for free for their priority employer amounting to about 2–3 days a year. However, in case of debt relations, the labourer is tied into beck-and-call relations to the moneylender-cum-employer, and has to work for him whenever he required.

17. This dividing line was more political than religious and did not, for example, create a new intermarriage boundary.

18. Not that their votes would have mattered much: a group of young Thakurs informed us that they ensured a result to their liking by stuffing the ballot box with 600 false votes for the BJP.

19. An unusual aspect of the labour relation is that the Musahars are paid partially in *ganja* (hashish).

20. SC activities were much more low-key and less organized here, both before and after the emergence of the BSP on the scene. This was not the least due to the much more oppressive social relations maintained by the dominant landowners here (Lerche 1995; 1999).

8

Modelling Institutional Fate: The Case of a Farmers' Movement in Uttar Pradesh

Staffan Lindberg and Stig Toft Madsen

The Bharatiya Kisan Union (Indian Farmers' Union) featured prominently in the Indian news from about 1986 as a radical champion of
the farmers of Uttar Pradesh.[1] It appeared then as if the Bharatiya
Kisan Union (henceforth BKU) would be able to carry on the heritage
of Chaudhary Charan Singh who, from the 1950s till his death in
1987, had been the foremost political leader of the farmers of UP.
Charan Singh was a Jat by caste, and the BKU, too, emerged among
the Jats. During the 1990s, however the influence of the BKU seems to
have declined. During a visit to UP in March–April 1998, Madsen
found that the organization was seen to have become 'very weak'. Even
its leader, Chaudhary Mahendra Singh Tikait, publicly bemoaned this.
In this paper we discuss the 'institutional fate' of the BKU in UP by
looking at the internal and external predicaments the organization has
faced and the manner in which it has responded. Talking about the
institutional fate of BKU, we have in mind an expected or unexpected
sequence of events involving a certain entity, in this case a social movement, as a result of which this entity itself undergoes qualitative change
even though its name, its leader and its constitution may remain the

* The article has been written in collaboration with Mahipal Singh Tomar, K.K. Jain,
PG College, Khatauli, Muzaffarnagar. Madsen and Tomar carried out fieldwork in UP, and
Lindberg and Narinder Singh Sandhu, State Institute of Rural Development, Nabha,
Punjab did so in Punjab. Madsen and Gaurang Sahay, Janata-Vedic Inter College, Baraut,
carried out additional fieldwork in February 2001. The study forms a part of a research
project on Farmers' Movements and Organizations in India, Taiwan and Thailand financed
by the Danish Council for Development Research and the Swedish Agency for Research
Cooperation with the Developing Countries (SIDA/SAREC). Our thanks to Kate Toft
Madsen for language editing.

same. Apart from this institutional analysis, the paper also attempts a comparison with another organization within the so-called new farmers movements in India, i.e. the BKU's namesake in Punjab.

MODELLING INSTITUTIONAL FATE

Among pioneering studies of the processes of institutionalization, those of Max Weber and Roberto Michels stand out (Gerth and Mills 1946: 297–301, Michels 1949). Zald and Ash have summarized the inquiries of Weber and Michels into organizational transformations in this way:

As an MO [movement organization] attains an economic and social base in society, as the original charismatic leadership is replaced, a bureaucratic structure emerges and general accommodation of the society occurs. The participants in this structure have a stake in preserving the organization, regardless of its ability to attain goals. Analytically there are three types of changes involved in this process; empirically they are often fused. The three types of change are goal transformation, a shift to organizational maintenance, and oligarchization. (Zald and Ash 1969: 461–2)

According to Zald and Ash, this model may be taken as the starting point for a more flexible institutional analysis envisaging other institutional outcomes. 'There are a variety of other transformation processes that take place including coalitions with other organizations, organizational disappearances, factional splits, increased rather than decreased radicalism, and the like' (Zald and Ash 1969: 462).

Accepting this model as a general frame of reference, we note that transformations may not take place just along the social movement–bureaucratic organization axis. A parallel process of organizational transformation may occur when traditional institutions formalize: informal, but rooted and valued, institutions unfold themselves to become formal and modern organizations capable of dealing with contemporary issues. This process was not of primary concern to classical sociologists, but contemporary social thought deals extensively with this form of transformation. The process is often valued positively. For example, the contemporary environmental discourse typically presumes that age-old indigenous institutions embody values and practices which are valid models for contemporary sustainable natural resource management. Similarly, the possibility of a transformation of a traditional moot into a modern legislative body or a court is a part of contemporary social philosophy, although currently overshadowed by the hopes pinned on traditional environmental wisdom.

On the basis of the model outlined, one might expect the institut-ional fate of the BKU to have been one of gradual transformation from a movement organization or from a traditional institution into a more formalized and specialized farmers' organization. However, this has not happened. Rather, the BKU has witnessed a period of decline dur-ing which it has become both less of a movement and less of a modern organization.

We see this change not as a linear development of progress or lapse, but as an oscillatory process. This oscillation takes place between traditional institution and modern organization or between mass move-ment and modern organization. However, it also occurs between tradi-tional institution and movement, and between movement and what we will call a machine of sin or rent-seeking faction. In the first case, a traditional institution may turn into a movement only to sink back into its old form once the energy of the movement has been spent. In such a case, a social movement is the extraordinary and 'hot' or active *ava-tar* of what is otherwise a 'cold' enduring social institution. In the second case, an organization would oscillate between being a movement orga-nization with a high degree of consensus and participation, and being a parasitic rent-seeking machine of sin extracting resources from vari-ous parts of its environment. Figuratively, the trajectory of the BKU leads to the following model, which features four entities between which relations of transformation or oscillation occur (Figure 8.1).

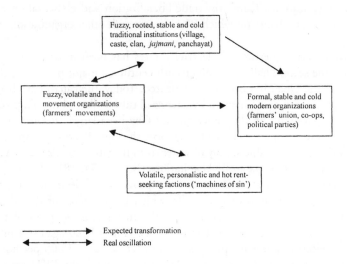

FIG. 8.1: ORGANIZATIONAL FORMS AND INSTITUTIONAL FATES

THE BKU AGENDA

Before looking closer at the institutional fate of the BKU, we would
like to present some of the major issues on which the BKU has mobilized. Like the other new farmers' movements in India, the BKU has
raised issues related to the economics and profitability of farming,
thereby contributing to the political pressure generated all over India
for higher minimum support prices for major crops. The Commission
on Agricultural Costs and Prices sets the support prices. This organization, therefore, has remained in the centre of the political storm (Varshney
1995). The BKU has also demanded continued high subsidies on chemical fertilizers. Another concern that the BKU has shared with other
organizations is the demand for a moratorium on the repayment of
institutional debt. The BKU scored a victory on this point in 1990
when the Government of India under V.P. Singh conceded a loan waiver
for loans up to Rs 10,000.

The BKU has also joined other groups resisting the 'globalization' of
world trade promoted by the World Trade Organization (WTO). The
attempts by the WTO to extend global legal protection to private intellectual property rights have been opposed in India by the eco-feminist
Vandana Shiva, Suman Sahai of the Gene Foundation, and by many
others (A. Gupta 1998). The BKU has participated in several anti-
WTO agitations together with the Karnataka Rajya Ryota Sangha
(Karnataka State Farmers' Association) and various Left and communist organizations. Currently, trade liberalization and globalization are
the overriding issues on which BKU unites with other organizations in
India.

In UP, the question of electricity rates has been most persistent.
Since the second half of the nineteenth century, a major portion of the
area in the Doab has been canal irrigated. Today, the canals have been
complemented or augmented by energized tube wells and the old problem of 'gambling on the monsoon' has now been largely reconstituted
as a question of assured field irrigation through electric pump sets.
Securing a dependable supply of water from irrigation canals has played
a relatively minor role in BKU agitations (Rana 1994: 181). The major
conflict arena of the BKU remains the provision of electricity for private irrigation pumps or tube wells, which irrigate most of the wheat
and cane raised in the area. In fact, the first major agitation of the
BKU was a mass protest in Baraut in September 1986 against a hike
in the electricity rate for pump sets from Rs 22.50 to 30.00 per horse
power per month (Gupta 1997: 31). Subsequently, the BKU gained

several *de jure* and *de facto* victories on the issue of electricity, including the reversal of the rates back to Rs 22.50 (Gupra 1997: 35).
Protected by the BKU, a very large number of farmers have refused to
pay their electricity bills, causing a loss of tens of millions of rupees to
the UP State Electricity Board (Gupta 1997: 20). About 80–5 per cent
of the rural electricity bills went unpaid at the end of the 1980s. This
figure has now dropped to around 35 per cent (interview with N.D.
Goyal, Superintendent Engineer (Rural), Muzaffarnagar, 30 March
1998). The frequency of non-payment of electricity bills seems to be
the highest in the heartland of the BKU, around Shamli, Budhana and
Kandla, where Jats have controlled many villages.[2] In the eastern areas
of Meerut and Muzaffarnagar districts, the Jats are less tightly organized and other land-owning castes have played a larger role.[3] That
may be the reason why more rural households have apparently started
to pay their bills in the eastern parts of the district.

The question of land ownership and its redistribution has also been
on the BKU's agenda. In this respect, the BKU has fought a rear-guard
battle to prevent land from falling into the hands of the low castes.
Indeed, the very origin of the BKU in the neighbouring state of Haryana
may be traced to a government decision in 1978 to allot 120 acres of
land to the Scheduled Castes in a Jat-dominated Haryana village called
Kanjhawla. Jats from across Haryana, Delhi, Rajasthan and UP mobilized on this issue, arguing that the land be declared common grazing
ground for all the villagers (Rana 1994: 16). The various mobilizations
of the land-controlling *Jat kisans* are meant to prevent any possibility of
low castes staking claims to the lands of the Jats, or to the common
land that the Jats have an eye on. BKU mobilizations aim to retain the
hegemony of the landed castes in their respective villages, whosoever
these landed castes might be. Tikait has said as much in closed gatherings even in the presence of representatives of agricultural labourers
and of organizers with a Naxalite (or Maoist) orientation:

We have only this *dhoti* and *kurta* [loincloth and shirt]. If you want the labourers
to touch these, we will beat them. We will not give them even a small cutting
from this cloth. . . . If you want to have a fight, let us go for where the real
treasure is. . . . The fight of the farmers and the labourers should be against the
capitalists. (Tikait at a joint anti-WTO rally preparatory meeting, Gandhi Shanti
Pratisthan Meeting Hall, Delhi, 13 May 1998; information courtesy of Mahipal
Singh Tomar)[4]

During its heyday, the BKU was able to close off villages to the
authorities (including the police), thus leaving the small castes under

control of the relatively autonomous farmers' panchayats (see Rana 1994: 178–9). Such control extended naturally into non-agricultural matters. With the rise of the Bahujan Samaj Party (BSP) (see Jens Lerche, and Craig Jeffrey, this volume), the moving frontier between the areas controlled by the land-owning and politically mobilized farmers and the BSP-dominated state shifted in favour of the state.

WHAT KIND OF A UNION?

The BKU is nominally a trade union registered under the Trade Union Act. The union has a rather elaborate constitution (Gupta 1997: 158; 195–6). It is doubtful, however, whether this constitutional ambition has ever been a blueprint for action. Though it is the aim of the BKU to represent farmers in the whole of India, Tikait's BKU is a regional association with its base in UP. The support base of the BKU used to include Saharanpur, Muzaffarnagar, Bijnor, Moradabad, Meerut, and Bulandshahr—essentially, north-west UP as defined in the introduction to this volume—with peripheral support in the districts of Rampur, Bareilly, Budaun, Aligarh, Etah, Mathura and Agra (Kant 1995: Map 2:2). In Punjab, there is a separate BKU, older than its UP namesake. The BKU was originally intended to cover the whole of the country, and it is possible to hold that Mahendra Singh Tikait is, indeed, the head of the several BKUs in India. Thus, he was re-elected as president of the BKU in 1997 in Chandigarh (*The Hindu* 4 September 1997). However, that did not make him the immediate head of BKU-farmers in Punjab. At most, it made him the formal head of a coordinating committee of a number of BKUs and allied organizations in various federal states of India.

Ostensibly, a farmer joins the BKU by paying Rs 5 for ordinary membership, or Rs 50 for lifelong membership as well as Re 1 for each acre of land owned, and a donation of one kilo of grain (Gupta 1997: 194). Such members elect the office-bearers to the Village Committee, who in turn elect members to the Block Committee, and so on upwards to the District Committee, the State Committee, and the National Executive,

The village members will choose from amongst themselves a President, Vice-President, Secretary, Joint-Secretary, and Treasurer. These office-bearers will have to be amongst the members. This committee will have up to fifteen people. In bigger villages, it can be up to twenty-one members.

(a) *Block committee*: The village-head will be considered a committee member but each village will choose and send one representative each. From these the block committee will be made with one President, two Vice-Presidents, one Chief-Minister, three Ministers, and one Treasurer. The office-holders will have to be life members.

(b) *District committee*: The block Pradhan will be considered a member of the district committee. The block committee will choose thirty-one representatives and send them to the district committee. It will have one Pradhan, four Upa-Pradhan, one Chief-Minister, three Ministers, one Treasurer. They will all be chosen from among the life members only.

Note: Please do not give donations to any man who comes from another village to collect it on behalf of the Bharatiya Kisan Union. Only a person belonging to the same village can collect donations. (Gupta 1997: 195)

The constitution goes on to outline the creation of the State Committee and the National Executive in a similar manner. Despite the rules, it is unclear who has paid their fees. According to the Treasurer of the BKU, the supporters from eastern UP tend to make cash donations, while the farmers from western UP prefer to support the BKU by making donations in wheat and rice. These donations are substantial, but they do not easily translate into membership rolls and budgets. The rules regarding elections are also honoured more in breach than in action. In fact, no one is elected: Tikait appoints all the office bearers. Consequently, there is also no agreement as to who are the office bearers. The standard answer to Dipankar Gupta's queries as to who were the top office bearers of the BKU, was: ' "There is of course Chaudhary sahab (Tikait), then Harpal Singh is the General Secretary, and then I. . . ." As each one said "and then I (*aur phir main*)" it was impossible to figure out who were the actual office bearers' (Gupta 1997: 71).

The lack of clarity as to membership and office-holding is underscored by the absence of written communications in the form of newsletters, which would inform members about what goes on in the organization. Some information is conveyed at the monthly panchayats, but these meetings are very loosely structured. Gupta has summed up the situation as follows: 'The organization is still run on informal lines for Tikait prefers it that way, and also because there is nobody in the Union who has the competence to set up a formal organizational structure. Those who could, and who were attracted to the BKU were, however, not fully trusted by Tikait' (Gupta 1997: 156).

Tikait and others could not, or would not, build the BKU into a formal organization. In addition, the BKU has not become an adjunct to an existing political party. Therefore, the BKU has had to remain a loosely structured mass movement organization relying on traditional institutions and occasional rent-seeking for its day-to-day running. The clan structure of the Jat caste has been the main traditional institutional infrastructure on which Tikait has been able to rely. Tikait himself is the hereditary headman of the Balyan clan (*gotra*). The villages dominated by Balyan Jats form the Balyan clan-territory (*khap*), with Sisauli as the centre (see Madsen 1991). Sisauli is also the headquarters of the BKU. According to Gupta (1997: 157), much organizational work of the BKU has been carried on by and through the Balyan clan and other, mainly Jat, clans. 'Through the *khap* money, material and activists were mobilized, which over time gave the *khap* chaudharies a lot more importance than they ever possessed in the recent past.'

The other major traditional institution on which the BKU has relied is the politico-juridical panchayat. BKU meetings are patterned on the panchayat. All senior males of the farmers' castes in the area deliberate on a loosely defined and ever-shifting agenda in an informal but often protracted manner, with a minimum of procedural rules. Disagreement is openly voiced, but consensual decisions are preferred to voting. The panchayats vary in size, and it is rarely clear what constitutes a quorum. A panchayat is called by a leader. If a leader calls an important BKU panchayat without inviting Tikait, this is likely to be an act of rebellion.

THE ISSUE OF PAYMENT THROUGH
COOPERATIVE SOCIETIES

To illustrate the manner in which the BKU seeks to realize its aims, this section will recount the main agitation conducted by the BKU in 1998. This agitation was about the mode of payment for cane. In western UP individual farmers are allotted an annual quantity of cane based on earlier deliveries to be sold to the mill in their designated area according to a cane-harvesting calendar. Farmers sometimes transfer this right to other farmers, an act that is against the rules. The farmers who deliver the cane are given a slip as acknowledgement. Prior to 1998, the factory itself made the payment to the cane cooperative societies, which in turn paid the farmer on presentation of the slip. As these societies are engaged in a series of dealings with farmers, some farmers may well be known to them personally. Moreover, the employees of the societies are often of local rural background. In Meerut and

Muzaffarnagar many are Jat by caste. Societies take a long time to pay the money to farmers, and when farmers turn up they may be 'harassed' for reasons good or bad.[5] Some time back, the BKU opined that it would be better for the farmers were payments to be made through the regular banks which are almost universally held to be more honest and straight, treating all customers as equals (*barabar*).

However, when the UP government decided to do just that, the BKU changed its opinion and protested. The BKU argued that if money were to be deposited in bank accounts, this would lead to struggles in the farming families. For example, absentee brothers or younger members of the family would be able to gain insight into the financial affairs of the (more or less) joint households generally run by the head of the family solely on trust. In effect, the BKU feared that transparency in financial matters would threaten ingrained authority structures in rural households. Another argument was that the government would eventually use the banks to deduct the dues and debts of the farmers to the Electricity Board before paying them for the cane. It was feared that the government would be able to do this because the banks—unlike the cooperatives—kept proper accounts. These, however, were not the only explanations forwarded for the BKU's sudden change of position. As is frequently the case in UP, a handful of supportive or alternative theories were in circulation to account for the shift. Thus it was alleged that the real reason for the BKU's objections was simply that the BKU wanted to support the Jat employees of the cooperative societies. These employees, it was held, had approached Tikait directly or through their family members to safeguard their rent-seeking activities. According to an alternative explanation, the episode was a clever ploy in which the BKU was not the villain but the victim. The issue came up at election time. By prompting Tikait to jump for it and subsequently leaving him high and dry in prison after he was arrested for obstructing the trains in Muzaffarnagar, the way had been cleared for aspirants to power—including Harinder Singh Malik who first supported Tikait's agitation and then left him to join the Samajwadi Party—to manipulate the leaderless BKU-followers in accordance with their own election plans.[6] Whatever may have been the chain of events leading to the agitation, it turned out to be a flop. Virtually everyone we spoke to agreed that payment through banks would be better for the farmers than the existing system. Thus the agitation took up the wrong issue at the wrong time, and as a result the movement was weakened and Tikait lost status.

'FROM TODAY, WE ABOLISH ALL POSTS'

The following extracts from a BKU panchayat held in Tikait's home village, Sisauli, on 29 March 1998 show how the BKU tried to deal with the situation which had arisen as a result of the failed agitation discussed earlier. During the agitation, Tikait was jailed for almost three months. This was his longest 'jail *yatra*' but despite its duration, very few BKU supporters courted arrest to join him in jail.[7] The period during which Tikait was jailed coincided with the campaigns for the general elections. By keeping him in jail during this period, the BJP government in UP successfully neutralized Tikait. Thus, the panchayat took place after Tikait had been humiliated by the BJP-government and betrayed by his own followers.

The date of the meeting had been decided at the Maha Panchayat in Lucknow on 17 March. It was to be an executive meeting of block level, district level, commissionary level, and state level presidents and secretaries of the BKU of UP. However, a few thousand people, *most of whom were from eastern and central parts of UP,* had gathered in Sisauli. This necessitated the break up of the gathering into two groups.

The executive meeting took place in Tikait's men's house away from the larger crowd gathered around the Kisan Bhawan.[8] It lasted from noon until around 4 p.m. The General-Secretary of the BKU in UP, Raj Pal Sharma, started the meeting by saying that normally panchayats would be held in Sisauli on the 17th of every month, but that this was a special meeting to discuss the current situation. He then announced the names of BKU executives at block and district level, and requested all others to leave the *ghar*. While some left, others kept coming. Tikait stood up and said that a maximum of five people from one district could be present. He said that it had been agreed in Lucknow which two people would represent a district at this meeting, but that so many more had come. Raj Pal Sharma said that the movement was not successful because of lack of coordination and disregard for the constitution of the BKU. He continued: 'Our national president was in jail for three months and because of this, we were not able to rescue him from jail. There should be no difference between words and action.'

Rajesh Chauhan, President of UP state BKU, said,

Strong decisions should be taken today, and Chaudhary Sahab, you should take all these decisions today and solve all disputes of different districts [regarding portfolio distribution]. Whomsoever you want to be on what post, that person will be on that post from today. Today you should decide regarding Muzaffarnagar district as well. Don't hesitate even for Muzaffarnagar [where a rebellion was brewing]! Had you done this already, there would have been no need for you to go to jail for three months.

Another speaker from Agra said, 'Why are people who have not been called still sitting here? We have done a lot of work when Tikait was in jail. Proceedings will start only when the rest of the people leave this place,' while a person from Bulandshahr pointed out that, 'We are here because we were asked to come here.' Tikait responded:

Listen! If I went to jail, I have not done so to oblige anybody. There was a problem of farmers regarding the manner of payment for cane, which I raised. I was in jail to keep alive the organization. In jail I was getting all the information from the newspapers about who went to jail where. . . . The panchayat in Allahabad took place when farmers were still in jail. You did not do anything. And there are still farmers in the jail. I trusted you when you asked me to start this agitation, though I already told you that this is not the time to fight with the government. 'We will fail,' I said. But still you people forced me to start this agitation and I could not get your proper cooperation. Tell me what these people want from us!—leave me alone! (*hamara picha chor do*). We could not succeed. Now, tell me what you want! Which issue (*kam*)? Let me know. There is a saying, *Kam ke waqt kam karo. Varna aram karo!* (When there is work to do, do it. Otherwise take rest!) Now abolish all units [of the BKU]. How many officials of the BKU went to jail? If all office-bearers had gone to jail, all jails would have been filled up! Even today we can smash the face (*chappat lagana*) of the CM: that is, if you cooperate.[9] Everybody has a printed letter-pad of BKU and this is the only work which has been done by you [i.e. all you do is to use the BKU letterhead for your non-BKU purposes]. The history of the organization is written by the blood of the martyrs—Akbar Ali, Jaipal Singh—and to their mothers we have to answer. We cannot play games with these great souls. You collect money in conspiracy with government officials, *tehsil* [sub-district] officials, doing all manner of wrong things, fighting to get contracts, getting involved in corruption. I do not understand what we need money for.

Pratap Singh, Vice-President, Kanpur, added:

If the organization today is weak, it is due to the factional politics (*gutbaji*). The office bearers are involved in wrong deals. BKU leaders approach MLAs and MPs for their personal gain. Then, naturally, the organization becomes weak. In all districts there is factionalism. Unqualified persons should be removed from the posts. I would request Chaudhary Sahab that strong decision should be taken today.

One speaker from Balyan *khap* said,

In the beginning it was a 'UUNIAN' ['union' pronounced in Hindi], now it has become a 'UNION' [i.e. now people with education and political ambitions have joined the organization]. If we had not listened to you educated people, it would have remained an 'UUNIAN'. Tikait should trust 'UUNIAN' people. The organization cannot work with 'UNION' people. There are 47 villages of Balyan *khap* here. And you want that we should do everything for you all the time? What have they done, the people like Rajesh Chauhan? I request the 47 villages of Balyan to leave this organization because everybody wants that Balyans should do everything for them. It is the history of Balyan *khap* that we sacrificed so many things in the past, and you people have now destroyed us. Go to your villages! Tikait-ji, I am telling you that one day you will lose your turban [headman ship of Balyan *khap*] as well, if you are in the grip of these people. . . .

Daryal Singh, the National Treasurer, said,

You people know that I am at the head-office here in Sisauli all the time. I am the Treasurer for the national BKU. Today we are holding a national panchayat. I am asking you, 'Do you know who has given me money and how much? Does anybody here know how we manage to cover our expenses at Sisauli headquarter?' Nobody has asked about that. I am resigning now.

He walked toward the public meeting place. Tikait smiled, knowing that Daryal Singh's was an empty threat and that he would not resign without Tikait's consent!

Then Chandra Pal 'Fauji' an ex-army man, block president of Khatauli, Muzaffarnagar District, said, 'For the last ten years I have taken an interest in the BKU during my army job. After leaving the army two years ago, I have been very active in this organization.' He started to describe how much good work he had done and how much he had suffered during agitations.

We captured SP's office [office of Superintendent of Police] at Muzaffarnagar and we decided to stop trains and did so. Even though Babaji [literally grandfather, i.e. Tikait] was not willing to accept this, we insisted to start a *rail roko* agitation. We did not listen to Chaudhary Sahab, and I was arrested from the station. BKU worked on the sound of Ransingha [a three feet long curved brass instrument which has been used to announce war or danger] in the past, but now the nonsense [*chekkar*] of portfolio distribution has destroyed our organization. So, all these posts should be abolished from now onwards!

Tikait left the centre of the meeting place and sat in a corner. Some office bearers went there showing him proof about what they had done during the agitation such as paper cuttings and diary notes. Some were showing Tikait allegedly false receipts issued by their opponents in BKU in the name of BKU. After five minutes Tikait came back to the centre of the stage and declared, 'From today, we abolish all the posts' (applause from majority). One person objected, 'There will be revolt in my district.' Tikait said, 'Sit down. I am not afraid of any revolt. Make a ten or eleven member committee which will take care of the organization and the affairs of the farmer.' Several people replied, 'You please form that committee yourself.'

The events at this meeting show that the BKU had developed ambitions of becoming a formal organization spanning the whole of UP. Though Jats of western UP have for long looked down on poor people from eastern UP, a large number of farmers from across the Ganga had become active in the organization. The meeting showed an ability to organize large-scale events. Still, the presence in Sisauli of large numbers of easterners during regular BKU meetings was an eyesore to many local people, not least to those opposed to Tikait.

A structure of authority had been created, though not exactly on the pattern of the BKU constitution, which specifies a larger number of representatives at district level (31), and at state level (61), and also a wider range of office-bearers than mentioned at this meeting. In the deliberations as to who was to participate in the executive meeting, no reference was made to the rules of the organization. Instead, reference was made to what was decided at a previous meeting. There was no procedure to reach and enforce a decision on participation. Even the rather arbitrary command by the leader that no more than five persons from each district could be present was unenforceable. Secondary leaders urged the primary leader to take action against those undermining the organization, but no detailed investigation was carried out against anybody. Instead, the question of alleged misconduct was bound up with the question of who had made personal sacrifices in the last agitation. This made it all the more difficult to decide who could participate: office bearers, those agreed upon in the last meeting, those who had sacrificed during the recent agitation, or the honest and hardworking members in general? At this point Tikait tried to break the stalemate first by acting as if he was the weak person being led by the movement, and then by challenging the gathering by questioning the very relevance of the meeting. He went on to contrast the high ideals set by the martyrs with the misconduct and cowardice of the present office-bearers. Tikait was supported by those who attributed the weakness to factionalism and the evil influence of educated people and politicians. This was supplemented by a threat from a person representing the original institutional base of the movement, i.e. the Balyan *khap*, to the effect that either all outsiders leave the organization, or the Balyans leave the organization. To further heighten the drama, the Treasurer of the BKU resigned—without any detailed discussion of accounts—whereupon the leader unilaterally abolished all posts of the BKU. Thus, the solution to the alleged mismanagement was not an investigation into any concrete act of mismanagement, but the abolition of posts held by those suspected of mismanagement. The matter of the letter-pads clearly shows the dilemma of the movement organization. To extend its sway over UP, the BKU had enrolled people from areas relatively unknown to the Jats of western UP. Armed with the weapons of bureaucracy, i.e. letter-pads on which letters could be written to the administration and others in the name of the BKU, these local leaders engaged in actions which the headquarters could not know about in any detail. Being basically averse to building up an administrative hierarchy, Tikait reacted to the crisis by dismantling the organizational structure. By this act of *organizational capacity destruction*, he hoped to smother internal dissent. As it was, the BKU remained formally without office bearers until a meeting in Hardwar on 15–17 August 1998. During this meeting, the old organizational structure was partly resurrected.

The organizational incapacity observed in 1998 can, in fact, be documented for an earlier period, probably from the start of the movement. In 1991, when Lindberg visited Sisauli for the second time—his first visit was in the spring of 1989—the BKU had built up an infrastructure with office facilities and an elaborate organization, but not all members followed the organizational rules. While some district presidents and other office bearers were more or less loyal to the organization (to Tikait, that is), others had started to go their own way, using the letterhead of BKU for their own purposes. In a national meeting in Kunda in 1992 there was a long discussion about these problems, and about whether BKU should form a political party. Tikait's view was that since the organization was weak because of lack of discipline and lack of sincerity among the volunteers, there was no point in forming a political party. At that time, too, Tikait had been in jail for eleven days following his agitation at Ram Kolla sugar factory, where farmers had not been paid for cane deliveries for eight months. The BKU had decided to court arrest, but very few activists actually did. Tikait criticized this and he also complained that nobody had come to see him while he was in jail. Lindberg interpreted these events as initial organizational difficulties that would be overcome as the BKU evolved. Now, years later, we may, perhaps, say that the movement has not been able to overcome these initial difficulties, and that the same pattern is repeated over and over again

DEFAULT ISSUES

Apart from the agricultural issues, which conventionally are of concern to farmers' organizations, the BKU has acted on issues only peripherally part of its formal agenda. Because any organization in South Asia which aspires to power sooner or later is expected to deliver justice (*insaf, nyaya*), and because, in any case, Tikait as a *khap* or *sarv khap* (all *khap*) headman is expected to sit in juridical panchayats, the BKU, too, has attained the status of a quasi-court.[10] Madsen has analysed one case in which Tikait played a judicial role dating from 1982, before the BKU became an important actor in the area (Madsen 1991). Apparently, Tikait has been engaged in several cases since then. It may be necessary to represent a particular group or faction to gain power, but to maintain power as a man of peace and compromise (a *panchayati admi*) it is advantageous not to be associated with a particular faction (Hitchcock 1971). We recount here one case to illustrate how difficult it may be for a leader, whose charisma is based partly on his role as traditional headman, to cash in on 'default issues'.

Around 1992, a Jat girl of Rathi clan from Dhundhahari village near Mansurpur married into a Balyan family in Barwala village near Shahpur town. When this girl died, her parents suspected that her in-laws had burned her to death. The people from the girl's village decided to approach Tikait for help, but he refused to call a panchayat. This refusal was interpreted by people in a cluster of Rathi-dominated villages as a sign that Tikait wanted to protect the Balyan family because he is himself Balyan. When asked why the Rathis had not approached their own headman, our informant replied that probably the Rathis do not have one, and that Tikait was the only influential Jat leader in the district. As a result of this affair, the Rathis from around Dhundhahari became angry with Tikait. Dhundhahari is the residence of a headstrong and radical female leader, Sohanviri, who for some time had supported the BKU. However, as a result of the strain building up between Sohanviri and Tikait, he replaced her with a Muslim woman from Muzaffarnagar city. Sohanviri subsequently formed a new organization, called the Kisan

Khap, at a gathering of 300–400 farmers in the compound of the Mansurpur sugar mill on 18 August 1998. However, she continued to attend BKU meetings. The case shows that the base on which Tikait originally built his career—his status as headman of the Balyan *khap*—became problematic as he expanded his scale of operation. As a big man he is required to settle disputes in his domain (Bentall and Corbridge 1996: 42). But it is difficult to do so without (appearing to be) taking sides.

Once enmity builds up within a group, it becomes difficult for the leader to carry out even rather non-controversial traditional tasks. One such task is the presentation of a turban (*pagri*) to the new head of a Jat family on the thirteenth day after the death of the father. At such a ritual in village Dhindawali near Bhagra, a certain Ved Pal Singh Balyan received turbans from a number of chaudharies from various *khaps*. However, Tikait, the head of Ved Pal's own *khap*, did not attend the ritual. In Tikait's absence another man from the Balyan *khap* offered Ved Pal the turban, urging him to take up the headmanship of the entire Balyan *khap*, the post which Tikait has held since he was young and which has been his base for building the BKU! Ved Pal declined the offer, but one of his younger brothers revealed to us that members of Ved Pal's family had already started processing disputes among Jats, and that they had also formed a Kisan Jagran Manch two years earlier, organizing farmers outside the BKU. We glimpse here the intimate relation between traditional values and expectations on the one hand, and the launching of movements and counter-movements on the other.

'MACHINES OF SIN'

So far, we have argued that the BKU aspires to be a formal membership organization open to all farmers but that, in reality, the BKU is a movement organization under charismatic leadership built on top of a clan-structure. But, as indicated in Figure 8.1, there is a fourth dimension to the BKU. In the eyes of some of its detractors, the BKU is a 'machine of sin', by which they mean that BKU has turned into a unit to maximize the material advantages of its leaders and members by questionable means. These advantages may be conceived of as a rent and the BKU may be seen as a 'rent-seeking unit'. 'Rent seeking' refers to non-productive activities directed towards creating opportunities for profits higher than would be obtained in an open, competitive market (Ostrom 1998: n 5).

In practice, it is difficult to draw a clear distinction between rent-seeking, political corruption, extortion and taxation. The following speech from a meeting illustrates how a critic perceives of the BKU as a machine of sin. It also provides a good example of what rent-seeking can be, in this case, the unauthorized auctioning of dead cattle. The meeting took take place on 9 September 1998 in village Mukundpur, not far from Shoron. The meeting was called to discuss *What we lost and what we gained in the last ten years under the leadership of Tikait.* The participants agreed that 'vehicles no longer raise dust in Sisauli', meaning that the BKU had become insignificant, but they were not sure how to react. Here follows the reasoning of Risal Singh 'Pradhan' from Dhindawali village:

There was no such word as 'organization' [*sangathan*] before Independence. . . . We were the people who started working for this organization. That Union [the BKU] has been kept in a secret way in the same manner as the police keeps an accused. Vir Bahadur was insulted at Sisauli [see n. 9]. Our elders never taught us this type of indiscipline. *Karma* [(good) work] is great, and discipline is an essential part of *karma*. Without discipline in an organization, it cannot work properly. Not only Tikait, but the members of his family, too, now have connections with the government. That is why people are unhappy with him. . . . There was a *jhor* in Harauli village which was turned into a political meeting. Tikait said there: '*Union to dhobion ki, teli, tange wallon ki hoti hai. In baton ko choro. Kucch aur bat karo*' [A Union is the sort of thing which washermen, oil pressers, horse-carriage drivers make. Not worth talking about. Talk about something else instead]. Tikait became too self-centred and started to think of himself as superior. . . .

Tikait has turned political! What happened to the electricity bills? He does not talk about education, health and social problems. All sorts of people have entered the BKU. BKU people have became involved in auctioning dead cattle saying that since the cattle are ours, therefore the leather is ours, too. They made money, but I ask where that money has gone? Nobody talks about this in Tikait's presence. The non-cooperation movement was against the British people on national issues, but after independence what is the use of these types of non-cooperation movements? All these are Tikait's machines of sin [*pap tantra*]. In the government where there is a ruling party, there is an opposition as well. But in the case of Tikait, if somebody says something which Tikait does not like, that person is considered anti-Tikait and an opponent. We oppose Tikait's wrong policies. He, too, has the right to say whatever he wants to say, but discipline is an essential element at every stage. At one time he supported one party, at another time he supported another party. The same was the case as regards political candidates and that only for his own self-interest.

The speaker notes that the BKU had made money by initiating unauthorized auctions. The Office of the Zila Panchayat collects about Rs 16 million annually in rural taxes, of which some Rs 5–6 million derive from auctioning the right to collect dead animals. In the Sisauli area, BKU activists had started issuing licenses to collect dead cattle as if the BKU were the government. In some cases, a contractor would have to buy licences both from the Zila Parishad and the BKU (interview with A.K. Pawar, 15 September 1998).

A whole range of accusations against the BKU was in circulation in the area. For example, the BKU supporters were said to steal food from pushcarts in Muzaffarnagar city during BKU agitations and behave rudely towards *bona fide* train-passengers while travelling ticketless to and from meetings and agitations. More seriously, it was said that Tikait had protected corrupt officials, with whom he shared clan or caste, against the genuine interests of the farmers. One case cited referred to a corrupt Jat employee in the Electricity Board, against whom Tikait had aborted a popular agitation. Another instance has already been cited (see p. 207). As the number of Jats employed outside agriculture increases and as Jats secure jobs that directly impact on the Jat farmers (unlike jobs in the army), it becomes increasingly difficult for the BKU to chose sides or balance its support.

This is also a dilemma for Tikait's family, which has initiated a process of economic diversification. One son works mainly on the farm. His reputation is the best. The second son works at a sugar mill, a job he got because the mill did not dare to refuse a request that he be employed. He is alleged to be rarely there to attend to this job. The third son resigned as policeman in Delhi or Haryana, and now works as a contractor taking up, *inter alia,* road contracts in rural areas of western UP. He resides in New Delhi, and his contact with farmers is basically that of a city dweller. Rumours in western UP persistently allege that he also acts as a political and financial intermediary in his father's dealings with high-level politicians and officials in Delhi and Lucknow. In February 2001, he was alleged to be supplanting Harpal Singh as the General Secretary of the BKU.

Formally, the BKU is 'apolitical', which means that it does not take part in party politics or run for electoral office. In practice, the BKU has extended or denied support to various politicians and parties over the years. Its connection to the heritage of Chaudhary Charan Singh is troubled: the BKU helped Ajit Singh, the son of Charan Singh, set up the Bharatiya Kisan Kamgar Party or BKKP, but later the relations between them soured. Since then, Ajit Singh has allied himself and his party with several other parties. A low point was reached in 1998 when Ajit Singh lost to the BJP in his father's old constituency, Baghpat, but, in one of those somersaults familiar to students of Indian politics, in 2001, he became Agriculture Minister in the BJP-dominated government.

When the BJP was on its way to power, the BKU extended some verbal support to this party (Gupta 1997: 81). Given that the Jats for decades have considered the BJP the party of the Banias and the Brahmins, this tacit support to the BJP was a turn-around. The BKU's support for the BJP on the Ayodhaya issue is said to have cost the movement the support of many Muslims and *kisans* from the Other Backward Classes (Bentall and Corbridge 1996: 44; Gupta 1997: 79, 158). In early 1999, Tikait even began talking favourably about the Congress, the party from which Jat farmers have distanced themselves since Charan Singh broke with it in the mid-1960s. In the 2002 UP Vidhan Sabha elections, several parties, including the BJP, the SP, and the BKKP, vied for votes from the class of farmers who used to support the BKU.

Farmers do not need to channel all their demands through one political party (Corbridge 1997: 433). Indeed, it has been possible for the BKU to gain influence by strategically supporting one or the other rising party as new windows opened up in the political opportunity structure. However, being an apolitical force, the BKU should ideally remain equidistant from all parties. Its failure to do so has served to bracket it with political parties in the eyes of many of its followers. Moreover, its declining ability to extract collective benefits for its political support undermines its status.

The BKU in Punjab

At this point it may be useful to look beyond the UP scene and ask: Is what we have seen in UP typical of farmers' movements in other parts of India? Is the oscillation between being a traditional institution, an active farmers' movement, a formally organized pressure group and a opportunistic and rent-seeking 'machine of sin' found elsewhere?

The closest relatives of the BKU in UP in the farmers' movement family are the BKUs in Punjab and Haryana. In this section, we will focus on the BKU in the Punjab. Compared to its relative in UP, the BKU in Punjab is older, dating back to the early 1970s. In terms of caste-wise recruitment, the Punjab BKU, too, mainly relies on Jats for support, but this is hardly surprising since the large majority of land-holding farmers in Punjab are Sikh Jats. Like the BKU in UP, the BKU in Punjab has a reputation for being secular and has tried to mobilize farmers as farmers, irrespective of their religion, for non-religious purposes. As we have seen, the BKU in UP was initially able to maintain this non-denominational character, but it subsequently took a stand on religious issues in favour of the BJP.

In Punjab, the mobilization drive of the BKU peaked in March 1984, when it staged a siege (*gherao*) of the governor's residence in the capital, Chandigarh, by roughly 40,000–60,000 farmers. The farm-ers' demands concerned agricultural support prices and a hike in the electricity tariff, but farmers also threatened to withhold grain from the market and deny officials and politicians access to the villages. After Operation Blue Star in June the same year, during which the Indian army attacked secessionist forces within the Golden Temple in Amritsar, the political opportunity structure for the open and relatively non-violent mass movement that BKU had led narrowed down consi-derably. Instead, the BKU was caught between the extremely violent, clandestine Khalistani secessionist movement and an increasingly re-pressive state apparatus. The various factions of the Khalistani move-ment recruited their cadres to a large extent from Sikh Jat farmers, and so did the police. The BKU had little room for manoeuvre in this battle.[11] Agricultural production and marketing were surprisingly un-affected by the period of terror. Hence, the BKU found little ground for mobilization on this account (Omvedt 1993: 121–4). The fact is that BKU was a weak force in Punjab from 1984 to around 1992.

After the defeat of the Khalistani movement, the Akali Dal re-emerged as the dominant political party of the state, and with it the BKU re-emerged as a movement. In 1997, the then Akali Dal government led by Prakash Singh Badal conceded the long-standing demand for cheaper electricity for irrigation purposes. In fact, the government announced that farmers would have to pay no user charges at all! The decision to meet—and even exceed—one of the basic demands of the BKU seems to have taken the air out of BKU for 'if the society changes in the direction of the MO's goals, the organization's reason for being no longer exists' (Zald and Ash 1969: 465). In a similar manner, in 1997, the Punjab government was able to negotiate a bonus of Rs 55 per quintal of wheat on top of the Rs 410 support price announced by the Commission on Agricultural Costs and Prices. In the following year, the chief ministers of Punjab and Haryana were able to put pressure on the newly installed BJP-led coalition government in Delhi to increase the support price to Rs 455. This price was further augmented with a bonus of Rs 60.

The Akali Dal-led government had also been able to pre-empt or dampen BKU agitations on other issues. For example, after coming to power the government had taken steps to deal with the serious water-logging affecting cotton-growing farmers in the south-western part of the state. When interviewed in the spring of 1998 many farmers, including former BKU activists, had expressed their satisfaction with the manner in which the government had solved their problem.

Because the Akali Dal has re-established its position as the political party of the Sikh farmers in Punjab, the BKU has been largely robbed of the opportunity to play different parties against each other by promising electoral support to the party most willing to support its demands. Instead, the BKU has split into several factions that 'mirror' or reproduce streams within the Akali Dal. Thus, the Akali Dal and the BKU both include capitalist and socialist constituencies. Within the BKU two main factions have emerged since 1988–9. One faction (which may be called the Liberal BKU), lead by Bhupinder Singh Mann and Balbir Singh Rajewal, stands for liberalization of the agricultural economy and free international trade in agricultural products and inputs. The other (which may be called the Nationalist BKU), led by Ajmer Singh Lakhowal, stands for a socialist position which sees state intervention as necessary for the development of agriculture. Leaders from both of these factions regularly try to negotiate privileged entry into the Akali Dal with reference to their BKU support base. In 1995, a further split took place within the latter faction when a group called BKU Ekta, under the leadership of Pashoura Singh of Fateh Garh Sahib District, was formed. This group stands for what we may call a radical nationalist position propagating strong state intervention in the interest of small and middle farmers. This group has a Maoist creed, and links up accordingly with established political forces outside the Akali Dal.

The contrast to UP is quite clear: In UP the BKU has not been subsumed under any political party in the service of which it has been able to deploy its followers. In particular, the BKU has not closely allied itself with the BKKP, the party ostensibly continuing the heritage of Charan Singh. The BKU has also had little opportunity or inclination to ally itself with Maoists. Instead, it has sought influence by maintaining its status as an 'apolitical force', extending qualified support to different parties in Lucknow as well as in Delhi. In fact, its direct links with Ajit Singh, Deve Gowda and V.P. Singh in New Delhi have often been more important than its links with leaders and parties in Lucknow. As the state of UP has undergone a process of political fragmentation, the BKU has found itself increasingly marginalized. The rise to power of the BSP-BJP coalition under the leadership of Mayawati is testimony to this.

The absence of enduring links with any particular party may have spared the BKU in UP from developing factions along the lines of a dominant party, thereby keeping the BKU loosely united. By laying its eggs in several political baskets, it has tried to adapt itself to the changing political scene in UP. Its loosely organized network has allowed farmers in different parts of the state to gain access to local politicians and bureaucrats, but the lack of access to a strong party has also made it difficult for the movement to extract sufficient payoffs to maintain its momentum. Hence, it has been forced to rely on assorted 'machines of sin' to provide individual and collective benefits to its followers.[12]

The BKU in UP has had to deal with the fact that the economic interests of the farming families are no longer limited to agriculture. As discussed above, economic diversification has sometimes landed the BKU in UP in a crisis of loyalty between the farming and non-farming interests of Jats. This problem is more severe in Punjab, where a large number of Sikh Jats have made investments outside their farm. In particular, many Sikh Jats now operate as commissioned agents on the grain markets. This puts a heavy strain on the BKU in Punjab, and the split of the BKU into various factions is not unrelated to this relatively recent development. In UP, the grain markets are still dominated by the trading castes, but the BKU has not been able to mount a concerted attack on the merchants and moneylenders in these markets. Many farmers in western UP operate small-scale cane processing plants (*kolhus*) producing unrefined sugar (*gur*). The BKU has not mobilized against these entrepreneurs either, thereby avoiding a split between farmers and small rural industrialists of the same or related caste. Altogether, the BKU in UP has taken a position corresponding to that of the 'Nationalist BKU' in Punjab.

Thus the history of the BKU in Punjab has been influenced by the fact that the movement organization has existed under the umbrella of a strong political party. Despite its perpetual factionalism, the Akali Dal has maintained a hold over the same section of farmers—the landed Sikh Jats—that the BKU appeals to. During the period of civil war in Punjab, the Akali Dal was pushed into the background by Khalistani forces. Though some BKU-followers may have joined these forces, the BKU did not, and hence it was swamped by the wave of terror and counter-terror. The oscillations which the BKU in Punjab has experienced are therefore of a different kind than those we have identified in UP.

THE TRAGEDY THAT IS UP

We have tried to demonstrate in this article how and why the 'institutional fate' of a farmers' organization changes over time, stressing the internal dynamics of that institution. This paper has tried to alert the reader to the likelihood of other outcomes than the standard transformation of a movement into a formal, bureaucratized and hierarchical organization. The transformation of the BKU into a political party has, so far, been ruled out by the principles of the movement. As we demonstrated in our discussion of the crisis management capacity of the BKU, its transformation into a non-political interest group is made difficult by its unwillingness and inability to invest in 'form' (Friedberg 1996). Further, the potential of the BKU to sustain and transform itself on the basis of clan, caste and panchayat was seen to be limited. In the absence of other options, we noted that the movement had to take recourse to various forms of rent extraction. In the end, the organization oscillates between various forms, unable to derive any lasting advantage from a process of formalization.

Our argument took its point of departure from classical sociological theory dealing with organizational transformation and formalization. According to a recent summary of the literature on formal organizations by Friedberg, this literature

always rests on the idea of a clear division, as if formalization introduced a sort of discontinuity or disruption into the field of action. On the one hand there is the world of formal organizations, which is characterized by control and submission, by capitalization of knowledge, by transparency and predictability, by clear structure and absence of competition, in short by all the features which, from a functionalist point of view, can 'explain' the success and multiplication of organizations. On the other hand there is the world of the 'market', of 'collective action' or 'social movement'—a world that is built on competition, process and change, on a sort of unstructured, disordinate and hazardous interaction, on fluidity, equality and the absence of hierarchy. (Friedberg 1996: 108)

We accepted the idea of such a basic distinction, and added two dimensions along which formalization might occur. However, recent organization theory has questioned the classical model, arguing that,

A large number of fields of action in a great variety of areas are structured and regulated according to a combination of formal and informal, explicit or implicit rules, regulations, conventions and contracts. In all of these fields, the 'constitutional rules' form but the basis of what could be called the 'constitutional practice' which backs up the constitution while deviating from it, which weakens the constitution on some points while strengthening it on others, and vice versa (ibid., p. 113). . . . In the end, formalization turns out to be an artificial dividing line, which marks a difference in emphasis rather than substance. (ibid.: 115)

Our reading of the case of BKU does not incline us to agree that formalization can be discounted as an artificial dividing line. Rather, we have argued that the manner in which the BKU in UP has dealt with its organizational dilemmas speaks of serious long-term shortcomings, and at least partly explains its institutional fate. Fuzziness leaves scope for the leader to exert charismatic control, but fuzziness does not always pay off.

We have also stressed that the fate of the BKU depends on the political opportunity structure within which it operates. Perhaps we should add that not only does the BKU operate within a certain structure, in the last instance it is a child of the environment to which it belongs. The inter-organizational environment, the state of UP, is characterized by failures rather than successes. A couple of decades ago the UP was 'the nerve centre of Indian politics' (Hasan 1998: 5) and a pioneer in 'carefully-conceived' land reforms (Brass 1993: 2088). Now the 'resilient inertia' (Drèze and Gazdar 1997: 93) of its state apparatus, the machinations of its politicians, and the unbridled 'quest for power' of its social movements (Hasan 1998) have conspired to push the state close to sub-Saharan standards of living (Drèze and Gazdar 1997: 39) and occasionally to the brink of anarchy. In this perspective, the failures of the BKU are but one instance of the tragedy that is UP.[13] The trouble is that UP's state failures are compounded by civil society's community failures.

NOTES

1. Recent literature on the BKU in UP includes Bentall (1995); Bentall and Corbridge (1997); Gupta (1997); Hasan (1998); Kant (1995); Rana (1994). New farmers' movements' are discussed in T. Brass (1994); Omvedt (1993); and Varshney (1995).

2. The ground water in the Budhana area is 16 m lower than in most other parts of the district. Farmers have to dig deep to reach an assured supply (interview with Ashok Kumar, Swami Kalyan Dev Krishi Vigyan Kendra, Bagra, Titawi, Muzafffarnagar on 1.4.98). At one point, Tikait argued for lower electricity rates for areas with deeper water-levels. This was opposed by farmers not living in Meerut and Muzaffarnagar (Singh 1992: 117, n. 87).

3. The spatial dimensions of the historical trajectories of the Doab may be culled from Stokes (1978).

4. In 1987 Tikait is reported to have said at a meeting where the rural poor were his hosts: '*Ek dhoti wala hai, ek langoti wale. Aur langoti wala dhoti wale ko dekh kar jal raha hai*' (One [the Jat rural rich] is wearing full clothes, another [the rural poor Chamar] is wearing underwear. The latter is jealous of the former). This zero-sum statement 'incensed' the rural poor (Singh 1992: 104).

5. The English term 'to harass' is often used for any action by public authorities which is deemed negative by a person interacting with the government, whether or not that person is entitled to a public good or not.

6. Information from Mahipal Singh Tomar.

7. One tactic of political campaigns in India is to fill the jails (*jail bharo abhyan*) to demonstrate injustice, the Gandhian logic being that only good people sacrifice by going to jail, and that only bad people jail good people (see also Bentall and Corbridge 1997: 42).

8. The Kisan Bhawan is a guest house with facilities like a basic swimming pool, three guest rooms, a common kitchen, a large meeting ground with a statue of Chaudhury Charan Singh, and the memorial items associated with the martyrs of the movement (*shahidi kisan*). The records of the BKU are kept in a steel cupboard in the Kisan Bhawan.

9. One of the boldest actions of Tikait occurred in 1987 when Vir Bahadur Singh, the Chief Minister of UP, had come to Sisauli village to negotiate with the BKU. Seated on the dais, the chief minister indicated that he would like to have some water: 'Tikait gestured that he should help himself from the water pitcher that was kept for this purpose near the microphone' (Gupta 1997: 70). This was a very impolite form of behaviour by any standard. A chief minister on visit to a village is to be waited on and served personally, or by a suitable servant.

10. According to lawyers in Muzaffarnagar, the BKU does not use the state legal machinery to further its causes.

11. See Porta (1995) for a study of the inter-connections between open mass movements and closed violent movements in Europe.

12. See Olson (1965) for the notion of collective and individual benefits.

13. The theme of UP as a 'tragedy' is not new: see Verma (1980).

9

Soft States, Hard Bargains: Rich Farmers, Class Reproduction and the Local State in Rural North India

Craig Jeffrey

Many scholars have referred to the emergence of a class of rich farmers in western UP (Jeffery and Jeffery 1997; Lerche 1995; Lieten 1996; Singh 1992; Wadley 1994) and other parts of northern and western India (Breman 1985; Rutten 1995). The relative wealth and power of this class is often viewed as a function of their control over the agricultural means of production, a propensity to hire labour, and a capacity to influence policy at state and Centre levels.[1] There has been much less work on the relationship between rural élites and local state institutions.[2] This paper serves as a corrective.[3] I shall explore how an agrarian élite in rural western UP has sought to consolidate and extend their local power by 'colonizing' and co-opting state institutions.

My approach to the state has been strongly influenced by the work of Barbara Harriss-White, one of the few to link the political power of rural élites at the state level with local social networks involving India's 'intermediate classes' and government officials (Harriss-White 1996b; Harriss-White 1997). Harriss-White analyses how merchants and state officials in Coimbatore District collude to manipulate the market, and state interventions in the market, to their advantage (Harriss-White 1996b: 299–302). Merchants openly and routinely bribe state officials and take advantage of unofficial markets in licences and skills (Harriss-White 1996b: 299–300). The ability of merchants to capture such resources is related to their colonization of the state. A number of traders have successfully acquired government jobs and infiltrated state institutions designed to reduce their power. Many merchants possess close kinship connections with those employed by the state, including politicians. In this context, state authority is perceived to reside increasingly in the 'private status'—the class, ethnicity, locality, gender and age—of dispersed state agents (Harriss-White 1996b: 301; see also Harriss-White 1997). The shape and nature of 'shadow states', existing parallel with the formal state, depend on the strategies of state officials and intermediaries and the ways in which they negotiate between their bureaucratic and non-bureaucratic roles (Harriss-White 1997: 11).

Drawing on these theoretical insights, this paper explores the economic and social strategies of Jat male farmers in Meerut District. After a brief description of Meerut District and the nature of fieldwork, I outline class differences in the three villages in which I worked, with reference to the dominant Jat caste and less advantaged groups. I then focus on the means by which rich Jat farmers seek to secure police protection and government employment.

I use land-ownership as a basis for examining links between material wealth and social and economic action. Utsa Patnaik has objected to the use of land-ownership as a tool of class analysis, arguing that there is no necessary relationship between the size of a landholding and propensity to practice capitalist agriculture and hire in agricultural labour (Patnaik 1971: A–128). This objection does not hold in Meerut District, where almost all Jat households are engaged in capitalist agriculture, and there is a close relationship between land size and propensity to hire labour. Patnaik also warns against using land as a proxy for class, since some rural households may have sold land in an effort to obtain control over alternative means of wealth accumulation. However, unlike rich agrarian capitalists in other parts of India, Jats in Meerut District have been loath to sell land in order to finance off-farm enterprise. My analysis anticipates a broader critique of using land as basis for stratification by exploring the extent to which, and why, land-ownership is correlated with other forms of economic and social power.

CLASS DIFFERENTIATION IN UP:
THE CASE OF MEERUT DISTRICT

This account draws on twelve months' fieldwork conducted in Meerut District, western UP. According to the 1991 Census, the population of Meerut District is 3.448 million, of which 37.0 per cent live in urban areas (Registrar General India 1991).[4] Scheduled Castes constitute 16.6 per cent of the population (Registrar General India 1991). In the 1931 Census, the population of Jats in Meerut District is said to be

12.1 per cent (Census of India 1931). According to the Settlement Report of 1940, they owned 24.7 per cent of the land (Cooke 1940, quoted in Singh 1992: 18).

Meerut District forms part of the flat and fertile Upper Doab. The rich loamy soils and high water table in this region support intensive sugar cane and wheat cultivation. Within Meerut District, these two crops covered 34.7 per cent and 31.8 per cent of the cultivated area respectively in 1987 (Singh 1992: 25). Following the widespread introduction of HYVs, chemical fertilizer, and electric tube well irrigation between the mid-1960s and mid-1980s, agricultural yields rose steeply and much of the land of the district is sown in an intensive sugar, wheat and fodder-based rotation (see Sharma and Poleman 1993). In 1987–8, 72.7 per cent of irrigation was provided by privately-owned tube wells, and many agricultural operations in the district are now mechanized (ibid.). There has also been a significant growth in manufacturing and service industries in Meerut District during the past thirty years (Sharma and Poleman 1993: 111–12).

My field research was concentrated in the township of Daurala and the two villages of Masuri and Khanpur. These settlements are located within 25 km of Meerut. In each settlement Jats constitute between a third and a half of the total population. Table 9.1 provides details of the total and Scheduled Caste (SC) populations of Daurala, Masuri and Khanpur and figures for the number of cultivators and agricultural labourers in each settlement.

I focus on the economic, social and political strategies of members of four Jat lineages. The genealogical tables of these lineages stretch back at least ten generations, and were constructed from the memory of respondents and the official records of the village genealogist (*bhat*) for each settlement. Information was collected on the structure and

Table 9.1: Basic Statistics Relating to Daurala Town and the Villages of Masuri and Khanpur, Meerut District

	Population	Scheduled Caste	Number of cultivators	Number of agricultural labourers
Daurala town	10,025	2,477	734	750
Masuri	4,373	1,484	360	328
Khanpur	4,913	520	427	438

Source: Village/Town Primary Census Abstract 1991.

landholding of all 250 income-sharing households within these four lineages, and the schooling and occupation of the members of each household.

   In addition, I conducted eighty intensive interviews on household strategies, social links and political activity, and affiliations of male household heads of selected rural and urban households within the lineage. Fifteen detailed interviews, spread between the three settlements, were aimed at establishing the economic condition, social connections and political activity and affiliations of randomly chosen Scheduled Caste (male) household heads. I collected basic occupational and schooling data for the wider kinship unit within which these households are located. Thirteen interviews were conducted in an identical fashion with a group of households comprising the most economically disadvantaged castes within the category of Other Backward Castes (OBCs). Following Pai and Singh (1997), I refer to these former service castes, which include Kumhars, Dhimars, Goswamis, Lohars, Telis and Julahas, as the Most Backward Castes (MBCs). Two Muslim male household heads were also interviewed. In addition, I conducted interviews with a number of policemen, lawyers, land officials and politicians aimed at establishing the link between class reproduction and the local state.[5]

CLASS DIFFERENTIATION AND AGRARIAN CHANGE

Jats own 90 per cent of the agricultural land in each of the three settlements, and 12 per cent of the Jats possess over 12 acres.[6] Only 32.9 per cent of the 73 SC households and 7.1 per cent of the 70 MBC households within the sample owned agricultural land. In all but one case these households owned less than 4 acres.

   Between 1965 and 1985, almost all Jats possessing over 12 acres of land intensified their agricultural production through investment in electric tube well irrigation and tractors, the adoption of improved varieties of sugar cane and wheat, and the application of chemical fertilizers. The resulting increase in agricultural yields, combined with favourable state procurement prices for cane and wheat, increased the rates of return from agriculture. An acre of sugar cane yielded a profit of around Rs 9,500 a year in 1997 (roughly the annual income of a farm servant).[7] Most farmers cultivating over 2 acres of land opt for intensive cash crop rotations based on sugar cane, employ tractors and tube wells, and apply chemical fertilizer. A substantial number of the larger farmers have recently included a relatively capital- and labour-intensive potato crop in their agricultural rotations.

Managerial pressures operating on richer farmers, combined with an increase in off-farm employment opportunities for rural labourers, are largely responsible for a decline in coercive forms of 'customary' labour. Male labourers are no longer at the beck and call of richer farmers during periods of peak agricultural labour demand (compare with Singh 1992: 70–1; see also Lerche 1998: A–31). The majority of farmers cultivating over 6 acres employ temporary workers for the most labour-intensive agricultural activities using task-specific, piece-rate contracts paid in cash. These contracts allow farmers to maintain control over decisions relating to agricultural production while passing the responsibility for the supervision of labour to the leader of the contract team.

A number of richer farmers have also attempted to avoid paying higher wages to local labourers by hiring labourers from Bihar on contracts of between six and nine months. The desire to combine agricultural land ownership with off-farm employment or social activity has also led a number of larger landowners to move over to mango cultivation run on the basis of yearly contracts. A shift amongst richer farmers towards less direct involvement in physical labour or supervision within agriculture, and the associated rise of temporary contract labour, has been noted by other scholars working in the Upper Doab (Lerche 1998; Singh 1992; Srivastava 1996).[8]

CLASS REPRODUCTION AND PUBLIC-SECTOR EMPLOYMENT

The move towards more 'managerial' agricultural regimes is associated with occupational diversification within rural households. For much of the twentieth century, rich Jat farmers have sought to reduce economic risk and raise their social status through investing in efforts at acquiring public-sector employment.[9] This is associated with a series of 'push' and 'pull' factors (see Jeffrey 1999). The most important push factor has been the rapid subdivision of agricultural land due to the system of partible inheritance. Pull factors include the social standing, local political purchase and illegal side-incomes that public-sector employment provides. Relative to off-farm business and a slowly expanding range of salaried posts in the private sector, government employment is lucrative and secure. Those with government posts obtain pensions and are often entitled to a range of other perks, such as subsidized travel, health care and education. In western UP, as in other areas of India, a 'government job', even a low-ranking post as a peon or state bus conductor, is perceived to secure a household's future.

The 'shift' into public-sector employment amongst Jats in western UP has been a gradual process. Before 1947, a small number of Jats from the largest landowning families were inducted into the British system of local administration. These men benefited from colonial stereotypes stressing the honesty of the Jats (Stokes 1986) and the spread of the Arya Samaj movement in western UP, which promoted schooling, social advancement and ideals of community service (see Dutta 1997).

My field research suggests a more pronounced move into off-farm employment amongst the Jats in the 1950s and 1960s. As Table 9.2 reveals, 14 per cent of Jats raised in households possessing more than 12 acres of agricultural land and born in the period 1922–46 entered 'higher' professional employme t, which I have defined as medicine and tertiary-level teaching, law, engineering and Grade I or II government service. An additional 25 per cent of Jats in this category entered less prestigious 'lower professional' employment: primary or secondary teaching, Grade III or IV positions in the police or state bureaucracies, and managerial or supervisory posts in private or public manufacturing units. In families possessing less than 12 acres, there is a more substantial move into salaried employment: 45 per cent moved into 'lower professional' positions. Significantly, none of the young Jat men from families possessing less than 12 acres of land entered 'higher professional' employment. It is also notable that very few Jats born between 1922 and 1946 established themselves in off-farm business.

The Jat move out of agriculture has continued since the early 1970s, in spite of positive discrimination in government employment for the so-called Other Backward Classes (OBCs), introduced in UP in 1977 and extended in the mid-1990s under Mulayam Singh Yadav.[10] Table 9.3 shows that 11 per cent of the men born after 1946 to richer Jat farmers have entered 'higher professional' employment. These men have effectively used low-ranking professional or white-collar employment in the public sector as a fallback option. Amongst those born after 1946 into rich farming families, there has been a cautious move into business. Since 1970, fourteen men raised in households owning more than 12 acres of land have engaged in off-farm enterprise. Three

Table 9.2: *Principal Occupation of Male Jats in the Four Lineages, Born between 1922 and 1946, by Employment and Landholding of Guardian*

[*nos.* (*in %*)]

Occupation of guardian	Occupation of Jat men born 1922–46					
	Farming	Business	Higher prof.	Lower prof. Low public sector	Unemployed	Total
Farmer or lower professional with more than 12 acres	60 (38)	0 (0)	14 (9)	25 (16)	0 (0)	63
Farmer or lower professional with 12 acres or less	50 (21)	2 (1)	0 (0)	45 (19)	2 (1)	42
Higher professional	7 (1)	20 (3)	40 (6)	33 (5)	0 (0)	15
Businessman	0 (0)	100 (5)	0 (0)	0 (0)	0 (0)	5
Total	48 (60)	7 (9)	12 (15)	32 (40)	1 (1)	125

Source: Interviews with Jat male heads of household conducted between January and December 1997 in Daurala, Masuri and Khanpur.

Note: In this and subsequent tables, percentages may not add up to 100 due to rounding.

Table 9.3. *Principal Occupation of Male Jats in the Four Lineages, Born after 1946, by Employment and Landholding of Guardian*

[*nos. (in %)*]

Occupation of guardian	Occupation of Jat men born after 1946						
	Farming	Business	Higher prof.	Lower prof. Low public-sector	Labour	Unmployed	Total
Farmer or lower professional with more than 12 acres	53 (42)	9 (7)	11 (9)	26 (21)	1 (1)	0 (0)	80
Farmer lower professional or labourer with 12 acres or less	32 (61)	6 (11)	2 (4)	35 (66)	18 (34)	7 (14)	190
Higher professional	23 (7)	7 (2)	39 (12)	32 (10)	0 (0)	0 (0)	31
Businessman	17 (2)	50 (6)	17 (2)	17 (2)	0 (0)	0 (0)	12
Total	36 (12)	8 (26)	9 (27)	32 (99)	11 (35)	4 (14)	313

Source: Interviews with Jat male heads of household conducted between January and December 1997 in Daurala, Masuri and Khanpur.

of them run shops, two are involved in urban land speculation, two are engaged in the trade of clothes and one runs a tractor dealership. In addition, one man supplies sand to a sugar mill on contract, one constructs roads on government contracts and two are involved in illegal trade in conjunction with their public-sector employment. Jats have been discouraged from entering into trade in agricultural products by the existence of dense and opaque non-Jat networks of merchants in western UP. In this respect, Jats differ from rich farmers in Tamil Nadu (Harriss-White 1996a: 92; Harriss-White 1996b: 238–9) and south Gujarat (Rutten 1995) where the use of cheap household labour and forms of state support have facilitated a move into agricultural trade amongst elite cultivating castes.

The figures for Jats born after 1946 support the notion that Jats born into households possessing less than 12 acres find it difficult to enter 'higher professional' employment. But young men in this category have been quite successful in securing low-ranking white-collar work. Table 9.3 shows that 35 per cent of Jats born after 1946 descended from Jats possessing 12 acres or less have entered 'lower professional' employment. Most of these men have entered low-ranking government, army, police, teaching, and factory employment. A small number of households possessing less than 12 acres have entered off-farm business, usually owning and running shops, small transport businesses, or agricultural processing units.

As in other areas of India, the occupational diversification of the rural élite in Meerut District has been bound up with increased investment in the formal schooling of children. Table 9.4 reveals a large increase in the schooling of Jats within the four lineages. A high school (Standard X) pass is necessary for most forms of public-sector employment and further qualifications may increase the ability of young Jats to negotiate examinations and interviews for government employment. Since the early 1980s, rich Jat farmers in the three villages have opted to send their children to urban English-medium non-state schools. These households have also begun to search for educational opportunities outside Meerut District and India. There has been an associated rise in forms of tuition outside school, coaching institutes and centres geared to prepare young Jats for competitive exams. Jat families also attempt to use the prevalent system of in-caste, arranged marriage to increase the chance of their sons obtaining jobs. Large dowries are used to negotiate access to well-placed grooms in this competitive market.[11]

The 'success' of Jat diversification strategies should not be over-

Table 9.4. *Schooling of Jat Males within the Four Lineages Born between 1898 and 1972*

[*nos. (in %)*]

	None	5th	8th	10th	12th	BA	MA	Total
1898–1922	42 (27)	28 (18)	8 (5)	11 (7)	8 (5)	2 (1)	3 (2)	100 (65)
1923–47	13 (15)	19 (22)	13 (15)	19 (22)	20 (23)	8 (9)	10 (12)	100 (118)
1948–72	7 (14)	6 (11)	7 (13)	19 (37)	19 (38)	14 (27)	30 (60)	100 (200)
Total	15 (56)	13 (51)	9 (33)	17 (66)	17 (66)	10 (37)	19 (74)	100 (383)

Source: Interviews with male heads of household in the four lineages. These were conducted between January and December 1997 in Daurala, Masuri and Khanpur.

Note: Percentage do not all add to 100 because of rounding.

stated. Table 9.3 shows that 18 per cent of the less affluent men born after 1946 have moved into semi-skilled or unskilled casual labour, usually as private drivers or factory workers. These men, like those who term themselves *berozgari* (unemployed), have usually spent large amounts of time engaged in a fruitless search for secure salaried employment. Nevertheless, and taken as a whole, the Jats in my sample have fared much better than the lower castes and Muslims in securing white-collar and professional employment. Table 9.5 shows that Jats have been about five times more successful than the low castes and Muslims that I surveyed in obtaining 'higher professional' employment and nearly three times as successful in securing low-ranking professional jobs. Most low-caste and Muslim households lack the assets and access to formal credit that would provide the basis for profitable off-farm business. As a result, the majority of SC, MBC and Muslim men in my sample are confined to unskilled or semi-skilled wage labour.

This general picture should not obscure the emergence of a numerically small but often politically important low-caste middle class since the 1960s. Table 9.5 shows that 34 SC, MBC or Muslim men in the three villages have managed to enter professional or public-sector employment. The emergence of a thin stratum of low-caste white-collar workers has been closely linked to their increased education: 30 per cent of male SCs, MBCs and Muslims born between 1947 and 1972 obtained a high school pass. This phenomenon is also a result of positive discrimination for SCs and MBCs. The five SCs who entered the police or public-sector clerical employment in the 1960s in the three sample villages all benefited from reservations, and subsequently assisted relatives in their search for public-sector positions.

The evidence presented in Tables 9.2, 9.3 and 9.4 suggests that the commercialization of agriculture and expansion of public-sector employment opportunities since 1947 has raised the social and economic position of the Jats in rural Meerut District. These processes have also encouraged class differentiation within the Jat caste. Elsewhere I have characterized this shift as a move amongst the rural élite from a direct mode of social reproduction, where advantage is passed down to the next generation through the transfer of property, to mediated reproduction, whereby privilege is simultaneously reproduced through the transmission of schooling credentials and other skills (Bourdieu 1996; see Jeffrey 2001). In contrast, the low castes and Muslims appear to have found it difficult to diversify into secure salaried employment and remain tied to poorly paid and insecure labouring work.

Table 9.5: *Principal Occupation of Male Jats in the Four Lineages and Males belonging to the Low Caste and Muslim Households Sampled*

[nos. (in %)]

	Farming	Business	Higher prof.	Lower prof. and low-rank public-sector	Labour	Unemployed	Total
Jats	158 (38.3)	35 (8.5)	43 (10.4)	127 (30.8)	35 (8.5)	15 (3.6)	413
SCs, MBCs and Muslims	3 (1.3)	32 (12.9)	5 (2.0)	29 (11.7)	171 (69.0)	8 (3.2)	248

Source: Interviews with Jat male heads of household and SC, MBC and Muslim male household heads conducted between January and December 1997 in Daurala, Masuri and Khanpur.

CLASS FORMATION AND THE LOCAL STATE

The power of the landed Jat élite is reproduced through a range of strategic efforts at manipulating, co-opting and colonizing village representative bodies (panchayats), the educational bureaucracy, and the protective arms of the state. These processes of co-option are poorly understood. In this section I shall focus on the Jat dual strategy of maintaining connections with local police officials and seeking public-sector positions for their children.[12]

(1) *Class Power and Access to the Police*

Rural people in Meerut District place a premium on maintaining 'good relations' with the local police service. Reliable and trusted contacts within the police are regarded as important in order to safeguard one's family and property. As Paul Brass (1997) has shown in his study of rural and small town violence in UP, police and judicial protection has become almost wholly privatized in this part of India: a valued resource in the competition for power and privilege.

Scarcities in information associated with the 'shadow state' in police protection and the desire for rents amongst local big-men, politicians and senior police officers appear to have encouraged the emergence of a range of mediators between rural clients seeking police help and low-ranking police officers. The following statement from a former MLA is consistent with many other descriptions of how farmers obtain police help.

CJ: You have said that it is difficult for farmers to get police help—so what do they actually do when there is a theft?
Ex-MLA: The farmer will approach the MLA with the problem. The MLA will then phone or go to the police station or SP's office [Superintendent of Police's office]. The police officer will either say 'give me this much and I will get your work done' or it will just work with influence. The MLA will go back [to the farmer] and say 'he has asked for 15,000 rupees', when in fact he only asked for 10,000. So politicians have become like commission agents. (former Member of the Legislative Assembly, Meerut, 21 November 1997)[13]

The key importance of politicians in obtaining access to the police and other state institutions encourages rural people to cultivate friendly relationships with local MLAs or MPs, but the numerous interviews that I conducted with rural people suggest that they rarely do this directly. Rather, rural people work through mediators—they might be described as 'lobbyists'—who live in the village and maintain close personal relations with politicians. These 'gatekeepers' of the local state tend to be younger and better educated than the large landowners who presided over land disputes and provided access to state officials before Independence. Their mediation may be the opportunity to extract a rent, individually or in league with a politician. This form of political activity may also provide a platform for a political career either inside the village or at the district or MLA constituency level.

It would be misleading to imply that the process of seeking police help is a neat or predictable process. Nevertheless, the stories that I collected while working in Daurala, Masuri and Khanpur usually pointed to quite a well-defined chain of negotiations within patron-client networks. In the first place, a member of the public usually seeks the assistance of a lobbyist—often a relation or member of the same caste/community. The lobbyist proceeds to approach a local politician who may agree to lend his weight to the cause by taking the case to a senior police official.[14] If the bribe or pressure persuades the senior official, (s)he may instruct local (junior) officials to take up the case. With the exception of the last stage of the process, the petitioner(s) may exert pressure or offer bribes in return for assistance at each point in the chain. In this context, the ability of a member of the public to secure state assistance is inversely proportional to the number of mediators through which they operate and the size of the bribes that they must pay in order to guarantee help.

There is a striking correlation between land size and the ability to activate these networks of assistance effectively. All but two of the nineteen Jats of the four lineages strongly suspected or known to possess a link with a local politician, and all Jats who regularly acted as lobbyists, owned over 12 acres of agricultural land.

The relative success of larger farmers in intervening within the field of local state relations is linked to their ability to pay large bribes. But it also relates to broader features of their lifestyle and consumption patterns. Several Jats referred explicitly to the value of possessing private transport in describing how they established a link with a politician or state official. Competition between agents for access to the state, and between state employees and lobbyists for rents, increases the importance of being able to make *timely* interventions in these collusive networks. This is likely to place those owning private transport and telephones at a significant advantage in co-opting public servants. Obviously, Jats possessing more than 12 acres of land are much

Table 9.6: Ownership of Selected Consumer Goods for a Sample of Jats within the Four Lineages according to Landholding and Location of the Household

	Motorcycle per cent (no.)	Car/jeep per cent (no.)	Telephone per cent (no.)	Number in sample
12 acres or less rural	33	6	2	
	(41)	(7)	(3)	124
12 acres or less urban	79	23	19	
	(41)	(12)	(10)	52
12 acres or less total	47	11	7	
	(82)	(19)	(13)	176
Over acres 12 rural	82	18	29	
	(14)	(3)	(5)	17
Over acres 12 urban	89	100	78	
	(8)	(9)	(7)	9
Over acres 12 total	85	46	46	
	(22)	(12)	(12)	26
All Jats in sample	51	15	12	
	(104)	(31)	(25)	202

Source: Basic lineage data collected during interviews with male heads of household in the four Jat lineages. These were conducted between January and December 1997 in Daurala, Masuri and Khanpur.

more likely to own a private motorized vehicle and telephone than poorer people (Table 9.6).

People's links with politicians are also often confirmed and maintained by their ability to entertain politicians in the village. Jats possessing large amounts of land have been much more active than poorer members of their caste in building the types of houses that impress local notables: 35.3 per cent of a sample of rural landowners possessing over 12 acres have spent more than Rs 3,00,000 on house construction in the past ten years. This compares to a figure of just 5.6 per cent for rural Jats owning 12 acres or less.

Low castes and Muslims find it much more difficult than the Jats, and especially rich Jats, to obtain fast and effective assistance from the police. In most cases, this is not a problem of self-confidence. As discussed elsewhere (C. Jeffrey 2001; Jeffrey and Lerche 2000) the rise of the Bahujan Samaj Party (BSP) in western UP has increased the political assertiveness of many SCs and enhanced their capacity to

seek assistance from the police and judiciary. But low castes and
Muslims are hampered in their attempts to obtain protection by their
lack of money for bribes and continued caste discrimination within
predominantly upper- or middle-caste state bureaucracies (see also Jeffery
et al. 2001). Furthermore, the lifestyle and consumption patterns of SCs
and MBCs are such that they lack the symbolic resources—what
Bourdieu calls 'cultural capital' (Bourdieu 1984)—required to negotiate effectively with brokers, officials and politicians. Thus low castes
and Muslims are frequently afraid of naming Jats in reports made to
the police and are sceptical of their chances of obtaining fair decisions
through the judiciary in the three villages in which I worked. In other
areas of Meerut District and western UP, and in villages where SCs
form a majority, SC assertion may be more sustained and effective
(see Pai and Singh 1997). But for low castes in Daurala, Khanpur and
Masuri, attempts at securing assistance from the police is usually perceived to involve economic and physical risk.

Securing Government Employment

The collusive networks that exist between the rural élite, politicians
and the police relate to the class-differentiated nature of access to
positions within government institutions such as the police. Corruption in the allocation of public-sector positions is particularly associated with the recruitment procedures managed by the Staff Selection
Commission (SSC) (at the Central level) and Uttar Pradesh Public
Service Commission (UPPSC) (at the state level). State-level recruitment run through the UPPSC is based upon a system of examinations
and interviews. Recruitment to the police force and allied services,
organized through the SSC, and the selection process associated with
army recruitment centres, may also involve physical tests.

Corruption is perceived to occur at various stages within the processes of recruitment overseen by these institutions. Several Jat students
referred to a market in examination papers leaked in advance of a public service exam. Nevertheless, conversations with students, brokers
and recruitment officers suggested that most corrupt activity occurs
after a candidate has successfully negotiated the written exam, or written exam and physical test. Respondents went as far as referring to a
'market' in government jobs at the interview stage. Jats maintained
that it is necessary to pay between Rs 40,000 and 80,000 to become
a police constable and Rs 30,000–50,000 to obtain a low-ranking

position in the army. A group of about twelve doctoral students in sociology at Chaudhury Charan Singh University provided a more exhaustive list during a discussion of bribery. They alleged that it is necessary to pay between Rs 60,000 and 1,20,000 to obtain a teaching position in a government secondary school; Rs 40,000 to 70,000 for a lower clerical position within the bureaucracy; Rs 20,000 to 60,000 to become a bus conductor in the UP Roadways; Rs 5,000 to 20,000 for a government or private-run factory job (group discussion, 17 January 1997). In addition, two rich farmers maintained that it is currently necessary to pay around Rs 1,00,000 to receive the necessary approval from the Education Commission to become a lecturer in a university or college (rich Jat farmer, Daurala, 10 October 1997; rich Jat farmer, Khanpur, 9 March 1997).

These 'shadow markets' in public-sector positions are notoriously opaque, and claims about the size and nature of bribery should not be taken at face value. But with alarming regularity, Jat parents (and many who have obtained public-sector positions) claimed that they had paid bribes to obtain government posts in Meerut District. This shadow market is said to have emerged in the late 1970s, partly as result of the extension of reservations to OBCs in 1977 in UP and the attendant increase in competition amongst the forward castes. However, the apparent ubiquity of bribery comes against the more general background of increased schooling and expectations without a concomitant rise in the number of private or public-sector clerical and professional jobs in UP (Dube 1998: 142–3). This scarcity has also led to the emergence of a market in government employment within the reserved sector. The 'price' of a government job in the reserved sector in Meerut District is said to be between a half and two-thirds of the figures quoted for the Jats (see Dube 1998: 129). As a low-caste man put it, 'there is no reserved sector, it is just money and influence [sifarish]' (Kumhar man, Khanpur, 14 September 1997).

The capacity of rich Jat farmers to obtain public-sector positions for their sons depends not only on their wealth but also on the nature of their contacts. A number of Jats claim to possess a 'link', 'source' or a jan-pehchan (a known and recognized person) within a government department who is able to assist in the recruitment process. Where the client is the son, nephew or brother of the patron, the link is especially strong and a bribe may prove to be unnecessary. The effectiveness of an attempt to secure a post also depends upon the power of a candidate's official contacts. This relates to the officials' ranks and the strength of their connections higher up within the administrative hierarchy (group discussion with three Delhi police officers, Khanpur, 10 October 1997).

Caste affinity may play a role in the means by which Jats establish and maintain links within the bureaucracy. Several Jats conceded that it is easier to establish a contact with a Jat than a non-Jat in government or a professional institution. As a Jat lecturer pointed out, upper-caste resentment at Jat progress may create feelings of Jat solidarity in professional institutions (Jat lecturer at Delhi University, New Delhi, 21 November 1997). The extension of reservations in public-sector employment for Other Backward Castes may have also fostered forms of Jat solidarity. But Jats were often ambivalent in their discussions of caste solidarity within government bureaucracies, and most of those that I interviewed maintained that money and influence are always more important than caste in the search for a government job.

My interviews within and outside government bureaucracies provide the basis for a rough taxonomy of middlemen in the recruitment process. The most important set of middlemen are the clerks employed by the state who act as *dalals* (dealers) between Jat candidates and recruitment officers or more senior officials. These dealers are likely to be especially important for rich farmers making their first move into off-farm salaried employment and lacking contacts/information regarding the recruitment process. Several Jats referred to how civilian clerks within the military take money from candidates in return for assistance in sepoy-level recruitment tests. Lower-level clerks tend to be more willing to engage in these practices since they are less likely than senior officers to face judicial proceedings should they be discovered.

A second type of dealer operates between households seeking a post and clerks, recruitment agents or higher officials in the relevant bureaucracy. These men do not possess formal positions within state bureaucracies but trade on their knowledge of recruitment processes and *jan-pehchan*. They frequently tour rural areas offering their services as fixers. The activities of these dealers are the frequent target of local hostility and I have heard references to them as 'vultures', 'wanderers' and 'blood-suckers'.

A third set of dealers comprises retired military or police officers. They operate between candidates and army or police recruitment officials. According to students in Meerut, these men usually wait until a candidate has passed their medical and physical test before arranging a deal. They then take a bribe with the promise that this will ensure their success in the interview or written test. These dealers also leak test papers to candidates and bribe physical examiners (Professor, Chaudhury Charan Singh University).

The virtual privatization of recruitment to low-ranking public-sector positions has had the effect of consolidating the process of class differentiation in rural areas. The large bribes required in order to obtain a government post make it impossible for most SCs and the poorest Jats within the four lineages to enter public-sector employment. Even those who can afford to pay substantial sums of money often lack the political clout and tenacity required in order to establish links with reliable brokers or state officials. In this context, dealers profit from the gullibility and desperation of poor and poorly connected clients. The four cases that I uncovered in which a dealer had cheated a cultivator by promising employment and then making off with the money all relate to Jats possessing less than 12 acres of land. Low castes maintained that they are also regular victims of unreliable and unscrupulous brokers. Notwithstanding positive discrimination, a person's prospects of obtaining secure salaried employment are largely circumscribed by his or her class position.

But the introduction of reserved places within the public sector, combined with the growing political confidence of SCs, has had an effect on SCs' capacity to secure government employment in Daurala, Khanpur and Masuri. A small number of low castes are acting as brokers for their fellow caste members 'charging us a little less and keeping their promises', as one low caste man observed in Khanpur (SC man, Khanpur, 14 October 1997). This tiny group of SC 'intellectuals', who are often graduates, may have a significant influence on the confidence and therefore mobility of their caste group (Pai and Singh 1997). A Daurala Jat spoke bitterly of how 'some educated SC troublemakers come back here to stir up trouble, telling their fellows that they are downtrodden' (rich Jat farmer, Daurala, 17 February 1997).

Conclusion

It would be unwise to generalize from the material that I present on caste and class relations. The capacity for rural élites to maintain their privilege in the face of challenges from low castes is likely to vary within individual districts and from village to village. My intervention is imagined as forming part of a broader effort to understand changing patterns and processes of social inequality and social exclusion in the Hindi belt.

My principle conclusions relate to the nature of élite strategies and links between class reproduction and the state. In Khanpur, Masuri and Daurala, rich Jat farmers have been relatively (but not wholly) effective in reproducing their advantage over the past eighty years through protecting their land, practising highly remunerative cash crop agriculture, moving into lucrative forms of off-farm employment, and investing in schooling. This finding is broadly consistent with research into rich farmers in other parts of India (Breman 1985: 113; Harriss-White 1996a: 92; Rutten 1986; Rutten 1995; Upadhya 1988). My study stands out in the importance that I have ascribed to public-sector employment in the social and economic strategies of a rural élite.

I have related class reproduction to relatively poorly understood dimensions of social change in UP: informal political networks associated with the competition for police protection and shadow markets in government employment. My contention is that patterns of agrarian class formation are increasingly defined by the ability of rural agents to influence local state practice and intervene successfully in government employment markets. This study is part of a broader effort to advance a notion of 'the state' that takes account of how government functions and practice are embodied in local institutions (Harriss-White 1997; Fuller and Harriss 2000). Critical analysis of the local state must explore how informal political networks frequently act to sustain gross inequalities in material wealth and exploitative and violent social relationships. Such explorations are likely to require a political economy approach that remains sensitive to questions of social organization and cultural identity.

NOTES

1. With the exception of the work of Harriss-White (1996; 1997), evidence tends to be anecdotal or based on single case studies. The privileged access of larger landowners to local state institutions has been noted for rural western Uttar Pradesh (Bliss and Stern 1982; Gupta 1998; Lerche 1998; Lieten 1996), coastal Andhra Pradesh (Upadhya 1988), Gujarat (Breman 1985) and Maharashtra (Attwood 1992; Carter 1974). There are also scattered references to collusion between rich farmers and the police (Balagopal 1991; Brass 1997; Breman 1997; Chowdhry 1997; Dube 1998).

2. This paper is based upon fieldwork conducted as part of a doctoral dissertation under the supervision of Stuart Corbridge at the Department of Geography, Cambridge University and funded by the UK's Economic and Social Research Council. I thank Dr Corbridge and the ESRC for support. I would also like to thank O.P. Bohra for assistance in the field and Roger Jeffery and Jens Lerche for comments on drafts of this paper.

3. Some empirical material in this paper is also cited in Jeffrey and Lerche (2000).

4. These official figures should be treated with caution. For an analysis of the difficulties associated with drawing conclusions from such data see Hill (1984).

5. For a discussion of the strategies required in order to conduct research into corruption and the ethical issues that such investigations raise see Jeffrey 1999, Chap. 3.

6. There are very few examples of Jats leasing land. Owned and operated agricultural holdings therefore rarely differ.

7. In July/August 1997, when the agricultural surveys were carried out, the exchange rate was about Rs 58 to £1 sterling. Jat farmers have an interest in underestimating yields, and downplay the profits they receive from sugar cane. The figure I offer is based on a yield of 220 quintals per acre and a price of Rs 65 a quintal, which is well below the current mill price and therefore takes into account the frequent problems faced by farmers in accessing sufficient supply slips from the mill. It does not enter into the account the opportunity costs associated with household supervisory or physical labour or the depreciation of land and agricultural machinery.

8. For a review of existing research on agricultural labour relations in western UP that places these observations in a broader context see Lerche (1998).

9. As a result of the continuing strength of patriarchal forces within Jat households, very few Jat women take salaried employment (see Chowdhry 1994; Jeffery and Jeffery 1997).

10. The Jats were not included in the OBC category until after I carried out my field research.

11. The implications of the instrumental use of the marriage market for schooling and safety of the female members of Jat households is explored in Jeffery and Jeffery (1997).

12. I have described the relationship between the Jats and the police in more detail elsewhere (see C. Jeffrey 2001).

13. As Robert Wade has argued in his research on corruption in south India, the enthusiasm amongst many politicians to extract rents is linked to the rising costs of contesting elections and remaining in power (Wade 1988: 92–5). One well-connected Jat maintained that it currently costs between Rs 2,00,000 and 5,00,000 to obtain a ticket from a political party, and about Rs 1 million to contest an election in Meerut District (rich farmer, Khanpur, 12 March 1997).

14. We did not encounter any examples of rural women acting as or through lobbyists.

10

The Newspapers of Lucknow
Journalism and Modernity

Per Ståhlberg

Since 1980, modern mass media and technologies of communication have entered India on a large scale. Television[1] and video and music cassettes have a massive presence in all urban milieus and play a considerable role in many people's daily lives—without fully displacing older mass media like the radio and cinema. Communication technologies such as the telephone and fax are nowadays widely available in Public Communication Offices (PCOs) which are readily found all over the cities—usually also with facilities for photocopying and sometimes equipped with computers. Internet connections can now be found in most district headquarters across UP, and mobile phone networks have already been established to cover most of the state.

The growth of electronic or 'new' media in India has many features worthy of study from a social science perspective. These media have the potential to transcend great distances, and more and more people have the opportunity to experience a world beyond their nearest surroundings. We have here an obvious angle to relate the study of Indian society to universal issues connected with modernity, globalization and the nature of the public. The Indian mass media industry could be viewed as part of a worldwide development, which links India to a global modernity (Appadurai and Breckenridge 1995). At the same time, however, ethnographic research readily provides examples of how globally spread technologies and cultural forms take specific expressions.[2] Global modernity is not a homogeneous project (Appadurai 1997; Hannerz 1996; Miller 1994).

The main reason for the rapid and diverse growth in new and electronic media in India is economic. The huge middle class—counted in hundreds of millions—enthusiastically embraces everything that is associated with a modern lifestyle. The speed of this development is striking and prominently advertised. Visitors frequently note those appealing conjunctions of 'typical Indian' and ultramodern phenomena that are the stock-in-trade of Western journalists, such as a cycle-riksha passenger using a mobile phone.

A less striking (but at least as notable) development has taken place within the well-established mass medium of the newspaper. In most parts of the world, the expansion of television and other electronic media has been accompanied by the decline of newspapers. This has not been the case in India. On the contrary, something like a 'printing revolution' has taken place since the end of the 1970s. The circulation of daily newspapers trebled between 1976 and 1992 and the dailies-per-thousand people ratio doubled. Furthermore, one feature of this development is that the growth has been most prominent among local and regional newspapers, not among those newspapers with national profile and circulation (R. Jeffrey 2000).

How should this development, which appears somewhat anachronistic, be interpreted? On the one hand, we could view the tremendous growth of regional and local newspapers as a trend opposed to the media stream that is moving in a national, transnational or even deterritorialized direction. In this case, regional and local newspapers could be interpreted as providing some kind of resistance to globalization. A well-rooted medium could successfully fight to save local concerns from drowning in the great events of the world. From another, not totally conflicting, perspective, we can view local and regional newspapers as part of the same phenomenon that is associated with the growth of electronic media. That is, local and regional newspapers are a form of mass medium strongly connected to the modernity of contemporary India. In this paper I draw on this latter perspective.

There is nothing original about looking at daily newspapers from a modernity perspective. The historical development of media technologies—from printed media to electronic communication—is an important part of several treatises on modernity (see, for example, Thompson 1995). A newspaper offers concrete illustrations of many of the main characteristics that usually are ascribed to modernity: a radical sense of presentness, the restructuring of time and place, reflexivity and publicness (Giddens 1990; Harvey 1989; Miller 1994: 58–81; Thompson 1995). But when interest is taken in places outside those parts of the world where modernity has its historical roots (Europe and North America), there seems to be a tendency to see modernity exclusively in 'the very latest' phenomena—such as cable-TV, Internet cafés or pizza restaurants.

But modernity has a history also outside Europe and North America. In India, as well as in many other places, it is often a legacy from colonial times—still visible, for example, in the bureaucracy, education system, city plans or railway-network. The newspapers too emanate from this colonial modernity, of which the English-language élite press is a clear sign. I argue here, however, that the regional/local press should not only be related to the established journalistic tradition. It has lately gone through such changes that it also forms part of the latest expressions of modernity.

To begin with, we should note that the newspaper 'boom' would hardly have been possible without the new and relatively cheap technologies that have become available. More attractive newspapers can easily be produced with computer editing, editorial offices can effectively communicate by modem, and printing can be done in several centres, which all give the possibility for wide distribution. Furthermore, in terms of their content, these newspapers should be interpreted in a contemporary mass medium context as well as in its relation to an older tradition of journalism. One could argue that in a sense the regional/local press represents something as 'new' as cable-TV.

I present here a picture of the regional/local press as a mass media product with great impact all over India. What does this press look like? What sort of material does it contain? How does it categorize its news and what kinds of ideas are there in circulation in the editorial offices? The aim is to give a basis for an interpretation of this part of the mass media industry in the context of an expanding Indian modernity.

My outlook is, however, specific, geographically as well as in time. The material to which I refer is collected from newspapers produced in Lucknow, the capital of Uttar Pradesh. I conducted fieldwork among journalists in this city during two periods, in 1996–7 and in 1998 (I spent in total nine months in Lucknow) (Ståhlberg 2002). I focused particularly on the Hindi-language newspapers and editorial offices, but I was also interested in the English-language press because it is still very much part of the local world of journalism. I am aware that the local/regional press in other states and regions in India can look quite different. The situation of the press in West Bengal or Kerala is, for example, different in fundamental ways.[3]

Newspapers in Lucknow

You will find the most well sorted newspaper-stand in Lucknow when you enter an arcade in front of the India Coffee House, at the busy intersection of Ashoka Road and Mahatma Gandhi Road. Every morning the owner of the stall arranges all his magazines and newspapers on a long table and directly on the pavement. The impressive selection of readings ranges from glossy film magazines with the latest gossip about the stars of the screen to the prime stage of India's intellectuals, the picture- and colour-less *Economic and Political Weekly*. The supply of newspapers usually consists of some 20 titles in Hindi, English and Urdu. In one row are placed the newspapers that arrive in the afternoon from New Delhi or Kolkata, in another row are the locally produced papers. The latter by themselves contain an amazing number of titles. One can easily understand the strong competition over the newsreaders of Lucknow.

During my fieldwork in 1996–7 there were six Hindi, three English and two Urdu language morning papers being published from Lucknow. Some of these were well known in the history of Indian journalism. One of them, *The Pioneer*, prided itself on having had Rudyard Kipling on its staff; another, *National Herald*, was founded by no less than Jawaharlal Nehru. Other newspapers have had a very brief history going back only a few years. Among all these publications there were certainly a few with very small circulation (such as the formerly important *National Herald*). But the competitive papers were numerous enough. The paper with the largest local circulation was the Hindi *Dainik Jagran*, which sold around 65,000 copies of its Lucknow edition every day.[4] The main Hindi-language competitors were *Aaj*, *Rashtriya Sahara* and *Swatantra Bharat*. The *Times of India* and the *Pioneer* competed for the English Language readers and *Qaumi Awaz*[5] was the leading Urdu paper. I was repeatedly told during my fieldwork that the city was over-supplied with newspapers. There was neither enough readership nor advertising revenue for so many publications.[6] A widely spread opinion was that at least a couple of the newspapers were bound to close down soon. But when I returned to Lucknow in January 1998, I was surprised by a contrary development. In the row of locally produced newspapers I found three new titles to choose from. The Delhi-based *Hindustan Times* had launched both their English- and Hindi-language editions from a newly constructed editorial building in central Lucknow. Furthermore, a newcomer on the Hindi language newspaper market, *Kuber Times*, had chosen Lucknow as one of three places (the other two being New Delhi and Mumbai) to publish from. None of the older newspapers had yet closed down.

In some ways it gives a misleading impression to call the newspapers that are produced in Lucknow 'local'. First, Lucknow is not just any big city in north India. It is the capital of Uttar Pradesh, the most populous state in India; it is a political and administrative centre for 160 million people. Naturally, this sets the Lucknow newspapers somewhat apart from other papers published in politically less significant cities in the region. Second, most of these papers are distributed all over north India. They are locally produced editions of regional papers that are simultaneously published from several centres. If you take the train from Lucknow to Agra (or, for that matter, Varanasi, Meerut, or Allahabad) and on the same day visit a newspaper-vendor, you will find several papers with the same name as in Lucknow. But they will have a different content, because other local editorial offices produce them. A few of the top stories are printed in all editions and several further stories go into more than one, but in most cases only the editorial pages are identical everywhere. On the one hand some regional north Indian newspapers are huge media organizations with total circulations that exceed half a million copies a day. On the other hand, these figures are divided between many local, distinct editions with more modest circulations. A big regional paper—such as *Dainik Jagran*—could be considered as a number of local cooperating newspapers with the same owner.

Moreover, not all the papers that are displayed in the locally produced row at the news-stand in Lucknow are perceived as local or regional. The English *Times of India* and *Hindustan Times* (and sometimes also the *Pioneer*) as well as the Hindi *Hindustan* are recognized as local editions of 'national' newspapers. What that implies is not self-evident. When the Indian press is discussed in the public, or is the subject of surveys, the newspapers are often categorized in two different ways: by language usage or by geographical dispersion. According to the first, the Indian daily press consists of two categories, 'English' and 'vernacular'. The other model differentiates between 'national', and 'regional' (and sometimes also 'local') newspapers. Both ways of categorizing have hierarchical connotations. The English language press has higher status than the vernacular, and 'national' papers are perceived as more serious than 'regional'. There is also a kind of leakage of status between the two models of categorization. Thus, an English language paper always seems to appear more 'national' than a Hindi paper, even though the latter might have a far wider circulation. Furthermore, a Hindi language paper that is published by an English-language publishing house follows the English edition in status. In the world of Indian newspapers, 'national' is something of a mark of quality: a 'national' paper is regarded as serious and is supposed to give prominence to news of all-India concern.

Why are so many newspapers being published from Lucknow? The commercial logic behind some of these establishments is not always obvious. Resident editors on some of the papers admitted that they had little hope of running the edition at a profit, at least in the short run. The main reason for launching a newspaper edition in Lucknow seems to be that the city has risen in political significance. Of course, as the capital of UP, Lucknow has always been interesting from a media point of view, but the turbulent political situation in the state during the 1980s and 1990s has accentuated this. Those political changes that India has gone through have been particularly evident in UP: the decline of Congress (I), the rise of Hindu nationalism and the greater importance of regional parties and low-caste movements. And because journalism in India is strongly focused on politics, a base in Lucknow is essential for every media organization that is active in the northern part of the country.

In the public debate on the Indian media, it is often argued that the real purpose behind some newspapers is to further the owners' interests in other commercial activities. A newspaper may run at a loss (and without appropriate journalistic care) because the purpose is to gain the political strength that comes with ownership of a newspaper—and which could be utilized in dealing with the government and politicians. This accusation is primarily aimed at those new media enterprises that have been started by successful companies with no previous experience in mass media. Among the Lucknow newspapers, *Rashtriya Sahara* and *Kuber* represent this type of organization. The former was previously known primarily as the name of an aviation company and the latter had its successes in finance and housing. There are also cases where companies outside the media have bought established newspapers or where old newspaper owners have expanded their commercial activities to other areas. Among the latter are the owners of *Dainik Jagran*, who are today involved with business in sugar, textiles and electronics.[7]

The criticism that successful industrial companies are launching unsound newspaper projects only to get a base for political influence is not altogether coherent. After all, the Hindi-language press at large is a commercially lucrative business and it is not very strange that some editions run at a loss for several years but are expected to generate a profit in the future. Furthermore, for some of the new owners the Hindi-language newspaper is part of a broader interest in the mass media; they are simultaneously launching projects in electronic media. All this is a trend that seems to continue. *Kuber* is not the last industrial group suddenly to launch a Hindi-language daily. In early 1998, for example, a south Indian group of companies advertised in north Indian papers; they wanted 'hundreds of professionals' for launching a new Hindi-language newspaper that would be published from several centres.[8] This group of companies, called *Sanghi*, described itself as 'a 2000 crore conglomerate with multidimensional, multi-locational interest that include textile processing, zip fasteners, rigid PVC, plantations along with its presence in vernacular daily with the launching of Vaartha—the Telugu national daily'.

APPEARANCE AND CONTENT

The Lucknow newspapers probably have clear identities—for the journalists as well as for the readers—already in their visual layout. Fonts, styles, policies for headlines, use of lines and colours, and disposition of the pages are a little different in all the papers. The outsider who takes a look at the local morning papers on display on the ground before some of the retailers in Hazratganj will, however, easily discern a considerable resemblance, despite the obvious fact that the English-, Hindi- and Urdu newspapers use distinct scripts. All are printed in the same broadsheet format (390 x 540 mm) and the page layout is based on eight columns. Pages are edited quite compactly with many articles, a lot of text and few pictures or illustrations. Headlines or pictures rarely exceed three columns. The newspapers are almost identical in the number of pages they contain, normally 16 (excluding supplements).

A customer who in 1998 took a look at what the newspaper-vendor in Lucknow had to offer of local dailies could choose from a variety of fairly attractive and well produced publications. All were printed with at least the first and last page in colour. This was not the case two years earlier, when only a couple of the Hindi-language papers were printed in colour. The English-language press was particularly hesitant to part with an ideal model of a 'serious' paper that prescribed black-and-white only. But with competition, even these papers had to convert to a more popular appearance. Anyhow, by comparison with the European equivalents, one has to conclude that overall the Lucknow newspapers appear quiet and serious; black screaming headlines and seducing pictures do not characterize this press.

What distinguishes the different newspapers is, however, the price. In 1998, most Hindi-language papers were priced at Rs 3 per copy. The newly started *Kuber Times* had rapidly succeeded in catching a substantial part of the market by charging only Rs 2. A paradox is that the English-language newspapers, which presumably have the wealthiest readers, are the cheapest to buy. In order to compete with the better and better produced vernacular papers in the middle of the 1990s, they had cut their price to Rs 1.50 per copy.[9]

POLITICAL NEWS

One of the main features of the Indian press since Independence is its obsession with politics (Yadava 1991). Political events and politicians at national and state level are followed closely. News on politics is probably the 'commodity' that to a great extent sells the newspapers.[10] Indian politics is of concern not only to the well-educated élite but is of a great general interest. Politics could actually be considered part of popular culture, much in the same way as cricket or movies from the Bollywood dream-factory. When moving around in Indian society you can hardly avoid hearing, over and over again, the hit song from the latest film, it is also unlikely that you should fail to be reminded about the political game. Political personalities like Atal Behari Vajpayee, Sonia Gandhi and Kanshi Ram, or subjects such as 'communalism', reservations and corruption are prominent in what has been called the 'public culture' of Indian modernity (Appadurai and Breckenridge 1995). They are commodities of political-cultural consumption. Of course much of the information that becomes public knowledge comes from newspapers.

It is also obvious in the editorial offices of Lucknow that political reporting is considered as the core of journalistic work. Most of the newspapers have one reporter assigned for each of the most important parties in the state: BJP, SP and BSP, and even some of the small parties are covered on a regular basis. The Chief Minister and Governor are also followed closely by special reporters. The main issues discussed during editorial morning meetings, when all reporters participate together with the resident editor, are above all the political reporting.

Other local topics are planned much more quietly. The political reporters have unquestionably the highest professional status and salary among the writing journalists (with the exception of columnists and writers of editorials that, of course, are also mainly concerned with politics). This status is reinforced by the plain fact that on a daily basis political reporters mingle with the most powerful political élite of the state.

Despite this, political journalism was seldom invoked when resident editors wanted to explain to me what distinguished their newspaper from their competitors. Some of them admitted that political reporting is very similar in all newspapers. Political journalism has a dignity that makes it self-evident and not a subject of improvement or change. This is not to say that political reporting is considered unproblematic. One big problem is that the reporters are very dependent on their sources, the leading politicians, for access to information. They have great difficulties in carrying out any independent reporting, and to a great extent the politicians dictate which issues become news.[11]

So political news has its limitations as a mean of competition between the newspapers. All newspapers must have it, but in much the same form. As one resident editor told me: 'All newspapers use the same material from the news agencies and we have reporters in the same places. Possibly we can carry three exclusive news-items each day but that the other papers also do.' It is outside the political reporting that it is possible to see how the different newspapers attempt to introduce journalistic models in which they can beat the competitors and attract more readers. I will describe two such fields that were ascribed great potential in several editorial offices: local reporting and feature journalism. First, however, I will give an overview of how the news is organized in the newspapers.

NEWS CATEGORIES—PLACES AND THEMES

The Lucknow dailies follow more or less the same model of classifying the news that is universally used. On top of each page a banner refers either to a geographical category or to a subject. The most common is the geographical banner and the Lucknow newspapers geographically divide the world broadly in the same way, but use somewhat different names. The geographical categories that are commonly found in the banners refer to Lucknow, Uttar Pradesh, India and The World.[12] One can note that the geographical system of classification that is used in banners is formally hierarchical, in the sense that the higher categories encompass the lower, like Russian dolls: Lucknow is part of Uttar Pradesh, which is part of India, which is part of the world. The exception is possibly a banner that one finds in most of the Hindi-language papers (but not in any of the English) that refers to administrative districts close to Lucknow (*zila, aaspaas*). But this category could also be interpreted as subaltern to Lucknow, since these pages present news from Lucknow's rural vicinity.[13]

The Lucknow dailies are also rather uniform if you look at the banners referring to subjects on the top of pages. In all newspapers you will find particular pages for 'economy', 'sport', 'editorial' and 'feature'. The difference in space that is devoted to these themes by the different newspapers is not dramatic. Most of them carry daily two pages on economy and one or two on sport (on both these subjects the Hindi press tends to have a little less than the English press). All papers have one editorial page and half of them devote the opposite page to columns of an analytic character. The last page is in all newspapers used for feature material, usually on themes that vary with the days of the week. Notably, universally common subjects such as 'politics' and 'culture' are not used as banners on top of pages in any of the Lucknow dailies. In the case of 'politics' that is not because news on this subject is missing in the newspapers. As I stated before, political news predominates to such an extent that it is useless as a category. The absence of a page on 'culture' does, on the other hand, reflect the north Indian newspaper's weak preoccupation with 'high' culture such as literature, art or classical music and dance—materials on popular culture like film, popular music and TV are placed on the feature pages.

If we return to the geographical categories used on top of the pages it is easy to detect a difference between the English and Hindi press. The latter newspapers all have around five pages with a banner that announces 'local' news while the English-language papers are content with two. 'National' news is, on average, given two pages in the English-language papers, and one or two pages are used for 'international' news. The Hindi papers often have one page in common for both 'national' and 'international' coverage.

The patterns of geographical categories that are used on top of the pages seem to confirm a general image of both the English- and Hindi-presses. The English-language newspapers appear to pay more interest to news of 'national' concern and the Hindi-language press seems more 'local'. But these patterns do not exactly mirror the quantity of news that the papers contain which can be ascribed to different geographical levels and places. For example, all Hindi papers—but none of those in English—carry several pages with a banner announcing 'various' on which news from state and national level are placed. We shall see that there are more reasons to qualify the commonly held impression of the Hindi-language press as being extremely 'local' in concern.

I wish to emphasize that geographical location, 'place', is a matter of great concern in journalism universally. For reporters all over the world, 'where?' is a question that should preferably be answered in the first paragraph of an article (together with what? who? why? and how?). Likewise, the way journalists use and juxtapose the numerous places and geographical categories that appear on the pages every day is an important subject if one wants to understand the newspaper as a cultural product. This is a feature of journalism that makes it essential in the perspective of modernity. The representation of space in mass media is fundamental to how people may experience themselves in the world. The consumer of mass media has an opportunity to extend his/her geographical horizon, to transgress the face-to-face context and build a notion of his/her place within the world. This should have some bearing on a person's sense of belonging. To a great extent the tools for imagining who and where you are may be constituted through the media (Thompson 1995: 31–43).

An analysis of how the newspapers of Lucknow shape the world can of course not be confined to a glance at the banners they use on the tops of pages. But already this superficial level of geographical categorization shows some notable tendencies. One is that the predominant geographical categories are 'nation' and 'local'. The Hindi-language press is clearest in its attempts to profile itself as 'local' by categorizing a third of all pages with this banner. The attempt of the English-language press to appear 'national' is less marked. One interesting feature is that neither the Hindi- nor the English-language newspapers are emphasizing the 'region', or any geographical category between 'nation' and 'local', in their terminology. Pages with a banner that refer to Uttar Pradesh generally amount to only one in all of the newspapers; the largest Hindi daily had in 1998 even discarded this page altogether. It should maybe once again be pointed out that Lucknow is the capital of an Indian state with a territory greater than Great Britain and with a population exceeding that of Germany and Great Britain taken together. Both in popular speech and demographically, UP is usually divided into a number of regions, the east, central and west UP, Uttarakhand and Bundelkhand.[14] None of the newspapers are using these, or similar categories, to structure news from the state or to situate Lucknow in a defined region. One could, for example, have expected that the newspapers in Lucknow would emphasize the historical region of Awadh which in other contexts plays a great role for the cultural identity of the city. But they do not. One could conclude that on this level the 'regional press' does not appear very 'regional' at all. The Lucknow newspapers, at least, do not bother much about constructing their own region.

This is not to say that the State of Uttar Pradesh is invisible in the news. 'Lucknow', as the name of the state capital, is often used as a metonym for all of UP, in the same way as Washington, London or New Delhi often refer to the political power in US, Great Britain or India. In particular, news stories from state-government departments (situated in the capital) that obviously concern all UP are most often placed on the Lucknow pages. And despite the fact that generally only one page in the newspapers is marked with a 'State' or 'UP' banner, the front page in all newspapers always gives prominence to state politics.

A closer look at front pages will reveal that among the main stories, the dominance of news ascribed to 'New Delhi' and 'Lucknow' is massive. Of all articles printed on the first page in eight of the Lucknow dailies during one week in December 1997, 32 per cent had 'Lucknow' and 34 per cent 'New Delhi' in the date line.[15] Counting only the three most important (conspicuously placed) news stories each day, the tendency is even clearer, with 51 per cent from New Delhi and 35 per cent from Lucknow. A notable feature is that if you look only at the front page, the Hindi papers do not appear more local than the English papers. Most conspicuously, the newspaper which devotes most space inside to 'local' news (*Dainik Jagran*), focused more on 'New Delhi' on the front page: out of the 18 most important news stories of the week, 'Lucknow' gets only 3, while 11 referred to 'New Delhi'.

Among the front page news items which do not carry 'New Delhi' or 'Lucknow' in the date line it is difficult to see a pattern. Places of both great and small significance from all over India and foreign countries are represented. You cannot discern any clear tendency to favour news from other places in Uttar Pradesh. It is also significant that metropolitan cities like Mumbai, Bangalore, Chennai and Kolkata do not have a prominent place on the front pages of the Lucknow newspapers. Out of a total of 794 news items in the sample, only 28 referred to any of these places (the majority to the financial centre, Mumbai). In the same sample there were 20 foreign news stories.

The newspapers' great preoccupation with Lucknow and New Delhi has a close connection to subjects that are considered newsworthy. The high frequency of these place-names in the beginning of front-page news does not imply that these cities are reported as places with a variety of urban aspects. As stated, most often 'New Delhi' and 'Lucknow' are metonyms. In the world of newspapers 'New Delhi' represents national concerns that are decided and organized from the national capital, while 'Lucknow' represents the same for Uttar Pradesh. These cities are interesting to the media because they are where the government departments and political institutions are to be found. From this it follows that for a newspaper to have 'a national perspective' is not a question of covering events from different places all over the country, but rather to report Centre-state issues.

LOCAL REPORTING

Local coverage was stressed as important in the competition between newspapers by the staff of most of the Hindi dailies. It was a journalistic field in which several editorial offices tried to improve in order to 'beat' the competing papers. The main part of the local coverage was, however, quite similarly organized in most of the offices. Generally it consisted of staff reporters assigned to a number of government departments or authorities, and was concerned with issues such as health, water supply, drainage, public works, electricity, telephones, communication, education and crime. Other stories could be about political, cultural, commercial or religious events that took place in the city— press releases were the main source of information in these cases. The local pages are not structured thematically but contain a mixture of issues, both big and small. One feature of the routine local reporting is that it is generally confined to one particular official level in society. If, for example, a reporter with the city hospitals on his beat comes across a story about extremely long queues for certain operations, he collects all information available from hospital official and doctors. But probably he does not include the responsible politicians in his sources, or talk to any patient waiting to be medically treated.

Attempts to improve local level reporting primarily aimed at two things: to have more material and to reach 'deeper down' in society. For this purpose some of the newspapers had a huge net of affiliated freelancers who contributed with small stories from residential areas and working places. In contrast to the stories from staff reporters, these stories to a great extent consisted of reporting from localities where people, sometimes named, complained about defects in public services, such as lack of water- or power-supply, leaking drainage, dirty environment or roads in a bad condition.

One of the main changes that took place in some editorial offices between my visits to Lucknow was how this type of reporting was organized. In Spring 1997, *Dainik Jagran* had taken the initiative by starting a kind of 'trainee-class', and enrolling 15–20 inexperienced free-lancers. They gathered around a big table in the editorial office every morning for three or even four hours. A senior journalist acted as their teacher, criticizing and suggesting improvements to news stories they had brought with them. In the newspaper, these stories could be de-tected by the byline, *samvad sutr* (news source). Some of the competing Hindi papers adopted the system very quickly and started their own 'trainee-classes'. None of the English newspapers did so. In these edi-torial offices, I often heard a severe criticism of the *samvad sutr*-system, which was believed to spoil journalistic competence, and was only a means to exploit young people's career dreams for very low payment. The latter criticism certainly had some basis. At least on *Dainik Jagran* there was an explicit promise that those who performed best in the 'trainee-class' should have a chance to advance to proper journalistic assignments.

The effort to improve local coverage fits well with the image of Hindi newspapers that circulated particularly among the journalists concerned. They often emphasized that the prime strength of the Hindi press is its closeness to the ordinary person's everyday life; Hindi jour-nalism is aware of people's worries and concerns, they say, in a way that the English élite press never can be. In my interviews and conver-sations with them, resident editors on Hindi newspapers were often eager to tell me about their good relationships with readers, how people approached them to express appreciation about certain news stories or disappointment when the newspapers had failed to report some event in their locality. As one of the resident editors explained to me, 'Ordi-nary people, the small people, feel that this newspaper is their own. That we are looking after their interests. We are one of them.' Another paper had a slogan on billboards around the city. It stated, '*Dainik Jagran*—not only a newspaper, also a friend.'[16]

FEATURE

The second field of journalism which leading editors often pointed out when they wanted to explain how they tried to improve their paper— or when they claimed to be better than the others—was 'feature'. All newspapers published each day at least one page, often in colour, devoted to specific subjects that generally varied with the days of the week. Furthermore, most papers published every week a number of supplements on various themes. Feature journalism is particularly interesting in two ways. First, the choice of themes and subjects discloses quite clearly which categories of people the newspapers want to reach, and where they hope to find more readers. Second, the feature pages may be read as a kind of discursive barometer on issues and questions that are, on a very general level, topical in the society. Some themes are common in almost all newspapers and appear regularly. Most papers devote, for example, one page every week to themes such as 'women', 'sport', 'film' and 'children'. Other common themes are 'TV', 'entertainment', 'education', 'environment', 'social issues', 'technology' and 'careers'. The last subject is, in several newspapers, the theme of a special weekly supplement. Much of the feature material is of a non-localized all-Indian character, produced from the head editorial office or bought from news agencies. In this sense 'features' could be seen as something diametrically opposed to local news reporting. But some editorial offices in Lucknow have chosen to give the feature material a local profile and they produce it themselves—often, however, by using freelance reporters.

An argument often heard when resident editors wanted to explain the importance of feature material was that the newspapers had to be for the whole family. A daily morning paper should ideally be a 'family newspaper' and of interest to women, youth and children as well as to men (who are supposed to be mainly interested in political news). This way of thinking was guided by the idea that the modern family had changed. It is not only the husband's voice that counts nowadays, but other members of the family also have opinions, for example, on the choice of newspaper. This is also evident on the feature pages. Relatively few subjects and themes are exclusively directed to male adult readers.

On the feature pages it becomes clear that the newspaper has to be understood in a wider mass media context in which the electronic media often dictate the cultural model. Several of the themes that are common on the feature pages directly refer to other mass media. In newspapers one can read about the latest Hindi films, the stars of 'Bollywood', and the soap operas on TV, or about the Internet and new computer technology. Other subjects—beauty contests, design, house furnishing or lifestyle—are clearly inspired by the content of TV or popular magazines. It is not rare to read in the regional press about modern ('Western') phenomena and commodities that even in the greatest metropolis of the country would appear very marginal. (At the time of writing this I am reading the Internet edition of one of the leading UP Hindi dailies, with one article about video-telephones and another about electronic trams in Britain.) The parallel between popular magazines and the reading that is offered on the feature pages is something that one is well aware of in the newspaper's editorial offices. Amongst those newspapers that put the most effort into features, it is an explicit policy to hang on to the attraction of colour magazines. With their aura of a modern urban lifestyle, these magazines are for many people inaccessible because they are expensive, and furthermore, the most sophisticated are in English. The newspapers can offer the same kind of desirable reading for a reasonable price. As one of the resident editors said: 'We should be both a newspaper and a feature magazine.'

It was, however, not difficult to trace an degree of ambivalence towards feature writing among the journalists. Features do not go well with the serious professional role that has been prevalent among journalists since Independence. It rarely happened that political reporters contributed to the feature pages. Features were considered 'light' material with which the 'proper' journalist should not meddle. Those editors who were responsible for the feature pages often complained that it was difficult to find good writers. The freelancers employed were, particularly on the English-language newspapers, remarkably often young unmarried women with a university education; that is to say, people who did not intend to make journalism a career but regarded it as an occupation for a few years before they were married. At the same time, several ambitious journalists talked about the lack of 'human interest' stories and serious social reporting in the Hindi press. But it seemed difficult to handle that kind of material on the pages of the newspapers. Outside strict news reporting, there is no clear genre between the intellectual writing on the editorial page and the 'light' material on the feature pages.

LUCKNOW NEWSPAPERS AND
TENDENCIES OF MODERNITY

One of the few ethnographical studies of modernity outside Western Europe and North America is Daniel Miller's monograph on mass consumption in Trinidad (Miller 1994). A core concept that he uses in analysing those cultural phenomena that he describes is 'dualism'. Miller found Trinidadian society to be permeated by dualistic distinctions, with regard to goods and persons as well as to values and social events. He argues that this dualism is an apt illustration of the universal tendency of modernity to manifest itself in contradictions, dilemmas or ambivalence. Even though I suspect that it is deceptive to look at any ethnographical material with 'dualisms' in mind—one tends to see them everywhere—some striking features of the newspapers in Lucknow and of journalism in India generally point in this direction.

To begin at a general level, within Indian journalism there is a clear dualism in the conceptual separation of the English-language press and the vernacular press,[17] which to a great extent merges with the opposition between the 'national' and the 'regional' press. Part of this dualism is also an opposition between the idea of the profession being a 'mission' and journalism as a commercial product. The English/national press is understood as the more responsible and serious while the vernacular/regional press is often blamed for 'selling news like soap or toothpaste'. Journalists working for Hindi newspapers do not of course subscribe to the latter description of their work, but do often admit that the English newspapers are more professional products. English-language journalists for their part readily acknowledge the vernacular journalists to be 'more in touch with the people'. It is not difficult to trace the ambivalence in this dualism. On the one hand we have a press that enjoys great respect and credibility but if it is read only by a few, it can not possibly claim to play a prominent role in forming popular opinion. On the other hand, there is a press that is accessible to many people but has low status and credibility. The two categories of journalists are trying to deal with this ambivalence in clearly distinct ways. Both subscribe to the idea that they are working in a profession which has an important role to play in the Indian democracy, and that they are somehow in the service of the public. The Hindi-language journalists naturally emphasize that they are speaking to the people in their own language; and argue that the problems of quality and credibility could be overcome (they often mention that Hindi journalism has already improved a great deal). The English-language journalists cannot, however, overcome the problem that they are only read by a miniscule fragment of the Indian population. Instead, they rely on the idea that they serve the people best because they are read by, and influence, power-holders in society.

Looking at the content of the Lucknow newspapers, one could see several tendencies to dualism. These are most clearly visible if one considers those areas or subjects that are left out. One obvious tendency towards a bifurcation is that most news seems to be classified either as 'national' or 'local', and that geographical categories in between are paid little attention. Another kind of division is that between 'serious' content (political news, the editorial, the economy) and trivial matter (feature, small local events) leaving a void between 'heavy' and 'light' reading.

A third tendency could be found in the practice of not mixing the general with the specific. By this I mean, for example, that reporting on large-scale political events is seldom related to their consequences for specific people. During my fieldwork in Lucknow I was present at several political 'rallies' when prominent politicians appeared on stage in front of a huge mass of people. The journalists followed with attention what was being said on stage, but I never saw—nor later read in their stories—that they turned to someone in the crowd to ask for comment. Another instance of this separation of the general and the specific could be found in the local reporting about certain problems in specific localities, which is very seldom explicitly related to the level of political power.

This last tendency could also be described as a significant difference between the national élite press and regional papers. Akhil Gupta has pointed out that the former, focusing almost exclusively on large-scale political events, tend to 'reify the state as a monolithic organization with a single chain of command' (Gupta 1993: 387). The latter, on the other hand, are clearer in delineating 'the multilayered and pluricentric nature of the state' because they write about different places, naming specific government departments and specific people. My point is, however, that this difference is also prevalent as a separation of levels within the regional press. These newspapers do contain both large-scale political materials and news stories from specific places. But they are to a great extent kept apart as a result of the division of work between different categories of journalists.

NOTES

1. Often transmitted by cable and with an increasing number of satellite channels.
2. The products of Bollywood, for instance, are not copies of Hollywood, video-vans are as far as I know an Indian innovation; and Indian news magazines with their extremely long and detailed political stories are unthinkable in most parts of the world.

3. See Robin Jeffrey on Indian-Language Newspapers which deal with the press in Hindi, Telugu, Bengali and Malayalam (R. Jeffrey 2000).

4. All information on the circulation of newspapers in India is known to be notoriously unreliable. Therefore I avoid giving precise figures. It is an open secret in the newspaper world that it is even possible to manipulate auditing by the Audit Bureau of Circulation (ABC).

5. *Qaumi Awaz* is the only paper with significant circulation that is still being published from the Herald Publishing House.

6. Advertising is limited because Lucknow is a political and administrative rather than a commercial centre.

7. Media critics have, for example, questioned the owner/editor of *Dainik Jagran* in connection with the establishment of a sugar mill (Vidura 1995: 12–14).

8. See, for example, *Dainik Jagran*, 24 December 1997.

9. The English-language press can charge more for advertising space and is therefore not so dependent on income from the sale of copies.

10. One of the factors to which Robin Jeffrey gives importance to explain the tremendous growth of the daily press is that political awareness has spread to a large section of the population who are eager to know more (Jeffrey 1993: 2004).

11. Generally Indian newspapers do not have any official political leaning. The exception in Lucknow is National Herald with its sister publications in Hindi and Urdu, which are owned by a trust close to the Congress (I) party. Nevertheless, every newspaper has a reputation, seldom totally denied in the editorial offices, of loyalty towards a particular party. In Lucknow the newspapers were in reality leaning either towards the BJP or the SP. In the case of *Dainik Jagran*, the most widely read paper, the reputation was obvious because its editor/owner was a BJP member of the Rajya Sabha.

12. Variations on banners that the different newspapers use for geographical categories are: (1) Lucknow, City, *rajdhani, sthaniya* or *apna shahar*; (2) Uttar Pradesh, UP, State, Region or *pradesh*; (3) India, Nation, *desh*; (4) The World, Foreign, *deshantar, videsh, pardesh, duniya*.

13. Only one of the newspapers uses the name of any district in the banner. *Hindustan* has one page named Rai Bareli/Barabanki.

14. See Lerche and Jeffery, this volume.

15. Newspapers surveyed were *Dainik Jagran, Hindustan, Swatantra Bharat, Rashtriya Sahara, Kuber Times, The Pioneer, The Times of India* and *The Hindustan Times*. I examined articles on the first page of these papers between 24 and 30 December 1997. These particular dates were chosen in order to reflect a reasonably representative week of news.

16. '*Dainik Jagran—akhbar hi nahi, mitr bhi.*'

17. The separation is not only conceptual but also exists in practice. The English- and the Hindi-language presses are to a great extent separate careers for journalists. I met very few journalists in Lucknow who had moved from one to the other.

11

Creative Television in the Siti of Varanasi: Television and Public Spheres in the Satellite Era

Simon Roberts

This paper examines some aspects of mass media in relation to public spheres in India and the city of Varanasi. It begins by outlining the formation of a national television network, and the subsequent development of satellite services and local networks in Varanasi. By tracing the rise and fall of the Doordarshan national network, in parallel with the development of global, regional and local networks in India, it explores the relationships between these mass mediated public spheres.

The primary objective is to draw out some contradictory tendencies in these televisual developments. The satellite revolution in India has been most often examined in terms of the global and the local. I argue here that it is also necessary to include consideration of the regional and national within any account of the contemporary television environment. Ethnographic illustration of the organization and content of local television services prepares ground for an examination of their relationship to extant public spheres in Varanasi. Two case studies explore aspects of gendered access to city life and to the use of local television by the local bourgeoisie.

Varanasi is a 'million plus' city in eastern Uttar Pradesh, part of an area known as *purvanchal*. Widely known for its religious importance to Hindus because of its location on the Ganga, it is also home to a significant Muslim population and to numerous regional-linguistic communities. Many accounts of the city (Eck 1983; Freitag 1989; Hertel and Humes 1993; Parry 1994) focus on aspects of sacred life, engaging with what might be called the 'performative intensity' of the city and its traditions. My account focuses on more profane aspects of life between August 1984 and December 1998. The news programme on one of the local channels is called *Siti Halchal.* In everyday talk, *halchal* means condition or state, but can extend from bustle or stir to commotion. With its varied content, *Siti Halchal* confirms that Varanasi is a busy city with no lack of televisual material. This paper examines such activity with reference to local, national and global television.[1]

THE SPECIAL PLAN AND THE ARRIVAL OF TELEVISION IN VARANASI

It can be said with some degree of certainty that for most people in Varanasi television did not arrive until 1984. However, we can and should be more precise. Indira Gandhi flew into Varanasi on 26 August, having switched on a transmitter in Jamshedpur, Bihar. Throngs of Congress (I) supporters greeted her helicopter around the relay station on the outskirts of the city. It was a hurriedly constructed building still lacking a mains electricity supply. Yet, with the press of a button, Varanasi came closer to Delhi and into the television age. The 108th Doordarshan centre had been inaugurated.

In the weeks and days preceding this visit the local press had become saturated with publicity about the event. Advertisers fought for the attention of would-be customers and reports of the building work at the site of the transmitter jostled with invitations to openings at new television shops. As one local journalist, surveying the landscape of the city, commented, 'On rooftops where there used to be booster antennae now there are small antennae. Most people can be seen busying themselves securing the means for buying a television set. It is estimated that the number of sets bought in the last week will have been in the thousands' (*Aaj* 26 August 1984).

In 1997, people still recalled streets awash with crowds encircling any shops that were selling televisions, and these were by no means limited to electrical stores. A new commodity had been introduced and, according to some, even teashops joined in the retailing opportunity. These shops all remained open on the Sunday that Indira came to Varanasi. From then on, programmes from Delhi Doordarshan would be available, rather than 'hazy, unclear and boring programmes' from Lucknow (*Aaj* 26 August 1984). At this early stage, only those living within 25 km of the city would receive the service, but this would later increase to upwards of 120 km. As antennae began to punctuate the skyline a writer in *Aaj* commented that 'the whole city is in the grip (*chapet*) of Doordarshan' (ibid.). Indeed, it could be said that as the network expanded, this was true of large parts of India.

The early experiments with television in India have been well documented and need not concern us in detail here (Mitra 1993a; Mitra 1993b; Rajagopal 1993; Singal and Rogers 1989), but it is necessary to consider some of the objectives that underlay the development of television. These were, principally, that it should act as a catalyst for social change, promote national integration, stimulate greater agricultural production through education, and highlight the need for social welfare measures including family planning (Kumar 1981: 88–9). It was axiomatic that television should be about education, information and entertainment and 'in that order' (Rajagopal 1993: 94).

I begin with this inaugural day as experienced through the eyes of Varanasi in order to locate it in the larger historical moment. The Asian games (Asiad) held in 1982 are usually seen as the critical point in the development of the television medium in the country (Mankekar 1993a; Pathania 1994; Pendakur 1991). However, the unstated aim of the 'Special Plan', under which a television centre was inaugurated in Varanasi, was the extension of Indira Gandhi's grip over the Indian nation.

The Asiad had been an opportunity to showcase the Indira regime, and the energy and finance that had sustained this project was now channelled towards making such events truly national: this required visibility. At the time of these games, there had been no special provision for increased reception, just an increase in transmission (Rajagopal 1993: 98). The 'Special Plan' concentrated less on the content of national television and instead gave precedence to increasing the visibility of a pre-existing repertoire of events.

National spectacles were highly eligible candidates for a televised repertoire of the 'nation'. Spectacles such as the Independence-day address from the ramparts of the Red Fort in Delhi, the Republic-day parade, and other state pageants, annual or quotidian, would be used to create a corporate national life. To this end the idea of national programming and colour television services had been launched, fittingly enough, on 15 August 1982 (Pendakur 1991: 242). The launch of the INSAT 1B satellite in 1983 allowed for the effective relay of national programming across the country. However, the first state event that Varanasi would see was to be much less triumphal. We should have anticipated the irony that a moment of much greater pathos would forge the city's relationship with television.

By 1983 the 'Special Plan' was in place. Originally 131 transmitters linked to Delhi were planned, but by the end of 1984 it was hoped that there would be 185, of which 20 would have 'programme originating capacity'. The expansion drive was meteoric in pace. In 1982 there were 19 transmitters, covering 26 per cent of the population and reaching 17 million home viewers. By 1987, these figures read 197, 70 per cent and 74 million respectively. The statistics for a shorter period, between March 1984 and 1985, are the clearest testament to the immense determination of Indira Gandhi, and her successor, to 'televise' India: in these twelve months the number of transmitters leapt from 46 to 172 (Government of India 1994: 235). In 1984, 'one new transmitter was commissioned every day for four months' (Gupta 1998: 32).

At a time when Indian 'unity' was threatened, the appeal of a national television network enacted in the spirit of integration must have been ineluctable. Since the 1970s, India had been experiencing the growth of regional and other diverse political formations. Assertiveness at state or local level (in Assam and the Punjab) was met by ever more muscular responses from the centre. As the political legitimacy of the centre waned, Doordarshan was developed as an effective counter to such 'anti-national' forces. The national network became one arm of the state apparatus, entrusted with a specifically national agenda (Mitra 1993a). The policy of placing the cleverly named 'relay centres' (*kendras*), in border and tribal regions[2] makes clear that Delhi was attempting to extend its reach, an example of what Mumford termed 'authoritarian technics' (1964: 3).

A committee charged with seeking to forge 'An Indian personality for television' reported, in 1984, that a result of the relay station expansion had been a 'Delhi-centric view of India' where 'the most trivial happening in Delhi becomes a national event, deserving of extensive television coverage, while important events elsewhere hardly merit a mention'. 'As a result, . . . 'while Delhi mostly sees itself, the rest of India sees mainly Delhi and occasionally glimpses of the rest of India as seen by Delhi. Surely, this unidimensional view of India is not an inevitable result of space technology?' (Government of India 1985: 27).

From the perspective of many states this was how the 'Special Plan' and its blueprint for television expansion was seen. The All India Sikh council protested against the propaganda of DD and All India Radio, fearing further alienation of their community (Gupta 1998: 44). In the southern states, which had long resisted the political and religious hegemony of the north, the national network programmes were opposed on linguistic grounds. As Mitra has cogently argued, DD was projecting a national image dominated by the Hindu practices of Hindi speaking north India (Mitra 1993b).

What is surprising, and more pertinent to this account, is that the more aware residents of Varanasi felt aggrieved by the course of the 'Special Plan'. Varanasi, by any measure within the 'mainstream' of Indian culture, was granted a transmitter after many other cities in Uttar Pradesh. Some residents resented this, mindful of their city's location on the cultural map, and attributed this decision to the political nature of the televisation campaign. 'Varanasi should have got this facility many years ago but those with "reach" [undue sway] in Delhi insured that places like Deoria, Sultanpur, Raibareli, Nainital, Allahabad, Bareilly, Agra and Gorakhpur were accorded greater priority than Varanasi' (*Aaj* 26 August 1984).

On the day of inauguration, the leader in *Aaj* complained that the religious, literary and artistic heritage of the city had been ignored. The centre should have been created earlier, it argued, and a full broadcasting and production centre established, not merely a relay transmitter. Varanasi, the city of legions of poets, littérateurs, musicians and religious figures (and traditions), had been insulted.

One current can be identified in the reactions which the televisation campaign precipitated. It points to an issue which later sections of this account take up in detail: narrowcasting as opposed to broadcasting. At geographical and cultural distance from Delhi, the states which Indira had planned to bring within Delhi's televisual and cultural orbit resisted the imposition of a national (for which they read Hindi and Hindu) culture. Meanwhile, cities such as Varanasi felt short-changed by a developing television network in which they had little voice.

Several writers have identified political prestige for the ruling party as a major incentive behind the expansion of the national network (Pathania 1994; Pendakur 1991). The early shyness that Indira in a personal capacity had shown for the mass media when Minister for Information and Broadcasting (Masani 1975: 156) seems to have dissipated when she became Prime Minister. The expanded Doordarshan network facilitated the propagation of a dynastic mythology in which visibility was crucial. The network established a framework through which, from any part of India, however distant from Delhi, the ceremonies and figureheads of state would be rendered visible. National radio was proverbially known as 'All Indira Radio' and Doordarshan might have been similarly known, had other events not forestalled this.

Talking to people thirteen years later about the inauguration, it was striking that the Prime Minister's visit was not remembered as well as the fruits of her action: that the people of Varanasi could be part of the national mourning and witness to the violent convulsions that followed her assassination. And it is this irony, that a leader who foresaw the broadcast of national spectacles, and became the immediate subject of one, that propelled Varanasi into the world of television. Barely two months after her visit to their city, people were crowded around every available television set watching coverage of the last rites of their leader.[3]

'I remember the women sitting right here in front of the set. With joined hands they said "Hai Mata, Hai Mata, you came to inaugurate our television [centre] and today we are looking at you, your body, you who knew everything, you knew, no?" She knew, she knew that when she died, the people will watch, how many people will watch me?' So remarked a woman recounting the scenes of grief in front of her television set on 3 November 1984. Elsewhere in the city, in a big house off a small alley, a local member of the Congress (I) who was 'personally' close to Indira Gandhi laid open his television to the neighbourhood, as his wife narrated.

They came crying through the alleys avoiding the curfew, they kept on coming. The television was placed for all to see but the crowds grew too big and the television was raised higher. Women sat in the front, crying and beating their chests. There was a curfew but the police let people move to watch television, they knew they couldn't stop people watching, they even gave people encouragement (*prerana*) and assistance. How could they stop people? Two or three thousand people came and my husband said to all 'come, watch'.

Thirteen years later many shopkeepers reported that the real surge in television sales came not during the run up to the inauguration but in the days following the assassination. This event indelibly etched the coming of television to their city to a specific and violent period of post-Independence history. During the early days of November 1984 television provided a window on a troubled world, for after Indira Gandhi's assassination, pogroms began against Sikhs in cities across north India. The distant *darshan* of the nation and its ceremonies that Indira had planned to offer Indian citizens through the expanded network was, for the residents of Varanasi, a rather catastrophic first *darshan*. The vainglorious Indira was centre stage in the first event that Varanasi saw of their televised theatre state.

NATION, REGION AND LOCALITY IN INDIAN TELEVISION

1984 has come and gone. The Orwellian prophecy of government control and manipulation of information had, at this point, seemed rather timely, but events in the years since have resulted in a very different

Table 11.1: Television Coverage in India, 1982–97

	1982	1987	1997
Transmitters	19	197	868
Population covered (per cent)	26	70	87
Home viewers (million)	17	74	296
Revenue (Rs million)	159	1,363	57,276

Source: *Doordarshan 1997*, New Delhi: Audience Research Unit, Doordarshan, Government of India, 1997.

media landscape. Centralized state media are in a position of considerably less influence. Having offered a general introduction to the development of national television in India and with a view to shifting focus to Varanasi, it is necessary to summarize briefly some of the main features of the contemporary televisual environment. The picture of television in Varanasi is a reflection of this larger picture.

State-induced development and progress had been key elements in the rationale for television expansion in the years up to 1984. Thereafter, the logics of global and local capitalism and consumerism have led Indian television and its viewers towards the twenty-first century. The primary agenda of national television is now entertainment, not development. In part this is a response to the competitive pressures faced from satellite channels, but the commercialization of programme content predated the 'satellite invasion of India'. It is clear that *Hum Log* ('We People') was the beginning of commercially driven television in India, and that was in 1984 (Singal and Rogers 1989).

Table 11.1 attests to the commercialization of DD (its revenue is now substantial) and to the continuing expansion of the DD network of transmitters. The figures for population coverage and home viewers indicate that television can truly be called a mass medium.

It is clear that the reach of television is now considerable.[4] However, it is obvious that bare figures will not reveal the complexity of the issue of access to television and there is no space to pursue this in detail here. What is more important at this point is to dwell on the idea of reach. The basis of Doordarshan in the 1980s was the Indian nation and, broadly speaking, a national service. The movement over the years has been a trend towards regionalization and localization. Doordarshan itself now conceives of its service in terms of a three-tier division between national, regional and local services. The Doordarshan handbook offers the following definitions for these three tiers:

National: Programmes of common interest for the entire country.
Regional: Programmes of interest to the people speaking a particular language
          or with a distinct regional identity.
Local: Programmes for a single ethno-linguistic zone. (Government of India
          1997: 24)

In Uttar Pradesh, the DD service comes from Lucknow, with occasional feeds of national programmes from Delhi. Two centres in Gorakhpur and Bareilly produce and broadcast limited amounts of more specific programming to their surrounding areas. Furthermore, because the ten Regional Language Satellite Services are now broadcast via satellite, they can be received outside their state of origin. In Varanasi, whose population includes large regional-linguistic communities, the availability of DD7 (Bangla), DD4 (Malayalam), DD5 (Tamil) and DD11 (Gujarati) is of considerable importance.

At the time of my fieldwork, press reports emerged suggesting that DD was establishing a local centre in Varanasi, similar to those in Gorakhpur and Bareilly. By late 1998 construction work had been completed and staff were being recruited and it appeared that the demands of the city for its own DD television station were, at last, being met. When this DD centre begins broadcasting programmes of and for Varanasi and environs, it will be doing so alongside two private local stations that have been broadcasting in the city since 1996.

The reach of DD is therefore becoming more localized. However, with satellites broadcasting overseas at the same time, its reach is extending beyond India. The picture of Doordarshan is therefore one of a more distant and more intimate *darshan*. A single rather unwieldy national channel has been supplemented by regional and local services, and it extends beyond territorial boundaries. The media scene in Varanasi reflects this breadth of scope: cable operators provide around 32 channels to their subscribers. These channels range from the DD regional services, MTV, Star TV, Sony TV, Pakistan TV to the two local channels: Siti Cable and Creative TV (CTV).

In the next section I describe the social organization of media in Varanasi and explore some of the implications of recent developments. Television services are now provided on a global, national, regional and local basis, and while nearly all these services arrive down one cable, they are subject to different modes of production and reflect the concerns of different viewing constituencies. The distinction between these four levels of television may seem to mirror the mode of production and represent an analytical imposition on what may be regarded by viewers as a single television service. However, there are grounds for drawing contrasts between DD and local television, and between local services and those more globally or nationally conceived. These different services represent and are seen (by viewers and administrators) as parallel, additional and often conflicting public spheres. To date, most popular and academic attention has been paid to the global nature of these televisual developments. Let us now try to draw out the interrelations of these different media spheres and their implications at a local level.

CABLEWALAS AND THE ORGANIZATION OF
SATELLITE TELEVISION IN VARANASI

> The sky was thick with TV. If you wore special glasses you could seem them spinning through the sky. . . (Arundhati Roy)

The arrival of satellite television was more anonymous than the expansion of the DD network. The pomp and curiosity accompanying the introduction of television to Varanasi arose from the part Indira Gandhi played in the televisation campaign and from her assassination. In the case of cable there was no highly publicized helicopter tour by a national leader. To all but the very well informed, the names of global and Indian media moguls remain unknown.

In Varanasi, there are two television networks and approximately 200 cable operators providing connections to approximately 60,000 households. For those with a connection, an average of 32 channels are available. Those without the financial means to take a connection, or who have decided against for other reasons, can receive only the terrestrial DD1.[5] The early cable operators were enterprising individuals employing minimal capital and technological know-how to piece together a small network among the houses in their neighbourhood (*mohalla*). Often this network was no more extensive than 10 to 15 nearby households and offered popular Hindi films on a single video channel. In the early 1990s, as satellite services became available, home-made dishes began to punctuate the city's skyline and a multi-channel environment emerged.

The narrow alleys of Varanasi are heavily congested both at ground level and above. Threaded between electricity poles, telephone cables, and other aerial obstacles lie the discarded remnants of kites abandoned by disappointed children. It is through this mélange that the job of connecting houses to the burgeoning cable network is conducted. Operators look on as their nimble assistants thread the cable through the obstacles above, connecting every 100 yards to a signal amplifier before the destination is reached. A one-off charge is made for initial connection (Rs 250), which (in 1997) covered the cost of the cable. Thereafter average charges per household connection at that time were Rs 100 per month.

With operators often providing services to *mohallas* where they grew up, a system arose in which linguistic and religious concerns (and ideas of propriety) were made explicit in the channels selected and films aired. During Ramazaan my operator moved Pakistan TV up in the sequence of channels displacing the TNT/Cartoon Network, allowing Muslims to view these topical programmes. Therefore the hallmark of these small neighbourhood networks was the striking degree of participation by subscribers in their operation. Requests could be made for particular films and complaints and suggestions easily offered in the nearby control room.

This small-scale, personalized and unregulated industry delivering satellite TV to substantial numbers of urban homes presented the government with something of a headache. The popularity of satellite channels was draining advertising revenues from the DD network and creating a regulatory nightmare (both in fiscal and censorship terms).[6] In large part these problems of regulation have been ameliorated by the entry of larger scale operators such as Siti Cable into the industry. What these attempts at control demonstrate, however partial their success has been, is the ambiguous attitude by DD towards an ever more global, regional and local television environment.

THE COMING OF SITI CABLE AND THE 'LOCAL TV CONCEPT'

We can get some idea of how the media scene in Varanasi has changed by briefly considering the professional biography of one cable operator. This will illustrate the slow but steady expansion of the industry and the place of small operators within a changing media environment. Describing the progression of his career, Rajiv presented a picture of changes in household media use:

When I was young I was mad for the cinema, I always wanted to hear songs and watch films. Thinking that I would become an *awara* (vagrant, wanderer) my father worried. I would always sit at local tape shops and with repairmen. I wanted to hear music all the time. I borrowed Rs 5,000 and with another man set up an [audio] tape library. Then I became interested in video cameras and managed to get hold of one, I trained myself in the house, made films of us all and then of weddings. I bought some video films too and had a video cassette player (VCP) and I hired that out . . . but then people started buying them. Then cable came . . . we had a few channels and few customers and then I got a loan from the bank. . . .

This account reflects the shifting trends in mass media and entertainment over the course of Rajiv's career. Once a participant in the audio-cassette revolution from the late 1970s onwards (cf. Manuel 1994), he was quick to see the potential of video as home entertainment and of the video camera as an important guest at any wedding. Rajiv, like most cable operators, moved with the times and the predilections of his neighbourhood clientele. In a cupboard, as a memento of his entrepreneurial youth, he stores the cassette library with which he began his business.

Nowadays, the Indian representatives of global media groups such as Star, ESPN and TNT visit Rajiv to negotiate deals for the provision of their channels. His case is slightly unusual since he has managed, against the odds, to maintain his own network, whilst most cablewalas are now tied to Siti Cable. On his rooftop there is a cluster of dishes and, unlike those of most of his fellow operators, they are functioning. To understand the cable scene in Varanasi it is necessary to appreciate the movement away from small, private operations towards one in which Siti Cable, an arm of Zee television (and therefore Rupert Murdoch) and the local bourgeoisie are involved.

Entering Varanasi at the start of 1996, Siti Cable quickly sought, by various tactics, to co-opt local satellitewalas into their network as service distributors, rather than self-employed satellite operators. In Varanasi, according to its promotion brochure, Siti Cable now covers 129 neighbourhoods with some 50,000 households connected, equating to some 2.5 lakh viewers.

Siti Cable, the largest cable television network in India has invaded the local as well as the national market through its excellent signal quality, coverage of exciting local events and the finest entertainment through city specific programmes . . . coverage that's not international, national or regional but intimately local. Neighbourhood happenings. News. *Tamashas* (show or spectacle). Local events.[7]

In 1997, Siti Cable was operational in 43 cities in India 'from Cochin to Jammu', including Noida, Kanpur and Varanasi in Uttar Pradesh.[8] In India as a whole they provide television services to 4.5 million homes through 8,000 km of cable. The rationale behind the channel is to inform people about local events and happenings, to report religious festivals and political meetings, inaugural and social gatherings. Another aim is both to uncover and provide a platform for new talent in a city that prides itself on creating world class exponents of the arts. As the manager noted, Siti is a 'local based news, events, talent, information and people based channel', and Siti Channel provides this very localized axis.

On Siti Channel, a daily news programme *Siti Halchal* covers events in the city. Other shows include musical and general knowledge quizzes for children, Hindi films and filmi shows. Significantly Siti Cable are pioneering live telecasts, particularly of their own *Siti Mahotsav* (festival) and the *Ganga Mahotsav*, both held annually in the city. Additionally, in the morning 'Siti Text' offers travel information, market prices, weather reports, local news headlines and information about events in the city.

Creative TV (CTV) is a similar though smaller concern, backed by limited amounts of more local capital. Predominantly staffed by the young and enthusiastic, CTV has an eye on expansion throughout the eastern belt of Uttar Pradesh, and on working for other international news-gathering organizations. CTV operates as a cable network and production company. In 1998 their service extended to Mughal Serai, Mirzapur and Jaunpur. Sultanpur was their next target. The manager talked of a cultural and televisual renaissance in eastern UP, viewing the area around Varanasi as leader in this resurgence and CTV as leading the way in Varanasi. Although unequivocally a commercial setup, social causes remain high on the agenda. Their reports are often controversial in nature, informing viewers about police brutality, the failure of municipal policy, and environmental issues. Commissions have been carried out for NGOs (including a piece on child labour) and links are maintained with Amnesty International. Local PCO shops are linked into their news gathering system, informing them of any newsworthy event breaking in the city.

In the cramped studio and editing suite at the heart of their offices, a cardboard cut-out of the ghats at Varanasi is shuffled into position. Meanwhile, the young newsreader, having changed out of her jeans and into a sari, receives her instructions for the news presentation. The lights spark into action and the cameras begin filming. Like their colleagues at Siti Channel, reporters at CTV have spent much of the day filming their 'visuals' around the city while the news reader wrote the news with the help of the local papers. The opening sequence begins with shots of the city and the nightly news show, *Parikrama*, is under way.

In many ways the news programmes on both these channels show little significant departure from the journalistic style of the local press in the city. Invitations to attend press conferences, seminars and cultural programmes are accepted by all journalists and the commentary for the news borrows heavily from what has been published elsewhere. The video cameramen are issued instructions for the day and collate footage from events as they circuit the city on scooters. These might be high profile visits by political leaders like Kalyan Singh, or more quotidian neighbourhood happenings, such as filming a procession or protest file past, a strike or activities in a temple or on the ghats. A news conference at the Press Club might offer a less visually stimulating item in the daily round up of events, such as a large religious festival or small *mohalla* celebration, a murder or a meeting of the Rotary Club in the city. Any or all of these may be included in the fifteen items shown each evening.

In all this, municipal affairs predominate; this reflects the considerable attention given to city administration and politics in teashops and other 'communicative centres'. The three most publicly discussed of the municipal issues are those of *pani*, *bijli* and *safai*: water, electricity and cleaning. Daily, the newspapers and local television report on demonstrations by formal or informal neighbourhood groups against the neglect of their *mohalla* by municipal agencies. This municipal trinity of issues, and the *dharnas, bands, hartals, gheraos* and *chakka jams*[9] that they give rise to, are central in the representation of the city by the local networks.

Advertising on Siti Channel is predominantly local: shops offering the latest fashions, spectacles, 'suitings and shirtings', 'exclusive' television showrooms and upmarket sari and cloth shops. The target of the advertisements are clearly the nascent urban bourgeoisie, those who want mobile telephones and the chance to live in the apartment blocks (complete with supermarket, marble and mosaic floors and built-in cable television sockets) that are springing up around the city. An observer, writing about India's experience of television, has argued that a television policy has emerged that: 'simultaneously serves its own propaganda needs as well as the demands of the indigenous and transnational capitalists, along with entertainment prerogatives of the middle/upper-middle class, while the communication and other needs of the majority of Indians are pushed aside' (Pendakur 1991: 259).

While in some regards this diagnosis is a fair assessment of television in India, in Varanasi local television has added an important dimension to the communication environment in the city. By considering women's access to news and views in the city, and the place of the local bourgeoisie with respect to local television, it will be possible to assess more carefully this sort of claim.

WOMEN, THE MALE PUBLIC SPHERE AND LOCAL TELEVISION

Reading through the October editions of the local paper *Aaj* between 1984 and 1997 I was impressed by one article titled, 'In protest against the insulting behaviour of a police inspector women come out onto the street, a *dharna* (picket) at Bhelupur police station' (*Aaj* 25 October 1988). While my newspaper survey over these years was clearly partial and I would not claim that such a protest is *sui generis*, it struck me as sufficiently unusual at the time to make a note of it. Men, in my experience, are the major protagonists in such protests and during the period of my fieldwork I did not witness any such demonstrations by women.

On a daily basis, women's participation in arenas where news and views are exchanged, primarily tea and pan shops, is practically non-existent. These sites, where newspapers are read and events of local and larger significance discussed, constitute a public sphere strikingly similar to that discussed by Habermas in that women are excluded from it (Habermas 1989 [1962]). I have written at length about teashops, newspaper consumption and their place within the communicative framework of the city elsewhere and cannot discuss in detail their importance here (Roberts 1999).

Similarly, there is a significantly male basis to public space in the city. The normative statement that much public space in urban north India is male space is contentious perhaps only in its generality. Certainly it can be argued that women's and men's perceptions of public space are different. The allocation of space for women in public arenas is suggestive of the requirement that, for women to participate in ostensibly male spaces, a demarcation of this space is required. At many cinemas in the city there are separate queues for women, for a *Krishna lila* a whole section of the auditorium may be marked out for unaccompanied women. Space for women needs to be determined in the predominantly male public sphere. In quotidian contexts, where space is less clearly demarcated by gender, women represent their forays into it as somewhat problematic. Their personal space is essentially violable and this knowledge of possible violation is inscribed on women's bodies (cf. Mankekar 1993b: 482).

The events that are packaged into the nightly news shows are the primary material of local newspapers and the sites of their discussion: pan and chai shops. Newsworthy items are often organized, attended, perpetrated and celebrated by men. Festivals, of a neighbourhood or more citywide significance (Durga or Saraswati Puja), are often organized by men's associations (Sarma 1969), and, although such festivals are not exclusively 'male', men predominate and a rather over-enthusiastic masculinity pervades. Some neighbourhood processions or performances do not begin until after dark and continue into the night: neither men nor women would advise the attendance of women.[10]

If the claim that (male) 'public spaces grow more violent, disorderly and uncomfortable' is accepted, then its corollary, that 'those who can afford it consume their spectacles in the company of their friends and family, on television' (Breckenridge 1995: 10), is one that has considerable implications for women. The introduction by Siti Channel of news from around the city and telecasts of musical and other events, was significant in that it opened up the household to a far greater range of news and views (both discursive and visual) from around the city. I found that men, but more especially women, greeted this development with enthusiasm. The commencement of daily local news programmes has created fresh avenues for communication between the city and the house.

Earlier, we noted that the first national event seen by most in Varanasi was the funeral of Indira Gandhi. This illustrates, on a national scale, the manner in which gendered access to certain events can be transformed by television. Except in certain Punjabi communities, women do not attend the last rites of their relatives (cf. Parry 1994: 152), though national television provided access to this funeral and it is likely that for many women this would have been the first they had witnessed.

On a daily basis, then, women's access to city events, affairs and issues has been heightened by local television. The news on Siti Cable and CTV allows women to view, in their own or neighbours' houses, areas and activities in the city which their seclusion or restricted mobility would otherwise not allow. When the predominantly male journalists of the papers in the city report, as they sometimes do, that the 'discussion markets of the city are hot' (*charcha ka bazaar garam hai*), they are noting that customers at tea and pan shops are doing discursive overtime, debating prescient issues. The assumption is that men are the main transactors in these 'markets'. It would be unwise to suggest that women are somehow granted unhindered access to such sites through the coverage of a similar range of stories on local television and that they are therefore participating in this sphere of activity on a par with men. However, their access to these events, its vicariousness notwithstanding, is viewed as a significant and welcome addition to their lives. Such access is obtained second hand, through participation in others' experiences as relayed on television. Women are not, therefore, participating in and constituting this public sphere of activity in the way that men are: their access is partial though significant.

Electronic media such as the telephone (Papanek 1973: 321) and television or VCR, can de-link social situations from their physical locations (Meyrowitz 1985), and by so doing recast the issue of access. What television affects is, in the words of Meyrowitz, a transformation of the 'traditional relationship between physical location and access to social information' (Meyrowitz 1985: 61). Siti Cable unhinges gender from the question of access by allowing domestic contact with events that are either temporally, geographically or socially off-limits. Women are, by their own reckoning, better placed to engage in discussions of news items which may have consumed their menfolk in 'his hotel' (teashop). Siti Cable has, as one woman put it, made them aware (*jagvana*) of city events because they can see them at home.

It is likely that when a man has not been to a far off *mohalla* in the city, his wife will not have been there either. In a large city those connected to the Siti Cable network can 'visit' a distant neighbourhood and see and hear about its festivals, concerns, and activities. There is the possibility for sustained, if less intimate, access to unknown areas of the city through local television. Although a report on the local television news may reach both men and women, it is, by women's reckoning at least, of greater significance that they have access to such things because '*gents log* (people) could go there anyway and see for themselves'. As the same woman described it: 'Those places you cannot wander to, those places you can see sitting in the house.'

When I asked the manager of Siti Cable about the impact of his services in the city he responded in a similar way. He commented that 'what today some people are talking about, this spreads to the cross-roads where people discuss it and we carry it into the house.

Therefore people sitting at home receive a lot of information.' What he expressed as the transportation of words from the mouth of the people (*janmukh*) has implications of a visual nature. If, as has been common, we think about purdah, be it the social institution of exclusion or the act of veiling as a seclusion or protection that is highly visual in nature, the use of electronic media, and particularly television, make us rethink this purported opacity. There are dangers in over-stretching the potential local television offers for participation but it can be seen to remove, however partially, walls or veils between the house and the world.

The variable impact of this televisual development for men and women is most clearly seen in terms of visibility. For women the visibility gained is one of visual access, however partial this may be. For men, however, local television provides a new forum through which enhanced visibility is created. The newspaper articles that cover city events, be they demonstrations, seminars or festivals are usually replete with a long list of the names of major participants. The addition of television cameramen at such events gives all participants and especially the organizers an added avenue for visual publicity.

NATIONAL NEWS AND LOCAL NEWS

Varanasi has produced its fair share of national political figures and in most other fields of life too its major contribution to national life is rarely denied. The city's position within the cultural and religious geography of the nation is, by any measure, quite central. It was for this reason that the residents of the city complained vociferously in 1984 when they learned that other cities in Uttar Pradesh had received relay stations before Varanasi, and were dismayed to hear that Gorakhpur was to be granted programme production and broadcast facilities ahead of their city (Gorakhpur's *kendra* was commissioned in November 1984). The announcement of the full DD *kendra* in Varanasi was greeted with a certain degree of sang-froid, since two private stations were already operating in the city and few expected the studio to become operational with much alacrity. In this context, how is the relationship between Doordarshan and Siti Cable/CTV news broadcasts viewed?

Conducting neighbourhood surveys on media use and during my more intensive ethnographic work with a smaller number of houses, several attitudes towards Doordarshan national news became clear.

The most striking was the disdain with which cable-connected households viewed the service, in terms of its content and trustworthiness. It
has become received wisdom that television viewers are apt to treat
with some suspicion the editorial decisions of DD and the partial
treatment granted to government ministers (see Rajagopal 1993). I
encountered little doubt that the news on other satellite channels fared
better than DD, in terms of 'proper' and 'truthful' reporting. However,
displaying patriotism that would have flattered the architect of the
'Special Plan', some household heads professed to watch only DD news
as a matter of principle.

Those with cable connections could afford to be more critical and
had better grounds for qualitative comparison. One word that was
frequently used to describe the news programmes of Star TV and especially Zee TV (by far the most popular news programme) was *josh*
(enthusiasm). However, it was also said of Siti that their news was
done with *josh*. One man quipped that Salma Sultan, a news reader on
DD when he was a Delhi student in 1969, still read the news, whilst
the satellite news programmes are presented by more lively, youthful
and forthright presenters. DD news resembles something akin to
'visual radio'; the private satellite channels employ much more visually
satisfying presentational techniques.

Since Doordarshan does not have a production team based in
Varanasi, if events in the city are to be filmed the crew from Gorakhpur
is employed. The irony is that this footage is then usually broadcast to
this city and its environs, not Varanasi. The arrival of Siti Cable and
CTV in Varanasi has had the result of making DD's absence from the
city more obvious and has perhaps highlighted the perceived distance
between DD news and the life of the city. The contrast that can be
drawn between local news and DD news is therefore the geographic
and experiential distance between the source of the news and the point
of its reception—an obvious point perhaps, but one that lies at the
heart not only of the popularity of the Siti/CTV broadcasts but also at
the shift in DD operations from broadcasting to narrowcasting.

As viewers watched events on television at which we ourselves had
been present, a phrase that was often used was '*hamare samne hua*' (it
happened in front of me). Indeed any event, reported on local television or in the press, that had occurred at geographical proximity to
the viewer but that they had not necessarily themselves seen might be
greeted with this phrase. The implication is that 'it might just as well
have happened in front of me, because I know this street, or have

participated in this or that activity there before, or with these people'. Such a statement points to the almost seamless relationship between an actual event in an area of the city and its representation in the city media. Absence from an event that is later televised does not preclude a sense of presence. A character in a novel by Don Delillo remarks that 'for most people in the world there are only two places. Where they live and their television set. If a thing happens on television, we have every right to find it fascinating' (1984: 66). A postscript should be added to this in the light of local television. Televised events that happen in places which are entirely familiar and are peopled by friends and colleagues are even more likely to be captivating. News on DD or on satellite channels, whatever its presentational qualities and geographical setting, is news of places which many may not have ever visited. It may be more appealing or even enchanting for just this reason, but the second place that Delillo's character points to is more likely to be closer rather than farther from home where local television is available.

Many householders were apt to note that their evenings had changed since the advent of Zee TV news. The shift was most clearly expressed in terms of commensality: the entire household would watch the news together while eating their evening meal rather than eating at separate times.[11] The reason given for this was that news was entertaining and could be watched by all: there was something for everyone. Zee and the other channels would seem to be consciously producing news for the entire television household, whilst DD news remains devoted to the Machiavellian politics of New Delhi. Similarly, the *Siti Halchal* news programme, while staying focused on municipal affairs and local politics, finds space to cover events in which the world of women and children feature strongly. School events are frequently broadcast, as are the events of women's charitable and welfare organizations, such as the Udyami Mahila Rojgaar Cooperative. Therefore, the newspaper report that I found in the *Aaj* archive was noteworthy for its unusual reference to women's activities, whilst Siti Cable is much more inclined to report stories that bear on their world.

An employee of All India Radio in New Delhi commented that narrowcasting was the 'slogan for the next century'. His point was that the old broadcasting model of source::medium::consumer would be replaced by one which began and ended with the consumer. The viewer or listener becomes the source and recipient of the programming. It would be fair to note that with regard to news the narrowcasting model remains at present a slogan for DD. However, the case of local news in Varanasi would suggest that what has emerged can be termed narrowcasting. With 'city specific programmes . . . coverage that's not international, national or regional but intimately local', and which includes within its broadcasting orbit 'neighbourhood happenings, news, *tamashas* (show or spectacle) and local events', Siti Cable is clearly bringing its viewers closer to the source of their programming. The enthusiasm for watching local news should be read as a hearty endorsement of narrowcasting.

However, as suggested above, households without a cable connection lie outside not only the orbit of the global and private Indian channels but also that of Siti Cable or CTV. Instead, they remain within the realm of the DD network. The term 'network' (an interconnected group or system) implies a process of inclusion but must, therefore, be viewed in terms of exclusion too. The rationale behind the national network was of an all-encompassing, almost forcible inclusiveness, in which the states of India were tied to Delhi through relay stations. The satellite television networks, whose 'footprints' tread silently on the neighbourhoods below, while represented as inclusive and open, might also be viewed in terms of their exclusionary tendencies. The presence of satellite networks, and of pay channels on them, suggests that viewing choice has become an economic transaction, and some will necessarily be excluded for this reason.

Pendakur's comments cited above, which suggest that Indian television policy developed in ways which excluded large sections of the population, might be seen in a fresh light in terms of broadcasting and narrowcasting. Broadcasting admits all under its ambit and, as is the case with DD1, is available to all (who own a television). This section has shown that local television, as an example of narrowcasting, enables enhanced and novel forms of access. However, at the same time it depends, almost by definition, on a rather more limited constituency of viewers. The following section will examine this claim with reference to one event organized annually by Siti Cable in Varanasi: the Siti Mahotsav.

LOCAL TELEVISION AND THE BOURGEOIS PUBLIC SPHERE

The party allegiance of the two primary networks in Varanasi is unclear. There is nothing in the coverage on either network to suggest that the economic backers of either network are pursuing an overtly political agenda through the network. Staff at both networks deny any sense of compulsion from their proprietors to take a particular editorial line. CTV, as noted earlier, has completed commissions for progressive organizations and pursues a policy of exposé rather than sycophancy. On some issues it has become the bête noire of the local administration. And so, while both networks run local news that is more or less adversarial, neither represents an open platform for new social movements or progressive organizations.

What is much clearer is the socio-economic orientation of the channels, evidenced by the providers of capital for their operation and the advertisers on these channels. Capital for the foundation of CTV came from a 'mutual benefit' company that specializes in savings and investments for individuals. Another mutual benefit company is the primary sponsor of the Siti Mahotsav. Advertisement slots on both channels frequently feature publicity for these and other such companies. In such advertisements a family is typically presented reaping the benefits of their association with such companies: finally able to afford college education for their son, the lavish wedding of their daughter or a new, more expansive and modern home.

Although programming on both these channels is directed to a wide audience, in which children, women and men get their fair share of attention, the advertisements suggest that the target audience is the nascent urban bourgeoisie. Promotions for cellular phones, the new 'exclusive' Videocon showroom, 'commercial-cum-residential' complexes and fashion stores for style conscious and affluent youths are at the core of their commercial publicity. News features often double as elaborate advertisements, particularly when new shops or shopping complexes are opened. During the course of my field work, air-conditioned clothing shops selling Levis, Nike, Ray Bans and other imported fashions were frequently opened and advertised on the channel.

In terms of socio-economic or commercial moorings, a strong distinction between local television in Varanasi and DD should not be drawn. As several commentators have noted, the development of DD during the 1980s was one which simultaneously co-opted the nascent bourgeoisie as both consumers within a liberalizing economy and as viewers of Hindu constructions of India (Lutgendorf 1995; Pendakur 1991). As developmental and education programming has been set aside, more glamorous and glitzy programming has emerged. Indeed, the experience of DD in the early 1980s was that companies were unwilling to advertise until the developmental tenor of programmes such as *Hum Log* had been toned down. In part, therefore, the de-

mands of advertisers guide television. As Symthe has argued, the primary impulse of modern television is not to deliver messages to the
audience, but effectively to deliver the audience to the advertiser (cited
in Pathania 1994).

This said, Siti Cable is producing local programming that reflects
a wide range of city activities. They cover many of the numerous
festivals that punctuate life in the city and its various linguistic and
religious communities, and there is little to suggest that the activities
of certain social groups are excluded for reasons other than space. A
Brahmin-dominated seminar on 'Sanskrit and globalization' might jostle
for space with coverage of running battles between the police and
students at Banaras Hindu University. A cultural and musical event
organized by the Yuva Agrawal Samiti might sit alongside a report of
disgruntled Muslim weavers in the Shivpur area, complaining about
the delay of the Municipal Corporation in alleviating problems caused
by flooding. The involvement of CTV in helping resurrect the Burva
Mangal, a festival of music held on the ghats, is perhaps indicative of a
programming policy which includes the entire city and its inhabitants.
This festival characterized the *mauj* and *masti* (abandonment and in-
souciance) of pan-Varanasi culture but ceased to occur during the 1920s
(Kumar 1988: 126–31). 'Anyone who knows anything about Banaras
knows that the symbol of the city is the Burva Mangal' (Kumar 1988:
126). Attempts to re-establish this event are an indication of the desire
for equal dispensation of coverage to all constituencies on local television and to provide a service to the whole city and its diverse and
unified traditions.

However, an event like the Siti Mahotsav is more specifically orientated towards the local bourgeoisie. A discussion of this event[12] will
help to illustrate the class-based nature of this emergent bourgeois public sphere, for this, and the other televised events which Siti Cable are
pioneering, are peopled by just this nascent class.

THE SITI MAHOTSAV

In October 1997, as Siti Cable approached its second anniversary, it
organized the Siti Mahotsav. The Mahotsav featured nightly performances of music including *bhajan, ghazal, shastriya* and *lok sangeet*
(classical and folk music) and an evening of comic Hindi poets (*kavi
sammelan*), Muslim poets (*mushayra*), and *qawaali*. The final night concluded with a performance by the famous playback singer, Abhijit

Bhattacharya. Every evening, following the Siti news, the programme was telecast live from a complex surrounded on one side by a huge shopping complex and on another by a tall apartment block.

A mutual benefit house sponsored the event and funds were raised by establishing a 'commodity' arena within the compound where local (i.e. Banarsi) and multinational companies displayed, marketed and sold their goods. These included a *pan masala* mix, Compton Greaves water heaters, famous Mishrambu *thundai*, Lakme cosmetics, Hindustan Lever domestic products and Rita ice-creams. All this represented a consumer spectacle around which the well-heeled audience could walk sampling their own sense of socio-economic arrival. The stage and surrounding areas were garlanded with advertisement hoardings while the television coverage had a constant band on the bottom third of the screen stating which company had brought each night to the airwaves: Top Con optics, stockists of imported sunglasses, were prominent.

The audience was the upwardly mobile middle class and the admissions policy seemed fairly restrictive so that this would remain the case. Outside, the hordes were held back by the Home Guard and PACs wielding *lathis*, whilst inside the comparatively spacious compound well-dressed family groups enjoyed the performances at leisure. Young men circulated, in smart slacks and shirts, the marque of Benetton (recently opened in the city) highly visible on their shirts and the rings of their cellular phones frequently audible. Entrance to this event was provided through invitations acquired by connections (*jan-pehchan*); those without such a 'source' had either to struggle outside or, if they had a cable connection, watch it at home.

On the final night, when I was returning to my neighbourhood, the owner of a late night chemist shop told me that 'there is a live broadcast coming, we've been watching it all night'. The next day, in Shivala, the Pandey family told me they had not left their home to watch the Siti Mahotsav. Mr Pandey said that after the debacle at the filming of Zee TV's *SaReGaMa* and *Antaakshari* at Dr Rajendra Prasad Ghat, he did not fancy the idea. Mrs Pandey added that there was little point since the broadcast came to their set with a clear (*saf*) picture and they could watch it in comfort at home. What they failed to mention was that they had no means of gaining entrance to the compound and the event live. Therefore, those whose social standing was insufficient to enable them to access the Mahotsav could watch it at home, and it was clear that many people did so.

Mr Pandey's reference to the filming of these two events acts as an instructive comment on the exclusionary basis of this and other televised events. During filming by Zee TV of these two popular shows a similarly inclusivist entrance policy, combined with huge levels of interest, led to police lathi charges and what appeared to be (from the inside, since I was included) a virtual riot. The 'discussion markets of the city' reverberated about these events for several days, the primary conclusion being that Zee only wanted a certain type of people to attend their event. Zee TV, in the words of Varma, did not want the 'tidiness of the middle class' own image' (Varma 1998) to be ruptured by the untidy masses of Varanasi.

At the Siti Mahotsav, the family groups crowded onto rooftops of houses adjoining the site of the event and the crowds jostling outside made a contrast with those enjoying the spacious and comfortable surroundings within. This contrast was the clearest indication that a similar self-image was being nurtured for the television audience. As access to the actual event itself was strictly controlled, this should serve to remind us that those without television or without a cable connection were denied even televisual admission into the event, unless they watched at a friend's home.

Television viewers in Varanasi have warmly welcomed Siti Cable and CTV. When, during a strike in February 1997, their services were halted, complaints were furious. One woman told me her life had become 'half, it was as if someone had died'. Their local services are regarded as productions of and for the whole city. However, this should not obscure the tendency of these channels to act as vehicles for a particular socio-economic stratum. The Siti Mahotsav illustrates that the interests of owners and advertisers often predominate; the new televised events are probably the only spectacles in Varanasi which purposefully exclude would-be participants.

MASS MEDIA AND GLOBAL, NATIONAL AND LOCAL PUBLIC SPHERES

This paper began with the arrival of television in Varanasi and the irony that the first national event seen by Varanasi was the funeral of their prime minister on a network devised to relay Delhi statecraft across the country. It has ended with a discussion of televised events made in the city, for local television and for Zee TV's global audience. Clearly much has changed on and off television.

The rationale of the DD network, particularly in the 'special plan', was of a nation conceived to encompass its constituent parts: an overarching national public sphere cemented by broadcasting. A network conceived to propagate a specifically national identity by linking the regions to the capital has been progressively overlaid by more locally and regionally orientated networks. The impetus for a movement towards narrowcasting has come from within DD itself, with a tacit acknowledgement that breadth cannot serve all of its purposes all of the time. Accordingly, it has developed ten Regional Language Satellite Services and increased its Local Services. However, pressure has also arisen from the emergence of local stations such as Siti Cable and from the private channels that now cater for regional communities. The multitude of south Indian channels (Sun, Vijay, and Raj in Tamil; Gemini and Eenadu in Telegu) demonstrates that the era of national broadcasting has come to a close.

Many opposing tendencies are therefore in evidence. The national rhetoric of DD has been diluted to encompass regionalism and global media companies provide non-local services, though it should be noted that they are 'Indianizing' their output. Private Indian channels offer regional language service, and at a city level local networks supply 'intimately local' coverage. Depending on the perspective, television is local, regional, national, 'Indianizing' global or global. If you lived in Varanasi and watched the programmes produced by Zee TV in the city, a further permutation is conceivable.

What the globalization, regionalization and localization of media has fragmented is the possibility of such a single Indian national public sphere of the type envisaged in the Special Plan. Mass mediation has changed the nature of the public sphere in a manner more complex than that assumed by Habermas (1989 [1962]). It is now possible, in the perspective of television, to talk of multiple and overlapping public spheres that articulate different regional, political and socio-economic interests.

Discussion of the public sphere draws on Habermas' (1962) work *The Structural Transformation of the Public Sphere* and on recent work discussing aspects of his ideas (Calhoun 1992). Habermas' public sphere is 'a form intimately connected with the institution of the print media. In his original formulation this is a quite tightly drawn concept that denotes the space between state and civil society, in which men of letters engaged in critical debate on matters concerning state authority. As a result of dissatisfaction with the idealized nature of such a sphere and with the treatment of mass media in his original work (Garnham

1992), recent work has attempted to redraw the concept to include mass mediated public spheres.

In the early stages of Habermas' argument, print media are held to be vital in the constitution of the public sphere. However, he then argues that it was the rise of literacy that caused the essential character of the public sphere to be lost. 'The "principle" of the public sphere, critical public discourse, seemed to lose in strength in proportion as it extended as a sphere'. For this reason his idea of the public sphere has been criticized as an idealized literate bourgeois form in which other mass media can play little part in generating and increasing access to 'currently significant "public" information' (Calhoun 1992: 8, 21). Habermas initially denied the possibility of multiple or competing public spheres, a weakness that he has now accepted (Habermas 1992). This discussion of mass media suggests that a much broader conceptualization of the public sphere(s) than that pictured by Habermas is necessary in terms of the print media, literacy, rational communicative action and political process. Mass media can create the very conditions for the existence of multiple public spheres.

This paper has juxtaposed various public spheres of varying scale to examine the ways in which these operate in parallel, in competition or to articulate different interests. The first case study examined the (male) public and political public sphere in Varanasi. On the one hand it was argued that the lively world of political and social debate and commentary that is a distinctive feature of this sphere has been given added currency by the emergence of local television. On the other, it was argued that transformations in women's access to this sphere have been enabled by this televisual development. Men and women have different stakes in, and opinions about, this televisation, and care was taken to stress that women's access is in no sense complete. However vicarious it may be, this access is a significant development, transforming the relationship between social status and access to social (or political) information. The mass media define their own boundaries of community, and television has partially ruptured the boundary between men and print media by giving it a form suitable for domestic consumption.

The second case study examined from another angle the idea of mass media and their communities. It suggested that whilst local television in Varanasi serves all those who have access to a cable connection, it is often focused on the nascent bourgeoisie. In many respects, therefore, these local networks are following a path beaten by DD since the mid-1980s in which, without directly excluding other sections of society, it has articulated the interests of the national bourgeoisie.

National developments since my first period of fieldwork have pointed to the conflicts between these new mass-mediated spheres. The belated tabling of the Prasar Bharati Bill[13] (which had been marooned in Parliament for over a decade) laid out a new regulatory framework through which the Indian state attempted to regain control of the media. L.K. Advani had first formulated the Prasar Bharati legislation in response to the Emergency excesses of Indira Gandhi (Masani 1990: 80). Framed in times of ultimate state control over media, it was enacted in an era when the state no longer had such control. Much has been made of government concerns over the intrusion by Pakistan TV into Indian territory. This example illustrates the residual desire of the state to maintain a national mass-mediated public sphere, free from intrusion.[14]

In Uttar Pradesh there is no direct political involvement in regional or local television channels. However, the connection between political parties and television channels in south India suggests that the partisan ownership and use of channels in Uttar Pradesh may be a trend in the future.[15] With the emergence of several regional public spheres, Delhi can no longer claim to be the chief nodal point in the communications network, particularly in respect of political broadcasting. The inability of any single national party to form a majority government has been an important trait of Indian politics since 1991. Although the connection is conjectural there is a clear parallel between the growing regionalization of media and the regionalization of politics.

NOTES

1. Fieldwork was conducted in Varanasi between August 1996 and December 1997 and was funded by an ESRC grant. A brief return visit was made in December 1998. I wish to acknowledge the assistance of Bharat Kumar, Rakesh Mishra and the staff at the Hindi Pracharini Sabha. I am particularly indebted to Bina Singh Mishra for her language instruction.

2. In 1984, Rs 36.43 crore were sanctioned for the north-east in an attempt to reach 80 per cent of the people in the region (*Aaj* 26 August 1984, special supplement).

3. Doordarshan covered the entire ceremony with a special broadcast between 12.30 and 4.30 p.m.

4. Home viewers are those who have access to television at home. Doordarshan estimated that in 1997 a further 152 million had access to television in other places. At the beginning of 1997 there were 57.7 million television homes in the country, with an estimated total audience of 448 million. Rural viewers, in 1996, accounted for 49 per cent of all viewers. Total population in these figures is recorded as 930 million (Government of India 1997: 43–4).

5. Contrary to what the Indian government first thought, the demand for satellite connections has not just come from the urban élite, and satellite television cannot be simply labelled as a class-based phenomenon. While there are obviously families who cannot afford a connection (or even a television), my research shows that financial reasons are often less important in decisions about cable connections than other factors. These usually centre on children, their 'proper' upbringing, education and current cricket fixtures (Roberts 1999).

6. A number of reports in the local press illustrate government attempts to regulate the industry in Varanasi (*The Pioneer* 27 August 1997; *Dainik Jagran* 20 February 1997) and conflict between global media corporations and operators in the city (*Aaj* 5 August 1997; 'Next month Sahara Cup: cricket lovers of the city destitute').

7. Source: promotional brochure of the Essel Group of Companies. This group also owns Zee TV India, Zee Cinema and EL TV. It is also interesting to note that Siti Cable plan to become Internet Service Providers, something which they are well placed to do because the 8,000 km of cable they have used can be used for two-way communication at a high bandwidth level.

8. Expansion to other towns in UP—Allahabad and Lucknow—went ahead soon after.

9. These are all varieties of protests available to activists. They are, respectively, pickets, closure, strikes, besieging an official (to press for demands) and the closure of a road passing through the area for which attention or action is sought.

10. In Varanasi there is such a huge range of events that any generalization about their gendered nature is obviously problematic. Those unwilling to accept my strictly segmented account might consider Nita Kumar's comment on the type of events she attended: 'I was the only woman in the whole gathering of thousands' (Kumar 1988: 242). For further reflection on the 'perils' facing women at such events see also her fieldwork memoirs (Kumar 1992: 179–84 and *passim*).

11. The obvious and important point that gendered and generational hierarchies in the household often mitigate against all members of the home watching television together, has been glossed over here for reasons of space.

12. Another example of a new style event: 'Bajaj Auto Ltd. Presents Amrita Bendre and Group from Mumbai. A Grand Musical Night. For the first time in Varanasi, on the occasion of Launching of NEW Bajaj Classic SL on Friday 24th October 1997. . . . Mr Karamveer Singh (I.G. Police) will grace the occasion as chief guest. . . . For a free test ride please visit. . . .' This event received extensive coverage on Siti, but was not televised live.

13. The Prasar Bharati (lit. spread Indianness) Act reframed existing communications legislation in the light of a significantly changed media environment, and instituted DD and AIR in positions legally akin to the BBC. The intention was to clarify national policy on supra-national media, and allow DD and AIR practical and legislative freedom to respond to industry changes.

14. In October 1998, the Uttar Pradesh state government shut down private networks in Varanasi (and elsewhere in Uttar Pradesh). This decision was made on the basis

of several factors. First, the hard-hit cinema industry had lobbied for protection from the broadcasting of films which were damaging its revenues and threatening future film production. A news feature on Zee TV (29 November 1998) on the decline in film attendance and revenues reported claims by the Indian cinema industry that the 40,000 cable operators were inflicting Rs 200 million damage per year. Second, conflict over unpaid revenues (entertainment tax) had come to an impasse. Finally, the broadcast of news programming entails government registration, and night bulletins on local channels were in contravention of this requirement. This move reflects the tensions and possible conflicts that arise when several mass-mediated spheres emerge alongside each other.

15. The political battle over control of channels in southern India indicates the role of media in regional party politics. In Tamil Nadu two parties oppose each other through their own networks. This battle is between Sun TV, which is a DMK supporter, and Vijay TV, which fights Jayalalitha's (AIDMK) battles. Sun was partly responsible for the downfall of the corrupt Jayalalitha regime. It whipped up antipathy against her by showing the lavish wedding of her foster son, and then, when raids were carried out on her mansion, broadcast the entire proceedings.

Bibliography

Agnihotri, S.B. 1997. 'Sex Ratio Imbalances in India: A Disaggregated Analysis'. Ph.D thesis: University of East Anglia.

Alvarez, C. 1992. *Science and Development: The Twilight of Modernity.* Delhi: Oxford University Press.

Amin, S. 1995. *Event, Metaphor, Memory: Chauri Chaura, 1922–1992.* Berkeley: University of California Press.

Anon. 1997a. 'Corruption and the bureaucracy'. *Frontline.* Madras.

———. 1997b. 'Transfers—the Damocles' sword bureaucrats dread'. *The Hindu.* Madras.

———. 1998. 'Uttar Pradesh: In the grip of the mafia'. *India Today International.* New Delhi.

———. n.d.-a. *Sewa Bharti.* New Delhi.

———. n.d.-b. *Sewa Sankalp.* Agra: Sewa Bharti Agra Mahanagar.

Appadurai, A. 1997. *Modernity at Large.* Delhi: Oxford University Press.

Appadurai, A. and C.A. Breckenridge. 1995. 'Public Modernity in India'. Pp. 1–20. In *Consuming Modernity: Public Culture in a South Asian World,* ed. C.A. Breckenridge. London: University of Minnesota Press.

Attwood, D.W. 1992. *Raising Cane: The Political Economy of Sugar in Western India.* Boulder, London and Delhi: Westview Press and Oxford University Press.

Bailey, F.G. 1963. *Politics and Social Change: Orissa in 1959.* Berkeley: University of California Press.

Balagopal, K. 1991. 'Post-Chundur and other Chundurs'. *Economic and Political Weekly* 26, 2399–2405.

Bardhan, P. 1984. *The Political Economy of Development in India.* Oxford: Basil Blackwell.

Basu, A.M. 1996. 'Girls' schooling, autonomy and fertility change: what do these words mean in South Asia?'. Pp. 48–71. In *Girls' Schooling, Women's Autonomy and Fertility Change in South Asia',* eds. R. Jeffery and A.M. Basu. New Delhi and London: Sage in association with the Book Review Literary Trust.

Bayly, C.A. 1973. 'Patrons and Politics in Northern India'. *Modern Asian Studies* 7, 349–88.

Bénéï, V. 2000. 'Teaching Nationalism in Maharashtrian Schools'. Pp. 194–221. In *The Everyday State and Society in Modern India*', eds. C.J. Fuller and V. Bénéï. New Delhi: Social Science Press.

Bennett, L. 1983. *Dangerous Wives and Sacred Sisters*. New York: Columbia University Press.

Bennett, L. et al. 1991. *Gender and Poverty in India*, Washington DC: The World Bank.

Bentall, J. 1995. 'Bharat versus India: Peasant Politics and Urban-rural Relations in North-West India'. Ph.D thesis: University of Cambridge.

Bentall, J. and S. Corbridge. 1997. 'Urban-rural relations, demand politics and the new agrarianism in northwest India: The Bharatiya Kisan Union'. *Transactions of the Institute of British Geographers n.s.* 21, 27–48.

Berreman, G.D. 1963. *Hindus of the Himalayas: Ethnography and Change*. Delhi: Oxford University Press.

Bhalla, G.S. and G. Singh. 1997. 'Recent Developments in Indian Agriculture—A State Level Analysis'. *Economic and Political Weekly* 32, A-2–A-18.

Bhalla, S. 1999. 'Liberalisation, Rural Labour markets and the Mobilisation of Farm Workers: The Haryana Story in an All-India Context'. *Journal of Peasant Studies* 26, 25–70.

Bhatkoti, D.N. 1987. 'Elites and Political Change in Tehri: A Study in the Politics of Mass Movement and Regional Development'. Ph.D thesis: Garhwal University.

Billig, M. 1995. *Banal Nationalism*. London: Sage.

Bliss, C.J. and N.H. Stern. 1982. *Palanpur: The Economy of an Indian Village*. Oxford: Clarendon Press.

Bose, A. 1988. *From Population to People* (Vol. 1). Delhi: B.R. Publishing Corporation.

Brass, P.R. 1980. 'The politicization of the peasantry in a North Indian State: II'. *Journal of Peasant Studies* 8, 3–36.

———. 1985. 'Caste, Caste Alliances, and Hierarchy of Values in Aligarh District'. Pp. 207–79. In *Caste, Faction and Party in Indian Politics*, ed. P. Brass. Delhi: Chanakya Publications.

———. 1993. 'Chaudhuri Charan Singh: An Indian Political Life'. *Economic and Political Weekly* 28, 2087–90.

———. 1994. *The Politics of India since Independence*. Cambridge: Cambridge University Press.

———. 1997a. 'General Elections, 1996, in Uttar Pradesh: Divisive Struggles Influence Outcome'. *Economic and Political Weekly* 32, 2403–21.

———. 1997b. *Theft of an Idol: Text and Context in the Representation of Collective Violence*. Princeton, New Jersey: Princeton University Press.

Brass, T., ed. 1994. *New Farmers' Movements in India*. London: Frank Cass.

Breckenridge, C.A., ed. 1995. *Consuming Modernity: Public Culture in a South Asian World*. London: University of Minnesota Press.

Breman, J. 1985. *Of Peasants, Migrants and Paupers: Rural Labour Circulation and Capitalist Production in West India.* New Delhi: Oxford University Press.

———. 1997. 'Silencing the voice of agricultural labourers in south Gujarat'. *Kingsley Martin Memorial Lecture.* Cambridge.

Brown, P. 1998. *Pouvoir et persuasion dans l'antiquité tardive.* Paris: Seuil.

Butola, B.S. 1992. *Political Economy of Underdevelopment: A Case Study of Uttar Pradesh Himalayas.* New Delhi: Har-Anand and Vikas.

Byres, T.J. 1988. 'Charan Singh (1902–1987): An assessment'. *Journal of Peasant Studies* 15, 139–89.

Calhoun, C., ed. 1992. *Habermas and the Public Sphere.* Cambridge: MIT Press.

Carter, A.T. 1974. *Elite Politics in India: Political Stratification and Political Alliances in Western Maharashtra.* London: Cambridge University Press.

Census of India. 1931. *United Provinces of Agra and Oudh,* Vol. XVIII, Part II. Allahabad: Government of the United Provinces.

Cernea, M., ed. 1991. *Putting People First: Sociological Variables in Rural Development.* Oxford: Oxford University Press for the World Bank.

Chambers, R. 1983. 'Seasonality, Poverty and Nutrition: A Professional Frontier'. Paper presented to the EFNAG National Workshop on Poverty and Malnutrition, Coimbatore, 1983.

Chanana, K. 1990a. 'The Dialectics of Tradition and Modernity and Women's Education in India'. *Sociological Bulletin* 39, 75–91.

———. 1990b. 'Structures and Ideologies: Socialisation and Education of the Girl Child in South Asia'. *Indian Journal of Social Science* 3.

Chandra, K. and C. Parmar. 1997. 'Party Strategies in the Uttar Pradesh Elections, 1996'. *Economic and Political Weekly* 32, 214–22.

Chatterjee, P. 1986. *Nationalist Thought and the Colonial World: A Derivative Discourse?* London: Zed Press.

Chew, S. and R. Denmark, eds. 1996. *The Underdevelopment of Development: Essays in Honor of Andre Gunder Frank.* Thousand Oaks: Sage Publications.

Chowdhry, P. 1994. *The Veiled Woman: Shifting Gender Equations in Rural Haryana 1880–1990.* New Delhi: Oxford University Press.

———. 1997. 'Enforcing cultural codes: gender and violence in northern India'. *Economic and Political Weekly* 32, 1019–28.

Cohen, A.P. 1985. *The Symbolic Construction of Community.* London: Ellis Harwood Limited and Tavistock Publications.

Cohn, B. 1954. 'The Camars of Senapur: A Study of the Changing Status of a Depressed Caste'. Ph.D thesis: Cornell University.

Cooke, C.H. 1940. *Final Settlement Report of Meerut District.* Allahabad: Superintendent Printing and Stationery.

Corbridge, S.E. 1995. 'Federalism, Hindu Nationalism and Mythologies of Governance in Modern India'. Pp. 101–27. In *Federalism: The Multiethnic Challenge,* ed. G.E. Smith. London and New York: Longman.

————. 1997. '"The Merchants Drink our Blood": Peasant Politics and Farmers' Movements in Post-Green-Revolution India'. *Political Geography* 16, 423–34.

Das, K. n.d. *Seva Sadhna Aur Siddhi*. Agra: Sewa Bharti Uttar Pradesh.

Das, V. 1976. 'Masks and faces: an essay on Punjabi kinship'. *Contributions to Indian Sociology* (*n.s.*) 10, 1–30.

————. 1979. 'Reflections on the Social Construction of Adulthood'. In *Identity and Adulthood*, ed. S. Kakar. Delhi: Oxford University Press.

Desai, N. 1995. 'Women's education in India'. Pp. 23–44. In *The Politics of Women's Education: Perspectives from Asia, Africa, and Latin America*, eds. J.K. Conway and S.C. Bourque. Ann Arbor: University of Michigan Press.

Dhruvarajan, V. 1989. *Hindu Women and the Power of Ideology*. Granby, Mass.: Bergin and Garvey.

Dogra, B. 1994. 'Uttarakhand: pawns in a chess game'. *Economic and Political Weekly* 29, 3130.

Drèze, J. and H. Gazdar. 1997. 'Uttar Pradesh: The Burden of Inertia'. Pp. 33–128. In *Indian Development: Selected Regional Perspectives*, eds. J. Drèze and A. Sen. Delhi: Oxford University Press.

Drèze, J. and A. Sen, eds. 1998. *India: Economic Development and Social Opportunity*. Oxford: Clarendon Press.

Dube, S. 1998. *In the Land of Poverty*. London and New York: Zed Press.

Dube, S.C. 1955. 'A Deccan Village'. Pp. 180–91. In *India's Village*, ed. M.N. Srinivas. Bombay: Asia Publishing House.

Dubey, K.N. 1992. *Processes of Socio-Economic Development*. Jaipur: Rawat Publications.

Duncan, I. 1997. 'Agricultural innovation and political change in north India: the Lok Dal in Uttar Pradesh'. *Journal of Peasant Studies* 24, 246–68.

————. 2000. 'Dalits and Politics in Rural North India: The Bahujan Samaj Party in Uttar Pradesh'. *Journal of Peasant Studies* 27, 35–60.

Dutta, N. 1997. 'Arya Samaj and the making of Jat identity'. *Studies in History* 13, 97–119.

Eck, D. 1983. *Banaras: City of Light*. London: Routledge and Kegan Paul.

Egnor, M.T. 1986. 'Internal Iconicity in Paraiyar "Crying Songs"'. Pp. 294–344. In *Another Harmony: New Essays on the Folklore of India*, eds. S.H. Blackburn and A.K. Ramanujan. Delhi: Oxford University Press.

Elliott, C. 1984. 'Women's education and development in India'. Pp. 243–56. In *Women and Education*, ed. S. Acker. London: Kogan Page.

Engineer, A.A. 1982. 'The guilty men of Meerut'. *Economic and Political Weekly* 17, 1803.

————. 1988. 'Meerut, shame of the nation'. Pp. 16–32. In *Delhi-Meerut Riots: Compilation, Documentation and Analysis*, ed. A.A. Engineer. Delhi: Ajanta.

Escobar, A. 1992. 'Culture, economics and politics in Latin American social movements theory and research'. Pp. 62–88. In *The Making of Social Movements in Latin America: Identity, Strategy and Democracy*, eds. A. Escobar and S.E. Alvarez. Boulder, Colorado: Westview Press.

———. 1995. *Encountering Development: The Making and Unmaking of the Third World.* Princeton, NY: Princeton University Press.

Foster, G.M. 1965. 'Peasant society and the image of limited good'. *American Anthropologist* 6, 293–315.

Frankel, F.R. 1978. *India's Green Revolution: Economic Gains and Political Costs.* Princeton, New Jersey: Princeton University Press.

Freitag, S., ed. 1989. *Culture and Power in Banaras: Community, Performance and Environment, 1800–1980.* Berkeley: University of California Press.

Garnham, N. 1992. 'The Media and the Public Sphere'. Pp. 359–76. In *Habermas and the Public Sphere*, ed. C. Calhoun. Cambridge: MIT Press.

Giddens, A. 1990. *The Consequences of Modernity.* Stanford, California: Stanford University Press.

Giri, A. 1998. *Global Transformations: Postmodernity and Beyond.* Jaipur: Rawat.

Government of India. 1955. *Lok Sabha Debates on the Report of the States Reorganisation Commission*, Vols. I–III. New Delhi: Lok Sabha Secretariat.

———. 1985. *An Indian Personality for Television: Report of the working group on software for Doordarshan.* New Delhi: Ministry of Information and Broadcasting.

———. 1994. *Mass Media in India 1993.* New Delhi: Ministry of Information and Broadcasting.

———. 1997. *Doordarshan 1997.* New Delhi: Audience Research Unit, Doordarshan.

Government of Uttar Pradesh. 1994. *The Kaushik Committee Report.* Lucknow: Uttarakhand Vikas Vibhag.

Graham, B. 1990. *Hindu Nationalism and Indian Politics: The Origins and Development of the Bharatiya Jana Sangh.* Cambridge: Cambridge University Press.

Grillo, R.D. 1997. 'Discourses of Development: The View from Anthropology'. Pp. 1–33. In *Discourses of Development: Anthropological Perspectives*, eds. R.D. Grillo and R.L. Stirrat. Oxford: Berg.

Guha, R. 1989. *The Unquiet Woods: Ecological Change and Peasant Resistance.* Delhi: Oxford University Press.

Gupta, A. 1993. 'Blurred Boundaries: The Discourse of Corruption, the Culture of Politics, and the Imagined State'. *American Ethnologist* 22, 375–402.

———. 1998. *Postcolonial Developments: Agriculture in the Making of Modern India.* Durham, North Carolina and London: Duke University Press.

Gupta, D. 1997. *Rivalry and Brotherhood: Politics in the Life of Farmers in Northern India.* Delhi: Oxford University Press.

Gupta, N. 1998. *Switching Channels: Ideologies of Television in India.* Delhi: Oxford University Press.

Gupta, S. 1999. 'Any move on Kalyan Singh may change equations'. *The Times of India*, 9.

Gyaneshwar and J. Chaturvedi. 1996. 'Dharma Yudh: communal violence, riots and public space in Ayodhya and Agra city, 1990 and 1992'. Pp. 177–200. In *Riots and Pogroms*, ed. P. Brass. London: Macmillan.

Haberman, D.L. 1994. *Journey Through the Twelve Forests: An Encounter with Krishna.* Oxford: Oxford University Press.

Habermas, J. 1989 [1962]. *The Structural Transformation of the Public Sphere: An Inquiry into a Category of Bourgeois Society.* Cambridge: Polity.

———. 1992. 'Further Reflections on the Public Sphere'. Pp. 421–61. In *Habermas and the Public Sphere*, ed. C. Calhoun. Cambridge: MIT Press.

Hannerz, U. 1996. *Transnational Connections.* London and New York: Routledge.

Hansen, T.B. 1998. 'The Ethics of Hindutva and the Spirit of Capitalism'. Pp. 291–314. In *The BJP and the Compulsions of Politics in India*, eds. T.B. Hansen and C. Jaffrelot. Delhi: Oxford University Press.

Harrison, S. 1960. *India: The Most Dangerous Decades.* Princeton, New Jersey: Princeton University Press.

Harriss-White, B. 1996a. 'The Green Revolution in south India'. *Politica Internazionale* 5, 81–94.

———. 1996b. *A Political Economy of Agrarian Markets in South India: Masters of the Countryside.* New Delhi: Sage.

———. 1997. 'The State and the Informal Economic Order in South Asia— A Speculative Discussion Based on Case Material'. Paper presented to the Colloquium on Exploratory/Informal Economies: Substance and Methods of Study, Moscow School of Social and Economic Sciences, 1997.

Harvey, D. 1989. *The Condition of Postmodernity.* Oxford: Basil Blackwell.

Hasan, Z. 1989. 'Power and Mobilization: Patterns of Resilience and Change in Uttar Pradesh Politics'. Pp. 133–203. In *Dominance and State Power in Modern India: Decline of a Social Order*, eds. F. Frankel and M.S.A. Rao. Delhi: Oxford University Press.

———. 1994. 'Shifting ground: Hindutva politics and the farmers' movements in Uttar Pradesh'. Pp. 165–94. In *New Farmers' Movements in India*, ed. T. Brass. London: Frank Cass.

———. 1998. *Quest for Power: Oppositional Movements and Post-Congress Politics in Uttar Pradesh.* Delhi: Oxford University Press.

———. 2001. 'Transfer of Power? Politics of Mass Mobilisation in UP'. *Economic and Political Weekly* 36, 4401–9.

Hatim, S. 1976. *Panchayati Raj in India, With Special References to Uttar Pradesh.* Aligarh: AMU.

Haynes, D.E. 1987. 'From Tribute to Philanthropy: The politics of gift in a Western Indian City'. *Journal of Asian Studies* 46, 339–60.

Hertel, B. and C. Humes. 1993. *Living Banaras: Hindu Religion in a Cultural Context.* Albany: State University of New York Press.

Hill, P. 1984. 'The poor quality of official socio-economic statistics relating to the rural tropical world; with special reference to south India'. *Modern Asian Studies* 18, 491–514.

Hitchcock, J.T. 1971. 'Structural Paradox and Value Conflict in the Dominant Caste of a North Indian Village'. In *Themes in Culture: Essays in Honor of Morris E. Opler*, eds. M.D. Zamora, J.M. Mahar and H. Orenstein. Quizon City, Philippines: Kayumanggi Publishers.

Hobart, M., ed. 1993. *An Anthropological Critique of Development: The Growth of Ignorance*. London: Routledge.

Hulme, D. and P. Mosley. 1996. *Finance Against Poverty*. London and New York: Routledge.

Ilaiah, K. 1996. 'Beef, BJP and Food Rights of People'. *Economic and Political Weekly* 31, 1444–5.

International Institute for Population Studies. 1995. *National Family Health Survey (MCH and Family Planning)—Uttar Pradesh, 1992–93*. Bombay: International Institute for Population Studies.

Jaffrelot, C. 1998a. 'The Bahujan Samaj Party in North India—No longer just a Dalit party?' *Comparative Studies of South Asia, Africa and the Middle East* 18, 35–51.

———. 1998b. 'The Sangh Parivar Between Sanskritisation and Social Engineering'. Pp. 22–71. In *The BJP and the Compulsions of Politics in India*, eds. T.B. Hansen and C. Jaffrelot. Delhi: Oxford University Press.

———. 1999. *The Hindu Nationalist Movement and Indian Politics, 1925 to the 1990s*. New Delhi: Penguin India.

Jafri, S.N.A. 1985 (1931). *The History and Status of Landlord and Tenants in the United Provinces*. New Delhi: Usha Publications.

Jeffery, P. 2000. 'Identifying Differences: Gender Politics and Community in Rural Bijnor, UP' in Leslie, J. (ed.) *Gender Constructs in India Religion and Society*. Delhi: Oxford University Press.

Jeffery, P. and R. Jeffery. 1994. 'Killing My Heart's Desire: Education and Female Autonomy in Rural North India'. Pp. 125–71. In *Woman as Subject: South Asian Histories*, ed. N. Kumar. Calcutta and Charlottesville: Bhatkal and Sen and Virginia University Press.

———. 1996a. 'What's the Benefit of being Educated? Girls' Schooling, Women's Autonomy and Fertility Outcomes in Bijnor'. Pp. 150–83. In *Girls' Schooling, Women's Autonomy and Fertility Change in South Asia*, eds. R. Jeffery and A. Basu. New Delhi and London: Sage in association with the Book Review Literary Trust.

———. 1996b. *Don't Marry me to a Polwman: Women's Everyday Lives in Rural North India*. Boulder: Westview Press.

———. 'Gender, Community and the Local State in Bijnor, India'. In *Resisting the Sacred and the Secular: Women's Activism and Politicized Religion in South Asia*, eds. P. Jeffery and A. Basu. New Delhi: Kali for Women.

Jeffery, P., R. Jeffery and A. Lyon, 1989. *Labour Pains and Labour Power: Women and Childbearing in India*. London: Zed Books.

Jeffery, R. and A.M. Basu. 1996. 'Schooling as Contraception?' Pp. 15–47. In

Girls' Schooling, Women's Autonomy and Fertility Change in South Asia, eds. R. Jeffery and A.M. Basu. New Delhi and London: Sage in association with the Book Review Literary Trust.

Jeffery, R. and P. Jeffery. 1997. *Population, Gender and Politics: Demographic Change in Rural North India*. Cambridge: Cambridge University Press.

Jeffery, R., P.M. Jeffery and A. Lyon. 1983. 'Female Infanticide and Amniocentesis'. *Economic and Political Weekly* 18, 655–7.

Jeffrey, C.J. 1999. 'Reproducing Difference: The Accumulation Strategies of Richer Jat Farmers in western Uttar Pradesh, India'. Ph.D thesis: University of Cambridge.

———. 2001. 'A Fist is Stronger than Five Fingers: Caste and Dominance in Rural North India'. *Transactions of the Institute of British Geographers* 25: 1–30.

Jeffrey, C. and J. Lerche. 2000. 'Stating the difference: state, discourse and class reproduction in Uttar Pradesh, India'. *Development and Change* 31, 857–78.

Jeffrey, R. 1993. 'Indian-Language Newspapers and Why They Grow'. *Economic and Political Weekly* 28, 2004–11.

———. 2000. *India's Newspaper Reduction: Capitalism, Politics and the Indian-language Press 1977–99*. New Delhi: Oxford University Press.

Joshi, M.P. 1990. *Uttaranchal Himalaya: An Essay in Historical Anthropology*. Almora: Shri Almora Book Depot.

Joshi, M.P. and V.S. Negi. 1994. 'Was there a Central Pahari? An appraisal of Grierson's Classification of Three Pahari Language Groups'. Pp. 259–74. In *Himalaya Past and Present*, Vol. I, eds. M.P. Joshi, A.C. Fanger and C.W. Brown. Almora: Shri Almora Book Depot.

Joshi, S.C. 1988. 'State of education and literacy'. Pp. 341–46. In *Kumaun land and people*, ed. K.S. Valdiya. Naini Tal: Gyanodaya Prakashan.

Kant, A. 1995. 'Agrarian Mobilisation in Western Uttar Pradesh: A Study of the Bhartiya Kisan Union'. Ph.D thesis: Jawaharlal Nehru University.

Kantowsky, D. 1970. *Dorfentwicklung Und Dorfdemokratie, Formen und Wirkungen von Community Development und Panchayati Raj*. Bielefeld: Bertelsmann Universitätsverlag.

Kapani, L. 1992. *La notion de Samskara*. Paris: Collège de France-De Boccard.

Karlekar, M. 1994. 'Women's nature and access to education in Bengal'. Pp. 59–82. In *Women, Education and Family Structure in India*, eds. C.C. Mukhopadhyay and S. Seymour. Boulder: Westview Press.

Kenny, J.T. 1995. 'Climate, race and imperial authority: the symbolic landscape of the British hill station in India'. *Annals of the Association of American Geographers* 85, 649–714.

Khan, R. 1992. *Federal India: A Design for Change*. Delhi: Vikas Publishing House.

Khan, S.R. 1993. 'South Asia'. Pp. 211–46. In *Women's Education in Developing Countries: Barriers, Benefits, and Policies*, eds. E.M. King and M.A. Hill. Baltimore: Johns Hopkins University Press.

Khanna, B.S. 1994. *Panchayati Raj in India: Rural Local Self-Government, National Perspective and State Studies*. New Delhi: Deep and Deep.

Khare, R.S., J. Singh and K.N. Maurya, eds. 1982. *20-Point Programme: Health Sector Monthly Monitoring: Calendar of Activities (1982–83) Uttar Pradesh*. Lucknow: Directorate of Medical, Health and Family Welfare Uttar Pradesh.

King, E.M. and M.A. Hill, eds. 1993. *Women's Education in Developing Countries: Barriers, benefits, and policies*. Baltimore: Johns Hopkins University Press.

King, R.D. 1997. *Nehru and the Language Politics of India*. Delhi: Oxford University Press.

Korten, D. 1990. *Getting to the 21st Century: Voluntary Action and the Global Agenda*. West Hartford: Kumarian.

Krengel, M. 1997. 'Migration and the danger of loss: some aspects of cultural identity in Kumaon/Indian Himalaya'. Pp. 171–87. In *Perspectives on history and change in the Karakorum, Hindukush, and Himalaya*, eds. I. Stellrecht and M. Winiger. Koln: Rudiger Koppe Verlag.

Kumar, K. 1981. *Mass Communication in India*. Bombay: Jaico Publishing House.

Kumar, N. 1988. *The Artisans of Banaras: Popular Culture and Identity 1880–1980*. Princeton: Princeton University Press.

———. 1992. *Friends, Brothers, and Informants: Fieldwork Memoirs of Banaras*. Berkeley and London: University of California Press.

Kumar, P. 1999. 'Dalits and the BSP in Uttar Pradesh: Issues and Challenges'. *Economic and Political Weekly* 34, 822–6.

Kurian, N.J. 1999. 'State Government Finances. A Survey of Recent Trends'. *Economic and Political Weekly* 34, 1115–25.

———. 2000. 'Widening Regional Disparities in India: Some Indicators'. *Economic and Political Weekly* 35, 538–50.

Lerche, J. 1995. 'Is Bonded Labour a Bound Category? Reconceptualising Agrarian Conflict in India'. *Journal of Peasant Studies* 22, 484–515.

———. 1998. 'Agricultural Labourers, the State and Agrarian Transition in Uttar Pradesh'. *Economic and Political Weekly* 33, A29–A35.

———. 1999. 'Politics of the Poor: Agricultural Labourers and Political Transformations in Uttar Pradesh'. Pp. 182–241. In *Rural Labour Relations in India*, eds. T.J. Byres, K. Kapadia and J. Lerche. London: Frank Cass.

Lieten, G.K. 1994. *The North Indian Kulak and His Deficient Democracy*. The Hague: IDPAD.

———. 1996a. *Development, Devolution and Democracy: Village Discourse in West Bengal*. New Delhi and London: Sage.

———. 1996b. 'Hindu Communalism: Between Caste and Class'. *Journal of Contemporary Asia* XXVI, 236–52.

———. 1996c. 'Panchayats in Western Uttar Pradesh: Namesake Members'. *Economic and Political Weekly* 31, 2700–5.

———. 2001. 'Development Priorities, Post-Modernist Assumptions and Pre-modernist Aspirations'. *Asian Journal of Social Science* 29, 567–84.

———. Forthcoming. 'Faltering Development and the Post-Modernist Discourse'. *Social Scientist.*

Lieten, G.K. and R. Srivastava. 1999. *Unequal Partners: Power Relations, Devolution and Development in Uttar Pradesh.* New Delhi: Sage.

Lutgendorf, P. 1995. 'All in the (Raghu) Family: A Video Epic in Cultural Context'. Pp. 217–53. In *Media and the Transformation of Religion in South Asia,* eds. L. Babb and S.S. Wadley. Philadelphia: University of Pennsylvania Press.

Lynch, O. 1969. *The Politics of Untouchability: Social Mobility and Social Change in a City of India.* New York: Columbia University Press.

Madan, T.N. 1989 [1965]. *Family and Kinship.* Delhi: Oxford University Press.

Madsen, S.T. 1991. 'Clan, Kinship, and Panchayat Justice among the Jats of Western Uttar Pradesh'. *Anthropos* 86, 351–65.

———. 1996. *State, Society and Human Rights in South Asia.* New Delhi: Manohar.

Mandelbaum, D. 1988. *Women's Seclusion and Men's Honor.* Tucson: University of Arizona Press.

Mankekar, P. 1993a. 'National texts and gendered lives: an ethnography of television viewers in a north Indian city'. *American Ethnologist* 20, 543–63.

———. 1993b. 'Television Tales and a Woman's Rage: A Nationalist Recasting of Draupadi's Disrobing'. *Public Culture* 5, 469–92.

Manuel, P. 1994. *Cassette Culture: Popular Music and Technology in North India.* Chicago: Chicago University Press.

Mari Bhat, P.N. 1996. 'Contours of Fertility Decline in India: A District Level Study Based on the 1991 Census. Pp. 96–177. In *Population Policy and Reproductive Health,* ed. K. Srinivasan. New Delhi: Hindustan Publishing Corporation.

Marx, K. and F. Engels. 1969. *Selected Works.* Moscow: Progress Publishers.

Masani, M. 1990. 'The Akashvani-Bombay University Debate'. Pp. 80–93. In *Autonomy for the Electronic Media: A National Debate on the Prasar Bharati Bill,* ed. K. Thomas. Delhi: Konark.

Masani, Z. 1975. *Indira Gandhi: A Biography.* London: Hamish Hamilton.

Mawdsley, E.E. 1996. 'The Uttarakhand Agitation and the Other Backward Classes'. *Economic and Political Weekly* 31, 205–10.

———. 1999. 'A New Mountain State: Politics, Territory and Development in the Indian Himalaya'. *Mountain Research and Development* 19, 101–12.

McAdam, D., J.D. McCarthy and M.N. Zald, eds. 1996. *Comparative Perspectives on Social Movements: Political Opportunities, Mobilising Structures and Cultural Framings.* Cambridge: Cambridge University Press.

Measham, A.R., K.D. Rao, D.T. Jamison, J. Wang and A. Singh. 1999. 'Reducing Infant Mortality and Fertility, 1975–1990: performance at All-India and State Levels'. *Economic and Political Weekly* 34, 1359–67.

Mendelsohn, O. 1993. 'The Transformation of Authority in Rural India'. *Modern Asian Studies* 27, 805–42.

Mendelsohn, O. and M. Vicziany. 1998. *The Untouchables: Subordination, Poverty and the State in Modern India*. Cambridge: Cambridge University Press.

Metcalf, T.R. 1979. *Land, Landlords and the British Raj*. Berkeley and Los Angeles: University of California Press.

Meyrowitz, J. 1985. *No Sense of Place: The Impact of Electronic Media on Social Behaviour*. New York: Oxford University Press.

Miller, B.D. 1981. *The Endangered Sex: Neglect of Female Children in Rural North India*. Ithaca: Cornell University Press.

Miller, D. 1994. *Modernity: An Ethnographic Approach; dualism and mass consumption in Trinidad*. Oxford: Berg.

Mishra, S. 2000. 'Uttaranchal: Sad State'. In *India Today*.

Mitra, A. 1993a. *Television and Popular Culture in India: A Study of the Mahabharat*. New Delhi and London: Sage.

———. 1993b. 'Television and the Nation: Doordarshan's India'. *Media Asia* 20, 39–43.

Moller, J. 1993. 'Insiders and Outsiders: Conceptual continuities from Household to Region in Kumaon, North India'. Ph.D thesis: London School of Economics and Political Science, University of London.

———. In Press. 'Anti-reservation protests and the Uttarakhand pro-autonomy movement'. *South Asia Research*.

———. Forthcoming. 'Symmetry and consanguinity in the kinship system of Kumaon, North India'. In *Himalaya: Past and Present*, Vol. IV, ed. M.P. Joshi. Almora: Shri Almora Book Depot.

Mukhopadhyay, C.C. and S. Seymour eds. 1994. *Women, Education and Family Structure in India*. Boulder: Westview Press.

Mumford, L. 1964 [1934]. *Technics and Civilisation: The Interplay of Artefact and Culture*. New York: Harcourt, Brace and World.

Nand, N. and K. Kumar. 1989. *The Holy Himalaya: A Geographical Interpretation of Garhwal*. Delhi: Daya Publishing House.

Nanda, A.R. 1991. *Census of India. [Series 1. Paper 1 of 1991. Provisional Population Totals]*. New Delhi: Registrar General and Census Commissioner, India.

Nandy, A. 1987. *Tradition, Tyranny, and Utopias*. Delhi: Oxford University Press.

Nelson, L.E., ed. 1998. *Purifying the Earthly Body of God: Religion and Ecology in Hindu India*. New York: State University of New York Press.

Oldenburg, P. 1992. 'Sex Ratio, Son Preference and Violence in India: A Research Note'. *Economic and Political Weekly* 27, 2657–62.

Olson Jr, M. 1965. *The Logic of Collective Action, Public Goods and the Theory of Groups.* New York: Schocken Books.

Omvedt, G. 1993. *Reinventing Revolution. New Social Movements and the Socialist Tradition in India.* Armonk, New York: M.E. Sharpe.

Oommen, M.A. ed. 1995. *Panchayati Raj Development Report.* New Delhi: Institute of Social Sciences.

Ostrom, E. 1998. 'A Behavioral Approach to the Rational Choice Theory of Collective Action: Presidential Address, American Political Science Association, 1997'. *American Political Science Review* 92, 1–22.

Pai, S. and J. Singh. 1997. 'Politicisation of Dalits and Most Backward Castes'. *Economic and Political Weekly* 32, 1356–61.

Papanek, H. 1973. 'Purdah: Separate Worlds and Symbolic Shelter'. *Comparative Studies in Society and History* 15, 289–325.

Parry, J. 1974. 'Egalitarian Values in a Hierarchical Society'. *South Asian Review* 7, 95–121.

———. 1989. 'On the moral perils of exchange'. Pp. 64–93. In *Money and the Morality of Exchange*, eds. J. Parry and M. Bloch. Cambridge: Cambridge University Press.

———. 1994. *Death in Banaras.* Cambridge: Cambridge University Press.

Pathak, S.N. 1987. *Land Reforms and Change in Rural Society.* Allahabad: Chugh Publications.

Pathania, G. 1994. 'Ambivalence in a STAR-ry Eyed Land: Doordarshan and the Satellite TV Challenge'. *SAGAR* 1, non paginated.

Patnaik, U. 1971. 'Capitalist development in agriculture: A note'. *Economic and Political Weekly* 6, A-123–A-130.

Pendakur, M. 1991. 'A Political Economy of Television: State, Class and Corporate Influence in India'. Pp. 233–49. In *Transnational Communications: Wiring the Third World*, eds. G. Sussman and J. Lent. Newbury Park: Sage.

Peterson, S.B. 1997. 'Hierarchy versus networks: alternative strategies for building organisational capacity in public bureaucracies in Africa'. Pp. 157–75. In *Getting good government: capacity building in the public sectors of developing countries*, ed. M.S. Grindle. Boston, Mass: Harvard University Press.

Porta, D.D. 1995. *Social Movements, Political Violence, and the State: A Comparative Analysis of Italy and Germany.* Cambridge, New York, Melbourne: Cambridge University Press.

Rajagopal, A. 1993. 'The rise of national programming: the case of Indian television'. *Media, Culture and Society* 15, 91–111.

Rajan, S.I. and P. Mohanachandran. 1998. 'Infant and Child Mortality Estimates'. *Economic and Political Weekly* 33, 1120–40.

Ram, N. 1995. *Beyond Ambedkar: Essays on Dalits in India.* Delhi: Har-Anand Publications.

Ramakrishnan, V. 1998. 'A climbdown'. In *Frontline* 15 August, 1–14.

Ramesh, J. 1999. 'Future of Uttar Pradesh: Need for a New Political Mindset'. *Economic and Political Weekly* 34, 2127–31.

Rana, M.S. 1994. *Bharatiya Kisan Union and Ch. Tikait.* Meerut: Paragon Publications.

Randhawa, M.S. 1970. *The Kumaon Himalayas.* New Delhi: Oxford and IBH.

Rangan, H. 1996. 'From Chipko to Uttaranchal: development, environment and social protest in the Garhwal Himalayas, India'. Pp. 205–26. In *Liberation Ecologies: Environment, Development, Social Movements,* eds. R. Peet and M.J. Watts. London and New York: Routledge.

Rau, M.C. 1981. *Govind Ballabh Pant: His Life and Times.* New Delhi: Allied Publishers.

Rawat, A.S. 1989. *History of Garhwal 1358–1947: An Erstwhile Kingdom in the Himalayas.* New Delhi: Indus Publishing Company.

Reddy, R.G., ed. 1977. *Patterns of Panchayati Raj in India.* New Delhi: Macmillan.

Reeves, P. 1991. *Landlords and Government in Uttar Pradesh: A Study of Their Relations until Zamindari Abolition.* Delhi: Oxford University Press.

Registrar General and Census Commissioner, India. 2001. *Census of India 2001: Provisional Population Totals* (Paper 1 of 2001) (Series 1). Delhi: Controller of Publications.

Registrar General of India. 1991. *Census of India: Village and Town Directory and Primary Census Abstract, Meerut District, Uttar Pradesh.* New Delhi: Office of the Registrar General.

———. 1988. *Child Mortality Estimates of India* (Census of India 1981, Occasional Papers 5 of 1988). New Delhi: Ministry of Home Affairs, Government of India.

———. 1961. *Census of India.* New Delhi: Ministry of Home Affairs, Government of India.

Renou, L., ed. 1956. *Hymnes spéculatifs du Veda.* Paris: Gallimard-UNESCO.

Roberts, S. 1999. ' "Another member of our family": Aspects of Television Culture in Varanasi, North India'. Ph.D thesis: University of Edinburgh.

Rosenthal, D.B. 1970. *The Limited Elites: Politics and Government in two Indian Cities.* Chicago: Chicago University Press.

Rudolph, L.I. and S.H. Rudolph. 1967. *The Modernity of Tradition: Political Development in India.* Chicago: University of Chicago Press.

———. 1987. *In Pursuit of Lakshmi: The Political Economy of the Indian State.* Hyderabad: Orient Longman.

Rutten, M. 1986. 'Social profile of agricultural entrepreneurs: economic behaviour of middle-large farmers in central Gujarat'. *Economic and Political Weekly* 21, A-15–A.23.

———. 1995. *Farms and Factories.* New Delhi: Sage.

Sah, S.P. 1993. 'Smaller States lead to faster development'. Pp. 9–14. In *The*

Separate Hill State, eds. D.C. Doundiyal, V.R. Dhoundiyal and S.K. Sharma. Almora: Shri Almora Book Depot.

Salmen, L.F. 1987. *Listen to the People: Participant-Observer Evaluation of Development Projects*. New York: Oxford University Press for the World Bank.

Samal, P.K. 1993. 'The status of women in central Himalaya: a cultural interpretation'. *Man in India* 73, 87–95.

Samata Sanghatana. 1991. 'Upper caste violence: study of Chunduru carnage'. *Economic and Political Weekly* 26, 2079–2804.

Sarma, J. 1969. 'Puja Associations in West Bengal'. *Journal of Asian Studies* 28, 579–94.

Saxena, N.C. 1985. 'Caste and Zamindari Abolition in UP'. *Mainstream.*

Schlanger, J.E. 1971. *Les métaphores de l'organisme*. Paris: Vrin.

Seymour, S. 1995. 'Family structure, marriage, caste and class, and women's education: exploring the linkages in an Indian town'. *Indian Journal of Gender Studies* 2, 67–86.

Shankar, K. 1993. 'Agricultural Labourers in East Uttar Pradesh'. *Economic and Political Weekly* 28, 1211–14.

Sharma, R. 1994. 'Constructing "Dalit" Identity'. *Link* 37, 13–15.

Sharma, R. and T. Poleman. 1993. *The New Economics of India's Green Revolution: Income and Employment Diffusion in Uttar Pradesh*. Berkeley and London: University of California Press.

Singal, A. and E. Rogers. 1989. *India's Information Revolution*. New Delhi: Sage.

Singh, J. 1992. *Capitalism and Dependence: Agrarian Politics in Western Uttar Pradesh, 1951–1991*. New Delhi: Manohar.

———. 1995. *Political Economy of Unaided and Unrecognised Schools: A Study of Meerut District of Western Uttar Pradesh*. Karnal: Indira Gandhi National Open University, Regional Centre for Haryana.

———. 1998. 'Ambedkarisation and Assertion of Dalit Identity: Socio-Cultural Protests in Meerut District of Western Uttar Pradesh'. *Economic and Political Weekly* 33, 2611-18.

Srivastava, R. 1989. 'Interlinked Modes of Exploitation in Indian Agriculture During Transition: A Case Study'. *Journal of Peasant Studies* 16, 493–522.

———. 1994. 'Planning and Regional Disparities in India'. Pp. 147–219. In *The State and Development Planning in India*, ed. T.J. Byres. Delhi: Oxford University Press.

———. 1995. 'India's Uneven Development and Its Implication for Political Processes: An Analysis of Some Recent Trends'. Pp. 219–47. In *Industry and Agriculture in India since Independence: Social Change and Political Discourse in India, Structures of Power Movements and Resistance*, ed. T.V. Sathyamurthy. Delhi: Oxford University Press.

———. 1996. 'Agrarian change and the labour process'. Pp. 228–50. In *Meanings of Agriculture: Essays in South Asian History and Economics*, ed. P. Robb. New Delhi: Oxford University Press.

———. 1999. 'Rural Labour in Uttar Pradesh: Emerging Features of Subsistence, Contradiction and Resistance'. Pp. 263–315. In *Rural Labour Relations in India*, ed. T.J. Byres, K. Kapadia, and J. Lerche. London: Frank Cass.

Ståhlberg, P. 2002a. 'The Illicit Daughter: Hindi-Language Newspapers and the Regionalisation of the Public Sphere in India'. Pp. 207–36. In *Contesting Good Governance: Crosscultural Perspectives on Representation, Accountability and Public Space*, eds. E. Poluha and M. Rosendahl. London and New York: Routledge Curzon.

———. 2002b. *Lucknow Daily: How a Hindi Newspaper Constructs Society*. Stockholm Studies in Social Anthropology, 51. Stockholm: Almqvist and Wiksell International.

Stokes, E. 1978. *The Peasant and the Raj*. Cambridge: Cambridge University Press.

———. 1986. *The Peasant Armed: the Indian Revolt of 1857*. Oxford: Clarendon Press.

Stone, I. 1984. *Canal Irrigation in British India*. Cambridge: Cambridge University Press.

Swarup, R. 1991. *Agricultural Economy of Himalayan Region with Special Reference to Kumaon*. Naini Tal: Gyanodaya Prakashan.

Thompson, J.B. 1995. *The Media and Modernity*. Cambridge: Polity Press.

Thorner, D. and Han-Seng. 1996. *Agricultural Regions in India*. Karachi: Oxford University Press.

Traill, G.W. 1980 [1828]. 'Statistical sketch of Kumaon'. *Asiatic Researches* 1, 137–234.

Tripathi, A.K. 1997. *Kalyan Singh*. Delhi: Rajkamal Prakashan.

Tsui, A.O., K.K. Singh, B. Buckner, J. Dietrich, J. DeGraft-Johnson, P. Bardsley, P.P. Talwar, T. Strickland and L. Betts. 1997. *Performance Indicators of the Innovations in Family Planning Services Project: 1995 PERFORM Survey in Uttar Pradesh*. State Innovations in Family Planning Services Project Agency.

Ullrich, H. 1994. 'Asset and liability: the role of female education in changing marriage patterns among Havik Brahmins'. Pp. 187–212. In *Women, Education and Family Structure in India*, eds. C.C. Mukhopadhyay and S. Seymour. Boulder: Westview Press.

Upadhya, C.B. 1988. 'The Farmer-Capitalists of Coastal Andhra Pradesh'. *Economic and Political Weekly* 23, 1376–82, 1433–42.

Varma, P. 1998. *The Great Indian Middle Class*. New Delhi: Penguin.

Varshney, A. 1995. *Democracy, Development, and the Countryside: Urban-rural Struggle in India*. New Delhi: Cambridge University Press.

Vatuk, S. 1972. *Kinship and Urbanization*. Berkeley: University of California Press.

Verma, K. 1980. 'The tragedy of a backward state'. *The Overseas Hindustan Times*, 10.

Verma, A.K. 2001. 'UP: BJP's Caste Card'. *Economic and Political Weekly* 36, 48: 4452–5.

Vlassoff, C. 1996. 'Against the odds: the changing impact of schooling on female autonomy and fertility in an Indian village'. Pp. 218–34. In *Girls' Schooling, Women's Autonomy and Fertility Change in South Asia*, eds. R. Jeffery and A.M. Basu. New Delhi and London: Sage in association with the Book Review Literary Trust.

Wade, R. 1988. 'Politics and Graft: Recruitment, appointment and promotions to public office in India. Pp. 73–110. In *Corruption, Development and Inequality: Soft touch or hard graft?*, ed. P. Ward. London and New York: Routledge.

Wadley, S.S. 1994. *Struggling with Destiny in Karimpur*. Berkeley and London: University of California Press.

Walker, B. 1983. *Hindu World*. Delhi: Munshiram Manoharlal Publishers.

Whitcombe, E. 1972. *Agrarian Conditions in Northern India: The United Provinces under British Rule, 1860–1900 (Vol. 1)*. Berkeley and Los Angeles: University of California Press.

———. 1980. 'Whatever Happened to the Zamindars?'. Pp. 156–80. In *Peasants in History: Essays in Honour of Daniel Thorner*, ed. E.J. Hobsbawm. Calcutta: Oxford University Press.

Yadava, J.S. 1991. 'Press System in India'. *Media Asia* 18, 132–42.

Zald, M.N. and R. Ash. 1969. 'Social movement organisations: Growth, decay and change'. Pp. 461–85. In *Studies in Social Movements. A Social Psychological Perspective*, ed. B. McLaughlin. New York: The Free Press.

Zérinini-Brotel, J. 1998. 'The BJP in Uttar Pradesh: From Hindutva to Consensual Politics?'. Pp. 72–100. In *The BJP and the Compulsions of Politics in India*, eds. T.B. Hansen and C. Jaffrelot. Delhi: Oxford University Press.

Index